Virginia Maxwell

İstanbul

The Top Five

1 Topkapı Palace
Tour this history-soaked palace
(p91)

2 Kariye Müzesi
View the exquisite mosaics and
frescoes (p111)

3 Grand Bazaar
Browse in the world's most
famous bazaar (p102)

4 Bosphorus
Savour the sights along the great
waterway (p217)

5 Aya Sofya
Visit one of the world's most
magnificent buildings (p79)

Contents

Published by Lonely Planet Publications Pty Ltd
ABN 36 005 607 983

Australia Head Office, Locked Bag 1, Footscray,
Victoria 3011, ☎ 03 8379 8000, fax 03 8379 8111,
talk2us@lonelyplanet.com.au

USA 150 Linden St, Oakland, CA 94607,
☎ 510 893 8555, toll free 800 275 8555,
fax 510 893 8572, info@lonelyplanet.com

UK 72-82 Rosebery Ave, Clerkenwell, London,
EC1R 4RW, ☎ 020 7841 9000, fax 020 7841 9001,
go@lonelyplanet.co.uk

Printed through Colorcraft Ltd, Hong Kong.
Printed in China

The Author

VIRGINIA MAXWELL

Virginia knows exactly why İstanbul has been called the City of the World's Desire, as she desires nothing more than to return and sample its manifold delights again and again. With her partner Peter and young son Max, she has tramped its cobbled streets, explored its bazaars and marvelled at the friendliness and good humour of its locals. With good friends Jill, Kate, Catherine, Dave and Janet, she's checked out bars, relaxed in *çay bahçesi* and eaten trayloads of meze; and with sister Elizabeth, she's hopped on and off ferries, eaten *lokum* and watched dervishes whirl. There's no doubt at all that she'll be back again soon.

PHOTOGRAPHER
PHIL WEYMOUTH

Australian born, Phil Weymouth and h family called Tehran, Iran, home from th late 1960s until the revolution in 197 After studying photography in Melbourn Phil returned to the Middle East in the mi 1980s to live and work as a photographer i Bahrain. Phil now runs a freelance phot graphic business based in Melbourne. H continues to travel extensively in Austral and internationally, writing stories an taking pictures. He found İstanbul to b a city full of surprises, great food, mus and friendly people, with history on ever corner.

Introducing İstanbul

Turkey's major city is like a juicy, sugar-dusted morsel of *lokum* just waiting to be devoured. Its flavours are rosewater, pistachio, almond and cinnamon – all rich, complex and redolent of the exotic east – but its packaging is different, reminiscent of the elegantly boxed treats sold in Paris' Fauchon or London's Fortnum and Mason. East meets West here, all in one delicious mouthful.

Food's a fitting analogy when discussing İstanbul, not only because the city's restaurants, cafés and markets offer a bewildering and uniformly excellent range of taste-bud tempters, but because the city is a banquet even if you're not eating. You can marvel at the greatest examples of Byzantine art and architecture in the world, submerge yourself in the world of the seraglio while wandering through palaces and imperial kiosks or lose yourself in the labyrinthine Grand Bazaar – and that's just on day one. Itineraries here are a moveable and ever-fascinating feast.

The resurgence in popularity of that most basic Turkish staple – the chewy, sesame encrusted *simit* – is one of the clearest examples of the pride that locals are increasingly displaying in their heritage. The days of Doritos a la Turca or the McTurko Burger ruling the fast-food roost are well gone, overtaken by the bread-rings made by Simit Sarayı outlets across town or the milk puddings sold at the many *muhallebicis* opening in shopping malls and on every major street. İstanbullus are starting to realise that when you're on a good thing it makes sense to stick to it.

On the world stage pin-up pianist-composer Fazıl Say performs his *Dervish in Manhattan* in concert halls in London and New York while Rifat Ozbek struts his stuff on international catwalks – all to a distant but no less emphatic ovation by their proud countrymen and women. When these and other locals-made-good come back to İstanbul the red carpet is well and truly rolled out, inspiring a host of aspirants whose art, music, fashion and film endeavours are making the city an enormously exciting and vibrant place to be.

Lowdown

- **Population** Officially 9.6 million, unofficially up to 20 million
- **Time zone** GMT/UTC + 2 hours
- **Three-star hotel room** Around €60
- **Turkish coffee** Around €1.10
- **Ferry ticket** Less than €0.50 one way
- **Fish sandwich** €0.80
- **City no-no** Asking to sit in the nonsmoking section
- **Essential accessory** An Akbil tag
- **Best view** Back to Old İstanbul from the Galata Bridge

The physical fabric of the city is being reinvigorated, too. Great monuments such as Justinian and Theodora's Küçük Aya Sofya and Mehmet the Conqueror's Tiled Kiosk are being given the loving restorations they so richly deserve; and fascinating suburbs such as Karaköy and Balat are being rediscovered, their cobbled streets cleaned up and their buildings given the spring cleaning of their lives. In these suburbs a harmonious mix of people go about their daily tasks – they may be of Armenian, Kurdish, Jewish or Greek heritage, but if asked they'll proudly label themselves as İstanbullus first and foremost, residents of the place so rightfully dubbed the 'City of the World's Desire'.

The best way to explore the city is by foot. As you walk along you'll hear müezzins duelling from the tops of their minarets and ferries honking their bass-toned horns while transporting passengers from Europe to Asia and back again. Sound systems in houses and shops pay homage to the current local darlings of the airwaves, overlaid by a constant and infectious strain of laughter and animated conversation – İstanbul is neither quiet nor restrained when it comes to celebrating daily life.

As if by magic, the historical layers of the city reveal themselves to passers-by on every street. You'll see Byzantine cisterns and churches here, Ottoman *hamams* and mosques there and 19th-century decorative flourishes everywhere. In fact, it's not an exaggeration to say that İstanbul is one of the most architecturally important cities in the world, full of buildings worthy of an intake of breath when first spotted and a 'favourite building' tag when better known.

These physical layers of the city are matched by the many layers and influences that make up the character of the contemporary city. On any one street, for instance, there might be a traditional Turkish meyhane packed with boisterous family groups, a marble-and-glass brasserie serving up international fusion food to Prada-clad couples, a *çay bahçesi* full of nargileh-puffing Anatolian gents and a cappuccino-dispensing café catering to a clientele of headscarf-adorned women. Though their education, income, interests, religion and (sometimes) language may be different, every one of these people is a true İstanbullu. Together they make the city the friendly, inclusive, exhilarating, utterly marvellous place it is. May it ever be so.

VIRGINIA'S TOP İSTANBUL DAY

After popping into a local börekçi for a breakfast of freshly baked *ıspanaklı börek* and a glass of tea, I walk to the symbolic heart of the city, Sultanahmet Park. I dodge past the crowds outside the Blue Mosque and make my way to the most beautiful building in the world: Aya Sofya. After a contemplative hour or so I saunter up the historic thoroughfare of Divan Yolu, stopping for a baklava and coffee at busy Çiğdem Pastanesi on the way. After wandering around the Grand Bazaar and assuring the good-humoured touts that I have no money to spend, I walk through the Old Book Bazaar and around İstanbul University to the Süleymaniye Camii so that I can marvel at Sinan's most wonderful creation. I'm feeling hungry by this stage, so I join the sea of locals on the bustling streets of Tahtakale and wander past the shops and street vendors down towards Eminönü. After gobbling a fish sandwich I hop on a ferry to Kadıköy and do the round trip because this is absolutely my favourite pastime when I'm in the city. Next I walk across the Galata Bridge and up through the narrow streets of Karaköy and Tünel to İstiklal Caddesi to meet friends for a drink at Leb-i Derya or Kat 5, followed by a rowdy dinner at one of the places on Nevizade Sokak. Raki, meze and good friends, all in the best city in the world – life doesn't get any better than this!

City Life

City Life

İSTANBUL TODAY

This meeting point of East and West has rarely been as full of confidence and hope for the future as it is today. In its guise as Constantinople the city was powerful and mysterious, but as the 21st century kicks off, modern İstanbul is poised on the brink of a total rebirth and is joyfully shouting this news to the world.

The biggest change on the horizon is, of course, tied up in the country's bid to join the European Union (EU). A decision as to whether accession talks with Turkey should be formally opened will be made at the Brussels summit in December 2004, but the outcome sure ain't in the bag. Spain, Germany, the UK and Italy openly back Turkey's membership, but the Scandinavian countries have reservations mainly to do with human rights, France doesn't seem keen and Greece (traditionally a foe) is unlikely to actively intervene on Turkey's behalf. Though optimistic, the Turks are nowhere near certain of success.

In fact, many visitors to İstanbul can't understand why Turkey's bid would even be questioned. They saunter down sophisticated İstiklal Caddesi in Beyoğlu or Teşvikiye Caddesi in Nişantaşı, pop into cafés and bars and say to themselves 'Of course Turkey should be admitted into the EU – why on earth isn't it already a member?!' It's only when they leave the city and travel into the less affluent and religiously conservative rural regions that the issue becomes less clear cut.

Whatever the ultimate decision, one thing is clear: Turkey's EU bid has forever changed the country. Initiatives to bring it into line with its European neighbours in the areas of human rights, environmental protection, economic management, freedom of speech and the introduction of democratic processes have had an enormous effect, particularly in İstanbul. There are still improvements that need to be made in all of these areas if candidacy is to be seriously considered, though, as İstanbullus themselves will freely admit.

One of the most important of these areas is human rights. In 2003 the much-lauded 'Harmonisation' legislation was passed through parliament. This legislation aimed to rid the country of its history of torture and ill treatment of prisoners, assure the right to immediate legal counsel for state security court detainees, lift restrictions on non-Turkish broadcasters on private radio and TV stations, and abolish article 8 of the anti-terror law (the crime of spreading separatist propaganda). Measures to achieve these aims include ending incommunicado detention in prisons and assuring the possibility of retrial for those whom the European Court of Human Rights ruled had suffered a violation of the European Convention of Human Rights.

Liberals throughout the country were ecstatic – it looked as if the Turkey excoriated by Amnesty International year after year was to finally change its ways.

Alas, in practice the legislation doesn't seem to have changed the status quo. Kurdistan Workers Party's (PKK) leader Abdullah

Cityscape, Sultanahmet (p78)

Öcalan continues his solitary incarceration on the island of İmrali off Bursa, denied visits from his lawyer and family, while the pro-Kurdish political party Hadep (People's Democracy Party) was recently banned by a Constitutional Court ruling. On top of this, allegations of police abuse continue unabated, with charges of rape and torture of female political prisoners being levied against İstanbul police, and the former head of the city's Organised Crime Branch being discharged from the force for ignoring torture committed under his authority. And though Nobel Prize nominee Leyla Zana and three of her DEP party parliamentary colleagues were released from prison in June 2004 pending an appeal against their 15-year prison sentences for alleged links to the outlawed PKK, the European Parliament and international human rights organisations continue to argue that the 10 years the MPs spent in jail constituted a gross abuse of human rights, and that the four never received a fair trial. Such criticisms elicit nothing but silence in Ankara.

Such behind-the-scenes thuggery was, of course, more than matched by the tragic 2003 bomb attacks by Muslim fundamentalists that saw 26 locals killed and hundreds injured at the Neve Shalom and Beth Israel synagogues in Beyoğlu, followed by 31 killed and many more injured in bomb attacks on the nearby British Consulate and HSBC Bank. İstanbullus were horrified: this wasn't the inclusive and peaceful city that they believed in. What was happening? What was happening, of course, was geopolitics as practiced by extremists and nothing the locals could do or say could make any difference.

These weighty issues aside, the city is supremely optimistic about the future that it has in store, and so it should be. After all, its standard of living is rising, its monuments are being restored to their former glory, its streetscapes are getting a real spit 'n' polish and its novelists, fashion designers, artists and writers are building international reputations. It even hosted Eurovision 2004. Can things get any better than that? We bet they can…

CITY CALENDAR

During the warmer months İstanbul is awash with arts festivals and music events, giving the visitor plenty of choice when it comes to entertainment. Most of the big-name arts festivals are organised by the **İstanbul Foundation for Culture and Arts** (☎ 212-334 0700; www.istfest .org; İstiklal Caddesi, Luvr Apt No 146, Beyoğlu 80070). Tickets to most events are available from **Biletix** (www.biletix.com). For a list of public holidays refer to p246.

APRIL & MAY
INTERNATIONAL İSTANBUL FILM FESTIVAL
☎ 212-334 0700; www.istfest.org
Now in its 23rd year, this annual festival, held around April/May, attracts big crowds. The program features retrospectives and new releases from Turkey and around the world. If you're keen to see the cream of the latest Turkish cinema releases and a few local film stars, this is the place to do it. Venues are mainly on and around İstiklal Caddesi in Beyoğlu.

INTERNATIONAL İSTANBUL DANCE FESTIVAL
☎ 212-232 9830; www.crrks.org in Turkish
Held in late April to early May, this showcases local and international choreographers and companies. International guests have included the Irish Modern Dance Theatre and Compagnie Fetes Galantes. Most performances are at the **Cemal Reşit Rey Concert Hall** (p177) in Harbiye.

CHILDREN'S DAY
The national public holiday on 23 April is celebrated on Beyoğlu's İstiklal Caddesi with a

morning parade. Children march, twirl batons, perform folk dances and make a racket with brass instruments, all watched by crowds of proud parents and indulgent onlookers.

INTERNATIONAL İSTANBUL THEATRE FESTIVAL
☎ 212-334 0700; www.istfest.org

Turkey's major theatre festival alternates every year with the **International İstanbul Biennial** (opposite), and is next scheduled for 2006. The Theatre Festival is usually held in May. Big-name international companies share the stages with top local talent. The result is often inspired. The main venue is the **Atatürk Cultural Centre** (p177) on Taksim Square, but performances have also been staged at atmospheric venues such as the **Great Byzantine Palace** (p86) and **Rumeli Hisarı** (p223). Very few performances are in English.

INTERNATIONAL ÜLKER PUPPET FESTIVAL İSTANBUL
☎ 212-232 0224; karagozek@hotmail.com

Turks take their puppetry seriously, and this one-week festival held at the start of May highlights Turkish *Karagöz* puppetry as well as international acts. Performances are at small venues and cultural centres throughout town.

ORTHODOX EASTER
☎ 212-531 9670/6; Ecumenical Orthodox Patriarchate; Sadrazam Ali Paşa Caddesi, Fener

The celebratory Easter Sunday mass is the biggest event of the year at the home of the Greek Orthodox community in Fener.

JUNE & JULY

INTERNATIONAL İSTANBUL MUSIC FESTIVAL
☎ 212-334 0700; www.istfest.org

Now in its 32nd year, this festival is held in early June to early July. It includes performances of opera, dance, orchestral concerts and chamber recitals. Acts are often internationally renowned and venues are suitably grand – **Haghia Eirene** (p177) in Sultanahmet, the Atatürk Cultural Centre on Taksim Square and **Yıldız Şale** (p127) in Yıldız to name but three.

INTERNATIONAL İSTANBUL JAZZ FESTIVAL
☎ 212- 334 0700; www.istfest.org

This festival was once part of the International İstanbul Music Festival, but branched out on its

own in 1994 and has subsequently gone from strength to strength. It usually runs for two weeks in the beginning of July. A weird hybrid of conventional jazz, electronica, drum 'n' bass, world music and rock, its headline performers have included Joan Baez, Nick Cave, Miles Davis, Charlie Haden, Lou Reed, and Massive Attack. Venues include Cemil Topuzlu Open-Air Theatre (Cemil Topuzlu Açık Hava Tiyatrosu), Cemal Reşit Rey Concert Hall, **Nardis Jazz Club** (p176), **Babylon** (p181) and cafés around town.

EFES PILSEN ONE LOVE
☎ 212-252 5167; www.pozitif-ist.com

A newcomer to the city's music scene, this two-night festival is held at Park Orman in June and features pop and electronic music. Up to 15,000 young İstanbullus turned up in 2003 to hear Moby and Manu Chao, and big crowds made it to hear acts including Peter Gabriel and John Cale in 2004.

AUGUST
ROCK'N COKE
☎ 212-252 5167; www.pozitif-ist.com

Turkey's biggest open-air music festival is held over two days at the Herarfen Airfield. In 2004 it featured headline acts Iggy and the Stooges, The Ramsus, Neneh Cherry and 50 Cent.

SEPTEMBER, OCTOBER & NOVEMBER
AKBANK JAZZ FESTIVAL
☎ 212-252 3500; www.akbanksanat.com In Turkish

The older sister to the International İstanbul Jazz Festival is now in its 13th year. A boutique event, its October program usually features traditional and avant-garde jazz, as well as Middle Eastern fusions and a special program of young jazz. Venues include the Cemal Reşit Rey Concert Hall, Babylon, **Roxy** (p182) and the **Akbank Culture & Arts Centre** (p177) in Beyoğlu. Recent headline acts have included Betty Carter and Muhal Richard Abrama.

EFES PILSEN BLUES FESTIVAL
☎ 212-252 5167; www.pozitif-ist.com

This two-day İstanbul event in October or November has been entertaining fans of the Blues since 1990. Headline international acts have included names such as Long John Hunter & the Bad Blues Band, Philadelphia Jerry Ricks and the Zydeco Brothers.

Mrs Erdoğan's Headscarf

Emine Erdoğan, the wife of Turkey's prime minister, hasn't been seen at too many official functions over the past 12 months. In fact, her name hasn't been included on any recent guest lists issued by the office of the country's president, Ahmed Necdet Sezer. The reason for her exclusion isn't that she speaks out of turn, gets blind drunk or exhibits poor table manners. She does none of these things. No, the reason the prime minister's wife is being ostracised is because she insists on wearing a headscarf.

No issue is as hotly debated in Turkey as the Constitutional Court's imposition of a national ban on headscarves being worn in the public domain. The fact that girls and women are being forced out of schools and universities as a result of the ban is considered by many to be a national disgrace, but others argue that the headscarf is a challenge to the national identity that cannot be countenanced; allow the headscarf, they argue, and the secular state fought for by Atatürk's generation is totally undermined. National newspapers such as the pro-Islamic daily *Zaman* point out that any argument that defines secularism as totally against every kind of social and public manifestation of religion is both naive and misguided, but they haven't yet managed to prompt the ruling Justice & Development Party (AKP) to force a constitutional amendment overturning the ban.

The reason the AKP hasn't yet done this is simple: it fears that such an action would lead to the National Security Council (NSC) forcing it to resign for flouting the constitutional ban on religion and politics, as happened to its Refah predecessor in 1997. This isn't to say that the AKP won't go ahead and press for an amendment regardless, for passions run high on this issue. The wives and daughters of a majority of cabinet members wear the headscarf and they and many Turks were outraged when the president refused to invite them to a National Day reception in 2003. Equally contentious was the expulsion from the national parliament of a deputy from İstanbul, Merve Kavakçı, who insisted on taking her oath of office while wearing a headscarf. Ms Kavakçı was subsequently stripped of her parliamentary immunity and prosecuted. Democracy in action?

INTERNATIONAL İSTANBUL BIENNIAL

☎ 212-334 0763; www.istfest.org

The city's major visual-arts shindig takes place towards the end of every second year. An international curator nominates a theme and puts together a cutting-edge program, which is then exhibited in venues around town. In 2003 paintings, sculpture, installation and multi-media work by some 85 artists from 42 countries was on show in the **Aya Sofya** (p79), the **Basilica Cistern** (p83), the Mimar Sinan Fine Arts University and the Antrepo 4 Exhibition Hall.

ANNIVERSARY OF ATATÜRK'S DEATH

At 9.05am on the 10th of November a minute's silence is held to commemorate the death of the nation's revered leader. Sirens blare and the city comes to a standstill, with people, cars and buses literally stopping in their tracks.

DECEMBER

AKBANK SHORT FILM FESTIVAL

☎ 212-252 3500; www.akbanksanat.com in Turkish

Beloved by the black-clad Beyoğlu bohemian set, this artsy film culture event is held at the Akbank Culture & Arts Centre.

CULTURE

IDENTITY

Turkey has a population of approximately 68 million, the great majority being Sunni Muslim Turks. Though İstanbul's population is given officially as 9.6 million, estimates of its true size reach as high as 20 million. The discrepancy comes about due to the fact that at census time, many of the migrants who have moved to the city return to their villages or towns to be counted among their populations, thus ensuring the rural communities a stable level of municipal funding. Poor old İstanbul, which has to supply infrastructure and social support for its swathe of new residents, is left short-changed as a result – no wonder it's finding it difficult to cope!

The city has always been a melting pot of different ethnicities and religions, with Greek and Christian communities calling Byzantium home, and Jews being invited to settle here by Mehmet after the Conquest. The rights of these groups were reiterated under the 1923 Treaty of Lausanne, which effectively created the modern state of Turkey. There have been tensions, of course, because though these communities were assured the right to practice their religions by Mehmet, over the years they have joined the large numbers of Turkish citizens of Armenian and Kurdish descent in suffering discrimination, even violence, at the hands of the Muslim majority. It's true to say, though, that the city is generally inclusive and that its different communities make an important contribution to its social, cultural and political fabric. The major ethnic groups are as follows.

Turks

The Turkic peoples originated in Central Asia, where they were a presence to be reckoned with as early as the 4th century AD. The Chinese called them Tu-küe, which is perhaps the root of our word 'Turk'. The Tu-küe were related to the Hiung-nu (the Huns).

The normally nomadic Turks ruled several vast but short-lived empires in Central Asia before being pushed westward by the Mongols. Various tribes of the Oğuz Turkic group settled in Azerbaijan, northern Iran and Anatolia, the culmination of which saw them, as the Ottomans, finally overrunning Constantinople in 1453, and going on to conquer much of Eastern Europe.

Early Turks followed each of the great Asian and Middle Eastern religions, including Buddhism, Nestorian Christianity, Manichaeism and Judaism. During their western migrations they became more familiar with Islam, and it has been adopted by them ever since.

Kurds

Turkey has a significant Kurdish minority estimated at 12 million or more. Some ethnologists believe that the Kurds, who speak an Indo-European language, are closely related to the Persians, and that they migrated here from northern Europe centuries before Christ. There are also significant Kurdish populations in neighbouring Iraq, Iran and Syria as well. İstanbul numbers many Turkish Kurds among its citizens, including those who moved to the city over the last two decades either to seek work or avoid the insurgency in their own provinces.

Over the centuries the Kurds have struggled for autonomy from the various majority governments that have ruled them. In 1924 Atatürk banned any expression of Kurdishness in an attempt at assimilation. Major battles and atrocities ensued throughout the 1920s and 1930s and, since 1984, nearly 30,000 people have died. Today, some Kurds such as supporters

Textile shop, Sultanahmet

of the banned PKK (Kurdistan Workers Party's) demand a separate state, but most just want the right to read the newspaper in their own language, have their children taught in this language and watch Kurdish TV, which is beamed in from Northern Europe. They'd also like to identify themselves as Kurdish on their identity cards and in the national census.

Jews

İstanbul's Jewish community of around 24,000 forms the majority of Turkey's Jewish population of some 27,000. The Turkish Jewish community is the remnant of a great influx that took place in the 16th century when the Jews of Spain (Sephardim) were forced by the Spanish Inquisition to flee their homes. They were welcomed into the Ottoman Empire, and brought with them knowledge of many European scientific and economic discoveries and advancements. The Galata area in Beyoğlu and Balat on the Golden Horn have traditionally been the centres of the community in İstanbul.

> ## Top Five Travellers' Accounts of İstanbul
>
> - *Turkish Letters*, Ogier de Busbecq. A French observer of the Ottoman empire in the 16th century
> - *Eothen*, A W Kinglake. An eccentric and lively account of a 19th-century journey through the Middle East
> - *Innocents Abroad*, Mark Twain. Twain's account of his 'grand tour' including observations of İstanbul
> - *The Owl's Watchsong*, J A Cuddon. An Englishman's account of 1950s İstanbul
> - *A Byzantine Journey*, John Ash. Journey through the Byzantine realm inevitably passes through the empire's former capital

City Life – Culture

Greeks

Turkey's community of ethnic Greeks was in the millions during the Ottoman Empire, but most fled to Greece or abroad during the cataclysm of WWI and the Turkish War of Independence. Many others left as part of the League of Nations' exchange of populations between Turkey and Greece after WWI. The conflict with Cyprus in the 1960s raised tensions between the two countries, causing another exodus of Turkish Greeks to Greece and Greek Turks to Turkey. It is estimated that ethnic Greeks in Turkey now number fewer than 100,000, many of whom live in İstanbul's Fener district surrounding the Ecumenical Orthodox Patriarchate.

Armenians

The Armenians are thought by some to be descended from the Urartians (518–330 BC) of eastern Anatolia, but others think they arrived from the Caucasus area after the Urartian state collapsed.

Armenians have lived in eastern Anatolia for millennia, almost always as subjects of some greater state. They lived with their Kurdish and Turkish neighbours in relative peace and harmony under the Ottoman *millet* system of distinct religious communities, but with the rise of modern ethnic nationalism during the declining years of the Ottoman Empire, their community was decimated by emigration, conflict, massacre and deportation.

Though many Armenians remained loyal to the Ottoman sultan during WWI, others organised guerrilla bands in pursuit of an independent Armenian state on Ottoman soil. The resultant outrage of terrorism (new at the time, though all too familiar to us now) set off a powerful anti-Armenian backlash, resulting in widespread massacres of innocent Armenians in İstanbul and elsewhere.

With the support of the Imperial Russian army, a short-lived Armenian Republic was proclaimed in northeastern Anatolia in the closing years of WWI, and the victorious Armenians repaid defeated local Muslims with massacres in kind. On 3 December 1920, the Ankara government concluded a peace treaty with the Armenian government in Yerevan, by then a Soviet republic. By the end of the war, the Armenian population of Anatolia had been reduced to insignificant numbers.

The centre of İstanbul's Armenian community is in Kumkapı, where it has its own schools, churches and cultural organisations.

Local Etiquette

Under the Ottoman Empire, Turkish etiquette was highly organised and very formal. When Atatürk founded the new Republic, he sought to do away with the rigid behavioural codes that had characterised the Ottoman system – banning the fez and head veil was one of the first symbolic steps in this process. Although Atatürk's reforms have changed İstanbul and the rest of the country enormously, glimpses of traditional attitudes and behaviour often come through, usually in the form of social etiquette.

In general, you may find your dealings with Turks to be more formal than you're used to at home. Though they have adapted to the informality of 21st-century life, you'll still notice vestiges of the courtly Ottoman state of mind. Those foreigners who study Turkish language, for instance, are often bamboozled by the dozens of polite phrases – actually rigid formulas – that must be repeated on cue in many daily situations. Fortunately, most visitors aren't expected to use these, but you should try using the following rules when in İstanbul:

- Don't point your finger directly towards any person.
- Don't show the sole of your foot or shoe towards anyone (ie so they can see it).
- Don't blow your nose openly in public, especially in a restaurant; instead, turn or leave the room and blow quietly.
- Don't pick your teeth unless you are covering your mouth with your hand.
- Don't kiss or hug in public in the more conservative parts of the city such as Sultanahmet, Fatih and Eminönü (showing affection towards your children is an obvious exception to this rule).
- Do learn the local term for 'thanks' *(teşekkürler)* or 'thank you very much' *(çok teşekkür ederim)* and use them when appropriate.

Mosque Etiquette

- Always remove your shoes before stepping on the clean area just in front of the mosque door, or on the carpets inside. Worshippers touch their foreheads to the carpets and so, quite reasonably, they like them to be clean.
- Wear modest clothes when visiting mosques, as you would when visiting a church or synagogue. Don't wear shorts. Women should have head, arms and shoulders covered with a shawl, and wear modest dresses or skirts, preferably reaching at least to the knees. At some of the larger mosques in İstanbul headscarves and robes can be borrowed to ensure modesty; the loan is free, though a donation to the mosque is appreciated.
- The best time to visit mosques is mid-morning on any day but Friday. Mosques are crowded with worshippers on Fridays, so it's best to leave your mosque sightseeing to the other days of the week. Avoid entering mosques at prayer time (ie at the call-to-prayer at dawn, noon, mid-afternoon, dusk and evening, or 20 minutes thereafter).
- When you're inside a mosque, even if it is not prayer time, there may be a few people praying. Don't disturb them in any way, don't walk directly in front of them, and don't take flash photos.

LIFESTYLE

İstanbul isn't a wealthy city – as you'll see when you encounter the dilapidated Old İstanbul housing stock and beggars on the Eminönü underpasses – but it has an innate optimism that manifests itself in every facet of life and makes it a great place in which to live or visit.

As is the case in all large cities, there are extremes of wealth and poverty here. Industrialists such as Rahmi Koç established dynasties whose younger members drip money wherever they go. These privileged İstanbullus live in mansions on the Bosphorus, shop in Nişantaşı when they can't get to Paris or London and are fixtures at big-ticket social events such as the İstanbul Music Festival. Fortunately many also endow museums and fund philanthropic trusts along the way. The new industrialists – media magnate Aydın Doğan for instance – seem to be following this philanthropic lead, albeit in a tentative fashion. At the other end of the spectrum are the thousands of migrants from eastern Turkey who have come to this version of the Emerald City to find work and shelter. Hundreds of thousands of these marginalised members of Turkish society live in makeshift illegal housing known as *gecekondu*, often without running water and electricity, and have to compete with others for the menial jobs on offer, as unemployment is high (some estimates put it at more than 20%).

If there's a typical İstanbul lifestyle, it's probably somewhere between these two extremes. Apartment living is the norm, and gardens and outdoor terraces are unusual, leading to the few green spaces in the city being heavily used. Cramped living spaces are also one of the major factors contributing to the city's street culture. In warmer weather couples, families and groups of friends like nothing better than an after-dinner walk with a stop for a coffee or nargileh. This social instinct is shared by every city resident – groups in restaurants are invariably large, picnics in the park even larger. After all, what's the point of enjoying life if you can't do it with friends and family?

Women are joining the workforce in ever-increasing numbers and feature heavily in the public sector, largely as a result of Atatürk's passionate promotion of women's rights in the early years of the republic. (Women were given the vote in Turkey in 1934 and have been active in political life ever since; there was even a female prime minister between 1993 and 1996 – something quite extraordinary in a Middle Eastern context.) Not all women are joining the workforce, though. While it's quite common to encounter female doctors and lawyers throughout the city, it's equally common to encounter female migrants from the east who were pulled out of school aged 10 or so to work in the fields before being married a few years later and migrating to the city in search of a better life. National education reform aimed at keeping all children in school until 15 years of age will very likely change this scenario over the next decade.

Many city households now have two incomes and this has led to a boom in sales of consumer goods and cars. One consequence of so many women working is that the family unit is getting smaller, and many young couples are relying on grandparents and parents to act as child minders while they're out in the workplace.

In all, the city is characterised by its inclusiveness, friendliness and great *joie de vivre*. Neighbours, relatives, friends and colleagues catch its public transport, eat on its streets, complain about local corruption and celebrate its soccer successes together. Best of all, they're happy to include visitors in their busy and laughter-filled lives.

FASHION

Fashion in İstanbul is best described as eclectic. Every season the latest trends spotted on the catwalks in Paris, Rome or New York are reworked for and by the local market, hitting the shelves in a remarkably short period of time. Though international chains such as Zara do this supremely well, local store Yargıcı (p200) is the most popular outlet for main street fashion, and can always be relied upon for a fetching summer frock in the latest colours and style or an accessory *de jour*. Glam areas such as Nişantaşı and Teşvikiye (p199) are the places to go to access real European designer items, which are snapped up by the blond-tipped, tanned and immaculately groomed wives of the city's bankers, industrialists and politicians. Ensembles by İstanbul-born, but London-based, designer Rifat Ozbek often feature on their shopping lists. At the other extreme are the young suburban women sporting the latest in Islamic chic, invariably a long denim skirt instead of jeans, a fitted (but not too revealing) top and a colour-coordinated headscarf. Cleverly applied makeup to feature the eyes is all part of the demure but modern package. The most popular fashion trend of all is a perennial one – young Turks love their jeans, and currently wear them tight and slung low. Local chain Mavi (p196) is where aficionados both male and female choose to shop for their latest pair.

Window shopping

The local designer fashion scene is thriving and does a particularly inspired line in Ottoman-influenced styles created using rich fabrics and embroidery. Gönül Paksoy (described as the 'new Hussein Chalayan') is probably the queen of this trend, but there are plenty of aspirants dotted throughout Nişantaşı and Çukurcuma just waiting to hit the pages of *Wallpaper* or *French Vogue*.

The uncompromising Chalayan (known in Turkey as Hüseyin Çağlayan) is, of course, the king of the scene, albeit from a distance. Though his clothes are difficult to find in İstanbul, his influence is felt everywhere. After all, he's a local boy who's made it to the big time (well, nearly local – he is in fact a Turkish Cypriot who trained in London), and he's proud of his heritage. More of a conceptual artist than a fashion designer, he undertakes intense historical research as part of his creative process, and has referenced Byzantine, Ottoman, Georgian, Armenian and Greek historical styles in a number of his collections. He freely admits that he likes taking ideas from the past and putting them into contemporary garments, and this appropriation has characterised most of his collections. More radically, he talks about using DNA and archaeology as reference points – no doubt his graduate collection, which featured garments that he had buried in the ground for several weeks and then disinterred to observe the deterioration, was his first foray into such investigations. Chalayan's most recent projects have been in the fields of video and installation rather than fashion, and his work *Place to Passage* was exhibited at the **Proje4L art gallery** (p180) in Levent in 2004 to great local acclaim.

SPORT

If you're keen to strike up a conversation about sport in İstanbul, you'll need to talk about soccer. Quite simply, nothing else counts. Turkey's three largest soccer teams – Galatasaray, Fenerbahçe and Beşiktaş – are based here, and locals are extravagantly proud of all of them. Indeed, when Galatasaray became the first Turkish team to win a UEFA Cup (in 2000), locals went wild with excitement – in many eyes it was probably the most significant event since the Conquest. When the national team reached the semifinals of the World Cup in 2002 and ended up in third place, an estimated 1.5 million came out on İstanbul's streets to congratulate the players on their return. As most of the team members were sourced from the ranks of the city's big three clubs, it was seen as a local triumph as well as a national victory.

Many of the İstanbul teams have strong roots in local or ethnic communities. Translated, Fenerbahçe means 'Garden of the Lighthouse', a clear reference to the Greek community in old Phanar (today's Fener); and Galatasaray was formed by Muslim students of the French-run Galatasaray Lycee. No doubt this is one of the factors contributing to the strong rivalries between supporters of each club, which occasionally lead to violence in the stands.

The link between national pride and soccer might be strong, but it's almost eclipsed by the relationship between soccer and local fashion. Soccer chic is *de rigueur* for the young İstanbullu male, and many a wardrobe is put together in the team stores, which sell all manner of fashion and lifestyle accessories as well as the more prosaic club footballs and uniforms. Soccer even influences the local music scene, as recently shown when German-Turkish footballer Ümit Davala, who played on the legendary UEFA-winning Galatasaray team, released a rap album featuring a spot by local pop star Kayahan and backing vocals from Beşiktaş and Galatasaray players.

The only sport that comes close to soccer in terms of eliciting national pride is weightlifting. At the Athens 2004 Olympics Turkish weightlifters won three gold medals, and one of them, Halil Mutlu, won his third consecutive Olympic weightlifting gold medal, ensuring his place in the ranks of Turkey's all-time sporting heroes.

MEDIA

Turkey is going to have to lift its game when it comes to the promotion of a free and diverse media if it is to have its bid to join the EU taken seriously. At present 70% of the Turkish media is under the control of only two companies: the Doğan and Bilgin groups. Doğan owns eight newspapers, including *Hürriyet*, *Milliyet* and *Radikal*, as well as the CNN Türk and Kanal D TV channels. It controls between 40% and 60% of national advertising revenue and 80% of distribution channels, and also has interests in banking, tourism, electricity and fuel distribution. Bilgin owns *Sabah* newspaper, ATV TV and dozens of periodicals. Like Doğan, it has interests in many other industries.

In 2002 local and international media analysts were outraged when the Ankara government passed legislation smoothing the way for media groups to enter into public tenders and trade on the stock exchange. Seen by many as a move tailor-made for Aydın Doğan, the head of the Doğan Group, the legislation made it possible for Turkish media barons to bid for government contracts and acquire stakes in the many state-owned companies being earmarked for privatisation. Critics feared (and still do) that the media channels owned by these barons would be pressured to present government-friendly media analysis as a way of staying sweet with Ankara and promoting the financial interests of their parent companies.

The legislation had another – equally unpalatable – component that called for all Internet sites to submit their content to government censors before posting or updating it. Anyone responsible for material considered to be 'threatening to national security, sexually explicit or libellous' would be subject to large fines and jail sentences. Turkey's Internet service providers were so appalled that they closed their services for a day in protest.

It's not often that legislation prompts open criticism from within government ranks in Turkey, but in this case even the head of the government's own broadcasting watchdog agency was moved to publicly comment that the two-part legislation was a 'dark stain on Turkish democracy'. At around the same time, the government's repressive hold on freedom of speech in the country was highlighted by the censor's ban on the İstanbul Film Festival's screening of Handan Ipekçis' film *Big Man Small Love*. The film's storyline is about a small Kurdish girl who hides in a closet while police conduct a violent raid on the apartment where she lives with a group of suspected Kurdish activists, and the censor took exception to both its 'subversive' message and its Kurdish dialogue. The festival screening was cancelled despite the fact that the film was Turkey's official nomination for Best Foreign Film at the Oscars. Confusingly, this occurred at around the same time that other legislation aimed at removing constraints on minority language education and broadcasting (so pleasing Brussels) was being passed in Ankara. The jury's still out as to whether the demands of the EU for the sanctity and importance of a free press will prevail over the behind-the-scenes machinations of powerful tycoons.

LANGUAGE

Writing of Constantinople in 1857, Herman Melville said '...You feel you are among the nations', and when it comes to language, the city hasn't changed much. Melville saw this Babel-like reality as a curse, and after taking the reins of government half a century later, Atatürk and his republican colleagues agreed, establishing the modern Turkish language to take over from its 'contaminated' Ottoman predecessor, which was full of Arabic and Persian influences. All Turks were encouraged to learn and speak the new language and its Latin alphabet rather than Ottoman Turkish, regional dialects or foreign languages. Fortunately, contemporary Turkey is reclaiming its polyglot heritage as well as taking pride in their own national language and you'll have no trouble at all communicating in English and, to a lesser extent, French, German or Russian when you're here. Snippets of many foreign languages can be heard throughout Old İstanbul and you'll also notice that the city has particular quarters in which dialects are spoken: in Balat, for instance, Ladino, a medieval Spanish dialect, is still used by descendants of the Sephardic community that migrated here during the Spanish Inquisition. Armenian, Greek and some regional Turkish dialects are also spoken in different quarters of town.

By learning a few Turkish phrases you'll do your bit to charm the locals; see p254 for tips.

ECONOMY & COSTS

Turkey's economy is still struggling to recover from the crash of the national currency in February 2001, which led to the country having to be baled out of trouble by huge International Monetary Fund (IMF) loans. The crash was generally blamed on lax and corrupt government regulation of the banking sector, and it totally scuttled the government's proposed implementation of privatisation initiatives, which in turn made its three-year plan to reduce inflation to 7% by the end of 2002 impossible to achieve. Instead, the government is aiming for 12% in 2004 (still impressive in an historical context, as inflation stood at 63% in 1999 and at 34% in 2000) and the IMF has predicted that inflation will be 10.6% in 2005.

Interest rates are hovering at around 26% compared with 70% in 2002, which is considered a major achievement. Debt is still a huge problem, with the World Bank's 2004 Development Report placing Turkey seventh largest among the developing countries when it comes to debt (Brazil is the largest). Of the debt, US$83.9 billion is owed or guaranteed by the state and US$47.6 billion by the private sector.

Rampant inflation due to successive governments borrowing at high rates of interest from an increasingly cautious international market is the major factor influencing the historically plummeting value of the Turkish lira, something that exasperates all Turks, particularly those in business. The obvious manifestation of this is the raft of zeros on the national currency, something that most visitors to the country have trouble getting their heads around. Good news might well be just around the corner, though, as the falling inflation rate and appreciation of the lira has prompted the government to announce that six zeros will be stripped from the currency on January 1, 2005. Though many Turks remain sceptical that this will happen, it could be that those zero-related rip-offs by taxi drivers will soon be a thing of the past!

In the past few years governments have encouraged the free interplay of market forces and have achieved wonders when it comes to convincing the IMF and international markets that Turkey doesn't have to be a basket case when it comes to economic management. Relaxed market conditions have seen great growth in the number of new companies (making up about 10% of existing companies in 2003), although there is little foreign investment (less than 10% of GDP), which hinders the modernization of the economy and hampers access to the export market. One of the major factors driving Turkey's bid to join the EU is the economic benefits it would bring – even now, Turkey is the EU's seventh-largest export destination and the 13th-largest exporter to the EU, and if restrictions were relaxed this relationship would be even more beneficial to Turkey.

Though the country has traditionally been a net exporter of food (one of the few such countries in the world), its strong agricultural sector has now been superseded by even stronger commercial and manufacturing activity, much of which is centred in İstanbul. Turkey produces motor vehicles, appliances and consumer goods, and has undertaken many large engineering projects. The country's products are exported throughout the region. İstanbul's industrial plants are to the west and east of the city centre. The commercial centre is north of the historic city on the western side of the Bosphorus.

Tourism is now among the most important sectors of the Turkish economy. In 2002, 13.2 million visitors came to Turkey, bringing US$11.9 billion into the country with them. The government hopes for tourist numbers to increase each year by around 5.5%, though the political situation in the Middle East and the bombings in İstanbul in 2003 and 2004 will make this hard to achieve.

How Much?

Litre of petrol €1.10
Litre of bottled water €0.80
Efes Pilsen in a bar around €2
Souvenir T-shirt around €8.30
Fish sandwich €0.80
Glass of çay (tea) around €0.70
Taxi ride from Sultanahmet to Taksim €3.30
Movie ticket €2.80 to €6.60
Nargileh €2.80
Copy of the Turkish Daily News €1.40

In its 2003 World Economic Report, the IMF said that the improvement of the Turkish financial market has had a positive impact on economic activity and confirmed that the GDP, supported by private investment and consumption, rose by 5.8% in 2003. The IMF expects growth to rise by an average 5% in 2004 and 2005.

Though the Turks have historically fretted about the state of the national economy, the woes of the lira have benefited travellers who have foreign currency to spend. There are few major cities in Europe where a three-star hotel room for two costs €60 and a decent evening meal €10 to €15 per head, but İstanbul is one of them. Transport is dirt cheap and many sights are free – others are relatively inexpensive (Topkapı Palace being the obvious exception).

GOVERNMENT & POLITICS

Though the Turks are firm believers in democracy, the tradition of popular rule is relatively short. Real multiparty democracy came into being only after WWII, and has been interrupted several times by military coups, though government has always eventually been returned to civilians.

The continuing power of the military is embodied in the make-up of the National Security Council (NSC), which is made up of high-level government and military leaders and meets monthly to 'advise' the government. Its relationship with the ruling Justice and Development Party (AKP) national government is uneasy, largely due to the AKP's obvious Islamist sympathies and the military's firm allegiance to the ideal of the Turkish secular state. Many Turks see discord within the ranks of the NSC as inevitable, and fear that another coup is on the horizon; others point toward Prime Minister Recep Tayyıp Erdoğan's strong economic stewardship and focus on Turkey's bid to join the EU as signs that he and his government have a very different agenda to that of past Islamist governments, and are unlikely to force the NSC's hand.

İstanbul itself is actually two political entities: the city and the province. The city is organised as a *büyükşehir belediyesi*, or metropolitan municipality, with several large sub-municipalities under the overall authority of a metropolitan city government.

The current metropolitan city government is perceived to be doing a pretty good job of coping with the demands on city infrastructure that the continuing influx of migrants from the provinces is making. It's also considered by most to be doing an excellent job with the provision of municipal services such as transport and with the introduction of environmental programs such as the clean-up of the city's waterways. Accusations of corruption and cronyism are of course made from time to time (particularly about the submunicipality governing Sultanahmet), but overall, voter approval is quite high.

It's true to say that this positive view of İstanbul's municipal government kicked off during the office of Recep Tayyıp Erdoğan, the current prime minister, who was elected the Refah mayor of İstanbul in 1994. Before being ousted by secularist forces in the national government in late 1998, he made many changes and improvements, not least being to the population's overall confidence and pride in its home town. The current city mayor, Kadir Topbaş, worked as an adviser to Erdoğan before going on to become the mayor of Beyoğlu, one of the largest submunicipalities. An architect by profession, he concentrated on the suburb's urban fabric while in office and did much to improve the safety, amenity and appearance of its streets and public buildings. The fact that he was elected mayor of the city in March 2004 with a huge majority is testament to the fact that İstanbullus approved of what he did in Beyoğlu and want to see the same types of programs occur over the city as a whole.

ENVIRONMENT

İstanbul has been plagued by hyper-growth during the last few decades as villagers move to the city by the tens of thousands in search of a better life. This has placed great pressure on infrastructure and services and has also meant that many of the green areas in and around the city have been developed for housing, making open space a rare commodity indeed. Although there are a few protected areas around the city – the Princes' Islands (Kızıl Adalar) and the Beykoz Nature Forests near Polonezköy, for example – a low average of just over 1 sq metre of forest reserve is put aside per person; conservationists say the average in Europe is about 40 sq metres per person. Many of the freshwater lakes around the city have been inadvertently protected due to their status as water catchments, though the protected areas around them are shrinking as government policies bend to developers. Some of these lake areas have even made their way onto the list of endangered flora and fauna sites identified by conservationists: Büyükçekmece Lake in the west of European İstanbul, and the Ömerli Reservoir on the Asian side are two such examples. Ömerli faces a double threat because it is the proposed location for the Turkish Formula One Championship course – the local branch of the **Worldwide Fund for Nature** (www.wwf.org.tr) has called for an environmental impact assessment to be completed before the location is confirmed.

Waiting for the 'Quake

İstanbul lies over the North Anatolian Fault, which runs for about 1500km between the Anatolian and Eurasian tectonic plates. As the Arabian and African plates to the south push northward, the Anatolian plate is shoved into the Eurasian plate, and squeezed west towards Greece. This movement creates stress along the North Anatolian Fault, which accumulates, and then releases pressure as earthquakes. Thirteen major quakes in Turkey have been recorded since 1939, with the latest in August 1999 devastating İzmit and Adapazarı, about 90km east of İstanbul, leaving nearly 20,000 dead and 100,000 homeless. İstanbul remained relatively unscathed, although the suburb of Avcılar to the west of the city suffered hundreds of deaths when jerry-built dwellings collapsed.

This pattern of earthquakes leaves İstanbul in an unenviable position. Locals are half-panicked, half-fatalistic about the next one, but no-one doubts that it's coming. The city has been hit four times by major earthquakes in the last 500 years and experts predict that the strain placed by İzmit's earthquake on nearby stress segments along the fault could lead to another major quake within the next few decades.

As the destruction at Avcılar illustrated, much of the city's urban development in the last few decades has been poorly built and is unlikely to make it through a major quake. Sadly, the government doesn't seem to be forcing developers to raise their game when it comes to building quality, and when the big one comes the consequences are likely to be catastrophic. Then again, Aya Sofya has made it through more than its fair share of quakes and still crowns the first of the city's hills. Many locals look at it and take heart.

Air pollution in the city is a big problem. Though clean-burning Russian natural gas has replaced dirty lignite (soft coal) as the preferred winter heating fuel, air pollution is still significant, largely due to the ever-increasing number of cars jamming city roads. The national Ministry of Environment, established in 1991, is trying to implement programs to reduce smog across the country's large cities, but the International Energy Agency has criticised its efforts, saying that current measures don't go far enough.

The major environmental threat to the city is pollution of its waterways. Increased oil exports from the Caspian Sea region to Russian and Georgian ports and across the Black Sea has led to increased oil-tanker traffic (and risk of accident) through the narrow and winding Turkish Straits, which comprise the Dardenelles, the Sea of Marmara and the Bosphorus. With 50,000 vessels per year using this route and one in 10 of these carrying oil or liquefied natural gas, the threat of a major spill is very real. Accidents are increasing in frequency, with the worst probably being the March 1994 collision of the Greek tanker *Nassia* with another ship. Thirty seamen were killed in this incident and 20,000 tons of oil were spilled into the Straits a few kilometres north of İstanbul, triggering an inferno that raged for five days. The possibility of this happening closer to the city is very real, as was illustrated in November 2003 when a Georgian-flagged ship ran aground and broke in two – fortunately it was carrying dry goods rather than oil.

Ships using these waters also cause major water pollution by releasing contaminated water as they ballast their holds. Though government has made genuine efforts to flush water through the Bosphorus and Golden Horn (the relocation of the current-blocking 19th-century Galata Bridge and municipal rubbish-removal programs being perfect examples), the waters are still highly polluted and have contributed to a major decline of local fishing levels. Overfishing has also been a contributing factor.

You may see the occasional green recycling bin in the city, but there are few home recycling collections. Instead, enterprising recyclers scour the streets after dark, collecting aluminium and other recyclables to sell to collecting depots.

Arts

Arts

Turks have a unique attitude towards the arts, being as likely to read, view and listen to works created a century or a decade ago as they are to buy a newly released novel or album. This merging of the old and the new can be initially disconcerting for the foreign observer used to gravitating towards the fresh and new, but it makes for a rich cultural landscape and gives contemporary artists a solid base on which to build their practices. Traditional art forms such as carpets are pretty well bound by tradition and have remained unchanged over the centuries, but there's no lack of innovative contemporary art in İstanbul, particularly within the disciplines of music, literature and cinema.

CARPETS

Turkish women have been weaving carpets for a very long time. These beautiful and durable floor coverings were a nomadic family's most valuable and practical 'furniture', warming and brightening the clan's oft-moved homes. The oldest-known carpet woven in the double-knotted Gördes style (Gördes is a town in the mountains of northwest Turkey) dates from between the 4th and 1st centuries BC.

It is thought that hand-woven carpet techniques were introduced to Anatolia by the Seljuks in the 12th century, so it's not surprising that Konya, the Seljuk capital, was mentioned by Marco Polo as a centre of carpet production in the 13th century.

The general pattern and colour scheme of old carpets was influenced by local traditions and the availability of certain types of wool and colours of dyes. Patterns were memorised and women usually worked with no more than 45cm of the carpet visible. Each artist imbued her work with her own personality, choosing a motif or a colour based on her own artistic preferences, and even events and emotions in her daily life.

In the 19th century, the European rage for Turkish carpets spurred the development of carpet companies. The companies, run by men, would deal with customers, take orders, purchase and dye the wool according to the customers' preferences, and contract local women to produce the finished product. The designs were sometimes left to the women, but more often were provided by the company based on the customers' tastes. Though well made, these carpets lost some of the originality and spirit of the older work.

Carpets made today often use traditional patterns such as the commonly used eye and tree patterns, and incorporate all sorts of symbols that can be 'read' by those in the know. At a glance two carpets might look identical, but closer examination reveals the subtle differences that give each Turkish carpet its individuality and charm.

Traditionally, village women wove carpets for their own family's use, or for their dowry. Knowing they would be judged on their efforts, the women took great care over their handiwork – hand-spinning and dyeing the wool, and choosing what they judged to be the most interesting and beautiful patterns. These days the picture is more complicated. Many carpets are made to the dictates of the market rather than according to local traditions. Weavers in eastern Turkey might make carpets in popular styles native to western Turkey. Long-settled villagers might duplicate the wilder, hairier and more naive *yörük* (nomad) carpets.

Village women still weave carpets, but most of them work to fixed contracts for specific shops. Usually they work to a pattern and are paid for their final effort rather than for each hour of work. A carpet made to a fixed contract may still be of great value to its purchaser. However, the selling price should be lower than for a one-off piece.

Other carpets are the product of division of labour, with different individuals responsible for dyeing and weaving. What such pieces lose in individuality and rarity is often more than made up for in quality control. Most silk Hereke carpets (Hereke is a small town near İzmit, about 100km southeast of İstanbul) are mass-produced, but to standards that make them some of the most sought-after of all Turkish carpets.

Carpets (opposite), Grand Bazaar

Fearing that old carpet-making methods would be lost, the Ministry of Culture now sponsors a number of projects to revive traditional weaving and dyeing methods in western Turkey. Some carpet shops will have stocks of these 'project carpets', which are usually of high quality with prices reflecting that fact. Some of these carpets are also direct copies of antique pieces in museums.

Most carpet shops have a range of pieces made by a variety of techniques. Besides the traditional pile carpets, they usually offer double-sided flat-woven mats, such as kilims. Some traditional kilim motifs are similar to patterns found at the prehistoric mound of Çatal Höyük, testifying to the very ancient traditions of flat-woven floor coverings in Anatolia. Older, larger kilims may actually be two narrower pieces of similar, but not always identical, design stitched together. As this is now rarely done, any such piece is likely to be fairly old.

Other flat-weave techniques include *sumak*, a style originally from Azerbaijan, in which intricate details are woven with coloured thread by wrapping them around the warp. The loose weft ends are left hanging at the back of the rug. *Cicims* are kilims with small and lively patterns embroidered on the top.

As well as Turkish carpets, many carpet shops in İstanbul sell pieces from other countries, especially from Iran, Afghanistan and from the ex-Soviet Republics of Azerbaijan, Turkmenistan and Uzbekistan. The major difference is that Turkey favours the double knot and Iran favours the single knot. Turkish carpets also tend to have a higher pile, more dramatic designs and more varied colours than their Iranian cousins.

If you're keen to read more about Turkish carpets and rugs, it's worth getting hold of *The Classical Tradition in Anatolian Carpets* by Walter B Debby, *Kilims: The Complete Guide* by Alastair Hull or *Oriental Carpets: A buyer's guide* by Eessie Sakhai. Most serious collectors eagerly await their bimonthly copy of the excellent magazine *Hali*, published in the UK.

For information on buying a carpet when in İstanbul, see p196.

LITERATURE

Turkey has a rich but relatively young literary tradition. Its brightest stars are greatly revered throughout the country and bookshop shelves groan under the weight of new local releases. Unfortunately, not many of these are translated into English. From its refined Ottoman roots through the flowering of politically driven literary movements in the 19th and 20th centuries, it has progressed to being predominantly concerned with investigating what it means to be a Turk in the modern age, particularly if one is displaced (either by the physical move from country to city or by virtue of one's ethnic background).

Under the sultans, literature was really a form of religious devotion. Ottoman poets, borrowing from the great Arabic and Persian traditions, wrote sensual love poems of attraction, longing, fulfilment and ecstasy in the search for union with God. Occasionally they wrote about more worldly pleasures and triumphs, as Nabi Yousouf Efendi's 16th century *Eulogy of Constantinople* (republished in Chronicle Books' *Chronicles Abroad: Istanbul*) attests.

By the late 19th century the influence of Western literature began to be felt. This was the time of the Tanzimat political and social reforms initiated by Sultan Abdül Mecit, and in İstanbul a literary movement was established that became known as 'Tanzimat Literature'. Its major figures were Sinasi, Ziya Paşa, Namık Kemal and Ahmet Mithat Efendi, all of whom sought to broaden the appeal of literature and bring it into line with developments in the West.

The Tanzimat movement was responsible for the first serious attacks on the ponderous cadences of Ottoman courtly prose and poetry, but it wasn't until the foundation of the republic that the death knell of this form of literature finally rang. Atatürk decreed that the Turkish language should be purified of Arabic and Persian borrowings, and that in future the nation's literature should be created using the new Latin-based Turkish alphabet. Major figures in the new literary movement (dubbed 'National Literature') included poets Yahya Kemal Beyatli and Mehmet Akıf Ersoy, and novelists Halide Edib Adıvar, Ziya Gokalp, Ömer Seyfettin and Aka Gündüz.

Of these figures, İstanbullu Halide Edib Adıvar (1884–1964) was particularly interesting. A writer and vocal leader of the emerging women's emancipation movement in Turkey, she was an ally of Atatürk and a leading figure in the War of Independence. Her 1926 autobiographical work *Memoir of Halide Edib* recounts her privileged upbringing in Beşiktaş and Üsküdar, progressive education at the American College for Girls in Arnavutköy and subsequent marriage to a noted mathematician, who humiliated her by taking a second wife. After leaving him, she joined the Nationalists, remarried, worked closely with Atatürk and wrote a popular history of the War of Independence called *The Turkish Ordeal* (1928). In later years she worked as a university lecturer; wrote over 20 novels, the most famous of which was probably the 1938 work *Thewn and his Daughter;* and had a brief stint as a member of parliament. A fictionalised account of the early part of this fascinating woman's life can be found in *Halide's Gift*, an enjoyable novel by American writer Frances Kazan.

Though not part of the National Literature movement, İrfan Orga (1908–1970) is probably the most famous Turkish literary figure of the 20th century. His 1950 masterpiece *Portrait of a Turkish Family* is his memoir of growing up in İstanbul at the start of the century and is probably the best writing about the city ever published. Exiled from the country of his birth, he also wrote a swathe of nonfiction titles, including the fascinating *The Caravan Moves On: Three Weeks among Turkish Nomads*. English translations of both works are available internationally.

The second half of the 20th century saw a raft of local writers gain popularity in Turkey. Many were socialists, communists or outspoken critics of the government and spent long and repeated periods in jail. The most famous of these writers was poet and novelist Nâzım Hikmet (1902–1963). Internationally acclaimed for his poetry, Hikmet was in and out of Turkish jails for 30 years due to his alleged communist activity. Released in 1950 after a concerted lobbying effort by the Turkish and international intelligentsia, he left the country and died in exile. His masterwork is the five-volume collection of lyric and epic poetry entitled *Human Landscapes from My Country*. The most readily available English-language translation of his poems is *Beyond the Walls: Selected Poems*.

Yaşar Kemal (born 1923) is another major literary figure whose work has a strong political flavour. A former agricultural labourer and factory worker, he writes highly-regarded epic novels dealing with the human condition. Kemal's best-known work is probably the 1955 *Mehmed, My Hawk*, which deals with the lives of Kurds in Turkey. Two of his novels – *The Birds are Also Gone* and *The Sea-Crossed Fisherman* – are set in İstanbul. Kemal was short-listed for the Nobel Prize for Literature in 1999.

Aziz Nesin (1915–1995) was perhaps the most prolific of all the Turkish political writers of the 20th century. A satirist, he published over 100 books and was jailed several times for his colourful indictments of the country's overly bureaucratic system and social inequalities. *Out of the Way! Socialism's Coming!* is one of the few of Nesin's works to be translated into English.

Since Halide Edib Adıvar blazed the trail, there have been a number of prominent female writers in Turkey, chief among them Sevgi Soysal, Erendiz Atasü, Buket Uzuner and Latife Tekin.

During her short life, Sevgi Soysal (1936–1976) was known as the author of strong works promoting women's rights in Turkey. Her 1975 novel *Noontime in Yenişehir* won the most prestigious local literary prize, the Orhan Kemal Novel Award.

Another writer who focuses on the experiences of women in Turkey is Erendiz Atasü (born 1947), a retired professor of pharmacology. Her highly acclaimed 1995 novel *The Other Side of the Mountain* looks at three generations of a family from the end of the Ottoman Empire to the 1990s, focussing on a central female character. It's published in English through a grant from the Arts Council of England. Atasü has also written *That Scorching Season of Youth* (1999) and three volumes of short stories.

Buket Uzuner (born 1955) writes short stories and novels, the best known being *Sound of Fish Steps* (1992), which was greatly admired by the local literary set when it was first released.

Latife Tekin (born 1957) has built a reputation as Turkey's major magic-realist novelist. Her first novel *Dear Shameless Death* (1983), which told the story of a family's difficult migration to a big city, had a strongly political subtext and was well received by local readers. Tekin's subsequent novels have included the 1984 *Berji Kristin: Tales from the Garbage Hills*, another look at the displaced members of society; and *Night Lessons* (1986), *Swords of Ice* (1989) and *Signs of Love* (1995).

Turkish-born (but American-based) writer Alev Lytle Croutier, internationally known for her bestselling *Harem: The World Behind the Veil*, has also written a children's book set in İstanbul called *Leyla: The Black Tulip*.

Orhan Pamuk

Turkey hasn't yet garnered a Nobel Prize for Literature, but there's one darling of the local and international literary establishments who could conceivably snaffle the big prize in the future: the much-fêted Orhan Pamuk. Born in 1953, the İstanbul-based novelist has a small but impressive body of work that's already attracted its fair share of accolades, including the €100,000 IMPAC Dublin Literary Award, *The Independent* newspaper's Foreign Fiction Award of the Month and every local literary prize on offer. The only prize Pamuk hasn't accepted is the prestigious title of State Artist, which was offered to him in 1999 by the Turkish Government but which he knocked back as, he stated, his protest against the government's incarceration of writers, 'narrow-minded nationalism' and an inability to address the Kurdish problem with anything but force.

Most critics describe Pamuk's novels as post-modernist, citing similarities to the work of Umberto Eco and Italo Calvino. He often uses a 'point of view' technique whereby he presents the internal monologues of interdependent characters, splicing them together so as to construct a meticulous overall narrative, often around a murder-mystery theme. Though not the easiest books to read (some critics have called them difficult and self-absorbed), they're meticulously researched and extraordinarily evocative of place. Most are set in his home town, İstanbul.

Pamuk has written seven novels to date. His first, *Cevdet Bey & His Sons* (1982), is a dynastic saga of the İstanbul bourgeoisie. *The Silent House* (1983) and *The White Castle* (1985) both won local literary awards and cemented his reputation, but were nowhere near as successful as his bizarre Beyoğlu detective novel *The Black Book* (1990), which was made into a film (*Gizli Yüz*) by director Omer Kavur in 1992. After this came *The New Life* (1995) followed by his most lauded book to date, *My Name is Red* (1998). A murder mystery set among the calligraphers of the sultan's court in the 16th century, *My Name is Red* took six years to write and was described by the IMPAC judges as 'A rare *tour de force* of literary imagination and philosophical speculation'. Pamuk's most recent novel, *Snow* (2002), has been a runaway bestseller both within Turkey and internationally.

For the record, Pamuk says that the best book ever written about İstanbul is Italian writer Edmondo de Amicis' 1878 travelogue *Constantinople*.

MUSIC

Turks love music and listen to it in many forms, the most popular of which are the over-wrought vocal style called *arabesk* and the slick Western-influenced pop styles performed by artists such as Tarkan. Though many foreigners immediately conjure up the trance-like sounds of Sufi Mevlevi music when they try to categorise Turkey's musical heritage, the reality is worlds away, sitting squarely within the cheerful modern-day vulgarity of Eurovision-style musical romps. These forays into the international scene stem from a solidly populist tradition of *arabesk* and folk, and are packaged with a thickly applied veneer of Western pop. Some local product can't be easily pigeonholed – who knows where the ska beats of Turkey's 2004 Eurovision entry, *For Real*, by Athena, came from? – but overall there are four dominant genres today: folk, *arabesk*, fasıl and pop.

The Ottoman court liked to listen to traditional classical music, which utilised a system of *makams* (modalities), an exotic-sounding series of notes similar in function to the familiar Western scales of whole and half-tone intervals. The result was a lugubrious sound that owed a lot to Persian and Arabic classical influences. Usually improvised, it was performed by chamber groups. While the court was being serenaded by such music at its soirees, another classical genre, the music of the Sufi Mevlevis, was inspiring followers of the religious sect. Its complex and refined sound was often accompanied by vocal pieces featuring the words of Celaleddin Rumi (Mevlâna), the 13th-century founder of the sect.

After the founding of the republic, the performance of traditional classical music was actively discouraged by Atatürk and his government. The great man considered it to be too redolent of contaminating Arabic influences, and he encouraged musicians and the public to instead turn their attention to Western classical music. The fate of Sufi music under the republic was even more extreme. With the forced closure of the Sufi *tekkes* (lodges) in 1923, the music of the order was in effect banned, only re-emerging when Prime Minister Turgut Özal overturned the ban on Sufi worship after he came to power in 1983. Today there's a healthy recording tradition among Sufi musicians and regular performances at the sect's *tekke* at **Mevlevi Monastery** (p118) in Beyoğlu.

As well as encouraging Western classical music, the republican government began a programme of classifying, archiving and promoting *halk müziği* (Anatolian folk music). Spanning 30 years and involving 10,000 songs, the programme had its positives and negatives. On the

Music shop (p189), Tünel

plus side, parts of a rich musical heritage were documented and promoted. Less positively, any music that was deemed 'un-Turkish' (usually due to its roots in the music of ethnic minorities) was struck from the record or forced to conform with the dominant sub-genre.

Until the 1960s and 1970s it was still possible to hear Turkish troubadours (*aşik*) in action around the countryside, playing their particular variety of *halk müziği*. These *aşik* were members of the Alevî sect of central Anatolia and had a set repertoire of mystical songs always featuring the *saz* (Turkish long-necked, stringed instrument) and vocals. Fortunately their music has been revived in studio form, with artists such as Ruhi Su, Arif Sağ, Yavuz Top and Musa Eroğlu reinterpreting the music of the wandering *aşik* for modern audiences.

In the 1980s traditional *halk müziği* underwent a revival, popularised by musicians such as the soulful Belkis Akkale, who fused it with pop to form a new sub-genre known as *Türkü*. The extremely popular İbrahim Can and Nuray Hafiftaş followed Akkale's lead.

Even before Belkis et al were experimenting with *Türkü*, rock musicians such as Cem Karaca were using folk influences to develop a distinctive form of Anadolu rock featuring politically charged lyrics. Since his death in 2004, Karaca's *Hayvan Terli* album has gained a whole new audience for this type of music. The music of Zülfü Livaneli, a popular singer and *saz* player who incorporates Western instrumentation into his protest songs, clearly shows the influence of Karaca and is best known internationally for his music for Yılmaz Güney's film *Yol* (*The Road*).

The popularity of some musical genres defied the government's early attempts to promote a national music based solely on *halk müziği*. Two examples were fasıl and *arabesk*, and they're still going strong today.

An emotive mix of folk, classical and fasıl traditions, *arabesk*'s name attests to its Arabic influences, specifically Egyptian dance music. First popularised by a local lad, Kaydar Tatliyay, in the 1940s, it was frowned upon by the nationalist government because of its Arabic influences and mournful tone. In fact, the government went so far as to first restrict and then ban Arabic musical films and recordings from Egypt and Lebanon to stop further 'contamination' of local musical tastes. Turkish devotees ignored the ban and tuned in to Radio Cairo for regular fixes of their favourite sounds regardless.

Arabesk songs have traditionally been geared towards a working-class audience from central and eastern Anatolia and are inevitably about the oppressed – sometimes the singer is oppressed by love, sometimes by his unfair lot in life. Though artists such as Müslüm Gürses have their devoted followers, it's the phenomenally popular İbrahim Tatlıses who is the undisputed king of the genre. A Turk of Kurdish descent, Tatlıses is from the southeastern town of Urfa and has probably sold more CDs during his career than the rest of the Turkish *arabesk* fraternity put together.

As the soulful laments of *arabesk* were building the genre's national following, fasıl (sometimes referred to as Gypsy) music was taking the taverns and nightclubs of İstanbul by storm. Usually performed by Turks of Armenian, Jewish, Greek or Gypsy origin who had no religious scruples preventing them performing in places where alcohol was served, this lively music usually featured the *klarnet* (clarinet) and *darbuka* (drum played with the hands). Solo improvisations from the stars of the orchestra were commonplace, as were boisterous renditions of emotionally charged songs by vocalists. Today this is the most popular form of music played in the city's many meyhanes (p175).

On the streets you may hear the plaintive strains of *arabesk*, but they're likely to be overlaid by the powerful sounds of Turkish pop, which is pumped out of shopfronts and cars across the city. Dominated by solo artists rather than bands, pop's pantheon of performers have built their success on a long and rich tradition of popular solo vocal artists trained in *sanat* or art music. Many have also been influenced by *arabesk*.

The first of these vocal stars to build a popular following was the fabulously camp Zeki Müren, Turkey's very own Liberace. Müren released his first album in 1951 and went on to record in classical and *arabesk* styles. Like Liberace, he liked nothing better than frocking up (his stage performances saw him appear in everything from gladiator costumes to sequin-and-feather confections) and was particularly beloved by middle-aged women. He died on stage at a comeback concert in İzmir in 1996 but recordings such as *Kahir Mektubu* still sell like hotcakes.

Following in Müren's cross-dressing footsteps is talented vocalist Bülent Ersoy, whose restrained classical idiom is best heard in her reinterpretation of late-19th-century repertoire, *Alaturka 1995*. Born in 1952, Ersoy is known by her many fans as 'Abla' ('Big Sister') as a show of support for her gender change (male to female). Before her operation she was banned from performing because of her 'effeminate ways'; afterwards she managed to successfully lobby Prime Minister Turgut Özal (a big fan) for her right to perform and also for the general civil rights of transsexuals in Turkey.

Though Bülent has attained diva status, her profile comes nowhere near to attaining the royal status given to Sezen Aksu. Aksu's influence on Turkey's popular music industry has been enormous. She's done everything from overseeing the Turkish contributions to the annual Eurovision contest to recording innumerable blockbuster albums of her own, along the way grooming up-and-coming stars such as Tarkan and Sertab Erener. In among her musical accomplishments she's managed to be an outspoken and controversial commentator on feminism and politics. Her most popular album is probably *Deliveren* (2001), though everything she's done since hitting the music scene in the 1970s has been pretty impressive.

Newcomer Sertab Erener has a lot to live up to if she's to take over the throne from Aksu one day. The İstanbul-born winner of the 2003 Eurovision contest has hit the big time with her album *No Boundaries*, which has sold over four million copies. Her winning track 'Every Way That I Can' was performed and recorded in English (the first time that a Turkish Eurovision entry wasn't performed in Turkish) and has built her a loyal international following. The fact that her Eurovision performance saw her looking particularly fetching in harem pants while doing a belly dance has probably helped, too...

Finally, no discussion of current Turkish music would be complete without a mention of the pin-up boy of Turkish pop, Tarkan. His albums regularly sell millions of copies and his catchy brand of music is the stuff of which recording empires are made. Good looks and a *soupçon* of attitude are all part of the Tarkan package, and have landed him a mega-lucrative Pepsi contract among other endorsements.

His most successful album to date, *Ölürüm Sana* (I'd Die For You), featured tracks written by former collaborator Sezen Aksu and sold 3.5 million copies in Turkey alone; *Dudu* (Woman), released in 2003, looks as if it might do the same. His latest release is a self-titled perfume (we kid you not).

Top Read

Those interested in learning more about Turkish music should grab a copy of the *Rough Guide to World Music* (Volume 1) by Simon Broughton.

CINEMA

Just a year after the Lumière brothers presented their first cinematic show in 1895, cinema first appeared in Turkey. At first it was only foreigners and non-Muslims who watched movies, but by 1914 there were cinemas run by and for Muslims as well, and the Turks' great love for this art form was up and running.

The War of Independence inspired actor Muhsin Ertuğrul, Turkey's cinema pioneer, to establish a film company in 1922 and make patriotic films. The company's first release was *The Ordeal*, based on a novel about the War of Independence by eminent writer and republican Halide Edib Adıvar. Within a decade Turkish films were winning awards in international competitions, even though a mere 23 films had been made.

After WWII the industry expanded rapidly with new companies and young directors. Lütfi Akad's *In the Name of the Law* (1952), Turkey's first colour film, brought realism to the screen in the place of melodrama, which had been the main fodder for audiences throughout the 1940s.

By the 1960s, Turkish cinema was delving deeply into social and political issues. Metin Erksan's *Dry Summer* (1964) won a gold medal at the Berlin Film Festival and another award in Venice. Yılmaz Güney, the fiery actor-director, directed his first film *Horse, Woman, Gun* in 1966 and scripted Lütfi Akad's *The Law of the Borders*, which he also starred in. His 1970 film *Hope* was a turning point in the national cinema, kick-starting a trend towards simple neorealist treatments of contemporary social issues that continues today. In this and similar films the commentary about life in modern Turkey was bleak indeed, and the exploration of issues such as the poverty-driven drift from rural areas to congested urban environments introduced a theme that would return again and again. The titles of Güney's subsequent films were representative of the industry's lack of optimism about the future of the country and their industry: after *Hope*, he released *Lament* in 1971, followed by *Sorrow*. It's not surprising that the government imprisoned him for three years after the 1971 coup.

The 1970s brought the challenge of TV, dwindling audiences, political pressures and unionisation of the industry. This was highlighted at the inaugural İstanbul International Film Festival in 1976, when the jury determined that no film was worthy of the award for best film. Despite the depressed start to the decade, the quality of films improved, and social issues such as the plight of Turkish workers in Europe were treated with honesty, naturalism and dry humour. By the early 1980s, several Turkish directors were well recognised in Europe and the USA, though they were having trouble getting their films shown at home. Despite winning the Palme D'Or at the Cannes Film Festival, Yılmaz Güney's bleak *The Road*, which explores the dilemmas faced by a group of men on temporary release from prison, was banned for 15 years in Turkey before finally being released in 2000. Güney had worked on the film while in jail (his second jail term), passing directions on to co-director Şerif Gören. His last film, *Duvar* (1983), made before his untimely death aged only 46, was a wrist-slashing prison drama.

Though the industry wasn't booming things were looking up by the 1980s, with some excellent films having redemptive themes symbolic of the more optimistic political climate.

İstanbul Through Foreign Eyes

Writers and film-makers have long tried to capture the magic and mystery of İstanbul in their work. For a taste of the city, try the following:

- **Aziyadé** Few artists have been as deeply enamoured of the city as the French novelist Pierre Loti (1850–1923). This romantic novel introduced Europe to both Loti's almond-eyed Turkish lover and the mysterious and all-pervasive attractions of the city itself.
- **James Bond** The sultan of all secret agents pops up twice in İstanbul, first in the 1974 *From Russia with Love* and then in 1999's *The World is Not Enough*. The city provides a great backdrop for his suave manoeuvres and sophisticated seductions.
- **L'Immortelle** Alain Robbe-Grillet directed this 1963 film before going on to collaborate with Alain Resnais on *Last Year at Marienbad*, and both films score high on the Esoteric-O-Meter. Here, a man is obsessed with a woman who is being followed around İstanbul (gloriously shot) by a sinister man and his two dogs. Go figure.
- **Midnight Express** Alan Parker's 1978 film has three major claims to fame: Giorgio Moroder's insufferable score, Brad Davis' homosexual sex scene and the Turkish tourism industry's virtual demise when the film was released. Mention it to a Turk at your peril.
- **Murder on the Orient Express** Hercule Poirot puts ze leetle grey cells to good use on the famous train in this 1934 novel by Agatha Christie. It was made into a film by Sidney Lumet in 1974 and features a few opening shots of İstanbul.
- **The Inspector Ikmen Novels** Barbara Nadel investigates İstanbul's underbelly in a suitably gripping style. Whether they're set in Balat or Beyoğlu, her books are always evocative and well researched. See 'Barbara Nadel's İstanbul' (p114).
- **The Turkish Embassy Letters** This 18th-century memoir was written by Lady Mary Wortley Montagu, the observant wife of the British Ambassador to the Sublime Porte. Based on letters she sent during the posting, it's a fascinating account of life in and around the Ottoman court and city.
- **The Mask of Dimitrios** This 1944 spy thriller directed by James Negulesco is based on an Eric Ambler novel. A ripping yarn, it opens with a body being fished out of the Bosphorus. Sydney Greenstreet and Peter Lorre give great performances.
- **Tintin** You'll see the T-shirts everywhere in the Grand Bazaar, but true devotees should check out this 1961 film by Jacques Vierne, which has the Belgian boy detective accompanying Captain Haddock to İstanbul.
- **Topkapi** Melina Mercouri's funky outfits, Peter Ustinov's hilarious performance and great shots of İstanbul make Jules Dassin's 1964 comedy spoof worth a view.

The most successful film of the decade was probably the 1983 *A Season in Hakkâri*, directed by Erdan Kıral, which addressed some of the issues surrounding the plight of Turkey's oppressed Kurdish population.

The 1990s were an exciting decade for the national cinema, with films being critically and popularly received both in Turkey and internationally. Notable among the many releases were Zeki Demirkubuz's *Innocence* (1997), which followed the story of an ex-con trying to survive in a society that had changed radically since his incarceration a decade before; and Omer Kavur's *Journey on the Hour Hand* (1997), a very different type of film, which can best be described as an existential mystery.

Many of the most highly regarded films of the 1990s were set in İstanbul. These included *Journey to the Sun* by Yeşim Ustaoğlu, which won the top prize at the International İstanbul Film Festival in 1999; the wonderful 1995 *İstanbul Beneath My Wings* and 1998 *Cholera Street* by Mustafa Altıoklar; and *The Bandit* (1996) by Yavuz Turgul. Many of these films explore important social and political themes. *Journey to the Sun*, for instance, is about a boy from the provinces who comes to the big city and is frequently mistaken for a Kurd due to his dark skin. Needless to say, he's appallingly treated as a result.

Contemporary directors of note include Ferzan Özpetek, whose 1996 film *Hamam*, set in İstanbul, was a big hit on the international festival circuit and is particularly noteworthy for addressing the hitherto hidden issue of homosexuality in Turkish society. His recent release, *The Window Across* (2003), has proved almost as popular.

Nuri Bilge Ceylan's 2003 film *Distant* has received a rapturous response from critics and audiences alike, winning the Jury Prize at Cannes among other accolades. The story of two cousins – played by newcomers Muzaffer Özdemir and Mehmet Emin Toprak – who are both alienated from society, it's in the bleak but visually beautiful tradition of Güney's films. Another 2003 release, *Mud*, directed by Derviş Zaim, won the Unesco award at the Venice Film Festival.

Contrary to what film festival catalogues would encourage the international filmgoer to believe, the local industry does regularly venture into territory outside political commentary and lamentations on the emptiness of the human condition. A recent example was the blockbuster action/revenge flick *Wild Heart – Boomerang Hell*, directed by Osman Sınav, which stars local strongman Kenan Imırzalioğlu and features wonderful cinematography by Tevfik Senol.

Architecture

Architecture

Urban designers wanting to study world's best practice when it comes to putting together a city skyline need go no further than İstanbul. Forget Chicago and New York with their skyscraper canyons, or London with its gimmicky Eye and squat clock tower – İstanbul is the real thing. Here you'll find delicate minarets reaching towards the heavens, distinctive domes crowning hills, and austere and elegant medieval towers commanding views across the waters.

The buildings in this imperial city are a conservation architect's wet dream – Byzantine cathedrals and churches are located next to Ottoman mosques, *medreses* (theological schools) and *hamams* (steam baths); distinctive 19th-century timber *yalıs* (seaside villas) adorn both shores of the Bosphorus; and neoclassical embassy buildings are dotted along Beyoğlu's boulevards. There's little of note dating from the second half of the 20th century, so the city is consolidating its time-capsule status, undergoing a continuous programme of restoration to preserve its architectural heritage; and attempting to enact legislation to ensure that the revered Stamboul skyline isn't tampered with. Time capsule doesn't mean Disney-like, though: İstanbullus still worship in these historic mosques and churches, live in the timber houses, run restaurants in *medreses*, sweat out the anxieties of the week in *hamams* and attend cocktail parties in the embassies. Today's İstanbul is a living testimonial to the architects and patrons who have contributed to its contemporary form. It's also proof that back in the old days, they sure knew how to build great buildings.

The oldest surviving buildings are in Old İstanbul, with a number of Byzantine structures including churches, cisterns, fortresses and fortified walls remaining. Urban spaces such as the Hippodrome and ceremonial boulevards such as Divan Yolu also date from this era. In Beyoğlu, traces of the Genoese presence dating back to the final years of the Byzantine Empire can be found, as can buildings from every stage of Ottoman rule. Early essays in the development of a national architectural movement in the early 20th century are found on both sides of the Golden Horn (Haliç). These areas are where most visitors spend their

Sirkeci Railway Station (p90)

time, but there are discoveries galore through every part of the city. In fact, that's what makes the place so fascinating – the layers of history have a physical manifestation here. There might be stellae from a Roman ceremonial way on one corner and an Ottoman *han* (caravanserai) on another…you'll end up acting like an archaeologist, looking to make new discoveries each time you leave your hotel room. A good start is to follow the **walking tours** (p136), but really, everywhere you go you'll see great buildings

BYZANTINE ARCHITECTURE

The city spent 1123 years as a Christian city within the Roman Empire and there are a surprising number of structures surviving from this era. These take three main forms: churches; fortifications and public utilities; and urban design and decoration.

CHURCHES

In the early Byzantine period, most churches were basilicas – rectangular buildings with a central nave, columns down either side and two side aisles. At the opposite end to the entry was a semicircular apse where the sermons were held. The entry was via a narthex (courtyard) and an inner vestibule as well. Occasionally there was an outer vestibule, too. Early basilicas had pitched roofs and flat ceilings; later, domes were introduced.

During Justinian's reign architects were encouraged to surpass each other's achievements when it came to utilising the domed basilica form. By achieving interiors whose enormous domes appeared to hover unsupported, the glory of God and His empire would be demonstrated for all to marvel at. **Aya Sofya** (p79), built in 537 and with a dome diameter of over 30m, is of course the supreme example of this.

Interestingly, Byzantine church design eschewed any major exterior ornamentation. From the outside, these buildings were often dull, with their domes being the only striking external feature. Thus Aya Sofya, widely acknowledged as the most impressive structure in the world when it was built, was and still is totally unimpressive on the outside, its squat form and dull brick appearance in direct contrast to the magnificence within. The same rule applied to the later Church of the Holy Saviour (Chora Church, currently the **Kariye Müzesi**; p111) in the Western Districts, the drab exterior of which gives no hint of the rich and wonderful mosaic-and-fresco decoration inside.

Another early Byzantine basilica design was the centralised polygonal plan with supporting walls and a dome set on top, wrapped inside square or rectangular external walls. There was still an entrance narthex. The lovely **Küçük Aya Sofya Camii** (p89), built around 530, is a surviving example of this form.

Later, a mixed basilica and centralised polygonal plan developed. This plan took a polygonal form with a series of smaller domes and half-domes that surround and support a central dome, while four large columns provide further support. The T-shape basilica ground plan was squashed into a squarish shape. This design was the foundation for church design in İstanbul from the 11th century until the Conquest (1453) and many classic Ottoman mosques were inspired by this plan. The **Zeyrek Camii** (Church of the Pantocrator; p107), built in 1124, is a good example of this style.

Top Books on İstanbul's Architecture

There are two essential references for any visitors seriously interested in the architecture and urban design of İstanbul:

- *Strolling Through İstanbul* by Hilary Sumner-Boyd and John Freely. Presented in the form of walking tours, this fantastic guide to the city's buildings and urban design is erudite, easy to read and absolutely fascinating. What these guys don't know about the history of the city is probably not worth knowing at all. We couldn't have written the Neighbourhoods and Walking Tours chapters without it.

- *İstanbul: An Architectural Guide* by Christa Beck and Christiane Forsting. This handy pocket-sized book was written by two architects and looks at buildings from every period in the city's architectural development. It's one of the few easily accessible references to discuss the city's 20th-century buildings.

When Mehmet the Conqueror took İstanbul in 1453 many churches were converted into mosques; despite the minarets, you can usually tell a church-cum-mosque by the giveaway distinctive red bricks, characteristic of all İstanbul's Byzantine churches.

FORTIFICATIONS & PUBLIC WORKS

The greatest of the Byzantine fortress structures is, of course, the great Theodosian land **wall** (p115). Twenty kilometres long, it was built to protect the city from siege and did so until Urban's great cannon breached it in 1453. Constructed in the reign of Theodosius II (r 408–450), the wall remained relatively intact until the 1950s, when parts were removed to facilitate construction of major roads through the city. Consisting of a moat, an outer wall and towers, it is built of layered brick and stone and has a monumental appearance befitting its purpose.

The Byzantines built grand palaces along the wall, including the **Tekfur Sarayı** (p114) near Edirnekapı and the **Bucoleon Palace** (p86), along the sea walls. Remnants of both exist today.

Glossary of Architectural Terms

arasta - row of shops near a mosque, the rent from which supports the mosque

bedesten - vaulted, fireproof market enclosure or warehouse where valuable goods are kept

camii - mosque

hamam(ı) - a Turkish steam bath

han - caravanserai; a place where traders could bring goods from all parts of the empire, unload and trade right in the bazaar's precincts

hünkâr mahfili - see *imperial loge*

imaret - soup kitchen for the poor

imperial loge - an elevated pavilion, screened from public view so the Sultan could come, pray and go unseen, preserving the imperial mystique

kasrı - imperial lodge; these were designed as getaway or pleasure palaces for the rich

kilise(si) - church

köşk(ü) - pavilion, villa, kiosk; these were picnic pavilions set in parkland

kule(si) - tower

külliye(si) - mosque complex including *medrese*, hospital, *hamam*, *imaret* etc

medrese - muslim theological seminary providing a secular education taught in a series of rooms surrounding a courtyard

mihrab - the niche in a mosque indicating the direction of Mecca

mimber - the pulpit in a mosque

minare(si) - minaret; the tall fluted towers from which Muslims are called to prayer

şadırvan - fountain where Muslims perform ritual ablutions; usually found in a mosque's forecourt

saray(ı) - palace

sebil - public fountain or water kiosk

selamlık - greeting room

tekke(si) - dervish lodge(s); these ceremonial halls usually have a central area for the whirling *sema* (Sufic religious ceremony) and galleries above for visitors to observe

türbe(si) - tomb or mausoleum; these are usually built in the cemetery of the *külliye* for the patron and his or her family

yalı - seaside villa; these wooden palatial dwellings were built as summer retreats along the shores of the Bosphorus in the early 19th century

Constantine had named his city 'New Rome' and like the empire's Latin capital, İstanbul had its great public works. Chief among these was the stone **aqueduct** (p100) built by Emperor Valens between 368 and 373. The parts that are left today tower over Atatürk Bulvarı, one of the city's major motorways, and give a clear idea of how the complete aqueduct would have dominated the city's skyline when it was built. The aqueduct fed a series of cisterns built across the city, including the majestic **Basilica Cistern** (p83) built by Justinian, and **Binbirdirek** (Cistern of 1001 Columns; p84), which was built by Constantine. Both are of considerable architectural significance.

URBAN DESIGN & DECORATION

Looking at the urban chaos of İstanbul today, it's easy to forget that civic planning was once alive and well here. Like Rome, the city was built on seven hills and to a strict grid pattern that included ceremonial thoroughfares such as Divan Yolu, originally a colonnaded way built by Emperor Severus. **Çemberlitaş** (Hooped or Banded Column; p85), which was originally crowned with a statue of Constantine, is one of the monuments that lined the length of this ceremonial way. Every emperor worth his salt wanted to have a major public space carrying his name – Theodosius I built a forum where the present-day Beyazıt Square is located and Constantine had one near the site of the Nuruosmaniye Camii. Forums such as these punctuated the ceremonial ways and acted as sites for celebrations and great public gatherings.

The greatest of all the Byzantine public spaces is the **Hippodrome** (p86), originally built by Severus in 203, and extended and adorned by a succession of emperors – Constantine erected his **Spiral Column** there in 330 and Theodosius plonked his Egyptian **obelisk** (p87) next to it in 390. Another of Theodosius' decorative flourishes was the **Porta Aurea** (Golden Gate; p115), subsequently built into Theodosius' wall.

OTTOMAN ARCHITECTURE

After the conquest of Constantinople in 1453, the sultans wasted no time in putting their architectural stamp on the city. Mehmet didn't even wait until he had it under his control, building the monumental **Rumeli Hisarı** (Fortress of Europe; p217), on the Bosphorus as part of a clever plan to cut the city off from its Black Sea grain supplies. The fortress was the first of many Ottoman structures over the centuries to be built in elevated positions, so commanding extraordinary views and claiming their piece of the city skyline.

Ortaköy Camii (p127)

When he made it into the city itself, Mehmet kicked off a centuries-long Ottoman building spree with a palace on what is now Beyazıt Square and a magnificent mosque on the fourth hill. Neither exists today, though remnants of the mosque are integrated into its replacement, the **Fatih Camii** (p110). After these structures he started work on the building that more visitors to İstanbul traipse through than any other: **Topkapı Palace** (p91). Mehmet was the first of a long line of sultans to commission mosques and palaces, making them the signature buildings of the Ottoman Empire. With *hans* and *hamams*, they have proved to be lasting memorials to their patrons and architects.

MOSQUES

In the earliest years of the Ottoman Empire, the most commonly built mosque form was the vaulted pier type, a large square or rectangular space sheltered by a series of small domes resting on pillars, as seen in Edirne's **Eski Camii** (p226).

When Sultan Orhan I took Bursa and İznik in the early 14th century the Ottomans were exposed to Byzantine architecture, particularly ecclesiastical architecture. Exposure to this new style led to the formation of a completely new mosque architectural style: the T-shape plan, a blend of the style of Sassanian Persia and the Byzantine basilica form. The **Üçşerefeli Camii** (p226), which was built in Edirne in 1447, became the model for other mosques not only because it was one of the first forays into this T-shape plan, but also because it was the first Ottoman mosque to have a wide dome and a forecourt with a *şadırvan* (ablutions fountain).

Süleyman the Magnificent's main architect, **Mimar Sinan** (see the boxed text above), perfected the classic Ottoman mosque. Sinan strove throughout his life to match or surpass in his mosques the magnificence of Aya Sofya, particularly the breadth of its dome and resulting transparency of its interior. His prototype mosque form has a large forecourt with a *şadırvan* at its centre and domed arcades on three sides. On the fourth side of the court is the mosque, with a two-storey porch. The main prayer hall is covered by a large central dome rising considerably higher than the two-storey facade and surrounded by smaller domes and semidomes. Lattice or grillework partitions separate an area at the back for use by female worshippers, while men occupy the central space. The *mihrab* is in the far wall of the prayer hall. There was usually one minaret, though imperial mosques had either two or four; and one imperial mosque, the **Blue Mosque** (p84), designed by Mehmet Ağa, has six.

Each imperial mosque (and there are a lot of them in İstanbul) originally had a *külliye* (mosque complex) clustered around it. This was a philanthropic complex comprising buildings such as a hospital, asylum for the insane, orphanage, *imaret* (soup kitchen), hospices for travellers, *medrese*, library, *hamam* and cemetery in which the mosque's imperial patron, his or her family and other notables could be buried. Over time, many of these buildings

The Great Sinan

Libeskind might be revered, Gehry admired and Koolhaas worshipped, but none of today's star architects come close to having the influence over a city that Mimar Koca Sinan had over Constantinople during his 50-year career.

Born in 1497, Sinan was a recruit to the *devşirme*, the annual intake of Christian youths into the janissaries, becoming a Muslim (as all such recruits did) and eventually taking up a post as a military engineer in the corps. Süleyman the Magnificent appointed him the chief of the imperial architects in 1538.

Sinan designed a total of 321 buildings, 85 of which are still standing in İstanbul. He died in 1588 and is buried in a self-built *türbe* located in one of the corners of the Sülemaniye Camii, the building that many believe to be his greatest work. He himself believed the Selimiye Camii in Edirne to be his major triumph.

An Armenian Architectural Dynasty

Arriving as a boy in Constantinople from Kayseri in central Anatolia, Bali Kalfa Balyan is unlikely to have guessed that his descendants would form the most powerful architectural dynasty the Ottoman Empire would ever see. In fact, the son, grandsons and great-grandsons of this Armenian immigrant would design imperial buildings for six sultans over a span of a century, and be responsible for introducing many European architectural styles and innovations into the country.

Bali's son, Kirkor, trained in Paris and returned to Constantinople chock-full of Western architectural ideas. He became chief of the imperial architects under Mehmet II and designed the city's first baroque building, the Nusretiye Camii in Tophane. Kirkor's son, Garabed, followed in his father's footsteps, designing **Dolmabahçe Palace** (p124) and siring two more architects to follow the familial profession, Nikoğos and Sarkis, both of whom were sent to study at the Ecole des Beaux Arts in Paris. On returning, Nikoğos helped design Dolmabahçe with his father before branching out on his own with the **Ortaköy** (Bücük Mecidiye) **Camii** (p127) and **Küçüksu Kasrı** (p220). Sarkis designed **Beylerbeyi Sarayı** (p217) and the Mecidiye Pavilion at Topkapı. Together, the brothers designed **Çırağan Sarayı**. Another member of the clan, Simon, designed many of the pavilions at Yıldız with Sarkis. Yet another, Senekerim, was responsible for the fire-watch tower in the grounds of the University of İstanbul. The family can truly be said to have put its stamp on the city!

were demolished or altered; fortunately, many of the buildings in the magnificent **Süleymaniye Camii complex** (p106) are intact. Also fairly intact is the **Yeni Camii complex** (p99) in Eminönü, which features the **Spice Bazaar** (Mısır Çarşısı or Egyptian Market; p106) built to provide funds for the upkeep of the mosque complex, a *türbe* (tomb or mausoleum) and a *sebil* (public fountain or water kiosk).

Early Ottoman mosques often featured tiles on their interior walls. The kilns at İznik produced the most highly regarded tiles, with the best work being produced from 1555 to 1620. Sinan's **Rüstem Paşa Camii** (p105) is widely considered to be the city's showpiece of such tile decoration.

The design of mosques developed during the reign of Süleyman the Magnificent proved so durable that it is still being used, with variations, for modern community mosques all over Turkey.

PALACES

When Mehmet built his first palace near the remnants of Theodosius' forum he triggered a palace-building craze that his successors would feel themselves honour-bound to emulate. No palace would ever rival the glory of **Topkapı** (p91), with its innumerable pavilions and stellar position on Saray Burnu (Seraglio Point), but Sultan Abdül Mecit I tried his best with the grandiose neoclassical **Dolmabahçe Palace** (p124) and then tried again with the rococo **Küçüksu Kasrı** (p217), both designed by members of the same architectural family, the **Balyans** (opposite). Abdül Aziz I was keen to have a shot, too, commissioning the Balyans to design and build extravagant **Çırağan Sarayı** (p124) and **Beylerbeyi Sarayı** (p217). These and other buildings of the era have been collectively dubbed 'Turkish baroque'.

Until the Balyans imported European ideas of monumental palace architecture, the Ottomans had remained faithful to the distinctive pavilion style epitomised by Topkapı, **Aynalıkavak Kasrı** (p129), **Yıldız Parkı** (p127) and **Ihlamur Kasrı** (p126), all of which featured pavilions in a garden setting. The first signs of European architectural influences seeping into traditional Ottoman styles had been the floral, colourful embellishments typical of the so-called Tulip Period. The Fountain of Sultan Ahmet III, just outside the gate to the First Court of Topkapı, and the Dining Room of Ahmet III in Topkapı's Harem are good examples of this.

Clock tower, Dolmabahçe Palace (p124)

HANS & HAMAMS

Mosques and palaces dominate the landscape and skyline of the city, so visitors need to investigate a bit more carefully to discover those other quintessentially Ottoman building types: the *han* and the *hamam*.

The Ottoman *han* is basically an Arabic-style caravanserai, with the addition of workshops and storage space for traders' wares. Built by rich merchants, a *han* was typically a two- to three-storey arcaded building surrounding a courtyard that could be locked at night. Its arcades were backed by small rooms that provided accommodation and offices for traders. The best examples of *hans* are found near the Grand Bazaar (Kapalı Çarşı); see the **walking tour** (p140).

Hamams were usually built as part of the *külliye* of a mosque, and provided an important point of social contact for the local community as well as facilities for observance of good personal hygiene, considered particularly important by Muslims. Architecturally significant *hamams* include Sinan's exquisite **Baths of Lady Hürrem** (p83), now a carpet shop, and the still-functioning *hamams* of **Çemberlitaş** (p172). and **Cağaloğlu** (p172).

WOODEN HOUSES

The mosques, palaces, *hans* and *hamams* of the Ottomans were major structures, built in stone or brick and usually having impressive street frontages. The Ottoman timber house was something entirely different. It came in two forms: the wooden summer house known as the *yalı*, examples of which were built along the shores of the Bosphorus for members of the Ottoman nobility and foreign ambassadors; and the traditional city house of the rest of the population, sometimes set in a garden but usually part of a crowded urban streetscape.

These houses usually followed a symmetrical plan with a central entertainment space giving access to other areas. Overhanging eaves and grilled vertical windows and bay windows, allowing women to look out on the street without being observed, were ubiquitous features. They also meant that the women's quarters were usually dark. Within the house there were often two parts of the house: the harem for womenfolk and the *selamlık* (greeting room) for men. For an excellent description of such houses you should go no further than Irfan Orga's wonderful memoir of growing up in Constantinople, *Portrait of a Turkish Family*. Unfortunately, not too many of these houses survive, a result of the many serious fires that regularly raced through the Ottoman city.

Wooden house (above)

ISLAMIC ECLECTICISM

While the Balyans were constructing their Turkish baroque confections for the sultans, a host of other architects were being commissioned by other countries to design splendid embassy buildings in Beyoğlu. Most of these embassies were built on İstiklal Caddesi, where they are still standing today. Sir Charles Barry, designer of the Houses of Parliament in London, was responsible for the neoclassical **British Consulate General** (p142) built in 1845; and the Swiss-born Fossati brothers were lauded for their elegant **Russian Consulate General** (1837; p142) and **Netherlands Consulate General** (1855; p142) as well as for restorations to Aya Sofya. All these European influences were bound to have an effect on the vernacular architecture.

In the late 19th and early 20th centuries foreign or foreign-trained architects began to unfold a neoclassical blend of European architecture alongside Turkish baroque, with some concessions to classic Ottoman style. This style has been dubbed 'Islamic eclecticism'. Two influential learning institutions nurtured this new style: The School of Fine Arts and the School of Civil Engineering.

The School of Fine Arts (now the Mimar Sinan University) had opened in 1882, modelled on Paris' Ecole des Beaux Arts. One of its teachers, Frenchman Alexandre Vallaury, was head of the imperial architects and was responsible for a host of buildings in the city, including the 1899 İstanbul High School building (with Raimondo D'Aronco) and the earlier neoclassical **Pera Palas Oteli** (Pera Palace Hotel; p121). The High School was originally designed as a bank and with its innovative combination of Beaux Art style with Ottoman flourishes, such as pointed arches and timber grilles, was one of the first buildings to experiment with Islamic eclecticism.

The School of Civil Engineering (now İstanbul Technical University) was the other architectural think-tank in town. One of its teachers, a German named Jachmund, designed the 1889 **Sirkeci Railway Station** (p90), perhaps the best example of the new architectural style. Though it seems an architectural hodgepodge when looked at with modern eyes, its combination of Islamic structure and neoclassical decoration was greatly admired by the city's architectural fraternity when it was constructed.

Turkish students and members of the faculty at these schools were quick to follow the lead taken by Vallaury and Jachmund. The most influential of all were Vedat Tek, who had studied in Paris and taught at the School of Fine Arts with Vallaury, and Kemalettin Bey, who had studied in Berlin and with Jachmund at the School of Civil Engineering. Together Vedat Tek and Kemalettin Bey formed the First National Architectural Movement, in which elements from Ottoman architectural styles were fused with modern Western building technologies such as steel or reinforced concrete. This resulted in a distinctively Turkish architecture.

Tek designed the central post office in Eminönü (1909), combining traditional Ottoman elements such as tile work (which he designed himself) and pointed arches with a monumental neoclassical façade and large atrium. Kemalettin Bey had a prodigious oeuvre, much of it in Ankara. His best-known İstanbul buildings are the **Merit Antique Hotel** (1919–22; p209) in Laleli, an innovative apartment block that was sadly bastardised when converted into a hotel in the 1980s; and an office building, 4 Vakıf Han, in Eminönü (1912–26), which has recently been gutted.

Top 10 İstanbul Buildings

Picking 10 İstanbul buildings of note out of a field of thousands is a dirty job, but we guess someone has to do it. Here's our best attempt – please note: no correspondence about our choices will be entered into.

- **Aya Sofya** (p79)
- **Basilica Cistern** (p83)
- **Baths of Lady Hürrem** (p83)
- **Blue Mosque** (p84)
- **Botter House** (p142)
- **Küçük Aya Sofya** (p89)
- **Rumeli Hisarı** (p217)
- **Rüstem Paşa Camii** (p105)
- **Süleymaniye Camii** (p106)
- **Topkapı Palace** (p91)

ART NOUVEAU

Believe it or not, İstanbul has a small body of significant Art Nouveau buildings scattered throughout its suburbs. The style was introduced by Raimondo D'Aronco, an Italian architect who lived in the city from 1893 to 1909. D'Aronco was chief of the imperial architects from 1896 to 1908 and during this time designed a number of elegant Art Nouveau buildings and structures, including the tiny Laleli Fountain in Karaköy; the **Egyptian consulate** (p219) in Bebek; and a theatre, porcelain factory and greenhouse at **Yıldız Parkı** (p127). His best work in this style is the gorgeous **Botter House** (p142) on İstiklal Caddesi.

Other Art Nouveau buildings of note in the city include the rose-adorned **Flora Han** (architect unknown; Map pp282-3) in Eminönü and the **Hıdıv Kasrı** (p221) on the Bosphorus.

MODERNISM

When Atatürk proclaimed Ankara the capital of the new republic in 1923, İstanbul immediately lost much of its glamour and investment capital. Modernism was played out on the new canvas of Ankara, while İstanbul's dalliances went little further than the **İstanbul City Hall** (Map pp282-3), designed by Nevzat Erol and built in 1953 near Fatih; the **İstanbul Hilton Hotel** (p213), designed by SOM and Sedad Hakkı Eldem, and built in 1952; and the much-maligned **Atatürk Cultural Centre** (p177) by Hayati Tabanlioğlu, built in 1956 on Taksim Square.

Recent architecture in the city can hardly be called inspiring. In fact, the words 'a disgrace' mightn't be inappropriate. The **Akmerkez Shopping Centre** (p199) is an example of the genre: bland skyscrapers aping the worst functionalist architecture of the 1980s. The city's apartment blocks are also lessons in what not to do: the further out they are the taller and uglier they become (look out near Atatürk International Airport if you dare). Illegal housing (*gecekondus*) built by immigrants from Turkey's countryside is an ongoing headache for the city – especially since planning regulations are difficult to enforce in these areas. Old Stamboul's skyline hasn't been too badly corrupted (though shoddy rooftop additions in the Cankurtaran hotel region are occurring with worrying regularity), but the Beyoğlu skyline, historically dominated by the wonderful Galata Tower, has had to suffer indignities such as the erection of the appalling Ritz-Carlton tower. In all, recent times haven't been kind to the city in architectural terms.

Food & Drink

Food & Drink

More than anything else, Turks love to eat. Their national cuisine has been refined over centuries and is treated more reverently that any museum collection in the country. That's not to say it's fussy, because what differentiates Turkish food from other national noshes is its rustic and honest base. Here meze (hors d'oeuvres) are simple, kebabs austere, salads unstructured and seafood unsauced. Flavours explode in your mouth because ingredients are used in season and are treated with respect. Travelling your tastebuds here will make you very, very happy.

Regional culinary differences exist in the country and are reflected in the city's restaurants – most meyhanes will be run by people whose roots are in the Black Sea region and who love anything fishy, for instance – but the basic philosophy is unwavering: if it's freshly grown and prepared, it will make it into the menu and satisfy Turkish tummies. We heartily approve.

ETIQUETTE

It's not considered very important that everyone eats the same courses at the same pace. Similarly, the kitchen will deliver dishes as they are ready: it's quite normal for all the chicken dishes to arrive and then, five minutes later, all the lamb. You don't have to wait for everyone's food to arrive to begin eating.

Because most Turkish food comes in bite-sized portions, a fork is usually sufficient and simple restaurants may not bother giving you a knife at all. You can hold a piece of bread in the other hand and use it to push food onto the fork if necessary.

Turkish waiters have a habit of snatching your plate away before you've finished. This may be due to a rule of Eastern etiquette that holds that it is impolite to leave a finished plate sitting in front of a guest. Saying *kalsın* (let it stay) may slow them down. When you have finished, put your knife and fork together to indicate that the waiter can take the plate. If this has no effect (or you don't have a knife), say *biti, alabilirsin* (finished, you can take it) to the waiter.

Dipping bread in your soup is acceptable, though it's more a village custom and might be clucked over by city hens. It's the same with belching and slurping: in urbanised families it might be frowned upon, in the countryside you can go for it. Try to avoid blowing your nose in public; sniff or excuse yourself if you need to do this.

It's not unusual for people to smoke while others are eating, and you will rarely find non-smoking areas in restaurants. Opting for outdoor seating can be a good way of avoiding the haze.

Toothpicking should be done behind your hands, but you don't need to be particularly discrete.

The Best Meal of the Day

Even if you're not usually an early bird, you'll find yourself jumping out of bed ready to start the day in İstanbul. The reason isn't that the air is particularly salubrious, nor that you have an enormous checklist of sights to visit. No, it's the wonderful Turkish breakfasts on offer that lure slugabeds from their hotel rooms. The standard breakfast *(komple kahvaltı)* served by most hotels consists of fresh bread or *simit* (bread ring) with jam, *pekmez* (fruit syrup) or honey; plump black or green olives; sliced tomatoes and cucumbers; a hard-boiled egg; cheese – usually flavoursome white sheep's milk cheese, sometimes mild yellow processed cheese *(kaşar peynir)* – and copious amounts of tea or coffee. Sometimes freshly made yogurt and cakes are served, occasionally a homemade *börek* (sweet or savoury pastry) will appear. Yum!

HOW İSTANBULLUS EAT

Mealtime in İstanbul is treated with respect. The idea of eating in front of a TV or from a freezer is absolute anathema to Turks. Friends, family and communal tables are as essential to the cuisine as its staple foodstuffs and signature dishes. Restaurants in İstanbul are always full of large groups sharing not only meze, but conversation and belly laughs, usually over a bottle or two (or even three) of the national tipple, rakı.

The day starts with *sabahları* (morning food) or *kahvaltı* (breakfast), usually eaten between 6am and 8am. *Öğle yemeği* (lunch) kicks off around noon, is usually consumed quickly and is often enjoyed in a lokanta, pideci or kebapçı. *Akşam yemeği* (dinner), which is eaten any time after 6pm, is where the meyhane or *restoran* comes into its own; in İstanbul many of these places serve until midnight and meals can be drawn out over a long period.

STAPLES & SPECIALITIES

BREAD

Bread (*ekmek*) appears in a multiplicity of forms and is considered an essential part of any Turkish meal. The days will often start with a sesame-encrusted *simit* (bread ring) or crusty white loaf to accompany cheese and olives. Lunch may be a *pide* or *lahmacun* – both are Turkish versions of the pizza, the difference being that *lahmacun* has a thin, crispy base and *pide* has a more standard pizza base. *Lahmacun* comes with an onion, lamb and tomato topping; *pide* is usually topped with *peynirli* (cheese), *yumurtalı* (egg) or *kıymalı* (minced lamb). A *karaşık pide* will have a mixture of toppings. Another lunch or snack dish is *gözleme,* a thin pancake baked on a concave griddle over an open fire and filled with cheese, potato, spinach or mushrooms. Dinner is always served with baskets of bread to mop up meze and wrap around morsels of meat. Light and airy *lavaş* (thin crispy bread) is often served with the house speciality at kebab restaurants.

MEZE

Meze isn't just a type of dish, it's a whole eating experience. If you eat in a local household, your host may put out a few lovingly prepared dishes for guests to nibble on before the main course is served. If you choose to spend a few hours in a Beyoğlu meyhane, beckoning the waiter over so that you can choose 'just a few more' will make the meze comprise a whole meal. However you encounter the meze, it will be fresh and just begging to be accompanied by a drink and a good natter.

Turks credit Süleyman the Magnificent with introducing meze into the country. During one of his Persian campaigns, Süleyman learned from the cunning Persian rulers that food tasters were a particularly good idea for every sultan who wanted to ensure his safety. Once he was back home, Süleyman decreed that *çesnici* (taste) slaves be given small portions of his meals before he sat down to the table. These portions became known as meze, the Persian word for pleasant, enjoyable taste. What the sultan did was, of course, aped by his courtiers and, in turn, by the populace. Thus was the institution of meze was born.

Meze

Mezes are usually vegetable based, though seafood dishes pop up regularly on meze trays and trolleys in meyhanes. Most are cold, though occasional hot dishes are served. You will probably encounter the following dishes:

Ançüz Pickled anchovy.
Barbunya pilaki Red bean salad.
Beyaz peynir White goat's cheese.
Beyin salatası Sheep's brain salad.
Biber dolması Stuffed pepper.
Cacık Yogurt with cucumber and mint.
Çerkez tavuğu Cssian chicken, made with chicken, bread, walnuts, salt and garlic.
Enginar Cooked artichoke.
Fava Mashed broad bean paste.
Haydari Yogurt with roasted eggplant (aubergine) and garlic.
Humus Chickpea, tahini, lemon and spice dip.
Kalamares Fried calamari.
Kısır Bulgur salad.
Lakerda Sliced and salted tuna fish.
Mücver Deep-fried zucchini (courgettes) fritters.
Pastırma Air-dried beef.
Patlıcan kızartması Fried eggplant with tomatoes.
Peynirli börek Cheese pastry.
Yaprak sarma Vine leaves stuffed with rice, herbs and pine nuts.

SOUP

Soup (çorba) is equally at home on the breakfast, lunch or dinner table, always accompanied by bread. Lokantas and cheap restaurants will usually have bowls of mercimek çorbası (lentil soup) or ezo gelin çorbası (red lentil and rice soup) on offer. The country's most famous soup, işkembe çorbası (tripe soup), is widely hailed as a hangover cure.

SALAD

Simplicity is the key to Turkish salata (salads), with crunchy fresh ingredients being caressed by a shake of oil and vinegar at the table and eaten with gusto as a meze or as an accompaniment to a meat or fish main course. The most popular salad in İstanbul's restaurants in summer is çoban salatası (shepherd's salad), a colourful mix of chopped tomatoes, cucumber, onion and pepper. Mayonnaise-laced Rus salatası (Russian salad) is also popular.

MEAT

There are more meat (et) dishes in the Turkish culinary repertoire than you can poke a şiş (skewer) at. The most famous of these is the kebab – şiş and döner – but köfte (meat balls), saç kavurma (stirfried cubed meat dishes), güveç (meat and vegetable stews) and tandır (meat cooked in a clay oven) dishes are just as common. Offal dishes are also popular – if you're a bit squeamish about the yucky bits it's a good idea to know the words işkembe (tripe), kelle (head) and koç yumurtası (ram's balls) so that you can steer clear if they pop up on a menu. The most popular sausage is the spicy beef sucuk. Chicken is extremely popular; you'll find it roasted, boiled, stewed and skewered.

SEAFOOD

İstanbul is on the sea, and locals have always made the most of this fact, falling hook, line and sinker for fresh fish (balık) in any form. There are a number of excellent fish restaurants along the Bosphorus and a few top-notch ones in town, but the best place to enjoy the catch of the day is at meyhanes in Beyoğlu or Kumkapı, where the fish is dusted in flour and lightly fried. Delicious!

Kalkan (torbot) and uskumru (mackerel) are best consumed between March and June. Mid-July to August is the best time to feast on levrek (sea bass), lüfer (bluefish), barbunya (red mullet) and istravrit (horse mackerel), while winter means hamsi (fresh anchovy).

Kebabs & Köfte

The national dish is undoubtedly the kebab, and it comes in many forms. In İstanbul you'll find the following dishes everywhere:

Çöp şiş Small pieces of fatty lamb grilled on a skewer and then rolled in a thin pide with onions and parsley.

Döner kebap Compressed meat (usually lamb) cooked on a revolving upright skewer (usually over coals) and then thinly sliced.

Fıstıklı kebab Minced suckling lamb studded with pistachios.

İskender (Bursa) kebap Döner lamb served on a bed of crumbled pide and yogurt, then topped with tomato and burnt butter sauces.

Patlıcan kebab Cubed or minced meat grilled with eggplant (aubergine).

Tavuk şiş Chicken pieces grilled on a skewer.

Tokat kebab Lamb cubes grilled with potato, tomato eggplant and garlic.

Tasty köfte (meatballs) are nearly as common, and are mainly in the following forms:

Şiş köfte Wrapped around a flat skewer and barbecued.

Adana köfte Grilled, then served with onions, paprika, parsley and pide.

Çiğ köfte Raw ground-lamb mixed with pounded bulgur (wheat), onion, clove, cinnamon, salt and hot black pepper.

İçli köfte Ground lamb and onion with a bulgur coating, often served as a meze.

Tekirdağ köftesi Served with rice and peppers.

Urfa kebab A mild version of the Adana köfte.

VEGETABLES

If it weren't for the Turks' ongoing and passionate love affair with the kebab, they'd probably all be vegetarians. They're sensible about their vegetables, too. There's none of the silly Western fixation for preparing vegetables that are out of season – here tomatoes are eaten when they're almost bursting out of their skins with sweet juices, corn is picked when it's golden and plentiful, and peppers are stewed when they're so ripe they're downright sexy. Look for what's on the vendor's carts when you're walking around town – you'll see the same produce in restaurant dishes across town. You'll also notice two particularly Turkish ways of preparing them: the first known as *zeytinyağlı* (sautéed in olive oil) and the second *dolma* (stuffed with rice or meat).

RICE & BULGUR

Rice is used in soups, stuffings (mainly for *dolma*), puddings and *pilav*. It is usually cooked with a chicken or meat stock. *Pilav*, which is served in every lokanta as an optional accompaniment to dishes, is always made from long-grain rice. Its rustic equivalent, bulgur, isn't seen too often in İstanbullu restaurants and you'll probably only encounter it in the popular meze dish *kısır*.

In Praise of Patlıcan

If there's one vegetable that Turks adore more than any other, it would have to be *patlıcan* (eggplant or aubergine). It features in countless dishes and menus across the city and inevitably tastes wonderful. To prove the point, consider what is probably the most famous of all Turkish dishes – *imam bayıldı* (the imam fainted). A simple dish of eggplant slowly cooked with onion and garlic and served cold, it is so named because legend has it that an imam fainted with pleasure on first tasting it. We know just how he felt. A dish that has a similar effect is the decadent *beğendili tas kebabı*, lamb cubes cooked with onions and tomatoes and served on a bed of creamy pureed eggplant. Unquestionably swoon-inducing.

DESSERT

If you have a sweet tooth, prepare to put it to good use when in İstanbul. Though the locals aren't convinced of the idea of dessert to finish a meal (What's rakı for, if not to finish the meal?!), they love a mid-afternoon sugar hit and will often pop into a *muhallebici*, *baklavacı* or *pastane* for a piece of baklava swimming in honey, a gooey cake or a *fırın sütlac* (rice pudding) tasting of milk, sugar and just a hint of exotic spices. Turkish specialities worth sampling are *dondurma*, the local ice cream; *kadayıf*, dough soaked in syrup and topped with a layer of *kaymak* (clotted cream); and *künefe*, layers of *kadayıf* cemented together with sweet cheese, doused in syrup and served with a sprinkling of pistachio.

Kebab cooking

DRINKS

TEA & COFFEE

Drinking tea *(çay)* is the national pastime and it is seen as strange, even unpatriotic, not to swig the tannin-laden beverage at regular intervals throughout the day. Sugar cubes are the only accompaniment. You'll find these are needed to counter the effects of long brewing, although you can always try asking for it *açık* (weaker). Be warned that you'll risk severe embarrassment if you ask for milk if you're anywhere other than a tourist hotel or restaurant. In these places try saying '*Sütlu çay var mı*' (Do you have milky tea?). Tea is served in delicate tulip-shaped glasses, though if you're clocked as a tourist you may be given a cup and saucer and charged double the usual price (you will get double the amount of tea, though).

Apple tea *(elma çayı)* is a sweet concoction of chemicals, vaguely tasting like apples. It's popular with tourists, much to the amusement of some locals who hold it in disdain.

Surprisingly, Turkish coffee (*Türk kahve*) is not widely consumed. A thick and powerful brew that's tricky to prepare, it's drunk in a couple of short sips. If you order a cup, you will be asked how sweet you like it – *çok şekerli*' means 'very sweet', *orta şekerli* 'middling', *az şekerli* 'slightly sweet' and *sade* 'not at all'. If you order a cup, it will be accompanied by a glass of water, which is to clear the palate before you sample the delights of the coffee. Though you shouldn't drink the grounds in the bottom of your cup, you may want to read your fortune in them – check out the website of İstanbul's longest-established purveyor of coffee, Kurukahveci Mehmet Effendi (www.mehmetefendi.com), for a guide.

Most cafés in Sultanahmet and Beyoğlu serve decent Italian-style espresso and make cappuccino or caffe latte with fresh milk, though you'll pay for the privilege. Instant coffee (called *neskafe* regardless of what brand it is) is widely available.

OTHER NONALCOHOLIC DRINKS

Many locals don't drink the tap water and we recommend that you follow their lead. Bottled water *(şişe su)* is readily available and is usually placed on the table in all lokantas, meyhanes and *restorans*. You may see water-sellers in garish costumes pouring water into glasses and selling them to thirsty bystanders; note that this water is unbottled. Most of the fruit juice *(meyva suyu)* drunk in İstanbul is bottled, though cheap, freshly squeezed *portakal suyu* (orange juice) is available in most büfes and lokantas.

Ayran is a refreshing yogurt drink made by whipping yogurt with water and salt to the consistency of pouring cream. It is widely available and is a ubiquitous accompaniment to kebabs.

Boza, made from fermented bulgur with water and sugar, is certainly an acquired taste. This viscous mucus-coloured beverage, often served in a glass topped with dried chickpeas, has a reputation for building up strength and virility. The most famous *boza* bar in the city is **Vefa Bozacisi** (p166), near the Grand Bazaar, which has been serving up the stuff for nearly a century.

If you're in İstanbul during the cooler months (November to February), you should try the delicious and unusual taste of *salep*, a hot drink made from crushed tapioca root extract. Famed for its aphrodisiac properties, it is sold by street vendors and the occasional restaurant or *pastanesi* (pastry shop).

BEER, RAKI & WINE

Though Turkey is a Muslim country, it's people (particularly men) like nothing better than a convivial drink or two. Rakı is certainly the most popular of all alcoholic beverages, but beer (*bira*) claims second place. The local drop, Efes, is a perky pilsener that comes in bottles, cans and on tap. Another brand is Tuborg, which is made in Turkey under license to the Danish brewery.

Served in long thin glasses, rakı fires the passions and ensures a good evening at a meyhane. Most locals wouldn't dream of drinking anything else. Its aniseed taste perfectly complements meze and fish and its powerful punch (we're talking serious alcohol content here) assures many a rowdy table at restaurants around town. It's drunk neat or with water, which turns the clear liquid chalky white; if you want to add ice, do so after adding water, as dropping ice straight into rakı kills its flavour. Yeni is the most popular brand; Kulüp Rakısı is somewhat stronger, with a bit more aniseed; and Altınbaş is the strongest and most aniseed-laden.

Turkey grows and bottles its own wine (*şarap*) and many of the local tipples are perfectly drinkable, if unlikely to threaten French, Australian and Californian wine producers. The two largest producers are Doluca and Kavaklıdere. Duluca's best wines are its Özel Kav (Special Reserve) red and white; its Antik red and white are its second string wines (but are still quite drinkable). Its Villa Doluca wines are headache-inducing, so beware. Kavaklıdere's most popular wines are the quaffable Yakut red and Çankaya white; neither are as impressive as Doluca's Özel Kav vintages. Imported wine is very expensive due to the 400% import duty levied to protect the local industry.

WHERE TO EAT & DRINK

BALIK RESTORAN

Near the city's fish markets and along the Bosphorus you'll find the popular *balık restoran* (fish restaurants). Sometimes the fish on offer is displayed, but usually you'll need to ask the waiter what's fresh and ask to see the fish. This is important, as the occasional dodgy restaurant may try to serve you old fish. This trick is not just pulled out for foreigners – most locals ask to check the fish is fresh, so don't be embarrassed to do the same. The eyes should be clear and the flesh under the gill slits near the eyes should be bright red, not burgundy. After your fish has been given the all clear, ask the approximate price. The fish will be weighed, and the price computed at the day's per-kilogram rate.

BÖREKÇI

Börek (sweet and savoury pastries) are distinguished by their filling, cooking method and shape: they are square and cheesy, cigar shaped and meaty, plain and moist, pointy and potato chunky. *Kol böreği* is long and arm-shaped, and comes filled with cheese (*peynirli börek*), spinach (*ıspanaklı börek*), potatoes (*patates börek*) or meat. For the juicy *su böreği*

Fancy Some Bacteria with That?

Street vendors pound pavements across İstanbul, pushing carts laden with artfully arranged snacks to satisfy the appetites of commuters. You'll see these vendors next to ferry and bus stations, on busy streets and squares, even on the city's bridges.

Some of their snacks are innocuous – freshly baked *simit*, golden roasted corn on the cob, refreshing chilled and peeled cucumber – but others score high on the 'you must be mad!' scale. Sample these local treats and you're risking a major dose of the sultan's revenge (diarrhoea). Major offenders:

- **Midye dolma** (stuffed muscles) Delicious, exotic and packed with more bacteria than a Petri dish. Only for those who want to live very, very dangerously.
- **Pis pilav** (rice and chickpeas) Displayed in a glass cabinet, this rice dish often comes with boiled chicken. The direct translation is 'dirty rice', which gains a whole new meaning when you realise that the stuff often sits in the sun all day.
- **Çiğ köfte** (raw meatball) Raw meat kneaded by hand for hours with wheat, onion, clove, cinnamon, salt and hot black pepper and then formed into patties, usually by a profusely perspiring man with a cigarette in his other hand. Enough said.
- **Kokoreç** (lamb's intestines cooked with herbs and spices) The Turkish version of black pudding; locals love to snack on this smelly stuff. We feel queasy even thinking about it.
- **Balık ekmek** (Fish sandwich) The quintessential İstanbul snack. Innocuous and utterly delectable when freshly prepared, dangerous when not. Worth the risk.

(water börek), *yufka* (filo pastry) is boiled first, making it very soft. Then the *yufka* and the filling are layered into a round metal tray that revolves over a flame. As the *börek* cooks, it's flipped to a golden brown. *Su böreği* are a cross between a pastry and a lasagna – the good ones are succulent, not too oily and full of punchy flavour.

First-time visitors to İstanbul often become deeply infatuated with börekçis. Often a tiny window in the wall or a cupboard-sized kiosk with a few stools and benches, they offer a few types of *börek*, tea, instant coffee and a small selection of cold drinks, *ayran* always among them. They're a great place for a quick dirt-cheap breakfast or lunch, or a between-meal carbo tweak. Börekçi stock is often sold out by mid afternoon, and the best time to sample their wares is in the early morning, when the pastries have just come out of the oven.

BÜFES

The büfe is a kiosk, a food stand and a shop all rolled into one. It's a place where you can buy cigarettes, crisps, ice cream and confectionary, but where you can also snack on a *tost* (toasted sandwich), *döner kebap*, freshly squeezed orange juice, *ayran* and even alcohol. Many have stools where you can perch while eating your snack.

CAFÉS

Chic café-bars are nearly as easy to find in İstanbul as they are in Paris, London or New York. Most are clustered in Beyoğlu, but others are dotted in the suburbs on both sides of the Bosphorus and in other well-heeled neighbourhoods. Finding one in the Old City can be a challenge, though. Most serve coffee, a variety of teas (including herbal infusions) and food such as sandwiches, salads and pasta. Some also serve alcohol.

The ubiquitous tea garden (*çay bahçesi*) is found throughout the city. It is usually an outdoor, leafy garden serving tea, coffee and occasionally snacks (no alcohol) frequented by clusters of moustached gents playing backgammon, students lazing around a *nargileh* (water pipe), courting couples and families.

The Drinking chapter (pp163–170) recommends cafés and *çay bahçesi* through the city.

Turkish delight, Ali Muhiddin Had Bekir (p190)

KEBAPÇIS & KÖFTECIS

Kebapçıs are low-key, cheap eateries focused on grilled or roasted meat, but usually offering soup, simple salads, cold drinks and *ayran* as well. Don't expect tablecloths or waiterly flourishes – these are quick-fire joints, specialising in high turnover and no-frills nourishment. A köfteci is similar in style, but the food staple is grilled meatballs rather than grilled kebaps. If you spot the word *ocakbaşı* in the menu or the eatery's signage, it means the food will be cooked in front of you. Order your main meat course by the portion: *bir porsyon* (one portion) if you're not overly hungry; *bir buçuk porsyon* (one and a half) if you are, and *duble porsyon* (double) if you're ravenous.

LOKANTAS

This is the basic Turkish restaurant, varying from starkly simple to homely and charming. The food on offer is mostly cheap *hazır yemek* (ready food) laid out in dishes kept warm in a bain-marie. More often than not the kitchen is open and visible, right behind the food.

Your table may be covered with butcher's paper or a tablecloth; water and bread will arrive and keep on coming as long as you sit there. Even if there is a menu (and usually there isn't), you should go up and choose whatever takes your fancy. Don't feel the need to pile up a plate straight away. It's fine to choose one or two dishes and go back for more as you feel like it.

Most of the time the dishes won't be labelled, so you can practise your Turkish or take pot luck. A normal spread will include a soup, an eggplant dish, a chickpea stew, maybe some beans, a few meat stews (perhaps one chicken and a couple of lamb) and roast chicken. Look out for seasonal vegetable dishes, which are delicious with garlic yogurt. There will always be *pilav* available, either rice, *bulgur* or both. Though you can't count on getting dessert in a lokanta, it's fairly common to find *kadayıf* and *fırın sütlac*.

The core trade of lokantas in İstanbul is working people and shoppers looking for lunch. Some lokantas close in the late afternoon or offer a smaller selection for dinner (often leftovers from lunch).

MEYHANES

Imagine an Irish pub meeting a tapas bar with a dash of Turkish wedding party thrown in and you've conjured up a meyhane in İstanbul. Carousing at a meyhane is something that all visitors to the city should do. Packed on weekends, these are the places where groups of locals gather to spend the evening, usually ending up drunk as sailors. Musicians strumming fasıl (folk music) move from table to table entertaining the guests and playing requests. Revellers sing along, throw their arms around each other, clap boisterously and break into dance. Food is usually ordered a couple of dishes at a time – always meze, often fish and occasionally meat dishes, too. There are usually no menus, so you'll need to look and point. Everything will taste delicious, particularly after you've downed a few of the obligatory glasses of rakı that accompany a meyhane meal.

PIDECI

The Turkish version of the pizza parlour is a slice of heaven if you're after quick and tasty belly fuel. Choose from cheese and various meat toppings and sit back with an *ayran* or a cola, or get a *pide paket* (wrapped to go). Look for places using woodfire ovens – the *pide* always tastes better. Pidecis in İstanbul often also function as kebapçıs, in which case there will be a sign on the shopfront saying '*Pide ve Kebap*'.

RESTORAN

The line between a *restoran* and a lokanta can be blurry – a low end *restoran* is pretty much a lokanta under an alias. But, as you move up the price scale, closed kitchens, menus and alcohol will appear. And where there is alcohol, there is usually meze. There's a lot of crossover between main dishes at a lokanta and a *restoran*, but you're more likely to find *pirzola* (chops), *biftek* (steak) and 'international' meat dishes such as schnitzel at a *restoran*.

At the upper end of the scale are the many classy restaurants around town serving Ottoman, fusion, Mediterranean-influenced dishes and more. Ottoman restaurants specialise in *saray* (palace) cuisine refined over centuries in the kitchens of the sultans. It's delicately flavoured, beautifully presented and, if done well, totally delectable.

TATLICI

It's considered normal for a main meal at a restaurant to lead onto the *tatlıcı,* a specialist dessert place. As well as the classic *tatlıcı*, where you can overdose on baklava, *helva* (sweet prepared with sesame oil, cereals and honey or syrup) and *lokum* (Turkish delight), look out for the *muhallebici,* which specialises in milk-based puddings, and the *pastane* (or *pastanesi* or *baklavacı*), which tempts you with its baklava, European-style cakes and ice cream.

VEGETARIANS & VEGANS

Though it's normal for Turks to eat a vegetarian meal, the concept of vegetarianism is quite foreign. Say you're a vegan and Turks will either look mystified or assume that you're 'fessing up to some strain of socially aberrant behaviour. There is a sprinkling of vegetarian restaurants in Beyoğlu, a couple of which serve some vegan meals, but the travelling vegetarian certainly can't rely on specialist restaurants.

Meze is usually vegetable-based, and meat-free salads, soups, pastas, omelettes and *böreks,* as well as hearty vegetable dishes, are all readily available. Ask *'etsiz yemekler var mı?'* (is there something to eat that has no meat?) to see what's on offer.

The main source of inadvertent meat eating is *et suyu* (meat stock), which is often used to make otherwise vegetarian *pilavs*, soups and vegetable dishes. Your hosts may not even consider *et suyu* to be meat, so they will reassure you that the dish is vegetarian; ask *'et suyu var mı?'* (is there meat stock in it?) to check.

WHINING & DINING

Turkish parents regularly take their children out to eat, so you'll encounter no problems if you want to enjoy meals out with your family. Best of all, Turkish cuisine is very child-friendly, being simple and varied. Letting the youngest members of the party choose from the meze dishes on offer is always popular. Fried calamari (*kalamares*) is a staple at meyhanes and roast chicken and rice or potato features on every lokanta menu – kids inevitably approve. And of course the Turkish equivalents of fast food – *pide*, kebabs and *böreks* – tend to go down a treat. We've been known to present *tavuk şiş* (chicken

Turkish Delight

You can't leave İstanbul without having sampled real *lokum* (Turkish delight). We just won't allow it. The stuff you get here is the best in the world, and you can even buy it from the original shop of Ali Muhiddin Hacı Bekir, inventor of the gorgeously gooey gloop (p190).

The story goes that Ali Muhiddin came to İstanbul from the Black Sea mountain town of Kastamonu and established himself as a confectioner in the Ottoman capital in the late 18th century. Dissatisfaction with hard candies and traditional sweets led him to invent a new confection that would be easy to swallow, and he called his creation *rahat lokum,* the 'comfortable morsel'. *Lokum,* as it soon came to be called, was an immediate hit with the denizens of the imperial palace, and soon the translucent jellied jewels had fans all over the country.

Ali Muhiddin elaborated on his original confection, as did his offspring (the shop, which was established in 1777, is still owned by his descendants), and now as well as enjoying it plain (*sade*), you can buy *lokum* made with various fillings, including walnut (*cevizli*) and the classic pistachio (*şam fıstıklı*), or flavoured with orange (*portakkallı*), almond (*bademli*) or rosewater (*roze*). You can also get an assortment (*çeşitli*).

skewers) to a dubious six-year-old as 'Turkish chicken nuggets' – and can report that we got away with it! Fresh orange juice and soft drinks are almost always available to quench junior's thirst, too.

Some places have high chairs, but they're in the minority. To ask if one is available say '*Bebek için yüksek iskemleniz var mı?*' Kid's menus are only seen at food courts and Western-style hotel restaurants.

COOKING COURSES

The **Sarnıç Hotel** (☎ 212-518 2323; www.sarnichotel.com; Küçük Aya Sofya Caddesi 26) in Sultanahmet runs well-regarded Turkish cooking classes. Classes run for 4.5 hours and are given in English, French or Dutch. They cost €41 per person. The results are enjoyed over lunch on the hotel's rooftop terrace.

EAT YOUR WORDS
USEFUL RESTAURANT PHRASES

Table for ..., please.
... kişilik masa lütfen.
... kee-shee-leek mah-sah luuut-fehn.

What's that?
O nedir?
oh neh-deer?

What's the speciality here?
Buranın speşili nedir?
buu-rah-nihn speh-see-lee neh-deer?

What do you recommend?
Ne tavsiye edersiniz?
neh tav-see-yeh eh-dehr-see-neez?

Can I see the menu please?
Menüyü görebilirmiyim, lütfen?
meh-nuuu-yuuu ger-reh-bee-leer-mee-yeem, luuut-fehn?

Do you have a menu in English?
İngilizce menünüz var mı?
een-ghee-leez-jeh meh-nuuu-nuuuz vahr-mih?

What are today's specials?
Bugünün speşili nedir?
buu-guuu-nuuun speh-shee-lee neh-deer?

I'd like...
... istiyorum.
... ees-tee-yoh-ruum

I didn't order this.
Bunu sipariş etmedim.
buu-nuu see-pah-reesh eht-meh-deem.

This food is	...Bu yemek...	buu yeh-mahk ...
brilliant	mükemmel	muuu-kehm-mehl
burnt	yanık	yah-nihk
cold	soğuk	ohh-uuk
undercooked	az pişmiş	ahz peesh-meesh

I'd like something to drink.
İçecek bir şey istiyorum.
ee-cheh-jehk beer shey ees-tee-yoh-ruhm.

I'll have a beer.
Ben bira alayım.
behn bee-rah ah-leem.

Cheers!
Şerefe!
sheh-reh-feh!

May I see the wine list, please?
Şarap listenizi görebilir miyim, lütfen?
shah-rahp lees-teh-nee-zee ger-reh-bee-leer mee-yeem, luuut-fehn?

I'd like a glass/bottle of… wine.	Kadeh/Şişe… şarap istiyorum.	shah-rahp lees-teh-nee-zee ger-reh-bee-leer mee-yeem, luuut-fehn?
red	kırmızı	kihr-mih-zih
white	beyaz	beh-yahz
rose	roze/pembe	ohh-uuk

Where's the toilet?		
Tuvalet nerede?		tuu-wah-leht neh-reh-deh?
The bill, please.		
Hesap lütfen.		heh-sahp luuut-fehn.

FOOD GLOSSARY

A

almond	badem	bah-dehm
anchovy	hamsi, ançüvez	hahm-see, ahn-chuu-wehz
apple	elma	ehl-mah
apricot	kayısıı	kahy-ih-sih
aubergine	patlıcan	paht-lih-jahn

B

banana	muz	muuz
bean	fasulye	fah-suul-yeh
beef	sığır eti	sihh-ihr eh-tee
beer	bira	bee-rah
black pepper	kara biber	kah-rah bee-behr
bread	ekmek	ehk-mehk
butter	tereyağ	teh-reh-yah

C

cake	kek	kehk
carrot	havuç	hah-vuhch
cauliflower	karnabahar	kahr-nah-bah-hahr
cheese	peynir	pehy-nihr
chicken	tavuk/ piliç	tah-vuhk/ pee-leech
chilli	kırmızıbiber	kih-rih-mih-zih-bee-behr
chips (French fries)	kızarmış patates	kih-zahr-mihsh pah-tah-tehs
potato chips	çips	chihpz
chocolate	çokolata	chee-koh-lah-tah
coffee	kahve	kah-veh
corn	mısır	mih-sih
courgette	sakızkabağı	sah-kihz-kah-bah-ih
cream	krem	krehm

cucumber	salatalık	sah-lah-tah-lihk

D

date	hurma	huhr-mah
duck	ördek	er-dehk

E

egg(s)	yumurta(lar)	yuu-muur-tah-(lahr)
eggplant	patlıcan	paht-lih-jahn

F

fig	incir	een-jeer
fish	balık	bah-lihk
fruit	meyve	mehy-veh
fruit juice	meyve suyu	mehy-veh suu-yuu

G

garlic	sarımsak/ sarmısak	sah-rihm-sahk/ sahr-mih-sahk
grape(s)	üzüm(ler)	uuu-zuuum(lehr)
green capsicum (pepper)	yeşil biber	yeh-sheel bee-behr
green lentil	yeşil mercimek	yeh-sheel mehr-jee-mehk

H

honey	bal	bahl
hot (spicy)	acı	ah-jih
hot (temperature)	sıcak	sih-jahk

I

ice buz		buuz
ice cream	dondurma	doh-duhr-mah

J		
jam	reçel, marmelat	reh-chehl, mahr-meh-laht

L		
lamb	kuzu	kuu-zuu
lemon	limon	lee-mohn
lemonade	limonata	lee-moh-nah-tah
liver	ciğer/ karaciğer	jee-ehr/ kah-rah-jee-ehr

M		
medium (cooked)	orta pişmiş	ohr-tah peesh-meesh
milk	süt	suuut
mineral water	maden suyu	mah-dehn suu-yuu
mussel	midye	meed-yeh
mutton	kuzu	kuu-zuu

N		
noodles	(şerit halindeki) makarna	(sheh-reet hah-lihn-deh-kee) mah-kahr-nah

O		
octopus	ahtapot	ah-tah-paht
oil	ya	yah
okra	bamya	bahm-yah
olives	zeytin	zehy-teen
black	siyah	see-yah
green	yeşil	yeh-sheel
stuffed	doldurmuş	dohl-duur-muush
olive oil	zeytinyağı	zehy-teen-yahh-ih
omelette	omlet	ohm-leht

P		
pasta	makarna	mah-kahr-nah
pastrami	sığır pastırması, pastırma	sihh-ihr pahs-tihr-mah-sih, pahs-tihr-mah
peanut	yerfıstığı	yehr-fihs-tihh-ih
pear(s)	armut(lar)	ahr-muut(lahr)
pepper	biber	bee-behr
pickle	turşu	tuur-shuu
pineapple	ananas	ah-nah-nahs
pistachio	fıstık	fihs-tihk
plum	erik	eh-reek

R		
red cabbage	kırmızı lahana	kihr-mih-zih lah-hah-na
red capsicum (pepper)	kırmızı biber	kihr-mih-zih bee-behr
red kidney bean	kırmızı barbunya	kihr-mih-zih bahr-buun-yah
rice brown	pirinç esmer	pee-reench ehs-mehr
ripe	olmuş; olgun	ohl-muush; ohl-guun

S		
salad	salata	sah-lah-tah
salt	tuz	tuuz
sardine	sardalya	sahr-dahl-yah
sauce	sos, salça, terbiye	sohs, sahl-chah, tehr-bee-yeh
scampi	karides	kah-ree-dehs
skimmed milk	yağsız süt/ az yağlı süt	yah-sihz suuut/ ahz yah-lih suuut
(a) slice	dilim	dee-leem
soda water	soda	soh-dah,
soft drink	alkolsüz içecek, meşrubat	ahl-kohl-suuuz ee-cheh-jehk, mehsh-ruu-baht
soup	çorba	chohr-bah
spinach	ıspanak	ih-spah-nahk
squid	kalamar	kah-lah-mahr
steak	biftek	beef-tehk
stew	türlü, güveç	tuur-luuu, gyuuu-wetch
still water	dinlenmiş su	deen-lehn-meesh suu
strawberry	çilek	chee-lehk
sugar	şeker	sheh-kehr

T		
tea	çay	chahy
chamomile	papatya çayı	pah-paht-yah chah-yih
green	yeşil çay	yeh-sheel chahy
herbal	bitkisel çay	biht-kee-sehl chahy
lemon	limonlu çay	lee-mohn-luu chahy
milk	sütlü çay	suuut-luuu chahy
peppermint	naneli çay	nah-neh-lee chahy

toast	*kızarmış ekmek; tost*	kih-zahr-mihsh ehk-mehk; tohst		**W**		
				water	*daha su*	dah-hah suu
tomato	*domates*	doh-mah-tehs		**well done (cooked)**	*çok pişmiş*	choke peesh-meesh
tripe	*işkembe*	eesh-kehm-beh		wine	*şarap*	shah-rahp
tuna	*tonbalığı, orkinos*	tohn-bah-lih-ih, ohr-kee-nohs			*(şarabı)*	(shah-rah-bih)
				red	*kırmızı*	kihr-mih-zih
				white	*beyaz*	beh-yahz
V						
vanilla	*vanilya*	wah-neel-yah		**Y**		
vegetable(s)	*sebze(ler)/ bitki(ler)*	sehb-zeh(lehr)/ beet-kee(lehr)		yogurt	*yoğurt*	yohh-uurt
vegetarian	*etyemez*	veh-zheh-tahr-yehn/ vejetaryen/ eht-yeh-mehz		**Z**		
				zucchini	*sakızkabağı (bir tür sakızkabağı)*	sah-kihz-kah-bah-ih

History

History

THE RECENT PAST

İstanbul has undergone enormous change since the 1980s, witnessing more than its fair share of political and economic upheavals, as well as the introduction of major economic reforms that have reinforced the city's position as Turkey's industrial powerhouse and seen the population boom.

Under the presidency of economist Turgut Özal, the 1980s saw a free market–led economic and tourism boom in Turkey and its major city. Özal's government also presided over a great increase in urbanisation, with trainloads of peasants from eastern Anatolia making their way to the cities – particularly İstanbul – in search of jobs in the booming industry sector. The city's infrastructure couldn't cope back then and is still catching up, despite two decades of large-scale municipal works being undertaken.

The municipal elections of March 1994 were a shock to the political establishment, with the upstart religious-right Refah Partisi (Welfare Party) winning elections across the country. Its victory was seen in part as a protest vote against the corruption, ineffective policies and tedious political wrangles of the traditional parties. In İstanbul Refah was led by Recep Tayyip Erdoğan, a proudly Islamist candidate. He vowed to modernise infrastructure and restore the city to its former glory.

In the national elections of December 1996, Refah polled more votes than any other party (23%), and eventually formed a government vowing moderation and honesty. Emboldened by political power, Prime Minister Necmettin Erbakan and other Refah politicians tested the boundaries of Turkey's traditional secularism, alarming the powerful National Security

Kariye Müzesi (p111)

Council, the most visible symbol of the centrist military establishment's role as the caretaker of secularism and democracy.

In 1997 the council announced that Refah had flouted the constitutional ban on religion in politics and warned that the government should resign or face a military coup. Bowing to the inevitable, Erbakan did as the council wished. In İstanbul, Mayor Erdoğan was ousted by the secularist forces in the national government in late 1998.

National elections in April 1999 brought in a coalition government led by Bülent Ecevit's left-wing Democratic Left Party. After years under the conservative right of the Refah Partisi, the election result heralded a shift towards European-style social democracy, something highlighted by the country's successful bid to be accepted as a candidate for membership of the European Union. Unfortunately for the new government there was a spectacular collapse of the Turkish economy in 2001, leading to an electoral defeat in 2002 by the newly formed Islamic Justice and Development Party, led by Phoenix-like Recep Tayyip Erdoğan. With İstanbul's former mayor now the country's prime minister, few doubt that he will continue to look after the city's best interests at the same time as leading the nation into a new, European-flavoured future.

FROM THE BEGINNING

EARLIEST TIMES

Semistra, the earliest-known settlement on the site of İstanbul, was probably founded around 1000 BC, a few hundred years after the Trojan War and in the same period that kings David and Solomon ruled in Jerusalem. Semistra was followed by a fishing village named Lygos, which occupied Seraglio Point (Seray Burnu) where Topkapı Palace stands today.

Around 700 BC, colonists from Megara (near Corinth) in Greece founded the city of Chalcedon (now Kadıköy) on the Asian shore of the Bosphorus. Chalcedon became one of a dozen Greek fishing colonies along the shores of the Propontis (the ancient name for the Sea of Marmara). The historian Theopompus of Chios, cited in John Freely's *İstanbul: The Imperial City*, wrote in the latter half of the fourth century that its inhabitants 'devoted themselves unceasingly to the better pursuits of life'. Their way of life was apparently in stark contrast to that of the dissolute Byzantines, who founded their settlement across the Bosphorus at Seraglio Point in 657 BC.

BYZANTIUM

Legend tells us that Byzantium was founded by a Megarian colonist named Byzas, the son of the god Poseidon and the nymph Keroessa, daughter of Zeus and Io. Before leaving Greece, Byzas had asked the oracle at Delphi where he should establish his new colony. The enigmatic answer was 'Opposite the blind'. All made sense when he and his fellow colonists sailed up the Bosphorus and noticed the colony on the Asian shore at Chalcedon. Looking west, they saw the small fishing village of Lygos, built on a magnificent and easily fortified natural harbour of the Golden Horn (known to the Greeks as Chrysokeras) on the European shore. Thinking, as legend has it, that 'Those people in Chalcedon must be blind' to disregard such a superb position, Byzas and his mates settled here and their new town came to be called Byzantium after its founder.

The new colony quickly prospered, largely due to its ability to levy tolls and harbour fees on ships passing through the Bosphorus, then as now an important waterway. A thriving marketplace was established and the inhabitants lived on traded goods and the abundant fish stocks in the surrounding waters. In all, the early Byzantines were a fortunate lot. They walled their city to ensure its invincibility from attack, enslaved the local Thracian population to do most of the hard work and worshipped the Greek Olympian

AD 330	527–65
Constantine the Great founds Constantinople, the 'New Rome', capital of the Eastern Roman (Byzantine) Empire	Reign of Justinian, the height of eastern Roman power and influence

gods. Theopompus of Chios might have thought that the Chalcedons lived a good clean life when they first established their city on the opposite shore, but he had no such compliment for the Byzantines, writing that they 'accustomed themselves to amours and drinking in the taverns'.

In 512 BC Darius, emperor of Persia, captured the city during his campaign against the Scythians. Following the retreat of the Persians in 478 BC, the town came under the influence and protection of Athens and joined the Athenian League. It was a turbulent relationship, with Byzantium revolting a number of times, only to be defeated by the Athenians. During one of the revolts, the Athenian navy mounted an expedition against Byzantium and Chalcedon and sailed up the Bosphorus to establish a settlement at Chrysopolis ('the City of Gold'), site of the present-day suburb of Üsküdar. From this base they successfully besieged Byzantium.

The Spartans took the city after the end of the Peloponnesian War. Their rule was threatened in 400 BC, when Xenophon led the remnants of the Ten Thousand (the Greek army in the service of Cyrus the Younger) back to Greece from the Battle of Cunaxa in Persia by way of the Bosphorus and attacked the city. They were persuaded not to continue with their attack, though, and the Spartans ruled for another 10 years before they were ousted and Byzantium once again joined the League of Athens. It was granted independence in 355 BC but stayed under the Athenian umbrella, withstanding with Athenian help a siege by Philip, father of Alexander the Great, in 340 BC.

By the end of the Hellenistic period, Byzantium had formed an alliance with the Roman Empire. It retained its status as a free state, which it even kept after being officially incorporated into the Roman Empire in AD 79 by Vespasian, but it paid significant taxes for the privilege. Life was relatively uneventful until the city's leaders made a big mistake: they picked the wrong side in a Roman war of succession following the death of the Emperor Pertinax in AD 193. When Septimius Severus emerged victorious over his rival Pescennius Niger, he mounted a three-year siege of the city, eventually massacring Byzantium's citizens, razing its walls and burning it to the ground. Ancient Byzantium was no more.

The new emperor was aware of the city's important strategic position, and he soon set about rebuilding it. He pardoned the remaining citizens and built a circuit of walls that stretched roughly from where the Yeni Camii is today to the Cankurtaran lighthouse, enclosing a city twice the size of its predecessor. The **Hippodrome** (p86) was built by Severus, as was a colonnaded way that followed the present path of Divan Yolu. He also erected a gateway known as the Miliarium Aureum or, more simply, the Milion. A marble stellae from this gate can still be seen today (p139). Severus named his new city Augusta Antonina and it was subsequently ruled by a succession of emperors, including the great Diocletian (r 284–303).

CONSTANTINOPLE

Diocletian had decreed that after his retirement, the government of the Roman Empire should be overseen by co-emperors Galerius in the east (Augusta Antonina) and Constantine in the west (Rome). This resulted in a civil war, which was won by Constantine in AD 324 when he defeated Licinius, Galerius' successor, at Chrysopolis.

With his victory, Constantine became sole emperor (r 324–37) of a reunited empire. He also became the first Christian emperor, though he didn't formally convert until on his deathbed. To solidify his power he summoned the First Ecumenical Council at Nicaea (İznik) in 325, which established the precedent of the emperor's supremacy in church affairs.

669	717–18
Arab Muslim armies lay siege to the city for the first time but cannot penetrate its walls	A further Arab siege of Constantinople is unsuccessful

Constantine also decided to move the capital of the empire to the shores of the Bosphorus. He built a new, wider circle of walls around the site of Byzantium and laid out a magnificent city within. The Hippodrome was extended and a forum was built on the crest of the second hill, near today's Nuruosmaniye Camii. The city was dedicated on 11 May 330 as New Rome, but soon came to be called Constantinople. First settled as a fishing village over 1000 years earlier, the settlement on Seraglio Point was now the capital of the Eurasian world and would remain so for almost another 1000 years.

Constantine died in 337, just seven years after the dedication of his new capital. His empire was divided up between his three sons: Constantius, Constantien and Constans. Constantinople was part of Constantius' share. His power base was greatly increased in 353, when he overthrew both of his brothers and brought the empire under his sole control.

Constantius died in 361 and was succeeded by his cousin Julian. Emperor Jovian was next, succeeded by Valens (of aqueduct fame, p34).

The city continued to grow under the rule of the emperors. Theodosius I ('the Great') had a forum built on the present site of Beyazıt Square and a massive triumphal gate built in the city walls, the **Porta Aurea** (Golden Gate; p115). He also erected the **Obelisk of Theodosius** (p86) at the Hippodrome. His grandson Emperor Theodosius II (r 408–50) came to the throne as a boy, heavily influenced by his sister Pulcheria, who acted as regent until her brother was old enough to rule in his own right. Threatened by the forces of Attila the Hun, he ordered that an even wider, more formidable circle of walls be built around the city. Encircling all seven hills of the city, the walls were completed in 413, only to be brought down by a series of earthquakes in 447. They were hastily rebuilt in a mere two months – the rapid approach of Attila and the Huns acting as a powerful stimulus. The Theodosian walls successfully held out invaders for the next 757 years and still stand today.

Theodosius II's other achievements were the compilation of the *Codex Theodosianus*, a collection of all of the laws that had been enacted since the reign of Constantine the Great, and the erection of a new cathedral, the Sancta Sophia (Aya Sofya or Church of the Divine Wisdom), which replaced an earlier church of the same name that had been burned during a riot in 404.

JUSTINIAN & THEODORA

Theodosius died in 450 and was succeeded by a string of six emperors, the last of whom was Justin, the uncle of the man who was to become one of the most famous of all Byzantine emperors, Justinian.

During the 5th and 6th centuries, as the barbarians of Europe captured and sacked Rome, the new eastern capital grew in wealth, strength and reputation. Justinian (r 527–65) had much to do with this. A former soldier, he and his great general Belisarius reconquered Anatolia, the Balkans, Egypt, Italy and North Africa. They also successfully put down the Nika riots of 532, killing 30,000 of the rioters in the Hippodrome in the process.

Three years before taking the throne, Justinian had married Theodora, a strong-willed former courtesan who is credited with having great influence over her husband (see Powers Behind the Throne, p60). Together, they further embellished Constantinople with great buildings, including SS Sergius and Bacchus, now known as **Küçük Aya Sofya** (p89), **Haghia Eirene** (p91) and the **Basilica Cistern** (p83). Justinian's personal triumph was a new Sancta Sophia (today known as the **Aya Sofya**, p79), built to replace Theodosius II's church, which had burned to the ground during the Nika riots. The new cathedral was completed in 537.

Justinian's ambitious building projects and constant wars of reconquest exhausted his treasury and his empire. Following his reign, the Byzantine Empire would never again be large, powerful or rich.

814–924	1071
Armies of the Bulgarian empire besiege the city unsuccessfully	Emperor Romanus IV Diogenes defeated and captured by the Seljuk Turks at Manzikert

BESIEGED & DECLINING

From 565 to 1025, a succession of warrior emperors kept invaders such as the Persians and the Avars at bay. Though the foreign armies often managed to get as far as Chalcedon, none were able to breach Theodosius' great walls. The Arab armies of the nascent Islamic empire tried in 669, 674, 678 and 717–18, each time in vain. Inside the walls the city was undergoing a different type of threat: the Iconoclastic Crisis. This began in 726 when Emperor Leo III launched his quest to rid the empire of all forms of idolatry. Those who worshipped idols, including the followers of many saints, revolted and a number of uprisings ensued. The emperor was ultimately triumphant and his policy was adopted by his successors. It was first overturned in 780, when the Empress Eirene, mother of the child emperor Constantine VI, set out to restore icons. Reintroduced, it was finally put to rest by the Empress Theodora, mother of Michael III, another child emperor, in 845.

The powerful emperors of the Bulgarian empire besieged the city in 814, 913 and 924, never conquering it. Under Emperor Basil II (r 976–1025), the Byzantine armies drove the Arab armies out of Anatolia and completely annihilated the Bulgarian forces. For this feat he was dubbed Bulgaroctonus, the 'Bulgar-slayer'.

In 1071 Emperor Romanus IV Diogenes (r 1068–1071) led his army to eastern Anatolia to do battle with the Seljuk Turks, who had been forced out of Central Asia by the encroaching Mongols. However, at Manzikert (Malazgirt) the Byzantines were disastrously defeated, the emperor captured and imprisoned, and the former Byzantine heartland of Anatolia thus thrown open to Turkish invasion and settlement. Soon the Seljuks had built a thriving empire of their own in central Anatolia, with their capital first at Nicaea and later at Konya.

Powers Behind the Throne

Many powerful women have featured in İstanbul's imperial history. Our favourites are the following:

Theodora The wife of Justinian, Theodora was the daughter of a bear-keeper at the Hippodrome. A courtesan before she married, she subsequently became extremely devout and endowed a number of churches in the city. Justinian was devoted to her and she was widely acknowledged by contemporary historians to be the true power behind the throne. When the Nika riots broke out in 532, the Imperial Council counselled the Emperor to flee the city, but Theodora persuaded him to stay and fight. The riot was put down and Justinian went on to enjoy a 38-year reign with Theodora at his side.

Zoe Our favourite of all the empresses, feisty Zoe (r 1028–50) was 50 years old and supposedly a virgin when her dying father, Constantine VIII, insisted she marry the aged Romanus III Argyrus. Romanus had in fact been happily married for 40 years but neither Zoe nor her father were going to let that get in their way, threatening him with blinding if he didn't consent. When Constantine died, Romanus was crowned emperor and Zoe empress. Finding married life a tad dull, Zoe took as her lover the much younger Michael the Paphlagonian. After Romanus mysteriously drowned in his bath in 1034, Zoe quickly married her virile companion, who joined her on the throne as Michael IV. Eight years later, after Michael died from an illness contracted while on campaign, Zoe and her sister Theodora ruled as empresses in their own right. At the age of 64 Zoe wed again – an eminent senator, Constantine IX Monomachus, who eventually outlived her.

Roxelana The wife of Süleyman the Magnificent, Hürrem Sultan was more commonly known as Roxelana ('the Russian'). She was beautiful, powerful and a thoroughly nasty piece of work. Though allowed four legal wives and as many concubines as he could support by Islamic law, Süleyman was devoted to Roxelana alone and ended up marrying her. Secure in her position, she mastered the art of palace intrigue and behind-the-scenes manipulation, even convincing the sultan to have İbrahim Paşa, Süleyman's lifelong companion and devoted grand vizier, strangled when he objected to her influence. Unfortunately, she also made sure that her drunken son, Selim the Sot, would succeed to the throne by having the able heir apparent, Prince Mustafa, strangled.

1204	1261
Armies of the Fourth Crusade capture the city, sack it and put a Latin emperor on the throne	Michael VIII Palaeologus, emperor of Nicaea, recaptures Constantinople and re-establishes the Byzantine Empire

As Turkish power was consolidated in Anatolia to the east of Constantinople, the power of Venice – always a maritime and commercial rival to Constantinople – grew in the west. This coincided with the launch of the First Crusade and the arrival in Constantinople of the first of the Crusaders in 1096.

THE CRUSADES

Soldiers of the Second Crusade passed through the city in 1146 during the reign of Manuel I, son of John Comnenus II 'The Good' and his empress, Eirene, both of whose mosaic portraits can be seen in the gallery at Aya Sofya (p79). In 1171 Manuel evicted Venetian merchants from their neighbourhood in Galata. The Venetians retaliated by sending a fleet to attack Byzantine ports in Greece.

The convoluted, treacherous imperial court politics of Constantinople have given us the word 'Byzantine'. Rarely blessed with a simple, peaceful succession, Byzantine rulers were always under threat from members of their own families as well as would-be tyrants and foreign powers. This internecine plotting was eventually to lead to the defeat of the city by the Crusaders.

Galata Tower (p118)

In 1195 Alexius III deposed and blinded his brother, Emperor Isaac II, claiming the throne for himself. Fleeing to the West, Isaac's oldest son, Prince Alexius, pleaded to the Pope and other Western rulers for help in restoring his father to the Byzantine throne. At the time, the Fourth Crusade was assembling in Venice to sail to Egypt and attack the infidel. Knowing this, Prince Alexius sent a message to the Crusaders offering to agree to a union of the Greek and Roman churches under the papacy if the Crusaders could put his father back on the throne. He also promised to pay richly for their assistance. The Crusader leaders agreed, and Enrico Dandolo, Doge of Venice, led the crusaders to Constantinople, arriving in 1203.

Rather than facing the Crusaders, Alexius III fled with the imperial treasury. The Byzantines swiftly restored Isaac II to the throne and made Prince Alexius his co-emperor. Unfortunately, the new co-emperors had no money to pay their allies. They were also deeply unpopular with their subjects, being seen as Latin toadies. Isaac fell ill (he died in 1204), and the Byzantines swiftly deposed Alexius and crowned a new emperor, Alexius V. The new emperor foolishly ordered the Crusaders to leave his territory, conveniently ignoring the fact that they believed themselves to be owed a considerable amount of money by the Byzantines. Their patience exhausted, the Crusaders attacked. On 13 April 1204 they broke through the walls, and sacked and pillaged the rich capital of their Christian ally.

When the smoke cleared, Dandolo took control of three-eighths of the city, including Aya Sofya, leaving the rest to his co-conspirator Count Baldwin of Flanders. The Byzantine nobility fled to what was left of their estates and fought among themselves in best Byzantine fashion for control of the shreds of the empire.

After Dandolo's death, Count Baldwin had himself crowned emperor of Romania ('Kingdom of the Romans'), his name for his new kingdom. Never a strong or effective state, Baldwin's so-called empire steadily declined until, just over half a century later in 1261, it was easily recaptured by the soldiers of Michael VIII Palaeologus, formerly the emperor of Nicaea, where the Byzantine Empire in exile sat. The Byzantine Empire was restored.

1288	1326–31
Osman Gazi, a Turkish warlord on the Byzantine frontier near Bursa, founds the Ottoman state	Orhan Gazi, son of Osman, captures Bursa and Nicaea for the Ottomans; Bursa becomes the Ottoman capital

UPSTARTS FROM THE EAST

Two decades after Michael reclaimed Constantinople, a Turkish warlord named Ertuğrul died in the village of Söğüt near Nicaea. He left his son Osman, who was known as Gazi ('Warrior for the Faith'), a small territory. Osman's followers became known in the Empire as Osmanlıs and in the West as the Ottomans.

Osman died in 1324 and was succeeded by his son Orhan. In 1326 Orhan captured Bursa, made it his capital and took the title of sultan. A victory at Nicaea followed, after which he sent his forces further afield, conquering Ankara to the east and Thrace to the west. His son Murat I (r 1362–89) took Adrianople (Edirne) in 1371 and extended his conquests to Kosovo, where he defeated the Serbs and Bosnians.

Murat's son Beyazıt (r 1389–1402) laid siege to Constantinople in 1394 (unsuccessfully) and then defeated a Crusader army 100,000 strong on the Danube in 1396. Though temporarily checked by the armies of Tamerlane and a nasty war of succession between Beyazıt's four sons that was eventually won by Mehmet I (r 1413–21), the Ottomans continued to grow in power and size. By 1440 the Ottoman armies under Murat II (r 1421–51) had taken Thessalonica, laid siege to Constantinople and Belgrade (unsuccessfully), and had battled Christian armies for Transylvania. It was at this point in history that Mehmet II 'The Conqueror' (r 1451–81) came to power and vowed to attain the ultimate prize – Constantinople.

THE CONQUEST

By 1450, the Byzantine emperor had control over little more than Constantinople itself.

The first step in Mehmet's plan to take the city was construction of the great fortress of Rumeli Hisarı, which was completed in 1452. He also repaired Anadolu Hisarı, the fortress on the Asian shore that had been built by his great-grandfather. Between them, the two great fortresses then closed the Bosphorus at its narrowest point, blockading the imperial capital from the north.

The Byzantines had closed the mouth of the Golden Horn with a heavy chain (on view in İstanbul's **Askeri Müzesi**, p122) to prevent Ottoman ships from sailing in and attacking the city walls on the north side. Mehmet outsmarted them by marshalling his boats at a cove where Dolmabahçe Palace now stands, and having them transported overland during the night on rollers and slides up the valley (where the İstanbul Hilton now stands) and down the other side into the Golden Horn at Kasımpaşa. As dawn broke his fleet attacked the city, catching the Byzantine defenders by surprise. Soon the Golden Horn was under Ottoman control.

As for the mighty Theodosian land walls to the west, a Hungarian cannon founder named Urban had offered his services to the Byzantine emperor for the defence of Christendom. Finding that the emperor had no money, he conveniently forgot about defending Christianity and went instead to Mehmet, who paid him richly to cast an enormous cannon capable of firing a huge ball right through the city walls.

Despite the inevitability of the conquest (Mehmet had 80,000 men compared with Byzantium's 7000), Emperor Constantine XI (r 1449–53) refused the surrender terms offered by Mehmet on 23 May 1453, preferring to wait in hope that Christendom would come to his rescue. On 28 May the final attack commenced: the mighty walls were breached between the gates now called Topkapı and Edirnekapı, the sultan's troops flooded in and by the evening of the 29th they were in control of every quarter. Constantine, the last emperor of Byzantium, died fighting on the city walls.

THE CITY ASCENDANT

The 21-year-old conqueror saw himself as the legitimate successor to the imperial throne of Byzantium by right of conquest, and he began at once to rebuild and repopulate the city. Aya Sofya was converted to a mosque; a new mosque, the Fatih (Conqueror) Camii, was built on

1453	1520–66
Sultan Mehmet II (the Conqueror) builds Rumeli Hisarı and conquers Constantinople	Reign of Sultan Süleyman the Magnificent

the fourth hill; and the Eskı Saray (Old Palace) was constructed on the third hill, followed by a new palace at Topkapı a few years later. The city walls were repaired and a new fortress, **Yedikule** (p115), was built. İstanbul, as it was often called, assumed the role of the new administrative, commercial and cultural centre of the ever-growing Ottoman Empire. Interestingly, Mehmet encouraged Greeks who had fled the city to return and issued an imperial decree calling for resettlement; Muslims, Jews and Christians all took up his offer and were promised the right to worship as they pleased. The Genoese, who had fought with the Byzantines, were pardoned and allowed to stay in Galata, though the fortifications that surrounded their settlement were torn down. The **Galata Tower** (p118) was the only part allowed to stand.

Mehmet died in 1481 and was succeeded by Beyazıt II (r 1481–1512), who was ousted by his son, the ruthless Selim the Grim (r 1512–20), famed for executing seven grand viziers during his relatively short reign.

The building boom that Mehmet kicked off was continued by his successors, with Selim's son Süleyman the Magnificent (r 1520–66) being responsible for more construction than any other sultan. Blessed with the services of Mimar Sinan (c 1497–1588), Islam's greatest architect, the sultan and his family, court and grand viziers crowded the city with great buildings. Under Süleyman's 46-year reign, the longest of any sultan, the empire expanded its territories and refined its artistic pursuits at its court. None of the empires of Europe or Asia were as powerful.

RULE OF THE WOMEN

Süleyman's son Selim II ('the Sot', r 1566–74) and his successors lost themselves in the pleasures of the harem and the bottle, and cared little for the administration of the empire their forebears had built. While they were carousing, a succession of exceptionally able grand viziers dealt with external and military affairs.

Before the drunken Selim drowned in his bath, his chief concubine Nurubanu called the shots in the palace and ushered in the so-called 'Rule of the Women', whereby a series of chief concubines and mothers (*valide sultans*) of a series of dissolute sultans ruled the roost at court. Among the most fascinating of these women was Kösem Sultan, the favourite of Sultan Ahmet I (r 1603–17). She influenced the course of the empire through Ahmet, then through her sons Murat IV (r 1623–40) and İbrahim, ('the Mad', r 1640–48) and finally through her grandson Mehmet IV (r 1648–87). Her influence over Mehmet lasted only a few years and she was strangled in 1651 at the command of the *valide sultan* Turhan Hatice, Mehmet's mother.

For the next century the sultans continued in Selim's footsteps. Their dissolute and often unbalanced behaviour led to dissatisfaction among the people and the army, which would eventually prove to be the empire's undoing.

DECLINE, THEN REFORM OF SORTS

The motor that drove the Ottoman Empire was military conquest, and when the sultan's armies reached their geographical and technological limits decline set in for good. In 1683 the Ottomans laid siege for the second time to Vienna, but failed again to take the city. With the Treaty of Karlowitz in 1699, the Austrian and Ottoman emperors divided up the Balkans, and the Ottoman Empire went on the defensive.

By this time Europe was well ahead of Turkey in politics, technology, science, banking, commerce and military development. Sultan Selim III (r 1789–1807) initiated efforts to catch up to Europe, but was overthrown in a revolt by janissaries (the sultan's personal bodyguards). The modernisation efforts were continued under Mahmut II (r 1808–39). He founded a new army along European lines, provoking a riot among the janissaries, so that in 1826 he had to send his new force in to crush them, which it did. The bodies of janissaries filled the Hippodrome and the ancient corps, once the glory of the empire, was no more.

1789–1807	1839
Reign of Sultan Selim III, who adopted Western-style systems of politics and defence	Sultan Abdül Mecit implements the Tanzimat (Reorganisation) political and social reforms

Sultan Abdül Mecit (r 1839–61) continued the catch-up, implementing the Tanzimat (Reorganisation) political and social reforms. But these efforts were too little, too late. During the 19th century, ethnic nationalism, a force more powerful even than Western armies, penetrated the empire's domain and proved its undoing.

ETHNIC NATIONALISM

For centuries, the non-Turkish ethnic and non-Muslim religious minorities in the sultan's domains had lived side by side with their Turkish neighbours, governed by their own religious and traditional laws. The head of each community – chief rabbi, Orthodox patriarch etc – was responsible to the sultan for the community's wellbeing and behaviour.

Ottoman decline and misrule provided fertile ground for the growth of ethnic nationalism among these communities. The subject peoples of the Ottoman Empire rose in revolt, one after another, often with the direct encouragement and assistance of the European powers, who coveted parts of the sultan's vast domains. After bitter fighting in 1831 the Kingdom of Greece was formed; the Serbs, Bulgarians, Romanians, Albanians, Armenians and Arabs would all seek their independence soon after.

As the sultan's empire broke up, the European powers (Britain, France, Italy, Germany, Russia) hovered in readiness to colonise or annex the pieces. They used religion as a reason for pressure or control, saying that it was their duty to protect the sultan's Catholic, Protestant or Orthodox subjects from misrule and anarchy.

The Russian emperors put pressure on the Turks to grant them powers over all Ottoman Orthodox Christian subjects, whom the Russian emperor would thus 'protect'. The result was the Crimean War (1853–56), with Britain and France fighting on the side of the Ottomans against the growth of Russian power. During the war, wounded British, French and Ottoman soldiers were brought to İstanbul for treatment at the Selimiye Army Barracks, now home to the **Florence Nightingale Museum** (p131), and the foundations of modern nursing practice were laid.

Even during the war, the sultan continued the imperial building tradition. Vast Dolmabahçe Palace (p124) and its mosque were finished in 1856, and the palaces at Beylerbeyi (p124), Çırağan (p124) and Yıldız (p127) would be built before the end of the century. Though it had lost the fabulous wealth of the days of Süleyman the Magnificent, the city was still regarded as the Paris of the East. It was also the terminus of the *Orient Express*, which connected İstanbul and Paris – the world's first great international luxury express train.

Naming Rights

Even when it was ruled by the Byzantines, Constantinople was informally known as 'the city' (*polis*). The name İstanbul probably derives from this (the Greek for 'to the city' is *'eis ten polin'*). Though the Turks kept the name Constantinople, they also used other names, including İstanbul and 'Dersaadet' (city of peace and/or happiness).

The city's name was officially changed to İstanbul by Atatürk in the early republican years and the use of the name Constantinople was banned for having, it was thought, unfortunate imperial connotations.

ABDÜL HAMIT II & THE YOUNG TURKS

Amid the empire's internal turmoil, Abdül Hamit II (r 1876–1909) assumed the throne. Mithat Paşa, a successful general and powerful grand vizier, managed to introduce a constitution at the same time, but soon the new sultan did away both with Mithat Paşa and the constitution, and established his own absolute rule.

Abdül Hamit modernised without democratising, building thousands of kilometres of railways and telegraph lines and encouraging modern industry. However, the empire continued to disintegrate, and there were nationalist insurrections in Armenia, Bulgaria, Crete and Macedonia.

1876	1876–1909
The Tanzimat movement ends with the promulgation of the first Ottoman constitution	Sultan Abdül Hamit II abrogates the constitution and rules the empire with an iron hand

The younger generation of the Turkish elite – particularly the military – watched bitterly as their country fell apart, then organised secret societies bent on toppling the sultan. The Young Turk movement for Western-style reforms gained enough power by 1908 to force the restoration of the constitution. In 1909 the Young Turk–led Ottoman parliament deposed Abdül Hamit and put his hopelessly indecisive brother Mehmet V on the throne.

When WWI broke out, the Ottoman parliament and sultan made the fatal error of siding with Germany and the Central Powers. With their defeat, the Ottoman Empire collapsed, İstanbul was occupied by the British and the sultan became a pawn in the hands of the victors.

REPUBLICAN İSTANBUL

The situation looked very bleak for the Turks as their armies were being disbanded and their country was taken under the control of the Allies, but what first seemed a catastrophe provided the impetus for rebirth.

Ever since gaining independence in 1831, the Greeks had entertained the Megali Idea (Great Plan) of a new Greek empire encompassing all the lands which had once had Greek influence – in effect, the refounding of the Byzantine Empire, with Constantinople as its capital. On 15 May 1919, with Western backing, Greek armies invaded Anatolia in order to make the dream a reality.

Even before the Greek invasion an Ottoman general named Mustafa Kemal, the hero of the WWI battle at Gallipoli, had decided that a new government must take over the destiny of the Turks from the ineffectual sultan. He began organising resistance to the sultan's captive government on 19 May 1919.

The Turkish War of Independence, in which the Turkish Nationalist forces led by Mustafa Kemal fought off Greek, French and Italian invasion forces, lasted from 1920 to 1922. Victory in the bitter war put Mustafa Kemal (1881–1938) in command of the fate of the Turks. The sultanate was abolished in 1922, as was the Ottoman Empire soon after. The republic was born on 29 October 1923.

Cumhuriyet Anıtı (p123)

1909–18	1922–23
The 'Young Turks' depose Abdül Hamit II and rule as a virtual military junta	The Grand National Assembly, led by Mustafa Kemal (Atatürk), abolishes the Ottoman sultanate and proclaims the Turkish Republic

NO LONGER THE CAPITAL

The nation's saviour, proclaimed Atatürk (Father Turk) by the Turkish parliament, decided to move away, both metaphorically and physically, from the imperial memories of İstanbul. He established the seat of the new republican government in a city (Ankara) that could not be threatened by foreign gunboats. Robbed of its importance as the capital of a vast empire, İstanbul lost much of its wealth and glitter in succeeding decades.

Atatürk had always been ill at ease with Islamic traditions and he set about making the Republic of Turkey a secular state. The fez (Turkish brimless cap) was abolished, as was polygamy; Friday was replaced by Sunday as the day of rest; surnames were introduced; the Arabic alphabet was replaced by a Latin script; and civil (not religious) marriage became mandatory. In 1934 women were given the vote. The country's modernisation was accompanied by a great surge of nationalistic pride, and though it was no longer the political capital, İstanbul continued to be the centre of the nation's cultural and economic life.

Atatürk died in İstanbul in 1938, just before WWII broke out, and was succeeded as president by Ismet İnönü. Still scarred from the calamity of its involvement in the Great War, Turkey managed to successfully stay out of the new conflict until 1945, when it entered on the Allied side.

THE COUP YEARS

The Allies made it clear that they believed that Turkey should introduce democracy. The government agreed and called parliamentary elections. The first opposition party in Turkey's history – the Democratic Party led by Adnan Menderes – won the first of these elections in 1950.

Though he started as a democrat, Menderes became increasingly autocratic. In 1960 the military staged a coup against his government and convicted him and two of his ministers of treason. All three were hanged in 1961. New elections were held and a government was formed, but it and ensuing administrations were dogged by corruption charges, and constitutional violations and amendments. In 1971 the military staged another coup, only to repeat the process in 1980 and install a military junta, which ruled for three years before new elections were called. It seemed to many observers that the far left and extreme right factions in the country would never be able to reconcile, and that military coups would be a constant feature of the modern political landscape. However, voters in the 1983 election refused to see this as a *fait accompli* and, rather than voting in the military's preferred candidates, elected the reforming Motherland party of Turgut Özal. A new era had begun.

1973	1988 to the Present
The first Bosphorus Bridge, joining Europe and Asia, is opened on the 50th anniversary of the republic's founding	İstanbul's population booms, economic and social reforms are adopted and Turkey is accepted as a candidate for European Union membership

1 *Fish sellers near Eminönü (p152)*
2 *Man smoking nargileh (p164)*
3 *Backgammon, tea garden off İstiklal Caddesi (p120)* 4 *Boy in circumcision finery (p110)*

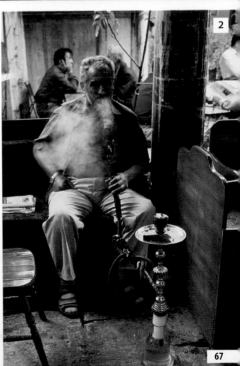

1 Bridge over the Bosphorus
(p217) *2* Fishers, Galata Bridge
(p101) *3* Food stalls near
Eminönü (p152) *4* sunset,
Golden Horn (p100)

1 *Yeni Camii (p99)* **2** *City view at night (p160)* **3** *Ferry (p239), Golden Horn* **4** *Boats in front of Ortaköy Camii (p127)*

1 Shoppers, Grand Bazaar (p102)
2 Entrance, Grand Bazaar (p102)
3 Market (p199), Süleymaniye 4
Carpet (p196), Süleymaniye

1 Calligraphy (p191), Grand Bazaar **2** Nargileh (p168) **3** Whirling dervishes (p119) **4** Tiles, Arasta Bazaar (p191)

1 *Ecumenical Orthodox Patriarchate (p109)* 2 *Detail, Church of St Stephen of the Bulgars (p108)* 3 *Dancers (p178), Hippodrome* 4 *Wedding, Neve Shalom Synagogue (p119)*

1 Market (p199), Süleymaniye
2 Tram (p243), İstiklal Caddesi
3 Light rail (p241), Sultanahmet
4 Men on balcony, İstiklal Caddesi
(p120)

1 Jogger, Yıldız Parkı (p127)
2 Basilica Cistern (p83) *3* Feeding pigeons, Yeni Camii (p99) *4* Child, Hippodrome (p86)

Neighbourhoods

Neighbourhoods

'AH STAMBOUL! OF ALL THE NAMES THAT CAN STILL ENCHANT ME, THIS ONE REMAINS THE MOST MAGICAL. AS SOON AS I HEAR IT, A VISION APPEARS BEFORE ME: VERY, VERY HIGH IN THE AIR, FAR OFF AT FIRST IN THE BLURRY DISTANCE, THERE IS THE SUGGESTION OF SOMETHING GIGANTIC, AN INCOMPARABLE OUTLINE OF THE CITY. THE SEA IS AT ITS FEET, A SEA CROSSED BY THOUSANDS OF SHIPS AND SMALL BOATS IN PERPETUAL MOTION; AND FROM THIS SEA RISES THE CLAMOUR OF BABEL, IN ALL THE TONGUES OF THE LEVANT; LIKE A LONG, HORIZONTAL CLOUD SMOKE FLOATS OVER THE MASS OF BLACK OCEAN-LINERS AND GILDED CAÏQUES ON THE MULTICOLOURED CROWDS SHOUTING OUT THEIR TRANSACTIONS, BARGAINING; THE SMOKE CEASELESSLY COVERS EVERYTHING WITH ITS VEIL. AND THERE, ABOVE THOSE BUOYS AND COAL DUST, THE IMMENSE CITY APPEARS, AS IF SUSPENDED IN AIR. MINARETS AS SHARP AS LANCES RISE IN THE MIDDLE OF THE CLEAR SKY, DOME UPON DOME PILED UP IN TERRACES, LIKE PYRAMIDS OF STONE BELLS; THE MOTIONLESS MOSQUES, UNCHANGED BY THE CENTURIES – HOLY MOSQUES WHITER, PERHAPS, IN FORMER ERAS, WHEN OUR WESTERN VAPOURS HAD NOT YET TARNISHED THE SURROUNDING AIR AND ONLY THE SAILING VESSELS OF OLD CAME TO ANCHOR IN THEIR SHADE – BUT STILL THE SAME, FOR CENTURIES CROWNING STAMBOUL WITH THE SAME GIGANTIC CUPOLAS, GIVING IT THIS SAME UNIQUE SKYLINE, MORE GRANDIOSE THAN ANY CITY ON EARTH.'

Pierre Loti said it all in his paean to the city, *Constantinople in 1890*. Ever since 657 BC when Byzas first sailed up to where the Golden Horn, the Bosphorus and the Sea of Marmara met, the promontory at the junction has been the centre of a city unlike any other. Each of today's older neighbourhoods hold remnants of ancient Byzantium, Roman Constantinople and Ottoman İstanbul, but have also developed their own modern signatures, often influenced by the ethnic or religious groups within their boundaries. By exploring these fascinating neighbourhoods full of historically and architecturally significant buildings and sites you'll certainly develop an understanding of the city and its people. You may even, like Loti and so many visitors since, develop a life-long infatuation with their charms.

ITINERARIES
One Day
With only one day you should try to get a feel for İstanbul's justly famous monuments and bazaars. After breakfast, start by visiting the wonderfully curvaceous **Blue Mosque** (Sultan Ahmet Camii; p100) and then walk across tiny Sultanahmet Park to the city's most beautiful and important building – the venerable **Aya Sofya** (p79). Next, investigate the watery depths of the **Basilica Cistern** (Yerebatan Sarnıçı; p83). For lunch make your way up Divan Yolu by tram or by foot to the **Grand Bazaar** (Kapalı Çarşı; p102) and **Havuzlu Restaurant** (p153), the bazaar's most popular eatery. Shopping is next – if you can't find something fabulous to take home you're just not trying hard enough! That mission accomplished, walk to the magnificent **Süleymaniye Camii** (p106), a triumph of Ottoman architecture. A quick coffee or tea in the courtyard of **Dârüzziyafe** (p106), a restaurant set in the mosque's former soup kitchen, or **Lale Bahçesi** (p166), a popular tea garden set in a nearby sunken courtyard, should then set you up for a wander

down through the busting mercantile area of Tahtakale to the **Spice Bazaar** (Mısır Çarşısı; p106) at Eminönü. After seeing (and smelling) this historic market, it's time to sample the kebabs at **Hamdi et Lokantası** (p153), which are as impressive as the panoramic views from the roof terrace. After dinner, walk, catch a tram or commandeer a taxi back to where you started the day, the Blue Mosque. Grab a seat at the Arasta Bazaar's **Café Meşale** (p164) and sit back to finish the night by enjoying a nargileh, listening to the live folk music and watching a dervish whirl.

Three Days

With three days you'll be able to fit in a number of the city's highlights. On day one, follow the itinerary set out above. Day two should be devoted to **Topkapı Palace** (Topkapı Sarayı; p91) and the İstanbul Archaeology Museums. Start at the palace and plan on spending at least four hours exploring. Enjoy lunch and the views on the terrace at **Konyalı restaurant** (p150) in the palace before making your way down the hill to the **İstanbul Archaeology Museums** (p88). After marvelling at treasures such as the sarcophagi from the Royal Necropolis at Sidon, have a drink or a late afternoon tea in the garden of the nearby **Konuk Evi hotel** (p164) in Soğukçeşme Sokak or in the flower-filled courtyard of the **Yeşil Ev hotel** (p165) near the Blue Mosque. Suitably refreshed, you should now either check out the shops around the Arasta Bazaar, Cankurtaran and Küçük Aya Sofya, or stroll around the **Hippodrome** (p86). For dinner, you should make your way across the Galata Bridge (Galata Köprüsü) to cosmopolitan **Beyoğlu** (p155) and have a meal with the locals at party central – Nevizade Sokak. After this, kick on to one of the many bars, music venues or nightclubs in the area.

For the third day, hop on a ferry and explore the Bosphorus (p217) by following the suggestions in the Excursions chapter. On the way back have dinner at one of the glamorous restaurants in **Beşiktaş** (p160) or **Nişantaşı** (p160), or dine waterside at one of the popular places at **Ortaköy** (p160).

One Week

A week is the minimum time needed to truly appreciate İstanbul. Follow the itineraries above for your first three days. On day four visit the extraordinarily beautiful Byzantine mosaics and frescoes at the **Kariye Müzesi** (p111) before enjoying an Ottoman lunch fit for a sultan at **Asitane** (p154). In the afternoon, follow the Western Districts **walking tour** (p144) or visit the holy **Eyüp Sultan Camii & Tomb** (p109). For dinner, check out the best kebabs in the city at **Develi** (p154), near the walls at Samatya. By day five, a ferry to the idyllic retreats of the **Princes' Islands** (p223) is in order. You should devote day six to shopping. Around İstiklal Caddesi in **Beyoğlu** (p195) is the best spot, particularly as the decadent **Patisserie Markiz** (p157) is waiting to supply sugar hits and coffee whenever you begin to run out of stamina. Alternatively, you could visit over-the-top **Dolmabahçe Palace** (Dolmabahçe Sarayı; p124) or the more restrained **Yıldız Parkı** (p127) and **Yıldız Şale** (p128) to gain a feel for how the sultans lived. Stay over this side for dinner and end the night at a music club – perhaps **Nardis** (p176) for jazz or **Andon** (p175) for fasıl music. Start your last day at the **Great Palace Mosaic Museum** (p86) in Sultanahmet and move on to the **Museum of Turkish and Islamic Arts** (p89) – both are fascinating. After lunch, a visit to a *hamam* (Turkish steam bath) is a wonderfully relaxing way to end your visit. Try **Cağaloğlu** (p172) or **Çemberlitaş** (p172) for maximum atmosphere. For dinner, make your way over to **Beyoğlu** (p155) or enjoy a fish dinner with the city's power brokers at **Balıkçı Sabahattin** (p149) in Sultanahmet.

ORGANISED TOURS

BUS TURİSTİK Map pp278-80

Tourist Bus; ☎ 212-230 0990; 1-day ticket weekdays adult/child €15/8, weekends €17/9, child under 5 years free; 🕐 10am-8.30pm Apr-Oct, 10am-5.30pm Nov-Mar

If you decide the convenience of being ferried from one sight to another and getting a tour of the city into the bargain outweighs the embarrassment of sitting in a bright yellow double-decker bus with booming recorded commentary, this service could be for you. Ticket boxes are located outside Aya Sofya and in Taksim Square or you can purchase tickets on the bus. There are 18 stops around town, including Sultanahmet, Eminönü (for the Spice Bazaar, Yeni Camii and Rüstem Paşa Camii), Edirnekapı (for Kariye Müzesi), Tepebaşı (for İstiklal Caddesi), Taksim Square and Dolmabahçe Palace. Get on and off as many times as you wish during one day – buses stop every 30 minutes.

KİRKİT VOYAGE Map pp278-80
☎ 212-518 2282; kirkit@kirkit.com; Mimar Mehmet Ağa Caddesi 39, Cankurtaran; tours €23-50

This small agency in the middle of the main hotel district in Sultanahmet specialises in tailoring walking tours for groups of two or more. You can choose from its 'Classic İstanbul', 'Ottoman İstanbul', 'Byzantine İstanbul' and 'Old Pera: The Hills of Beyoğlu' half- and full-day tours, as well as specialised tours such as 'İstanbul: The Unusual Way', which explores *hans* (caravanseries) around the Grand Bazaar. Other tours visit sights by public transport and minibus.

LES ARTS TURCS Map pp278-80
☎ 212-520 7743; nurdogan@lesartsturcs.com; İncili Çavuş Sokak 37/3, Sultanahmet; tours €25-50; ☪ 10am-10pm

These tours are operated by members of a collective of artists, writers and historians who are based in a public studio in Sultanahmet. Marketed as 'off-the-beaten-path walking tours', the half- and full-day programmes introduce participants to artists who live and work in the neighbourhoods around Old İstanbul, and visit sights of historical and artistic importance.

PLAN TOURS
☎ 212-234 7777; www.plantours.com; tours €29-74, 30% discount for child 2-7 years

Plan offers a range of half- and full-day tours of the city. Choose from half-day 'İstanbul Classics', 'Ottoman Relics' or Bosphorus cruise tours; or full-day 'Byzantine & Ottoman Relics', Bosphorus or Princes' Islands trips. There's also an 'İstanbul by Night' dinner (€54), a Bosphorus dinner cruise (€74) and a 2½-hour bus sightseeing tour around the city (€12.50) on offer. Pick-ups are from your hotel. Plan can also organise tailored tours of İstanbul's Jewish heritage that allow access to the Ahrida and other synagogues. Contact the company for details.

OLD İSTANBUL
Eating p149; Shopping p190; Sleeping p202

Nineteenth-century travellers called the Old City 'Stamboul', and only ventured into it during the day to visit its bazaar and mosques; at night they returned to their comfortable bases in Pera. Things are different these days, with most travellers staying around Sultanahmet and spending their days and nights exploring the fascinating streets, laneways and sights of Old İstanbul.

SULTANAHMET

Many visitors to İstanbul never make it out of Sultanahmet. And while this is a shame, it's hardly surprising. After all, not many cities have such a concentration of major sights, shopping precincts, hotels and eateries within easy walking distance. The heart of Byzantium, Constantinople and the Ottoman Empire, it's the area where emperors and sultans built their palaces, places of worship and major public buildings; where court officials lived, schemed and planned

advantageous marriages; and where conquering armies declared their victories with the obligatory rite of drunken pillage and plunder. Today, armies of tourists congregate around the Hippodrome, their only battles being with the touts selling carpets and the overwhelming number of sights and activities that make competing claims on their (alas!) limited holiday time.

Orientation

Occupying the promontory that runs from the eastern side of Eminönü on the Golden Horn (Haliç) to Küçük Aya Sofya on the Sea of Marmara, this neighbourhood is centred on the Byzantine Hippodrome and is where most of İstanbul's major sights and hotels are located. It incorporates a number of small suburbs, including the following: **Binbirdirek**, which takes its name from the Byzantine cistern and is home to shops and offices; **Cağaloğlu**, home to the city's most beautiful *hamam* and many shops; **Cankurtaran**, where a good percentage of the city's hotels and hostels are located; Çemberlitaş (the eastern half), a shopping district around busy Divan Yolu; Küçük Aya Sofya, a quiet residential area with some significant historical buildings and a few hotels; Sirkeci, with its shops, offices and train station; Sultanahmet proper, the area around Aya Sofya and the mosque that gives the suburb its name; and Topkapı, a green belt with a palace and next-door Gülhane Parkı, which runs down to the water at Seraglio Point (Saray Burnu).

The neighbourhood's major thoroughfares are Divan Yolu Caddesi, which runs from Aya Sofya up towards the Grand Bazaar; and Hüdavendigar Caddesi, which runs north from Divan Yolu down to Eminönü. Alemdar Caddesi, which runs north from the end of Divan Yolu, merges into Hüdavendigar Caddesi and leads down to Sirkeci and Eminönü.

Aya Sofya (below)

Neighbourhoods – Sultanahmet

Transport

The super-convenient Eminönü to Zeytinburnu tram runs through Sultanahmet along Hüdavendigar Caddesi and Divan Yolu. The T4 bus runs to and from Taksim Square every 30 minutes (approx) from 7.15am to 10pm, leaving from outside the Tourist Information Office at the end of the Hippodrome.

AYA SOFYA Map pp278–80

☎ 212-522 0989; Aya Sofya Square, Sultanahmet; adult/child 6 & over/child under 6 €8.30/2.80/free, official guide (45 mins) €20; ☻ Tue-Sun 9am-5pm, upper gallery closes 4.30pm; tram (Sultanahmet), bus T4 from Taksim Square

Called Sancta Sophia in Latin, Haghia Sofia in Greek and the Church of the Divine Wisdom in English, İstanbul's most famous monument has a history as long as it is fascinating. Built by Emperor Justinian (r AD 527–65), it was constructed on the site of Byzantium's acropolis, which had also been the site of two earlier Aya Sofyas – the first a basilica with a timber roof completed in 360 by Constantine's son and successor, Constantinius, and burned down in a riot in 404; and the second a building commissioned by Theodosius II in 415 and destroyed in the Nika riots of 532. Justinian's church, which dwarfed all other buildings in the city, was completed in 537 and reigned as the greatest church in Christendom until the Conquest of Constantinople in 1453, when

Mehmet the Conqueror took possession of it for Islam and immediately converted it into a mosque. As significant to Muslims as it is to Christians, it was proclaimed a museum by Atatürk in 1934. Current restoration work (partly Unesco funded) means that the interior is filled with scaffolding, but not even this can detract from the experience of visiting one of the world's truly great buildings.

On entering his great creation for the first time, Justinian exclaimed, 'Glory to God that I have been judged worthy of such a work. Oh Solomon! I have outdone you!' Entering the building today, it is easy to excuse his self-congratulatory tone. The exterior may be somewhat squat and unattractive but the interior, with its magnificent domed ceiling soaring heavenward, is so sublimely beautiful that many seeing it for the first time are quite literally stunned into silence.

The original achievement of Aya Sofya's architects, who did not have the benefits of today's technology and materials, remains

Sultanahmet Top Five

- Aya Sofya (above)
- Topkapı Palace (p91)
- Basilica Cistern (p83)
- Blue Mosque (Sultan Ahmet Camii; p84)
- Museum of Turkish & Islamic Arts (p89)

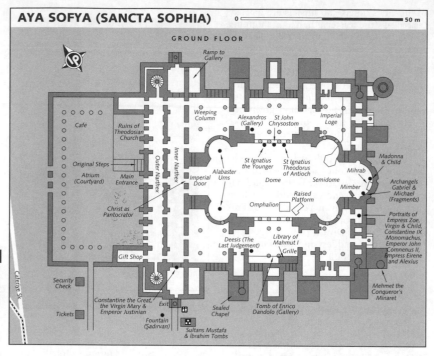

AYA SOFYA (SANCTA SOPHIA)

0 ▭▭▭▭▭▭▭ 50 m

GROUND FLOOR

Ramp to Gallery

Café

Ruins of Theodosian Church

Weeping Column

Alexandros (Gallery)

St John Chrysostom

Imperial Loge

Original Steps

Atrium (Courtyard)

Main Entrance

Inner Narthex

Outer Narthex

Imperial Door

Alabaster Urns

St Ignatius the Younger

Dome

St Ignatius Theodorus of Antioch

Raised Platform

Omphalion

Semidome

Mihrab

Mimber

Madonna & Child

Archangels Gabriel & Michael (Fragments)

Portraits of Empress Zoe, Virgin & Child, Constantine IX Monomachus, Emperor John Comnenus II, Empress Eirene and Alexius

Christ as Pantocrator

Deesis (The Last Judgement)

Library of Mahmut I

Grille

Gift Shop

Security Check

Tickets

Constantine the Great, the Virgin Mary & Emperor Justinian

Exit

Fountain (Şadırvan)

Sultans Mustafa & Ibrahim Tombs

Sealed Chapel

Tomb of Enrico Dandolo (Gallery)

Mehmet the Conqueror's Minaret

Caterye Sk.

unequalled. The Byzantines gasped in amazement at the sense of air and space in the nave and the 30 million gold mosaic tiles *(tesserae)* that covered the dome's interior. Most of all, they marvelled at the apparent lack of support for the enormous **dome**. How was it possible, they asked? The dome lasted just over two decades before an earthquake brought it down in 559. It was rebuilt to a slightly less ambitious design, with a slightly smaller base and steeper sides, and the basilica was reopened in 563. Over subsequent centuries it was necessary for succeeding Byzantine emperors and Ottoman sultans to rebuild the dome several times, to add buttresses and other supports and to steady the foundations.

The dome, which is 30m in diameter, is supported by 40 massive ribs constructed of special hollow bricks made in Rhodes from a unique light, porous clay, resting on four huge pillars concealed in the interior walls. Sinan, who spent his entire professional life trying to design a mosque to match the magnificence and beauty of Aya Sofya, used the same trick of concealing pillars when designing the great Süleymaniye Camii almost 1000 years later. To truly appreciate what a difference the concealment makes, we suggest that you compare

Aya Sofya's pillar-free central space with that of the nearby Blue Mosque, which features four huge freestanding pillars. You'll find that Aya Sofya shines in comparison.

In Justinian's time, a street led uphill from the west straight to the main door. Today the ticket kiosk is at the southwest side. To experience the church as its architects, Anthemeus of Tralles and Isidorus of Miletus, intended, walk to the atrium (courtyard) before the main entrance. Here are the sunken ruins of a Theodosian church (404–15) and the low original steps. Enter through the main entrance slowly, one step at a time, looking ahead: at first there is only darkness broken by the brilliant colours of innumerable stained-glass windows. It is these windows, with the many arcades, that give the building its famous 'transparency'. As your eyes adjust to the dark, two massive doorways appear, the first to the **outer narthex** and the second to the **inner narthex**. Far beyond them in the dim light, your eyes will alight on a semidome blazing with the gold mosaic portrait of the Madonna and Child. Take a few steps and stop just inside the threshold of the main entrance: the far mosaic is clear and beautiful and the apse beneath it makes a harmonious whole. Stand in the doorway between the outer and inner narthexes and look deep into the church again, and you'll see that the semidome of the Madonna and Child is topped by another semidome, and above that is the famous, gigantic main dome of the church.

Walk through the second door into the inner narthex and towards the immense **imperial door**, and you will be surprised to see that the 'gigantic main dome' is in fact only another semidome: Halfway to the imperial door, a row of windows peeks out above the larger semidome and betrays the secret. As you approach the imperial threshold the real, magnificent main dome soars above you and seems to be held up by nothing. During its years as a church (almost 1000), only imperial processions were permitted to enter through the central, imperial door. You can still notice the depressions in the stone by each door just inside the threshold where imperial guards stood. Also note the matched marble panels in the walls and the breccia (a type of rock made up of angular fragments) columns.

The chandeliers hanging low above the floor are Ottoman additions. Previously, rows of glass oil lamps lined the balustrades of the gallery and the walkway at the base of

Mosaics

Justinian was understandably proud of his basilica's great dome, but he was just as proud of its magnificent **mosaic** work. Originally, the great dome, the semidomes, the north and south tympana (semicircles) and the vaults of narthex, aisles and galleries were all covered in gold mosaics. Remnants exist and are a highlight of any visit, but one can only imagine what the place must have looked like when the entire interior glittered and gleamed with *tesserae*. Unfortunately, the later figurative mosaics (mostly 9th and 10th centuries) ended up as casualties of theology. First, the Byzantine church and state endured a fierce civil war (726–87) over the question of whether 'graven images' should be countenanced or not.

Though the Bible seems clear that images (icons, mosaics, statues) should not be worshipped, they were very popular and the iconoclasts (image-breakers) were ultimately defeated. Aya Sofya's mosaics stayed *in situ*. When the Turks took Constantinople, though, there was no debate. Islamic art, as laid out in the Quran, isn't supposed to depict people, animals, fish or fowl, nor anything else with an immortal soul.

Needless to say, the mosaics had to go. Fortunately they were covered with plaster rather than destroyed, and some were successfully uncovered and restored by Swiss architects Gaspere and Guiseppe Fossati, working for the sultan, from 1847 to 1849. Though once again covered (this time by paint), they were left in good condition for a final unveiling when the mosque was deconsecrated and the museum opened.

From the floor of Aya Sofya, 9th-century mosaic portraits of **St Ignatius the Younger** (c 800), **St John Chrysostom** (c 400) and **St Ignatius Theodorus of Antioch** are visible high up at the base of the northern tympanum (semicircle) beneath the dome. Next to these three, and seen only from the upstairs east gallery, is a portrait of **Alexandros**. In the apse is a wonderful mosaic of the **Madonna and Child**; nearby mosaics depict the archangels **Gabriel** and **Michael**, though only fragments of Michael remain. Above the imperial door in the inner narthex there is a striking depiction of **Christ as Pantocrator (Ruler of All)**. He holds a book that carries the inscription 'Peace be with you. I am the Light of the World' and to his right an emperor (probably Leo VI) prostrates himself. As you exit the inner narthex and enter the passage to leave the building, make sure you turn and look up above the door to see one of the church's finest late 10th-century mosaics. This shows **Constantine the Great**, on the right, offering **Mary**, who holds the **Christ child**, the city of Constantinople; **Emperor Justinian**, on the left is offering her Aya Sofya.

The upstairs galleries house the most impressive of Aya Sofya's mosaics and mustn't be missed. They can be reached via a switchback ramp at the northern end of the inner narthex. The magnificent **Deesis Mosaic (The Last Judgement)** in the south gallery dates from the early 14th century. Christ is at the centre, with the Virgin Mary on the left, and John the Baptist on the right.

At the eastern (apse) end of the south gallery is the famous mosaic portrait of **Empress Zoe** (r 1028–50). When this portrait was done she was 50 years old and newly married to the aged Romanus III Argyrus. Upon Romanus' death in 1034, she had his face excised from the mosaic and that of her virile new husband, Michael IV, put in its place. Eight years later, with Michael dead from an illness contracted on campaign, Zoe and her sister Theodora ruled as empresses in their own right, but did it so badly that it was clear she had to marry again. At the age of 64, Zoe wed an eminent senator, Constantine IX Monomachus, whose portrait remains only because he outlived the empress. The inscription reads 'Constantine, by the Divine Christ, Faithful King of the Romans'.

To the right of Zoe and Constantine is another mosaic depicting characters with less saucy histories: in this scene **Mary** holds the **Christ child**, centre, with **Emperor John (Johannes) Comnenus II** (the Good) to the left and **Empress Eirene** (known for her charitable works) to the right. Their son **Alexius**, who died soon after this portrait was made, is depicted next to Eirene.

the dome. Imagine them all lit to celebrate some great state occasion, with the smell of incense and the chants of the Orthodox (and later the Latin) liturgy reverberating through the huge interior space.

The Byzantine emperor was crowned while seated in a throne placed within the **omphalion**, the square of inlaid marble in the main floor. The nearby raised **platform** was added by Sultan Murat III (r 1574–95), as were the large **alabaster urns** so that worshippers could perform their ritual ablutions before prayer. During the Ottoman period the *mimber* (pulpit) and the mihrab (prayer niche indicating the direction of Mecca) were also added.

The large 19th-century **medallions** inscribed with gilt Arabic letters are the work of master calligrapher Mustafa İzzet Efendi, and give the names of God (Allah), Mohammed and the early caliphs Ali and Abu Bakr. Though impressive works of art in their own right, they seem out of place here and unfortunately detract from the purity of the building's interior form.

The curious elevated kiosk screened from public view is the **imperial loge** *(hünkar mahfili)*. Sultan Abdül Mecit (r 1839–61) had it built in 1848 so he could come, pray and go unseen, preserving the imperial mystique. The ornate library behind the omphalion was built by Sultan Mahmut I in 1739.

In the side aisle to the northeast of the imperial door is the **weeping column**, with a worn copper facing pierced by a hole. Legend has it that the pillar is that of St Gregory the Miracle Worker and that putting one's finger in the hole can lead to ailments being healed if the finger emerges moist.

Upstairs in the floor of the south gallery near the Deesis Mosaic you will see the **tomb of Enrico Dandolo** (c 1108–1205). Dandolo, who became doge of Venice in 1192, came from the prominent Venetian family that supplied Venice with four doges, numerous admirals and a colonial empire. During the Fourth Crusade (1203–04), he diverted the Crusader armies from their goal of an assault on the infidels to an assault on the friendly but rival Christian city of Constantinople. Aya Sofya was ransacked during the assault, with the altar being destroyed. Venice got the better part of the rich spoils from the sacking of the city, as well as numerous Byzantine territories. Dandolo ruled three-eighths of conquered Constantinople, including Sancta Sophia, until his death in 1205, when he was buried here. Tradition tells us that Dandolo's tomb was broken open after the Conquest of the city in 1453, and his bones thrown to the dogs. Also upstairs (this time in the western gallery) is a large circle of green marble marking the spot where the **throne of the empress** once stood.

As you exit the building, the fountain *(şadırvan)* to the right was for ablutions. To your left is the church's baptistry, converted after

Blue Mosque (p84)

the Conquest to a tomb for sultans Mustafa and İbrahim (the Crazy). These are not open to the public. Other tombs are clustered behind it, including those of Murat III, Selim 'the Sot' II (designed by Sinan and featuring gorgeous İznik tiles) and Mehmet III. Selim's tomb is particularly poignant as it houses the graves of five of his sons, murdered on the same night in December 1574 to ensure the peaceful succession of the oldest, Murat III. It also houses the graves of 19 of Murat's sons, murdered in January 1595 to ensure Mehmet III's succession. They were the last of the royal princes to be murdered – after this, the younger brothers of succeeding sultans were confined to the *kafes* (cage) in Topkapı instead. To the southeast of the building a wall hides excavations on a section of the Great Byzantine Palace. To the left of the entrance is a small Ottoman primary school built by Mahmut I in 1740.

Aya Sofya's first minaret was added by Mehmet the Conqueror (r 1451–81). Sinan designed the others for sultans Beyazıt II (r 1481–1512) and Selim II (r 1566–74).

BASILICA CISTERN Map pp278-80
The Sunken Cistern, Yerebatan Sarnıçı; ☎ 212-522 1259; www.yerebatansarnici.com; Yerebatan Caddesi 13, Sultanahmet; admission €7; ⏰ 9.30am-7.30pm summer, 9.30am-5.30pm winter; tram (Sultanahmet), bus T4 from Taksim Square
When those Byzantine emperors built something, they certainly did it properly! This extraordinary subterranean structure, built by Justinian in AD 532 (perhaps on the site of an earlier cistern), is the largest surviving Byzantine cistern in İstanbul. Now one of the city's most popular tourist attractions, it's a great place to while away 30 minutes or so, especially during summer when its cavernous depths stay wonderfully cool.

The cistern's roof is 65m wide and 143m long, and is supported by 336 columns arranged in 12 rows. It once held 80,000 cu metres of water, delivered via 20km of aqueducts from a reservoir near the Black Sea.

Constructed using columns, capitals and plinths from ruined buildings, the cistern's symmetry and sheer grandeur of conception are quite extraordinary. Don't miss the two columns in the northwestern corner supported by blocks carved into Medusa heads or the column towards the centre featuring a teardrop design – we don't know where these columns originally came from but it's great to speculate

Walking on the raised wooden platforms, you'll feel the water dripping from the vaulted ceiling and may catch a glimpse of ghostly carp patrolling the water. Lighting is atmospheric and the small café near the exit is certainly an unusual spot to enjoy a cup of tea.

Like most of the sites in İstanbul, the cistern has an unusual history. Known in Byzantium as the Basilica Cistern because it lay underneath the Stoa Basilica, one of the great squares on the first hill, it was used to store water for the Great Palace and surrounding buildings. Eventually closed, the cistern seems to have been forgotten by the city authorities some time before the Conquest. Enter scholar Petrus Gyllius, who in 1545 was researching Byzantine antiquities in the city and was told by locals that they were able to miraculously obtain water by lowering buckets in their basement floors. Some were even catching fish this way. Intrigued, Gyllius explored the neighbourhood and finally discovered a house through whose basement he accessed the cistern. Even after his discovery, the Ottomans (who referred to the cistern as Yerebatan Saray) didn't treat the underground palace with the respect it deserved – it became a dumping ground for all sorts of junk, as well as corpses. Fortunately, later restorations, most notably in the 18th century and between 1955 and 1960, saw it properly maintained. It was cleaned and renovated in 1985 by the İstanbul Metropolitan Municipality and opened to the public in 1987.

BASIN MÜZESİ Map pp278-80
Press Museum; ☎ 212-513 8458; Divan Yolu Caddesi, 84, Çemberlitaş; admission free; ⏰ 10am-6pm Mon-Sat; tram (Çemberlitaş), bus T4 from Taksim Square
This little museum doesn't have much of a collection, but the old printing presses may interest some. There's a café and a handicrafts shop selling stuff from the Subcontinent on the ground floor.

BATHS OF LADY HÜRREM Map pp278-80
Haseki Hürrem Hamamı; ☎ 212-638 0035; Aya Sofya Square 4, Sultanahmet; admission free; ⏰ 8.30am-5.30pm Tue-Sun; tram (Sultanahmet), bus T4 from Taksim Square
Traditionally, every mosque had a *hamam* included in or around its complex of buildings. Aya Sofya was no exception and this elegant symmetrical building, designed by Sinan from 1556 to 1557, was built just across the road from the great mosque by Süleyman in the name of his wife Hürrem Sultan, known to history

as Roxelana. The *hamam* was one of 32 Sinan designed and is widely thought be his best. It operated until 1910 and is now home to a carpet shop (run by the Ministry of Culture) rather than a steam-filled pleasure palace full of tourists looking for the quintessentially 'Turkish' experience (it has to be said that in many ways the carpet shop is the more authentic of the two!). Management, though, doesn't seem to mind if visitors wander through the building, admire the interior spaces and come out sans rug.

Designed as a 'double *hamam*' with identical baths for men and women, the centre wall dividing the two has now been breached by a small doorway. Both sides have separate entrances and the three traditional rooms: first the square *camekan* for disrobing (on the men's side, this has a pretty marble fountain and stained-glass windows); then the long *soğukluk* for washing; and finally the octagonal *hararet* for sweating and massage. The most impressive features are the domes, with their star-like apertures. Also of note are the four *eyvan* (niches) and the four semiprivate washing rooms in the *hararet*, as well as the *göbektaşı* (hot platform) in the men's bath, which is inlaid with coloured marble. In all, the place gives a good idea of how *hamams* are set up – perfect for those not convinced that they want to bare all in one of the city's still-functioning establishments.

BİNBİRDİREK CISTERN Map pp278-80

Cistern of 1001 Columns, Binbirdirek Sarnıcı; ☎ 212-517 8725; www.binbirdirek.com.tr; İmran Öktem Sokak 4, Binbirdirek; admission €5.50; ♥ 10am-6pm; tram (Sultanahmet), bus T4 from Taksim Square

Constantine built Binbirdirek in AD 330. During Ottoman times it was converted into a khan for silk manufacturers. Closed for decades, it has recently been restored and functions as a restaurant/café (meze plate €5, mains around €9) and venue for concerts. Not as impressive as the Basilica Cistern (largely because it has been emptied of its water reserves and has a false floor), the only time this place is really worth a visit is when it hosts the concerts – check the website or the board at its exit for details. The admission price includes one drink.

BLUE MOSQUE Map pp278-80

Sultan Ahmet Camii; ☎ 212-518 1319; Hippodrome, Sultanahmet; donation requested; ♥ closed during prayer times; tram (Sultanahmet), bus T4 from Taksim Square

With his eponymously named mosque, Sultan Ahmet I (r 1603–17) set out to build a monument that would rival and even surpass the nearby Aya Sofya in grandeur and beauty. So enthusiastic was the sultan about his grand project that he is said to have worked with the labourers and craftsmen on site, pushing them along and rewarding extra effort. Ahmet did in fact come close to his goal of rivalling Aya Sofya, and in so doing achieved the added benefit of making future generations of hotel owners in Sultanahmet happy – a 'Blue Mosque view' from the roof terrace being the number-one selling point of the fleet of hotels in the area.

The mosque's architect, Mehmet Ağa, who had trained with Sinan, managed to orchestrate the sort of visual wham-bam effect with the mosque's exterior that Aya Sofya achieved with its interior. Its curves are voluptuous, it has more minarets than any other İstanbul mosque (in fact, there was consternation at the time of its construction that the sultan was being irreverent in specifying six minarets – the only equivalent being in Mecca) and the courtyard is the biggest of all the Ottoman mosques. The interior is conceived on a similarly grand scale: the blue tiles that give the building its unofficial name number in the tens of thousands, there are 260 windows and the central prayer space is huge. No wonder its picture graces a million postcards!

In order to fully appreciate the mosque's design you should approach it via the middle of the Hippodrome rather than walking straight from Sultanahmet Park through the crowds. When inside the courtyard, which is the same size as the mosque's interior, you'll be able to appreciate the perfect proportions of the building. Walk towards the mosque through the gate in the peripheral wall, noting on the way the small dome atop the gate: this is the motif Mehmet Ağa uses to lift your eyes to heaven. As you walk through the gate, your eyes follow a flight of stairs up to another gate topped by another dome; through this gate is yet another dome, that of the ablutions fountain in the centre of the mosque courtyard. As you ascend the stairs, semidomes come into view: first the one over the mosque's main door, then the one above it, and another, and another. Finally the **main dome** crowns the whole, and your attention is drawn to the sides, where forests of smaller domes reinforce the effect, completed by the **minarets**, which lift your eyes heavenward.

The mosque is such a popular tourist sight that admission is controlled so as to preserve its sacred atmosphere. In the tourist season (May to September), only worshippers are admitted through the main door; tourists must use the north door. Shoes must of course be taken off and women who haven't brought their own headscarf or are too scantily dressed will be loaned a headscarf and/or robe. There's no charge for this, but donations for the mosque are requested.

Inside, the **stained-glass windows** and **İznik tiles** immediately attract attention. Though the windows are replacements, they still create the luminous effects of the originals, which came from Venice. The tiles line the walls, particularly in the gallery (which is not open to the public). There are so many of these tiles that the İznik workshops producing the finest examples could not keep up with demand, and alternative, less skilled, workshops were called in to fill the gap. The mosque's tiles are thus of varying quality.

You can see immediately why the mosque, which was constructed between 1606 and 1616, over 1000 years after Aya Sofya, is not as daring as its predecessor. Four massive **'elephant's feet'** pillars hold up the less ambitious dome, a sturdier solution lacking the innovation and grace of the dome in Justinian's cathedral.

The semidomes and the dome are painted in graceful **arabesques**. Of note in the main space are the **imperial loge**, covered with marble latticework, which is to the left of the mihrab; the mihrab itself, which features a piece of the sacred **Black Stone from the Kaaba** in Mecca; and the high, elaborate **mahfil** (chair) from which the imam (teacher) gives the sermon on Friday. The beautifully carved white marble **mimber** with its curtained doorway at floor level features a flight of steps and a small kiosk topped by a spire.

Mosques built by the great and powerful usually included numerous public-service institutions. Clustered around the Blue Mosque were a *medrese* (theological college); a soup kitchen *(imaret)* serving the poor; a *hamam* so that the faithful could bathe on Friday, the holy day; and shops (the Arasta Bazaar), the rent from which supported the upkeep of the mosque.

There's a sound-and-light show after dusk daily from May to September – see the board on Mimar Mehmet Ağa Caddesi for languages and time (usually around 7.30pm). Admission is by donation.

The *türbe* (tomb) of the Blue Mosque's great patron, the **Tomb of Sultan Ahmet I** (donation expected; 9.30am-4.30pm), is on the north side facing Sultanahmet Park. Ahmet, who had ascended to the imperial throne aged 13, died one year after the mosque was constructed, aged only 27. Buried with Ahmet are his wife, Kösem,

who was strangled to death in the Harem, and his sons, Sultan Osman II, Sultan Murat IV and Prince Beyazıt (murdered by Murat). Like the mosque, the *türbe* features fine İznik tiles.

CAFERAĞA MEDRESESİ Map pp278-80
☎ 212-513 3601; Caferiye Sokak; admission free; 8.30am-7pm; tram (Gülhane), bus T4 from Taksim Square

This lovely little building, which is tucked away in the shadows of Aya Sofya, was designed by Sinan on the orders of Cafer Ağa, Süleyman the Magnificent's chief black eunuch. Built in 1560 as a school for Islamic and secular education, today it is home to the **Turkish Cultural Service Foundation** (p244), which runs workshops in traditional Ottoman arts such as calligraphy, marbling and miniature painting. Some of the arts and crafts produced here are for sale and there's a pleasant tea garden in the courtyard serving simple snacks (soup €1.10, tea €0.50).

CARPET & KILIM MUSEUM Map pp278-80
Halı ve Kilim Müzesi; Blue Mosque, Sultanahmet; ☎ 212-518 1330; admission €1; 9am-noon & 1-4pm Tue-Sat; tram (Sultanahmet), bus T4 from Taksim Square

Up the stone ramp on the Blue Mosque's north side is this small museum, housed in the mosque's imperial pavilion. Though there are some great rugs in the collection, they aren't particularly well displayed – the collection in the nearby **Museum of Turkish and Islamic Arts** (p89) provides a more satisfying overview.

ÇEMBERLİTAŞ Map pp278-80
Tram (Çemberlitaş), bus T4 from Taksim Square

Close to the Çemberlitaş tram stop, in a plaza packed with pigeons, you'll find one of the city's most ancient and revered monuments: a derelict column known as **Çemberlitaş** (also known as the Hooped, Banded Stone or Burnt Column). Erected by Constantine the Great (r 324–37) to celebrate the dedication of Constantinople as capital of the Roman Empire in 330, the column was placed in what was the grand Forum of Constantine and was topped by a statue of the great emperor himself. It's looking considerably worse for wear these days, having had iron bands added for support within a century of it being built. The column lost its crowning statue of Constantine in 1106 and was damaged in the 1779 fire that ravaged the nearby Grand Bazaar.

Also in this vicinity is the historic **Çemberlitaş Hamam** (p172).

GREAT PALACE MOSAIC MUSEUM

Map pp278-80

Büyüksaray Mozaik Müzesi; ☎ 212-518 1205; Torun Sokak, Sultanahmet; admission €2.20; ☼ 9am-4.30pm Tue-Sun; tram (Sultanahmet), bus T4 from Taksim Square

When archaeologists from the University of Ankara and the University of St Andrews (Scotland) dug at the back of the Blue Mosque in the mid-1950s, they uncovered a stunning mosaic pavement dating from early Byzantine times. Restored from 1983 to 1997, it is now preserved in the Great Palace Mosaic Museum.

Thought to have been added by Justinian (r 527–565) to the Great Byzantine Palace on the Palatium Magnum (Palace Hill) originally built by Constantine, the pavement is estimated to have measured from 3500 to 4000 sq metres in its original form. The 250 sq metres that is preserved here is the largest discovered remnant – the rest has been destroyed or remains buried underneath shops, hotels and the Blue Mosque in the surrounding area.

The pavement is filled with bucolic imagery as well as intricate hunting and mythological scenes. Note the gorgeous ribbon border with heart-shaped leaves surrounding the mosaic. In the westernmost room is the most colourful and dramatic picture, that of two men in leggings carrying spears and holding off a raging tiger. Also here is an amusing depiction of a donkey kicking its load and rider off its back.

The museum has informative panels documenting the floor's rescue and renovation.

GÜLHANE PARKI Map pp278-80

Tram (Gülhane), bus T4 from Taksim Square

Gülhane Parkı was once the palace park of Topkapı. Now, crowds of locals come here at weekends to enjoy its shade, street food and the occasional live concert. The trees here are lovely and the views over the Golden Horn impressive, but many of the fountains and other features added in recent times are blots on the landscape – the wretched little zoo and the horrible concrete water feature near the main gate being the major offenders. The park is also home to the decaying and pretty dull **Tanzimat Müzesi**, which is open from 9am to 5pm daily. 'Tanzimat' (Reorganisation) was the name given to the political and societal reforms planned by Sultan Abdül Mecit in 1839 and carried out through the middle of the 19th century.

At the far (north) end of the park, up the hill, there is a series of terraces with a tea garden,

Great Byzantine Palace

Constantine the Great built the Great Byzantine Palace soon after he founded Constantinople in AD 324. It was renovated and added to by successive Byzantine leaders. The opulent palace was a series of buildings set in parklands and terraces, stretching from the Hippodrome over to Aya Sofya and down the slope, ending at the sea walls and the Bucoleon Palace. In the 13th century the palace was abandoned, and the ruins were filled in after the Conquest to become mere foundations to much of Sultanahmet and Cankurtaran. The mosaics in the Great Palace Mosaic Museum were part of the complex. In 1998 archaeologists unearthed frescoes in structures to the southeast of Aya Sofya, which are still being excavated today.

the **Set Üstü Çay Bahçesi**, offering basic refreshments and superb views over the Bosphorus.

To the right of the south exit is a bulbous little kiosk built into the park wall. Known as the **Alay Köşkü** (Parade Kiosk), this is where the sultan would sit and watch the periodic parades of troops and trade guilds that commemorated great holidays and military victories.

Across the street from the Alay Köşkü (not quite visible from the Gülhane gate) is an outrageously curvaceous rococo gate leading into the precincts of what was once the grand vizierate, or Ottoman prime ministry, known in the West as the **Sublime Porte**. Today the buildings beyond the gate hold various offices of the İstanbul provincial government.

HIPPODROME Map pp278-80

Tram (Sultanahmet), bus T4 from Taksim Square

The Hippodrome (Atmeydanı) was the centre of Byzantium's life for 1000 years and of Ottoman life for another 400 years. It was the scene of countless political dramas during the long life of the city. In Byzantine times, the rival chariot teams of 'Greens' and 'Blues' had separate political connections. Support for a team was akin to membership of a political party and a team victory had important effects on policy. A Byzantine emperor might lose his throne as the result of a post-match riot.

Ottoman sultans also kept an eye on activities in the Hippodrome. If things were going badly in the empire, a surly crowd gathering here could signal the start of a disturbance, then a riot, then a revolution. In 1826, the slaughter of the corrupt janissary corps (the sultan's personal bodyguards) was carried out here by the reformer Sultan Mahmut II. And in

1909 there were riots that caused the downfall of Abdül Hamit II and the repromulgation of the Ottoman constitution.

Though the Hippodrome might be the scene of their downfall, Byzantine emperors and Ottoman sultans outdid one another in beautifying it. Unfortunately, many priceless statues carved by ancient masters have disappeared from their original homes here. Chief among the villains responsible for such thefts were the soldiers of the Fourth Crusade, who sacked Constantinople, a Christian ally city, in 1204. After sacking Aya Sofya, they tore all the bronze plates from the stone obelisk at the Hippodrome's southern end in the mistaken belief that they were gold. The crusaders also stole the famous *quadriga*, or team of four horses cast in bronze, a copy of which now sits atop the main door of the Basilica di San Marco in Venice (the original is inside the museum).

The level of the Hippodrome rose over the centuries, as civilization piled up its dust and refuse here. A number of its monuments were cleaned out and tidied up by the British troops who occupied the city after the Ottoman defeat in WWI.

Near the northern end of the Hippodrome, the little gazebo in beautiful stonework is actually **Kaiser Wilhelm's Fountain.** The German emperor paid a state visit to Abdül Hamit II in 1901 and presented this fountain to the sultan and his people as a token of friend-ship. According to the Ottoman inscription, the fountain was built in the Hejira (Muslim lunar calendar) year of 1316 (AD 1898–99). The monograms in the stonework are those of Abdül Hamit II and Wilhelm II, and represent their political union.

The impressive granite **Obelisk of Theodosius** was carved in Egypt around 1450 BC. According to the hieroglyphs, it was erected in Heliopolis (now a Cairo suburb) to commemorate the victories of Thutmose III (r 1504–1450 BC). The Byzantine emperor, Theodosius, had it brought from Egypt to Constantinople in AD 390. He then had it erected on a marble pedestal engraved with scenes of himself in the midst of various imperial pastimes. Though Theodosius' self-promoting marble billboards have weathered badly over the centuries, the magnificent obelisk, spaced above the pedestal by four bronze blocks, is as crisply cut and shiny as when it was carved in Upper Egypt some 3500 years ago.

South of the obelisk is a strange column coming up out of a hole in the ground. Known as the **Spiral Column**, it was once much taller and was topped by three serpents' heads. Originally cast to commemorate a victory of the Hellenic confederation over the Persians, it stood in front of the temple of Apollo at Delphi from 478 BC until Constantine the Great had it brought to his new capital city around AD 330. Though badly bashed up in the Byzantine

Obelisk of Theodosius (above)

struggle over the role of images in the church, the serpents' heads survived until the early 18th century. Now all that remains of them is one upper jaw, housed in İstanbul's Archaeology Museum.

All that is known about the **Rough-Stone Obelisk** at the southern end of the Hippodrome is that it was repaired by Constantine VII Porphyrogenitus (r 913–59), and that its bronze plates were ripped off during the Fourth Crusade.

İSTANBUL ARCHAEOLOGY MUSEUMS Map pp278–80

Arkeoloji Müzeleri; ☎ 212-520 7740; Osman Hamdi Bey Yokuşu, Gülhane; admission €2.70; ☺ 9.30am-5pm Tue-Sun; tram (Gülhane), bus T4 from Taksim Square

It may not pull the number of visitors that flock to nearby Topkapı, but this is a stunner of a museum complex that shouldn't be missed. It can be easily reached by walking down the slope from Topkapı's Court of the Janissaries First Court, or by trudging up the hill from the main gate of Gülhane Parkı, just near the tram stop

The complex is divided into three buildings: the Archaeology Museum (Arkeoloji Müzesi), the Museum of the Ancient Orient (Eski Şark Eserler Müzesi) and the Tiled Kiosk (Çinili Köşk). These museums house the palace collections, formed during the late 19th century by museum director and archaeologist Osman Hamdi and added to greatly since the republic. While not immediately as dazzling as Topkapı, they contain a wealth of artefacts from the 50 centuries of Anatolia's history. Excellent interpretive panels are in both Turkish and English. A board at the entrance lists which of the exhibits are open and which are closed; unfortunately, budget cutbacks seem to be treating the museum harshly: the place seems inadequately staffed and sorely in need of an injection of funds to renovate long-closed galleries and reopen its bookshop and café. At the time of research the 'Anatolia and Troy', 'Thrace, Bithynia and Byzantium' and 'Anatolia's Neighbouring Cultures' exhibits upstairs in the Archaeology Museum were closed indefinitely, and the Tiled Kiosk was closed for renovation.

The first building on your left as you enter the museum complex is the **Museum of the Ancient Orient**. Overlooking the park, it was designed by Alexander Vallaury and built in 1883 to house the Academy of Fine Arts. It displays Anatolian pieces (from Hittite empires) as well as pre-Islamic items collected from the expanse of the Ottoman Empire. You can't miss the series of large glazed-brick panels depicting various animals such as lions and bulls. These beautiful blue-and-yellow panels lined the processional street and the Ishtar gate of ancient Babylon from the time of Nebuchadnezzar II (605–562 BC). Other treats here are the amazing 1st century BC alabaster statue heads from Yemen and the oldest surviving political treaty: a copy of the Kadesh Treaty drawn up in the 13th century BC between the Egyptians and Hittites. There are also clay tablets bearing Hammurabi's famous law code (in cuneiform, of course), ancient Egyptian scarabs and Assyrian reliefs.

On the opposite side of the courtyard is the **Archaeology Museum**, housed in an imposing neoclassical building. The major building in the complex, it features an extensive collection of Hellenic, Hellenistic and Roman statuary and sarcophagi.

A Roman statue of **Bes**, an impish half-god of inexhaustible power and strength who was thought to protect against evil, greets you as you enter the museum. Turn left into Room 1, and walk to the dimly lit rooms beyond, where the museum's major treasures – sarcophagi from the **Royal Necropolis of Sidon** – are displayed. These sarcophagi were unearthed in 1887 by Osman Hamdi in Sidon (Side in modern-day Lebanon). As soon as they were discovered they were swiftly whisked out of the country in a complex operation that involved them being carried on rails laid to the coast and then rafted out to sea, where they were hoisted onto ships and brought to İstanbul. In Room 2 you will see a sarcophagus that is Egyptian in origin; it was later reused by **King Tabnit of Sidon**. Also here is a beautifully preserved **Lycian sarcophagus** made from Paros marble dating from the end of the 5th century. It depicts horses, centaurs and human figures with beautifully rendered expressions on their faces. Next to this is the **Satrap sarcophagus** with its everyday scenes featuring the provincial governor. After admiring these, pass into Room 3 to see one of the most accomplished of all classical artworks, the famous marble **Alexander sarcophagus** – so named not because it belonged to the Macedonian general, but because it depicts him among his army battling the Persians (long pants, material headwear), who were led by King Abdalonymos and whose sarcophagus it was. Truly exquisite, it is carved out of pentelic marble and dates from the last quarter of the 4th century BC. Alexander, on horseback, has a lion's head as a headdress. Remarkably, the sculpture has remnants of its original red-and-yellow paintwork. At the end of this room the **Mourning Women sarcophagus** also bears traces of its original paintwork. Its depiction of the women is stark and very moving.

Turn back and walk past Bes through to Room 4, the first of the statuary galleries. It and Rooms 5 and 6 exhibit a selection of fine works, including a striking Attic **horse's head** in Room 6. **Alexander** makes another appearance (Room 7) – you'll see his bust and statue from the Hellenistic period. In Room 8 don't miss the **Ephebos of Tralles**, a statue of a young boy wrapped in a cape and leaning against a pillar. And in Room 9, which is crowded with busts, note the **Hadrianus statue**.

Artisans at Anatolia's three main sculpture centres – Aphrodisias, Ephesus and Miletus – turned out thousands of beautiful works, some of which have been collected in Room 10. There's a beautiful relief showing the struggle of **Athena and the Giants from Aphrodisias**, and a statue from Miletus showing **Apollo** wearing ornate sandals and playing a lyre. The last room has examples of sculpture from throughout the Roman Empire. Look out for the delicately carved statue of **Tyche**.

In the annex behind the main ground floor gallery there is an unimpressive mock-up of the facade of the **Temple of Athena at Assos** (Behramkale). On the mezzanine level above the Temple of Athena is an exhibition called '**İstanbul Through the Ages**', tracing the city's history through its neighbourhoods during different periods: Archaic, Hellenistic, Roman, Byzantine and Ottoman. This is well worth a visit.

While children will be bored stiff with the naff dioramas of early Anatolian life in the **Children's Museum** found off Room 1, they will no doubt be impressed by the large-scale model of the Trojan Horse, which they can climb into.

The last of the complex's museum buildings is the **Tiled Kiosk** of Sultan Mehmet the Conqueror. Thought to be the oldest surviving nonreligious Turkish building in İstanbul, it was built in 1472 as an outer pavilion of Topkapı Palace and was used for watching sporting events. The recessed doorway area is covered with tiles – some with white calligraphy *(sülüus)* on blue. The geometric patterns and colour of the tiles – turquoise, white, black – on the facade show obvious Seljuk influence.

Much of the interior of the kiosk is covered with triangular and hexagonal tiles of brown, green, yellow and blue. The excellent collection of Turkish faïence (tin-glazed earthenware tiles) highlights **İznik tiles** from the period in the 17th and 18th centuries when that city produced the finest coloured tiles in the world. When you enter the first room you can't miss the stunning **mihrab** from the İbrahim Bey Mosque, built in 1432. Also of note is the pretty **fountain** recessed into the wall in the room to the left at the back of the kiosk.

KÜÇÜK AYA SOFYA CAMİİ Map pp278-80

Little Aya Sofya, SS Sergius & Bacchus Church; ☎ 212-458 0776; Küçük Aya Sofya Caddesi; donation requested; tram (Sultanahmet), bus T4 from Taksim Square

Justinian and Theodora built this little church sometime between 527 and 536 (just before Justinian built Aya Sofya) and you can still see their monogram worked into some of the frilly white capitals. It was named after the two patron saints of Christians in the Roman army. The building, which was undergoing extensive renovation at the time of research, is one of the most beautiful in the city. Its dome is architecturally noteworthy and its plan –an irregular octagon – is quite unusual. Like Aya Sofya, its interior was originally decorated with gold mosaics and featured columns made from fine green and red marble. The mosaics are long gone, but the impressive columns remain. The church was converted into a mosque by the chief white eunuch Hüseyin Ağa around 1500; his tomb is to the north of the building.

The *medrese* cells, arranged around the mosque's forecourt, are now used by secondhand booksellers and bookbinders. In the leafy forecourt there is a tea garden and the simple **Yesevi Sofrasi Restaurant**, serving cheap, good-quality lunches for around €2.50.

MUSEUM OF TURKISH & ISLAMIC ARTS Map pp278-80

Türk ve İslam Eserleri Müzesi; ☎ 212-518 1805; Hippodrome 46, Atmeydanı Sokak, Sultanahmet; admission €2.50; ☺ 9am-4.30pm Tue-Sun; tram (Sultanahmet), bus T4 from Taksim Square

This impressive museum is housed in the Palace of İbrahim Paşa, built in 1524 on the western side of the Hippodrome.

İbrahim Paşa was Süleyman the Magnificent's close friend and brother-in-law. Captured by Turks as a child in Greece, he had been sold as a slave into the imperial household in İstanbul and worked as a page in Topkapı where he became friendly with Süleyman, who was the same age. When his friend became sultan, İbrahim was made in turn chief falconer, chief of the royal bedchamber and grand vizier. This palace was bestowed on him by Süleyman the year before he was given the hand of Süleyman's sister, Hadice, in marriage. Alas, the fairy tale was not to last for poor İbrahim. His wealth, power and influence on the monarch became so great that others wishing to influence the sultan became envious, chief among them Süleyman's powerful wife, Haseki Hürrem Sultan (Roxelana). After a rival accused İbrahim of disloyalty, Roxelana convinced her husband that İbrahim was a threat and Süleyman had him strangled in 1536.

The museum's exhibits date from the 8th and 9th centuries up to the 19th century. Highlights include the superb calligraphy exhibits, including writing sets, imperial edicts *(fermans)* with monograms *(tuğras)* and illuminated manuscripts. In the largest room (and last room on the 1st floor) have a look at the wooden inlaid Quran stands and chests from the 16th century, as well as the colourful Turkish miniatures. This room also has an extraordinary collection of enormous antique carpets – whatever you do, don't miss them.

The lower floor of the museum houses ethnographic exhibits. First up is a village loom on which carpets and kilims are woven. Next you'll see the insides of a *yurt* (Central Asian felt hut). An exhibit of the plants and materials used to make natural dyes for the textiles follows; then there's a black tent *(kara çadır)* made of goat hair, like those used by nomads in eastern Turkey, followed by some slightly dodgy domestic dioramas featuring stuffed-sack figures.

Labels are in Turkish and English. The coffee shop in the courtyard of the museum, which also has tables on the terrace overlooking the Hippodrome, is a welcome refuge from the press of crowds and touts in the area.

SİRKECİ RAILWAY STATION Map pp278-80
Sirkeci Istasyonu; Ankara Caddesi, Sirkeci; tram (Sirkeci), buses to Eminönü
The romance of the famous *Orient Express* and other locomotives of the era was reflected in the design for this train station, built as the terminus of European routes in 1881. Designed by a German architect, it is an excellent example of Islamic Eclecticism, an architectural movement introduced into İstanbul by European architects at the end of the 19th century. The structure replaced one of the Topkapı Palace pavilions and it reflects this Ottoman heritage, though

its clock tower, arches and large rose windows clearly reflect the neoclassicism popular in Europe at the time. These days the station is a slightly run-down terminus for European and suburban routes. The **Orient Express Restaurant** on platform 1 still functions, though the current menu certainly wouldn't have made the grade back in the glory days, reminding us of college dinners rather than grand predeparture celebrations. Still, train buffs may well enjoy a beer (€2.20) or coffee (€1.25) stop here.

SOĞUKÇEŞME SOKAK Map pp278-80
Tram (Gülhane), bus T4 from Taksim Square
Soğukçeşme Sokak, or Street of the Cold Fountain, runs between the Topkapı Palace walls and Aya Sofya. In the 1980s, the Turkish Touring & Automobile Association (TTAA) acquired all of the buildings on the street and decided to demolish most of them to build nine recreations of the prim Ottoman-style houses that had occupied the site in the previous two centuries. A vitriolic battle played out on the pages of İstanbul's newspapers ensued, with some experts arguing that the city would be left with a Disney-style architectural theme park rather than a legitimate exercise in conservation architecture. The TTAA eventually got the go-ahead (after the intervention of no less than Turkey's president) and eventually opened all of the re-created buildings as Ayasofya Pansiyonları (Aya Sofya Pensions), one of the first boutique heritage hotels in the city. Conservation theory aside, the colourful buildings and cobbled street are particularly picturesque and worth wandering past.

SOKOLLU MEHMET PAŞA CAMİİ
Map pp278-80
Şehit Çeşmesi Sokak 20-22, Küçük Aya Sofya; donation requested; tram (Sultanahmet or Çemberlitaş), bus T4 from Taksim Square
This mosque was built in 1571 during the height of Ottoman architectural development by the empire's greatest architect, Sinan. Though named after the grand vizier of the time, it was really sponsored by his wife Esmahan, daughter of Sultan Selim II. Besides its architectural harmony, typical of Sinan's greatest works, the mosque is unusual because the *medrese* is not a separate building but actually part of the mosque structure, built around the forecourt; compare it to the similar plan of the **Mihrimah Camii** (p144). If the mosque is not open, wait for the guardian to appear; he may offer photos for sale.

When you enter, notice the harmonious form, the coloured marble and the spectacular İznik tiles – some of the best ever made. The stained glass is also particularly fine. The mosque contains four fragments from the sacred Black Stone in the Kaaba at Mecca: one above the entrance framed in gold, two in the *mimber* and one in the mihrab. Interestingly, the marble pillars by the mihrab revolve if the foundations have been disturbed by an earthquake – an ingenious early warning device – though apparently they didn't move during the earthquake of 1999 as one was 'out of order'!

TOPKAPI PALACE Map pp278-80

Topkapı Sarayı; ☎ 212-512 0480; Soğukçeşme Sokak, Topkapı; adult/child €6.60/1.60, Harem & Treasury extra; ☽ 9am-5pm, closed Tue in winter; tram (Sultanahmet), bus T4 from Taksim Square

Home to Selim the Sot, who drowned in the bath after drinking too much champagne; İbrahim the Mad, who lost his reason after being locked up for four years in the infamous palace *kafes*; and Roxelana, beautiful and malevolent consort of Süleyman the Magnificent, Topkapı would have to be the subject of more colourful stories than most of the world's museums put together. No wonder it's been the subject of an award-winning feature film, an opera (Mozart's *The Abduction from the Seraglio*) and a blockbuster social history

(John Freely's wonderful *Inside the Seraglio*). Make sure you dedicate a day to exploring, because tourist attractions rarely come any better than this.

Mehmet the Conqueror built the first stage of the palace shortly after the Conquest in 1453, and lived here until his death in 1481. Subsequent sultans lived in this rarefied environment until the 19th century, when they moved to ostentatious European-style palaces such as Dolmabahçe, Çırağan and Yıldız that they built on the shores of the Bosphorus. Mahmut II (r 1808–39) was the last sultan to live in Topkapı.

Buy your tickets to the Palace and the Treasury at the main ticket office just outside the gate to the Second Court. Tickets to the Harem are available at the ticket box outside the Harem itself. Guides to the palace congregate next to the main ticket office. A one-hour tour will cost €30 for one. There are usually guides speaking English, German, French, Spanish, Russian, Italian and Arabic. Alternatively, an audio guide in English, French, Italian, Spanish or German will cost you €5.50. These and free maps of the palace are available at the audio booth just inside the turnstile entrance to the Second Court.

Before you enter the Imperial Gate (Bab-ı Hümayun) of Topkapı, take a look at the ornate structure in the cobbled square near the gate. This is the **Fountain of Sultan Ahmet III**, built in 1728 by the sultan who so favoured tulips.

Gate of Felicity (p94), Topkapı Palace

Neighbourhoods – Sultanahmet

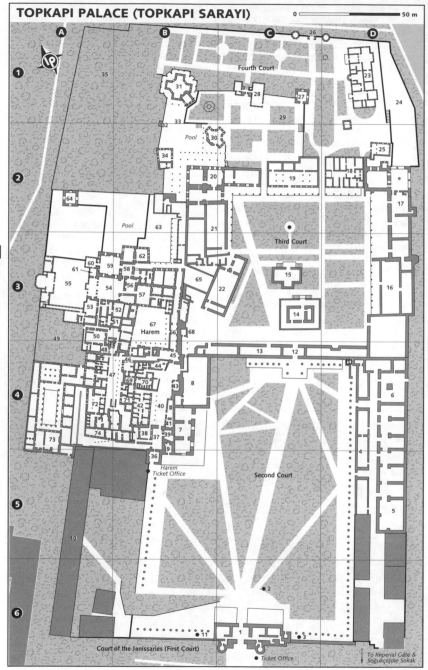

TOPKAPI PALACE (TOPKAPI SARAYI)

0 —————— 50 m

Fourth Court

Pool

Pool

Third Court

Harem

Second Court

Harem
Ticket Office

Court of the Janissaries (First Court)

Ticket Office

To Imperial Gate &
Soğukçeşme Sokak

It replaced a Byzantine fountain at the same spring. Typical of architecture during the Tulip Period, it features delicate Turkish rococo decorations (note the floral carvings).

As you pass through the Imperial Gate, you enter the First Court, known as the **Court of the Janissaries**, also known as the Parade Court. On your left is the former **Haghia Eirene**, also known as Aya İrini Kilisesi or Church of the Divine Peace. There was a Christian church here from earliest times and, before that, a pagan temple. The early church was replaced by the present one, commissioned by Justinian in the 540s. It is almost exactly as old as its close neighbour, Aya Sofya. When Mehmet the Conqueror began building his palace, the church was within the grounds and was most fortunately retained. It was used as an arsenal for centuries, then as an artillery museum and now occasionally as a concert hall (especially during the International İstanbul Music Festival). Its serenely beautiful interior and superb acoustics mean that tickets to concerts here are usually the most sought-after in town. If you're fortunate enough to be here during the festival, make sure you visit the temporary box office, located outside Haghia Eirene, to see if any tickets are available.

Janissaries, merchants and tradespeople could circulate as they wished in the Court of the Janissaries, but the Second Court was restricted. The same is true today, as you must have a ticket to the palace to enter the Second Court. Just past the ticket windows is a little fountain where the imperial executioner used to wash the tools of his trade after decapitating a noble or rebel who had displeased the sultan. The head of the unfortunate victim was put on a pike and exhibited above the gate you are about to enter.

The **Middle Gate** (Ortakapı or Bab-üs Selâm) led to the palace's **Second Court**, used for the business of running the empire. Only the sultan and the *valide sultan* (queen mother) were allowed through the Middle Gate on horseback. Everyone else, including the grand vizier, had to dismount. The gate was constructed by Süleyman the Magnificent in 1524, utilising architects and workers he had brought back from his conquest of Hungary.

To the right after you enter are models and a map of the palace. Beyond them, in a nearby building, you'll find imperial carriages made in Paris, Turin and Vienna for the sultan and his family.

The Second Court has a beautiful, park-like setting. Topkapı is not based on a typical European palace plan – one large building with outlying gardens – but is a series of pavilions, kitchens, barracks, audience chambers, kiosks and sleeping quarters built around a central enclosure.

The great **Palace Kitchens**, on your right, hold a small portion of Topkapı's vast collection of Chinese celadon porcelain, valued by the sultans for its beauty but also because it was

SECOND COURT		
Middle Gate	**1**	C6
Audio Tour Booth	**2**	C6
Imperial Carriages	**3**	C6
Palace Kitchens	**4**	D5
Chinese & Japanese Porcelain	**5**	D5
Helvahane (Temporary		
Exhibitions)	**6**	D4
Imperial Council Chamber	**7**	B4
Inner Treasury	**8**	B4
Kiosk	**9**	B4
Imperial Stables	**10**	A5
Book & Gift Shop	**11**	B6

THIRD COURT		
Gate of Felicity	**12**	C4
White Eunuchs' Quarters	**13**	C4
Audience Chamber	**14**	C3
Library of Ahmet III	**15**	C3
Dormitory of the Expeditionary Force		
(Costumes)	**16**	D3
Imperial Treasury	**17**	D2
Museum Directorate	**18**	D2
Treasury Dormitory	**19**	C2
Sacred Safekeeping Rooms	**20**	B2
Quarters of Pages in Charge of the		
Sacred Safekeeping Rooms		
(Paintings & Calligraphy)	**21**	B2
Mosque of the Eunuchs &		
Library	**22**	C3

FOURTH COURT		
Mecidiye Köşkü	**23**	D1
Konyalı Restaurant	(see 23)	
Cafe Terraces	**24**	D1
Sofa or Terrace Mosque	**25**	D2
Gate of the Privy Gardens	**26**	C1
Chief Physician's Room	**27**	C1
Kiosk of Mustafa Pasha	**28**	C1
Tulip Garden	**29**	C1
Revan Kiosk	**30**	B2
Baghdad Kiosk	**31**	B1
İftariye Baldachin	**32**	B2
Marble Terrace & Pool	**33**	B1
Circumcision Room	**34**	B2
Lower Gardens of the Imperial Terrace	**35**	A1

HAREM		
Carriage Gate	**36**	B5
Dome with Cupboards	(see 36)	
Hall with Şadırvan	**37**	B4
Black Eunuchs' Mosque	**38**	B4
Tower of Justice	**39**	B4
Courtyard of the Black Eunuchs	**40**	B4
Harem Eunuchs' Mosque	**41**	B4
Black Eunuchs' Dormitories	**42**	B4
Harem Chamberlain's Room	**43**	B4
Chief Black Eunuch's Room	**44**	B4
Main Gate	**45**	B4
Second Guard Room	(see 45)	
Concubines' Corridor	**46**	B4

Concubines' & Consorts'		
Courtyard	**47**	A4
Sultan Ahmet's Kiosk	**48**	A4
Harem Garden	**49**	A3
Valide Sultan's Quarters	**50**	A3
Sultan's Hamam	**51**	B3
Valide Sultan's Hamam	**52**	B3
Chamber of Abdül Hamit I	**53**	A3
Imperial Hall	**54**	A3
Terrace of Osman III	**55**	A3
Room with Hearth	**56**	B3
Room with Fountain	(see 56)	
Consultation Place of the Genies	**57**	B3
Beautifully Tiled Antechamber	**58**	B3
Privy Chamber of Murat III	**59**	A3
Library of Ahmet I	**60**	A3
Dining Room of Ahmet III	**61**	A3
Double Kiosk	**62**	B3
Favourites' Courtyard & Apartments	**63**	B2
Private Prison	**64**	A2
Harem Mosque	**65**	B3
Golden Road	**66**	B3
Courtyard of the Valide Sultan	**67**	B3
Birdcage Gate	**68**	B3
Harem Kitchen	**69**	B4
Imperial Princes' School	**70**	B4
Women's Hamam	**71**	B4
Women's Dormitory	**72**	A4
Harem Hospital	**73**	A4
Laundry Room	**74**	A4

Dolmabahçe Palace (p124)

reputed to change colour if touched by poisoned food. In a building close by are the collections of European, Russian and Ottoman porcelain, silverware and glassware. The last of the kitchens, the Helvahane, in which all the palace sweets were made, now hosts occasional temporary exhibitions.

On the left (west) side of the Second Court is the ornate **Imperial Council Chamber**, also called the Divan Salonu. It's beneath the squarish Tower of Justice, the palace's highest point. The Imperial Divan (council) met in the Imperial Council Chamber to discuss matters of state while the sultan eavesdropped through a grille high on the wall. During the great days of the empire, foreign ambassadors were received on days when the janissaries were to get their pay. Huge sacks of silver coins were brought to the Imperial Council Chamber. High-court officers would dispense the coins to long lines of the tough, impeccably costumed and faultlessly disciplined troops as the ambassadors looked on in admiration.

North of the Imperial Council Chamber is the **Inner Treasury**, which today exhibits Ottoman and European armour.

The entrance to the palace's most famous sight, the **Harem** (p96), is beneath the **Tower of Justice** (Adalet Kulesi) on the left-hand side of the Second Court. The tower is not part of the Harem tour; at the time of research it was being restored.

If you enter the **Third Court** after visiting the Harem, and thus by the back door, you should head for the main gate into the court and enter again to truly appreciate the grandeur of the approach to the heart of the palace. This main gate, known as the **Gate of Felicity** or Gate of the White Eunuchs, was the entrance into the sultan's private domain. As is common with oriental potentates, the sultan preserved the imperial mystique by appearing in public very seldom. The Third Court was staffed and guarded by white eunuchs, who allowed only a few very important people in. As you enter the Third Court, imagine it alive with the movements of imperial pages and white eunuchs scurrying here and there in their palace costumes. Every now and then the chief white eunuch or the chief black eunuch would appear, and all would bow. If the sultan walked across the courtyard, all activity stopped until the event was over.

An exception to the imperial seclusion was the ceremony celebrating a new sultan's accession to the throne. After girding the Sword of Osman, which symbolised imperial power, the new monarch would sit enthroned before the Gate of Felicity and receive the obeisance, allegiance and congratulations of the empire's high and mighty.

Before the annual military campaigns in summertime, the sultan would also appear before this gate bearing the standard of the Prophet Mohammed to inspire his generals to go out and conquer all for Islam.

Inside the Gate of Felicity is the **Audience Chamber**, constructed in the 16th century, but refurbished in the 18th century. Important officials and foreign ambassadors were brought to this little kiosk to conduct the high business of state. An ambassador, frisked for weapons and held on each arm by a white eunuch, would approach the sultan. At the proper moment, he knelt and kowtowed; if he didn't, the eunuchs would urge him ever so forcefully to do so.

The sultan, seated on the divans whose cushions are embroidered with over 15,000 seed pearls, inspected the ambassador's gifts and offerings as they were passed through the small doorway on the left. Even if the sultan and the ambassador could converse in the same language (sultans in the later years knew French and ambassadors often learned Turkish), all conversation was with the grand vizier. The sultan would not deign to speak to a foreigner and only the very highest Ottoman officers were allowed to address the monarch directly.

Right behind the Audience Chamber is the pretty **Library of Ahmet III**, built in 1719 by Sultan Ahmet III. Light-filled, it has comfortable reading areas and stunning inlaid woodwork.

To the right of the Audience Chamber (ie on the opposite side of the Harem exit) are the rooms of the **Dormitory of the Expeditionary Force**, which now house the rich collections of imperial robes, kaftans and uniforms worked in silver and gold thread. Also here is a fascinating collection of talismanic shirts, which were believed to protect the wearer from enemies and misfortunes of all kinds. Textile design reached its highest point during the reign of Süleyman the Magnificent, when the imperial workshops produced cloth of exquisite design and work. Check out the absolutely gorgeous silk kaftan of Sultan Süleyman II with its appliquéd tulip design.

Next to the Dormitory of the Expeditionary Force is the **Treasury** (p98).

Opposite the Imperial Treasury on the other side of the Third Court there's another set of wonders, the holy relics in the Suite of the Felicitous Cloak, nowadays called the **Sacred Safekeeping Rooms**. These rooms, sumptuously decorated with İznik faïence, constitute a holy of holies within the palace. Only the chosen could enter the Third Court, but entry into these special rooms was for the chosen of the chosen, and even then only on ceremonial occasions. During the empire, this suite of rooms was opened only once a year so that the imperial family could pay homage to the memory of the Prophet on the 15th day of the holy month of Ramazan. Even though anyone, prince or commoner, faithful or infidel, can enter the rooms now, you should respect the sacred atmosphere by observing decorous behaviour, as this is still a place of pilgrimage for Muslims.

In the east entry room, notice the carved door from the Kaaba in Mecca and, hanging from the ceiling, gilded rain gutters from the same place.

To the right (north) a room contains a hair of Prophet Mohammed's beard, his footprint in clay, his sword, tooth and more. There is a glass booth here from which a seated imam sometimes chants passages from the Quran. The 'felicitous cloak' itself resides in a golden casket in a small adjoining room along with the battle standard.

Also in the Third Court are the **Quarters of Pages in Charge of the Sacred Safekeeping Rooms**, where the palace school for pages and janissaries was located. These days the building features exhibits of Turkish miniature paintings, calligraphy and portraits of the sultans. Notice the graceful, elaborate *tuğra* (monogram) of the sultans. The *tuğra*, placed at the top of any imperial proclamation, contains elaborate calligraphic rendering of the names of the sultan and his father, eg 'Abdül Hamit Khan, son of Abdül Mecit Khan, Ever Victorious'.

Other buildings in the Third Court include the **Mosque of the Eunuchs** and a small **library**.

Pleasure pavilions occupy the northeastern most part of the palace, sometimes called the Tulip Gardens or Fourth Court. A late addition to Topkapı, the **Mecidiye Köşkü**, was built by Abdül Mecit (r 1839–61) according to 19th-century European models. Beneath this is the **Konyalı restaurant** (p150).

West of the Mecidiye Köşkü is the sultan's **Chief Physician's Room**. Interestingly, the chief physician was always one of the sultan's Jewish subjects. Nearby, you'll see the **Kiosk of Mustafa**

Life in the Cage

As children, imperial princes were brought up in the Harem, taught and cared for by its women and servants.

In the early centuries of the empire, Ottoman princes were schooled as youths in combat and statecraft by direct experience: They practised soldiering, fought in battles and were given provinces to administer. But as the Ottoman dynasty did not observe primogeniture (succession of the firstborn), the death of the sultan regularly resulted in a fratricidal bloodbath as his sons battled it out among themselves for the throne. In the case of Beyazıt II (r 1481–1512), his sons began the battles even before the sultan's death, realising that to lose the battle for succession meant their own death. The victorious son, Selim I (r 1512–20), not only murdered his brothers but even forced Sultan Beyazıt to abdicate and may even have had him murdered as he went into retirement.

Fratricide was not practised by Ahmet I (r 1603–17), who could not bring himself to murder his mad brother Mustafa. Instead, he kept him imprisoned in the Harem, beginning the tradition of cage life *(kafes hayatı)*. This house arrest, adopted in place of fratricide by later sultans, meant that princes were prey to the intrigues of the women and eunuchs, ignorant of war and statecraft, and thus usually unfit to rule if and when the occasion arose. Luckily for the empire in this latter period, there were able grand viziers to carry on.

In later centuries the dynasty adopted the practice of having the eldest male in the direct line assume the throne.

Pasha, sometimes called the Sofa Köşkü. Outside the kiosk, during the reign of Ahmet III, the **Tulip Garden** was filled with the latest varieties of the flower. Little lamps would be set out among the tulips at night.

Up the stairs at the end of the Tulip Garden are two of the most enchanting buildings in the palace, joined by a marble terrace with a beautiful pool. Murat IV (r 1623–40) built the **Revan Kiosk** in 1636 after reclaiming the city of Yerevan (now in Armenia) from Persia. In 1639 he constructed the **Baghdad Kiosk**, one of the last examples of classical palace architecture, to commemorate his victory over that city. Notice the superb İznik tiles, the mother-of-pearl and tortoiseshell inlay, and the woodwork.

Jutting out from the terrace is the golden roof of the **İftariye Baldachin**, the most popular happy-snap spot in the palace grounds. İbrahim the Mad built this small structure in 1640 as a picturesque place to break the fast of Ramazan.

On the west end of the terrace is the **Circumcision Room** (Sünnet Odası), used for the ritual that admits Muslim boys to manhood. Built by İbrahim in 1641, the outer walls of the chamber are graced by particularly beautiful tile panels.

TOPKAPI HAREM Map pp278-80

Soğukçeşme Sokak, Topkapı; adult/child €5.50/1.60; 🕑 every 30 min from 9.30am-4pm, closed Tue in winter

If you decide to tour the Harem – and we highly recommend you do so – you have no option but to take a guided tour. Tickets for this are available from the ticket office outside the Harem's entrance. There are usually lengthy queues here and numbers are limited to 60 for each 30-minute tour, so it's a good idea to head this way as soon as you enter Topkapı. The attendants usually have a break at lunchtime and so no tour is scheduled at 12.30pm.

Audio guides to the Harem are available at a booth situated right next to its ticket office. Tickets cost €1.90. While these audio guides can illuminate your visit, be aware that there appears to be a bit of a scam associated with them. Despite the fact that signs at the Harem's entrance say that the Harem tour is in Turkish only (which clearly prompts many English-speaking visitors to hire an audio guide), the truth is that the tour is more often than not in English. The only time it is likely to be in Turkish is on the weekend, when locals visit.

As popular belief would have it, the Harem was a place where the sultan could engage in debauchery at will (and Murat III did, after all, have 112 children!). In more prosaic reality, these were the imperial family quarters, and every detail of Harem life was governed by tradition, obligation and ceremony. The word harem literally means 'private'.

Every traditional Muslim household had two distinct parts: the *selamlık* (greeting room) where the master greeted friends, business associates and tradespeople; and the *harem* (private apartments), reserved for himself and his family. The Harem, then, was something akin to the private apartments in Buckingham Palace or the White House.

The women of the Harem had to be foreigners, as Islam forbade enslaving Muslims, Christians or Jews (although Christians and Jews could be enslaved in the Balkans). Girls, too, were bought as slaves (often having been sold by their parents at a good price) or were received as gifts from nobles and potentates. A favourite source of girls was Cssia, north of the Caucasus Mountains in Russia, as Cssian women were noted for their beauty.

Upon entering the Harem, the girls would be schooled in Islam and Turkish culture and language, as well as the arts of make-up, dress, comportment, music, reading, writing, embroidery and dancing. They then entered a meritocracy, first as ladies-in-waiting to the sultan's concubines and children, then to the sultan's mother and finally, if they were the best, to the sultan himself.

Ruling the Harem was the *valide sultan,* the mother of the reigning sultan. She often owned large landed estates in her own name and controlled them through black eunuch servants. Able to give orders directly to the grand vizier, her influence on the sultan, on the selection of his wives and concubines and on matters of state, was often profound.

The sultan was allowed by Islamic law to have four legitimate wives, who received the title of *kadın* (wife). If a wife bore him a son she was called *haseki sultan; haseki kadın* if it was a daughter. The Ottoman dynasty did not observe primogeniture (the right of the first-born son to the throne), so in principle the throne was available to any imperial son. Each lady of the Harem contrived mightily to have her son proclaimed heir to the throne, to thus assure her own role as the new *valide sultan*.

As for concubines, Islam permits as many as a man can support in proper style. The Ottoman sultans had the means to support many, sometimes up to 300, though they were not all in the Harem at the same time. The domestic thrills of the sultans were usually less spectacular, however. Mehmet the Conqueror, builder of Topkapı, was the last sultan to have four official wives. After him, sultans did not officially marry, but instead kept four chosen concubines without the associated legal encumbrances, thereby saving themselves the embarrassments and inconveniences suffered by another famous Renaissance monarch, King Henry VIII. The exception to this rule was Süleyman the Magnificent (r. 1520–66), who famously married his favourite concubine, Roxelana.

The Harem was much like a village with all the necessary services. About 400 or 500 people lived in this section of the palace at any one time. Not many of the ladies stayed in the Harem all their lives: The sultan might grant them their freedom, after which they would often marry powerful men who wanted the company of these well-educated women, not to mention their connections with the palace. And the relationship was twofold: The sultan was also happy to have the women, educated to be loyal, spread throughout the empire to help keep tabs on political affairs via their husbands.

The chief black eunuch, the sultan's personal representative in administration of the Harem and other important affairs of state, was the third-most powerful official in the empire, after the grand vizier and the supreme Islamic judge.

The earliest of the 300-odd rooms in the Harem were constructed during the reign of Murat III (1574–95). In 1665 a disastrous fire destroyed much of the complex, which was rebuilt by Mehmet IV and later sultans.

Although the Harem is built into a hillside and has six levels, the standard tour takes you through or past only a few dozen rooms on one level; fortunately these rooms are among the most splendid. Interpretive panels in Turkish and English have been placed throughout the building, although you will be hurried through the tour at such a pace that there is little or no time to read them. Linger at your peril – the attendants can be very overbearing!

The tour route may vary from time to time, as various rooms are closed for restoration and others are finished and opened to view. The following is a description of the tour at the time of research. The tour is largely broken into four sections: the apartments of the Eunuchs,

Harem, Topkapı Palace (opposite)

the concubines and the *valide sultan* and the rooms of the sultan.

You enter the Harem by the **Carriage Gate**, through which Harem ladies would enter in their carriages. Inside the gate is the **Dome with Cupboards**. Beyond it is the **Hall with Şadırvan**, a guard room decorated with fine İznik faïence; the green colours are unusual in İznik tiles. To the left is a doorway to the **Black Eunuchs' Mosque**, on the right the doorway to the Tower of Justice, which rises above the Imperial Council Chamber.

Beyond the Hall with Şadırvan is the narrow **Courtyard of the Black Eunuchs**, decorated in Kütahya tiles from the 17th century. Behind the marble colonnade on the left are the **Black Eunuchs' Dormitories**. In the early days white eunuchs were used, but black eunuchs sent as presents by the Ottoman governor of Egypt later took control. As many as 200 lived here, guarding the doors and waiting on the women of the Harem.

Near the far end of the courtyard on the left, a staircase leads up to the rooms in which imperial princes were given their primary schooling. These are not open to the public. On the right is the **Chief Black Eunuch's Room**.

At the far end of the courtyard, safely protected by the eunuchs, is the **Main Gate** into the Harem proper, as well as a **guard room** featuring two gigantic gilded mirrors. From this, the

Concubines' Corridor on the left leads to the Concubines' and Consorts' Courtyard. A concubine came by gift or purchase; the more talented and intelligent rose in the palace service to hold offices in the administration of the Harem; the less talented waited on the more talented.

Next you'll go through Sultan Ahmet's Kiosk to the Valide Sultan's Quarters, the very centre of power in the Harem. These rooms include a large salon, a small bedroom, a room for prayer and other small chambers. From these ornate rooms the *valide sultan* oversaw and controlled her huge 'family'. After his accession to the throne, a new sultan came here to receive the allegiance and congratulations of the people of the Harem. The later rococo mezzanine was added by the mother of Murat III in the 1580s. Of particular note in these quarters is the charming small *hamam* designed by Sinan.

As he walked these corridors, the sultan wore slippers with silver soles. As no woman was allowed to show herself to the sultan without specific orders, the clatter of the silver soles warned residents of the sultan's approach, allowing them to disappear from his sight. This rule no doubt solidified the *valide sultan's* control, as *she* got to choose the most beautiful, talented and intelligent of the Harem girls to be her personal servants, and thus introduced them to her son, the sultan.

The tour passes through the private *hamams* and toilets of the *valide sultan* to the Imperial Hall, decorated in Delft tiles. This grand room is the largest in the Harem and was where the sultan and his ladies gathered for entertainment, often with musicians in the balcony. Designed perhaps by Sinan during the reign of Murat III (r 1574–95), it was redecorated in baroque style by Osman III (r 1754–57). The smaller part of the room remains baroque; the larger part has had its 16th-century décor restored.

The tour then enters the Privy Chamber of Murat III (1579), one of the most sumptuous rooms in the palace. Dating from 1578, virtually all of the decoration is original. It is thought to be the work of Sinan. Besides the gorgeous İznik tiles and a fireplace, there is a three-tiered marble fountain to give the sound of cascading water and, perhaps not coincidentally, to make it difficult to eavesdrop on the sultan's conversations. The gold seating places are later 18th century additions.

Adjoining the Privy Chamber to the west is the Library of Ahmet I (1609), with small fountains by each window to cool the summer breezes as they enter the room. Perhaps Ahmet I retired

here to inspect plans of his great building project, the Blue Mosque. The adjoining Dining Room of Ahmet III (1705–06), with its wonderful rococo painted panels of flowers and fruit, was built by Ahmet III, the Tulip Sultan. It is known as the Yemiş Odası (Fruit Room).

Northeast of the Privy Chamber of Murat III is the Twin Kiosk, two rooms dating from around 1600. Note the painted canvas dome in the first room and the fine tile panels above the fireplace in the second. The fabulous stained glass is also noteworthy.

North and east of the Twin Kiosk is the Favourites' Courtyard and Apartments. The Turkish word for 'favourite', *gözde*, literally means 'in the eye' (of the sultan). Over the edge of the courtyard (really a terrace) you'll see a swimming pool. Just past the courtyard (but on the floor above) are the many small dark rooms that comprised the Private Prison *(kafes)* where the unwanted brothers or sons of the sultan were kept (see the boxed text on p95).

A corridor leads east to the Golden Road, a passage leading south. A servant of the sultan's would toss gold coins to the women of the Harem here, hence the name. It is among the oldest parts of the palace, having been built by Mehmet the Conqueror.

The Harem tour then re-enters the guardroom with the huge gilded mirrors, then exits through the Birdcage Gate into the palace's Third Courtyard.

TOPKAPI TREASURY Map pp278–80
Soğukçeşme Sokak, Topkapı; adult/child €5.50/1.60;
☺ 9am-5pm, closed Tue in winter

The Treasury, which is in the northeast corner of the Third Court, features an incredible collection of precious objects made from or decorated with gold, silver, rubies, emeralds, jade, pearls and diamonds. The building itself was constructed by Mehmet the Conqueror in 1460 and has always been used to store works of art and treasure. In the first room, look for the jewel-encrusted sword of Süleyman the Magnificent and the Throne of Ahmed I, inlaid with mother-of-pearl and designed by Mehmet Ağa, architect of the Blue Mosque. In the second room, the tiny Indian figures, mainly made from seed pearls, are well worth seeking out, as are the bizarre and vaguely sinister relics of the Arm and Skull of St John the Baptist, which are cased in jewels. Both had originally been in the possession of the Byzantines and fell into Ottoman hands after the Conquest.

After passing through the third room and having a gawk at the enormous gold and diamond candlesticks, each weighing 48kg, you come to a fourth room and the Treasury's most famous exhibit: the **Topkapı Dagger**. The object of the criminal quest in the 1964 movie *Topkapi*, it features three enormous emeralds on the hilt and a watch set into the pommel. Also here is the **Kaşıkçı (Spoonmaker's) Diamond**, a teardrop-shaped 86-carat rock surrounded by dozens of smaller stones. First worn by Mehmet IV at his accession to the throne in 1648, it's the world's fifth-largest diamond. It's called the Spoonmaker's Diamond because it was originally found at a rubbish dump in Eğrikapı and purchased by a street peddler for three spoons.

YENİ CAMİİ Map pp278-80
New Mosque; ☎ 212-527 8505; Yenicami Meydanı Sokak, Eminönü; donation requested; ferries, tram & buses (Eminönü)

Only in İstanbul would a 400-year-old mosque be called 'New'. The Yeni Camii was begun in 1597, commissioned by Valide Sultan Safiye, mother of Sultan Mehmet III (r 1595–1603). The site was earlier occupied by a community of Karaite Jews, radical dissenters from Orthodox Judaism. When the *valide sultan* decided to build her grand mosque here, the Karaites were moved to Hasköy, a district further up the Golden Horn that still bears traces of their presence.

Safiye lost her august position when her son the sultan died and the mosque was completed six sultans later in 1663 by Valide Sultan Turhan Hadice, mother of Sultan Mehmet IV (r 1640–07).

In plan, the Yeni Camii is much like the Blue Mosque and the Süleymaniye Camii, with a large forecourt and a square sanctuary surmounted by a series of semidomes crowned by a grand dome. The interior is richly decorated with gold, coloured İznik tiles and carved marble. It also has an impressive mihrab.

The mosque was created after Ottoman architecture had reached its peak. Consequently, even its tiles are slightly inferior products, the late 17th century having seen a diminution in the quality of the products coming out of the İznik workshops. You will see this if you compare these tiles with the exquisite examples found in the nearby **Rüstem Paşa Camii** (p105), which are from the high period of İznik tilework. Nonetheless, it is a popular working mosque and a much-loved adornment to the city skyline.

Recent municipal works have seen flagstones of the plaza around the Yeni Camii relaid. We can only hope that the cleaning of the mosque's stonework and eradication of the pesky pigeons that populate its entrance will be next on the agenda.

Across the road from the mosque is the **tomb of Valide Sultan Turhan Hadice**, the woman who completed construction of the Yeni Camii. Buried with her are no fewer than six sultans, including her son Mehmet IV, plus dozens of imperial princes and princesses. Further east, on Hamidiye Caddesi, are two of the best places in town to buy fresh Turkish delight, **Hafiz Mustafa Şekerlemeleri** (p190) and **Ali Muhiddin Hacı Bekir** (p190).

Max's İstanbul
An interview with Max Handsaker, aged six

İstanbul is awesome. For little kids like me, the best things are the ferries and the ice cream. The ferry trip down the **Bosphorus** (p217) was great, especially when we stopped at the **castle** (Rumeli Hisarı; p217). I climbed really high on the battlements and mum and dad freaked out because there were no fences or anything. It was way cool and just like when the knights would have been there. My favourite ice-cream shop is **Mado** (p161) and there are at least three (on İstiklal Caddesi, Teşvikiye Caddesi and Iskele Square). The cakes at that **cake shop** (Patisserie Markiz; p157) were yummy, too, particularly the tiramisu cake. And there's a good **toy shop** (İyigün Oyuncak; p196) opposite there that has Star Wars figures. Little kids jump on the back of the tram that goes up and down that street and they hang on while it's moving, but mum said I couldn't do that. I also liked the **Basilica Cistern** (p83) because it was sort of scary being underground and there was an upside-down head on a pillar. I got bored at Topkapı Palace and the big church near there (Aya Sofya) but mum and dad really liked them. I also liked taking the **ferry** (p131) to Üsküdar and going on the little boat to the **tower** (Kız Kulesi; p132) on an island. And there was a little train to go on at **Miniaturk** (p129), as well as a playground, but the little buildings were silly. The best **museum** (Rahmi M Koç; p129) was the one with all the trains and boats. That was so cool because there were lots of buttons to press and cars and stuff.'

THE BAZAAR DISTRICT

In Byzantine times the Golden Horn provided a perfect natural harbour for the city's commerce. So, suppliers of fresh vegetables and fruits, grain and staple goods set up shop here. Until a couple of decades ago, their successors in İstanbul's wholesale vegetable, fruit and fish markets performed the same services in the same area – to the west of the Galata Bridge, in Eminönü. With the drive to clean up and beautify the Golden Horn, the wholesale markets have been moved to the outskirts of the city, though some produce stalls remain around Tahmis Caddesi next to the Spice Bazaar, providing an echo of the not-too-distant past.

Commerce also reigns on the hill behind the Spice Bazaar, a frantically busy shopping precinct known as Tahtakale, where vendors with carts full of everything from *simits* (bread-rings) to strawberries make their way through narrow streets full of shoppers, delivery vans and tourists valiantly fighting their way through the chaos. At the top of the hill is the city's first and most evocative shopping mall – the famous Grand Bazaar (Kapalı Çarşı), established during the rule of Mehmet the Conqueror and going strong ever since. Getting lost in its maze of laneways is obligatory for all first-time visitors; those who have visited previously are quick to gravitate towards their favourite shops, coffee houses and restaurants. Near the bazaar are two of the grandest of all Ottoman buildings, the Süleymaniye and Beyazıt Camiis, wonderfully contemplative spaces to escape from the mercantile madness of the surrounding streets.

Orientation

The Grand Bazaar is the southern anchor of a vast market district that spills northward downhill through the area known as Tahtakale to Eminönü on the Golden Horn. To the west of the Grand Bazaar on Yeniçeriler Caddesi (the continuation of Divan Yolu) is Beyazıt Square, officially known as Hürriyet Meydanı, a bustling meeting place for shoppers and students from nearby İstanbul University. Behind the university is the grand complex of the Süleymaniye Camii, which has given its name to the surrounding suburb.

West of Beyazıt Square and Süleymaniye are the suburbs of Laleli and Kalenderhane, which end at the major road artery of Atatürk Bulvarı; visitors to İstanbul who are staying in Beyoğlu or the Western Districts inevitably follow this road from the airport, gasping in amazement when they catch their first glimpse of the majestic Aqueduct of Valens and the Golden Horn ahead.

South of the Grand Bazaar and Beyazıt Square are the residential suburbs leading down to the Sea of Marmara. At the foot of the hill are the cobbled streets of Kumkapı, once a fishing village and now a pleasant place to enjoy a fish dinner.

Bazaar District Top Five

- Grand Bazaar (p102)
- Süleymaniye Camii (p106)
- Spice Bazaar (p106)
- Rüstem Paşa Camii (p105)
- Beyazıt Camii (opposite)

AQUEDUCT OF VALENS Map pp282-3
Bozdoğan Kemeri; tram (Laleli), bus 61B from Taksim Square

Rising majestically over the traffic on busy Atatürk Bulvarı, this limestone structure is one of the city's most distinctive landmarks. Visitors often gasp in amazement on seeing it for the first time (amazement often turns into consternation when they notice excited fans from the nearby Vefa football stadium doing perilous victory dances waving their team's colours from its dizzy heights). It's not certain that the aqueduct was constructed by the Emperor Valens (r 364–78), though we do know it was repaired in 1019, in later times by several sultans and in the late 1980s. It's thought that the aqueduct carried water over this valley to a cistern at Beyazıt Square before finally ending up at the Great Byzantine Palace. After the Conquest it supplied the Eski (Old) and Topkapı Palaces with water.

BEYAZIT CAMİİ Map pp282-3

Mosque of Sultan Beyazıt II; ☎ 212-519 3644;
Yeniçeriler Caddesi; tram (Beyazıt), bus 61B from
Taksim Square

Dating from 1501 to 1506, this was the second
imperial mosque to be built in the city after
Mehmet the Conqueror's Fatih Camii (p110), and
was the prototype for other imperial mosques.
In effect, it is the link between Aya Sofya, which
obviously inspired its design, and the great
mosques such as the Süleymaniye, which are
realisations of Aya Sofya's design fully adapted
to Muslim worship. These days the Beyazıt
Camii is in need of a good sprucing up, as the
exterior stonework is extremely sooty and the
interior is similarly grimy.

Of particular note is the mosque's exceptional use of fine stone: marble, porphyry, verd
antique and rare granite. The mihrab is simple,
except for the rich stone columns framing it,
and the courtyard, with its 24 small domes and
central fountain, is particularly pretty.

Some of the other buildings of Beyazıt's
külliye (mosque complex) have been well utilised. The soup kitchen has been turned into a
library, while the medrese is now the Museum of
Turkish Calligraphic Art (p104). Unfortunately the
once-splendid hamam is still waiting to be restored. Beyazıt's türbe is behind the mosque.

BEYAZIT SQUARE & İSTANBUL UNIVERSITY Map pp282-3

Tram (Beyazıt), bus 61B from Taksim Square

Beyazıt Square is officially called Hürriyet
Meydanı (Freedom Square), though everyone
knows it simply as Beyazıt. Under the rule
of the Byzantines it was called the Forum of
Theodosius. Sections of the forum's columns
decorated with stylised oak-knot designs
were dug up from the square during the

1950s and can be seen on the other side of
Yeniçeriler Caddesi. Today the square is home
to street vendors, students from İstanbul University and plenty of pigeons, as well as a
few policemen who like to keep an eye on
student activities.

The square is backed by the impressive
portal of the University. After the Conquest,
Mehmet the Conqueror built his first palace
here, a wooden structure called the Eski Sarayı
(Old Seraglio). After Topkapı was built the Eski
Sarayı became home to women when they
were pensioned out of the main palace, eg for
valide sultans when their sultan sons died and
they lost their powerful position as head of the
harem. The original building was demolished in
the 19th century to make way for a grandiose
Ministry of War complex designed by Auguste
Bourgeois; this now houses the university. The
stone **tower**, visible from most of Old İstanbul,
was built as a lookout for fires. Both the university and tower are off limits to travellers.

CARTOON & HUMOUR MUSEUM

Map pp282-3

İstanbul Karikatür ve Mizah Müzesi; ☎ 212-521
1264; Kovacılar Sokak 12, Fatih; admission €0.80;
⊙ 10am-6pm Tue-Sat; tram (Laleli), bus 61B from
Taksim Square

Housed in the former medrese of Gazanfer Ağa,
the chief of the white eunuchs under Mehmet
III, this museum's collection highlights the fact
that Turkish cartoon artistry has been lively
and politically important since Ottoman times.
It's fascinating to see how cartoonists have
historically gotten away with criticising the authorities – print journalists have rarely been as
radical and lived to tell the tale. All exhibits and
signs are in Turkish so you may have difficulty
getting the in-jokes, but you can still enjoy the
pictures and the pleasant courtyard, with its
fountain and grapevines.

GALATA BRIDGE Map pp282-3

Galata Köprüsü; Tram, ferries & buses (Eminönü)

Nothing is quite as evocative as walking across
the Galata Bridge. At sunset, when the Galata
Tower is surrounded by shrieking seagulls and
the mosques atop the seven hills of the city
are thrown into relief against a soft red-pink
sky, the view from the bridge is spectacularly
beautiful. During the day, it carries a constant
flow of İstanbullus crossing to and from Beyoğlu
and Eminönü, a handful or two of hopeful anglers trailing their lines into the waters below
and a constantly changing procession of street

Transport

Eminönü is the transport nerve centre of the city:
Bosphorus and Marmara ferries dock here, Galata
Bridge traffic from Beyoğlu passes through, buses
leave Rüstempaşa Bus Station next to the water for
all parts of the city, and the tram starts its journey to
Sultanahmet and further on to Zeytinburnu, stopping
at the Çemberlitaş, Beyazıt, Üniversite and Laleli stops
in this neighbourhood. A little further on over Atatürk
Bulvarı is Aksaray Metro Station, which runs to the
otogar (main bus station) and on to the airport.

Buses go to and from the Western Districts and
Taksim Square from Beyazıt Square.

vendors hawking everything from fresh-baked *simit* to Rolex rip-offs. The smell of fresh fish sandwiches being prepared wafts across from the Eminönü ferry docks and the evocative scent of apple tobacco seeps up from the nargileh cafés below. This is İstanbul at its most magical.

Underneath the bridge, restaurants and cafés on its lower level serve all day and night – the locals tend to congregate at those on the Beyoğlu side looking towards the Bosphorus, and will often spend hours playing backgammon and drinking tea. They have plenty to look at, too, with ferries zooming past and cruise ships docking at the nearby international sea terminal at Karaköy. There's even a shop selling fishing equipment for those who aspire to emulate the anglers up on the bridge, who proudly display their catch in buckets and bowls.

The present, quite ugly bridge was built in 1992 to replace an iron structure dating from 1909 to 1912, which in turn had replaced two earlier structures. The iron bridge was famous for the ramshackle fish restaurants, teahouses and nargileh joints that occupied the dark recesses beneath its roadway, but it had a major flaw: it floated on pontoons that blocked the natural flow of water and kept the Golden Horn from flushing itself free of pollution. In the late 1980s the Municipality started to draw up plans to replace it with

a new bridge that would allow the water to flow. These plans were expedited by a fire in the early 1990s and the new bridge was built a short time afterwards. (The remains of the old, much-loved bridge were moved further up the Golden Horn near Hasköy.)

GRAND BAZAAR Map p103
Kapalı Çarşı, Covered Market; 🕙 **8.30am-7pm**
Mon-Sat; tram (Beyazıt), bus 61B from Taksim Square

Before you visit this, the most famous *souq* in the world, make sure you prepare yourself properly. First, make sure you're in a good mood, ready to swap friendly banter with the hundreds of shopkeepers who will attempt to lure you into their establishments. There's no use getting tetchy with the touts here – this is their turf and it would be delusional of you to think that you're anything more than putty in their hands (and lira in their cash registers). Second, allow enough time to look into every nook and cranny, drink innumerable cups of tea, compare price after price and try your hand at the art of bargaining. Shoppers have been doing this here for centuries and, frankly, it would be unbecoming for you to do any less. (For tips on bargaining, see p187.) Third: never, ever forget your baggage allowance. There's nothing worse than that sinking feeling at the airport check-in counter when you realise that your Grand Bazaar–induced shop-

Spice Bazaar (p106)

ping frenzy means that the dreaded term 'excess baggage' is about to become a reality and test your already sorely abused credit card to its limits. Last, prepare to enjoy yourself! This is the heart of the city in so much more than a geographical sense and has been for centuries. No visit to İstanbul would be complete without a stop here.

With over 4000 shops and several kilometres of lanes, as well as mosques, banks, police sta-

tions, restaurants and workshops, the bazaar is a covered world. Though there's no doubt that it's a tourist trap *par excellence,* it's also a place where business deals are done between locals and import/export businesses flourish. And it functions as the nucleus of a large commercial neighbourhood, with most of the surrounding streets (Mahmutpaşa Yokuşu is a good example) catering to every conceivable local shopping need.

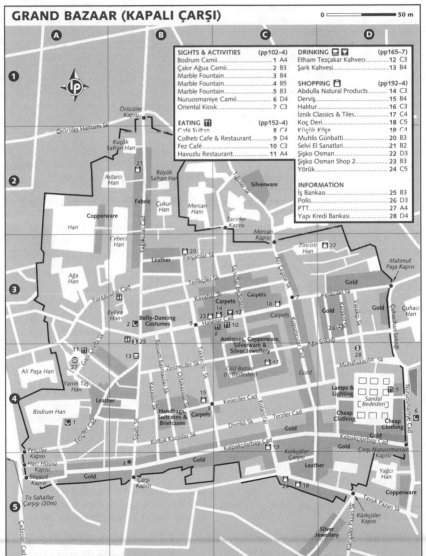

GRAND BAZAAR (KAPALI ÇARŞI)

0 — 50 m

SIGHTS & ACTIVITIES	(pp102–4)
Bodrum Camii..............................	1 A4
Çakır Ağua Camii.........................	2 B3
Marble Fountain..........................	3 B4
Marble Fountain..........................	4 B5
Marble Fountain..........................	5 B3
Nuruosmaniye Camii....................	6 D4
Oriental Kiosk.............................	7 C3

EATING 🍴	(pp152–4)
Café Sultan...............................	8 C4
Colheti Cafe & Restaurant...........	9 D4
Fez Café..................................	10 C3
Havuzlu Restaurant....................	11 A4

DRINKING 🍷🍷	(pp165–7)
Etham Tezçakar Kahvecı.............	12 C3
Şark Kahvesi..............................	13 B4

SHOPPING 🛍	(pp192–4)
Abdulla Natural Products............	14 C3
Derviş.......................................	15 B4
Halıtur.....................................	16 C3
İznik Classics & Tiles..................	17 C4
Koç Deri....................................	18 C5
Küçük Köşe................................	19 C4
Muhlis Günbatti.........................	20 B3
Selvi El Sanatları........................	21 B2
Şişko Osman..............................	22 D3
Şişko Osman Shop 2...................	23 B3
Yörük..	24 C5

INFORMATION	
İş Bankası..................................	25 B3
Polis...	26 D3
PTT...	27 A4
Yapı Kredi Bankası.....................	28 D4

Starting from a small masonry *bedesten* (warehouse) built in the time of Mehmet the Conqueror, the bazaar grew to cover a vast area as neighbouring shopkeepers decided to put up roofs and porches so that commerce could be conducted comfortably in all weather. Finally, a system of locked gates and doors was provided so that the entire minicity could be closed up tight at the end of the business day. Street names refer to trades and crafts: Kuyumcular Caddesi (Jewellers St), İnciciler Sokağı (Pearl Merchants' St), Fez-Makers St. Large sections of the bazaar have been destroyed by fire and earthquake a number of times in its history (most recently in 1954), but have always been rebuilt.

Just inside the Nuruosmaniye Kapısı (doorway), on the southeast corner of the market, you'll find a glittering street filled with the stores of gold merchants. This is called **Kalpakçılarbaşı Caddesi** and it's the closest thing the bazaar has to a main street. Most of the bazaar is on your right (north) in the crazy maze of tiny streets and alleys. You'll inevitably get lost when exploring them, but hey, that's part of the fun!

Make sure you pop into the **Sandal Bedesten** off Kalpakçılarbaşı Caddesi. This rectangular hall with a domed roof supported by 12 large pillars is also called the Yeni Bedesten or New Warehouse as it was built after Mehmet's central *bedesten* some time in the 17th century. Once the city's auction place for used and antique goods, these days it hosts a popular weekly carpet auction (1pm Wednesday). It's also home to **Colheti Café & Restaurant** (p152) and stores selling cheap clothes.

The **Old Bazaar**, also known as Cevahir Bedesteni (Jewellery Warehouse), is at the centre of the market. Thought to be the first building Mehmet the Conqueror built, its structure is similar to the Sandal Bedesten. Inside, you'll find innumerable small shops selling quality jewellery, silver, ceramics and antiques.

When wandering, seek out north–south Sipahi Caddesi and its famous **Şark Kahvesi** (p166) a worn-out but charming relic of Old İstanbul whose walls feature quirky images of dervishes on flying carpets. This is a great place to linger over a game of backgammon and a few cups of tea. Other places that make good coffee and tea stops in the bazaar are the pricey **Fez Café** (p153), the slightly less expensive **Café Sultan** (p152) and the bargain-basement **Etham Tezçakar Kahveci** (p166), all of which have adjoining spots on atmospheric Halıcılar Caddesi near the Old Bazaar. The Fez and the Sultan cafés also serve food. **Abdulla Natural Products**

(p192), one of the first of the new breed of designer-product shops that are popping up in and around the bazaar, is found here too.

The best place for a meal is without doubt **Havuzlu Restaurant** (p153), located in a *han* near the PTT in Gani Çelebi Sokak.

Near the junction of Halıcılar Caddesi and Kuyumcular Caddesi you'll find the crooked **Oriental Kiosk**, which was built as a coffee house and now functions as a jewellery shop. North from here, up Acı Çeşme Sokak, is the gorgeous pink **Zincirli Han**, home to one of the bazaar's most famous carpet dealers, **Şişko Osman** (p194).

Bibliophiles will want to head towards **Sahaflar Çarşısı** (Old Book Bazaar), which is found in a shady little courtyard west of the bazaar at the end of Kalpakçılarbaşı Caddesi. The book bazaar dates from Byzantine times. Today, many of the booksellers are members of a dervish order called the Halveti after its founder, Hazreti Mehmet Nureddin-i Cerrahi-i Halveti. They sell wares both new and old, and though it's unlikely you'll uncover any underpriced antique treasures, you'll certainly be able to find old engravings, a curiosity or two and books on İstanbul and Turkish culture in several languages.

To check out what to buy in the bazaar and where to buy it, refer to p192. One of the most intriguing aspects of a visit to the bazaar is its juxtaposition of tourist tat and precious objects, proving the point that the place really does cater to every possible shopping desire!

MUSEUM OF TURKISH CALLIGRAPHIC ART Map pp282-3
Türk Vakıf Hat Sanatları Müzesi; ☎ 212-527 5851; Hürriyet Meydanı, Beyazıt; admission €1.30; 🕥 9am-4pm Tue-Sat; tram (Beyazıt), bus 61B from Taksim Square

Housed in a small building at the western side of Beyazıt Square, this museum contains wall hangings and manuscripts illustrating mainly cursive calligraphic styles, many dating from the 13th century. There are also some examples of calligraphy on stone, tile and glass. Interpretive labels in English are sadly lacking. The building, once the *medrese* of Beyazıt Camii, is a series of rooms surrounding a leafy courtyard.

NURUOSMANİYE CAMİİ Map p103
Light of Osman Mosque; Vezir Hanı Caddesi; tram (Beyazıt), bus T4 from Taksim Square, bus 61B from Taksim Square

Facing Nuruosmaniye Kapısı, one of several doorways into the Grand Bazaar, this mosque was built in Ottoman baroque style between 1748 and 1755, started by Mahmut I and finished by his successor Osman III. Though meant to exhibit the sultans' 'modern' taste, the baroque building has very strong echoes of Aya Sofya, specifically the broad, lofty dome, colonnaded mezzanine galleries, windows topped with Roman arches and the broad band of calligraphy around the interior. Despite its prominent position on the busy pedestrian route from Cağaloğlu Square and Nuruosmaniye Caddesi to the bazaar, it is surprisingly peaceful and contemplative inside.

RÜSTEM PAŞA CAMİİ Map pp282-3

Mosque of Rüstem Pasha; ☎ 212-526 7350; Hasırcılar Caddesi; donation requested; tram, ferries & buses (Eminönü)

Plonked in the middle of the busy Tahtakale district, this little-visited mosque is a gem. Built in 1560 by Sinan for Rüstem Paşa, son-in-law and grand vizier of Süleyman the Magnificent, it is a showpiece of the best Ottoman architecture and tilework, albeit on a small scale. It is thought to have been the prototype for Sinan's greatest work, the **Selimiye** (p226) in Edirne.

At the top of the entry steps there's a terrace and the mosque's colonnaded porch. You'll notice at once the panels of İznik faïence set into the mosque's facade. The interior is cov-

ered in similarly gorgeous tiles and features a lovely dome, supported by four tiled pillars.

The preponderance of tiles was Rüstem Paşa's way of signalling his wealth and influence – İznik tiles being particularly expensive and desirable. It may not have assisted his passage into the higher realm, though, because by all accounts he was a loathsome character. His contemporaries dubbed him Kehle-I-İkbal (the Louse of Fortune) because, although he was found to be infected with lice before his marriage to Mihrimah, Süleyman's favourite daughter, even this did not prevent the marriage or his subsequent rise to great fame and fortune. He is best remembered for plotting with Roxelana to turn Süleyman against his favourite son, Mustafa. They were successful and Mustafa was strangled in 1553 on his father's orders.

The mosque is easy to miss because it's not at street level. Look to the left of the ablutions block on the street and you'll see a stone doorway marked by a silver plaque. A flight of steps next to this leads up to the mosque.

ŞEHZADE MEHMET CAMİİ Map pp282-3

Mosque of the Prince; Şehzadebaşı Caddesi; tram to Laleli, bus 61B from Taksim Square

Süleyman the Magnificent built this mosque between 1543 and 1548 as a memorial to his son, Mehmet, who died of smallpox in 1543

Men washing, Yeni Camii (p??)

at the age of 22. It was the first important mosque to be designed by Mimar Sinan. Although not one of his best works, it has two beautiful minarets and attractive exterior decoration. Among the many important people buried in tile-encrusted **tombs** here are Prince Mehmet, his brothers and sisters, and Süleyman's grand viziers, Rüstem Paşa and İbrahim Paşa. Admission to the complex is free, though you may be asked for a donation.

SPICE BAZAAR Map pp282-3
Mısır Çarşısı; Egyptian Market; ⏳ 8.30am-6.30pm Mon-Sat; tram, ferries & buses (Eminönü)

Need a herbal love potion or natural Turkish Viagra? This is the place to find them, although we wouldn't vouch for the efficacy of either! As well as spices (baharat), nuts, honey in the comb and olive oil soaps, the bustling spice bazaar sells truckloads of figs (incir), Turkish delight (lokum) and fruit pressed into sheets and dried (pestil). The number of shops selling tourist trinkets increases annually, yet this remains a great place to stock up on edible souvenirs, share a few jokes with the vendors and marvel at the well-preserved building. It's also home to one of the city's oldest restaurants, **Pandeli** (p153).

The market was constructed in the 1660s as part of the Yeni Camii complex, the rent from the shops supports the upkeep of the mosque and its charitable activities, which include a school, baths, hospital and public fountains. It was called the Egyptian Market because it is thought that it was initially endowed with taxes levied on goods imported from Egypt.

Between the market and the Yeni Camii is the city's major outdoor market for flowers, plants, seeds and songbirds. There's a toilet (tuvalet) down a flight of stairs, subject to a small fee.

On the west side of the market there are outdoor produce stalls selling fresh foodstuff from all over Anatolia. Also here is the most famous coffee supplier in İstanbul, **Kurukahveci Mehmet Efendi Mahdumları** (p192), established over 100 years ago.

SÜLEYMANİYE CAMİİ Map pp282-3
Mosque of Sultan Süleyman the Magnificent; ☎ 212-514 0139; Prof Sıddık Sami Onar Caddesi; donation requested; ⏳ tombs 9.30am-5.30pm; tram (Beyazıt), bus 61B from Taksim Square or buses, ferries & tram (Eminönü)

The Süleymaniye crowns one of the seven hills, and dominates the Golden Horn, providing a landmark for the entire city. It was commissioned by the greatest, richest and most power-

ful of Ottoman sultans, Süleyman I (r 1520–66), known as 'The Magnificent', and was the fourth imperial mosque built in İstanbul, following the Fatih, Beyazıt and Selim I complexes.

Though it's not the largest of the Ottoman mosques, the Süleymaniye is certainly the grandest. It was designed by Mimar Sinan, the most famous and talented of all imperial architects. Though Sinan described the smaller Selimiye Camii in Edirne as his best work, he chose to be buried here in the Süleymaniye complex, probably knowing that this would be the building that he would be best remembered by. His tomb is just outside the mosque's walled garden, next to the medrese building.

The mosque was built between 1550 and 1557; records show that 3523 craftspeople worked on its construction. Though it's seen some hard times, being damaged by fire in 1660 and having its wonderful columns covered by cement and oil paint at some point after this, a restoration in 1956 and decades of subsequent care mean that it's in great shape these days. It's also one of the most popular mosques in the city, with worshippers rivalling the Blue Mosque in number.

The mosque's setting and plan are particularly pleasing, with well-tended gardens and a three-sided forecourt surrounded by a wall with grilled windows and featuring a central domed ablutions fountain. Its four minarets with their beautiful balconies are said to represent the fact that Süleyman was the fourth of the Osmani sultans to rule the city.

Inside, the mosque is breathtaking in its size and pleasing in its simplicity. It is also remarkably light. Sinan's design is particularly ingenious due to the fact that the buttresses used to support the four columns are incorporated into the walls of the building, masked by galleries with arcades of columns running between the buttresses. Put simply, the architect, ever challenged by the technical accomplishments of Aya Sofya, took the floor plan of that church and here perfected its adaptation to the requirements of Muslim worship.

There is little interior decoration other than some very fine İznik tiles in the mihrab, gorgeous

It's Free
- Grand Bazaar (p102)
- Spice Bazaar (p106)
- Yıldız Parkı (p127)
- Hippodrome (p86)
- Florence Nightingale Museum (p131)

stained-glass windows done by one İbrahim the Drunkard, and four massive columns – one from Baalbek in modern-day Lebanon, one from Alexandria and two from Byzantine palaces in İstanbul. The painted arabesques on the dome are 19th-century additions, recently renewed. If you visit when the stairs to the gallery on the northeast side (ie facing the Golden Horn) are open, make sure you go upstairs and out to the balcony. The views from this vantage point are among the best in the city.

The *külliye* of the Süleymaniye, which is outside the walled garden, is particularly elaborate, with the full complement of public services: soup kitchen, hostel, hospital etc. Today the soup kitchen, with its charming garden courtyard, houses the **Dârüzziyafe Restaurant**. Though a lovely place to enjoy a cup of tea (€0.50), the food has been poor on our recent visits. **Lale Bahçesi** (p166), located in a sunken courtyard next to Dârüzziyafe, is also a great place to relax over tea. Both it and the nearby **Kanaat Lokantası** (p154), are extremely popular with locals. Those in need of an energy boost could make the short trip to **Vefa Bozacısı** (p166), the most famous place in the city to sample *boza*, the İstanbullu tonic drink made with fermented grain.

The mosque's **hamam** (p172) still functions, though it has a vaguely sleazy air.

Near the southeast wall of the mosque is the cemetery, with the **tombs** of Süleyman and his wife Haseki Hürrem Sultan (Roxelana). The tilework in both is superb. In Süleyman's tomb, little jewel-like lights in the dome are surrogate stars. In Hürrem's tomb, the many tile panels of flowers and the delicate stained glass produce a serene effect.

ZEYREK CAMİİ Map pp282-3
Church of the Pantocrator; İbadethane Sokak; tram (Laleli), bus 61B from Taksim Square

Zeyrek Camii was originally part of an important Byzantine sanctuary comprising two churches, a chapel and a monastery. The monastery is long gone and the northernmost church is derelict, but the southern church still has some features intact, including a magnificent marble floor. Empress Eirene had the church built before her death in AD 1124 (she features in a mosaic at Aya Sofya with Emperor John II Comnenus). The church and the attached chapel, built by John II, now function as a mosque. Outside prayer times a caretaker is usually available to show visitors around and will gratefully accept a donation in return. Ask him to pull back the carpet to reveal part of the splendid floor.

The Ottoman building to the east houses a posh restaurant, the **Zeyrekhane** (p153).

WESTERN DISTRICTS

As İstanbul grew over the centuries, its boundaries moved westward and a series of successive city walls were put up to protect the city. In these western suburbs populations of two major ethnic groups settled – the Jews in Balat and the Greeks in Fener. Today, their synagogues and churches are among the most interesting sights to visit in the neighbourhood. Though remnants of these populations still live around here, most of the current inhabitants are from the east of Turkey and are more conservative than the rest of the city's population. You'll notice, for instance, that headscarves are *de rigueur* here, with some women even wearing chadors. These areas are also conspicuously less affluent than the suburbs around Sultanahmet, Beyoğlu or the Bosphorus.

Orientation

The Western Districts begin at Atatürk Bulvarı to the south and follow the Golden Horn north as far as Eyüp, incorporating suburbs including Fatih, Fener, Edirnekapı and Balıkhane. The major streets are Mürsel Paşa Caddesi (at various points also called Demirhisar Caddesi, Abdülezel Paşa Caddesi, Ayvansaray Caddesi and Feshane Caddesi), which follows the shore of the Golden Horn; and Fevzi Paşa Caddesi (the continuation of Macar Kardeşler and Şehzadebaşı Caddesi), which runs from Beyazıt and punches through the walls at Edirnekapı.

Western Districts Top Five
- **Kariye Müzesi** (p111)
- **Eyüp Sultan Camii & Tomb** (p109)
- **Church of St Stephen of the Bulgars** (p108)
- **Fatih Camii** (p110)
- **Mihrimah Sultan Camii** (p113)

Neighbourhoods – Western Districts

AHRIDA SYNAGOGUE Map p281

Ahrida Sinagogu; ☎ 212-523 4729; Kürkçüçeşme Sokak 9, Balat; ferry from Eminönü, bus 99, 99A, 36CE, 44B & 399B/C/D from Eminönü, bus 55T from Taksim Square (Balat)

Balat once housed a large portion of the city's Jewish population. Sephardic Jews, driven from Spain by the judges of the Inquisition, found refuge in the Ottoman Empire in the late 15th and early 16th centuries and settled in this quarter of the city. Many of their descendants still live here and speak the native Spanish dialect of Ladino. Like all other religious 'nations' within the empire, the Jewish community was governed by its supreme religious leader, the Chief Rabbi, who oversaw its adherence to biblical law and who was responsible to the sultan for the community's good conduct. Today, you'll need to contact the current **Chief Rabbinate of Turkey** (☎ 212-243 5166) if you wish to visit this or the neighbouring **Yanbol synagogue**. Ahrida is the oldest and most beautiful of the two, having been built before the Conquest.

To visit, you must contact the rabbinate at least 24 hours before your visit. You'll need to fax a copy of your passport identification papers. Call between 9.30am and 5pm Monday to Thursday, 9.30am and 1pm Friday.

CHURCH OF ST STEPHEN OF THE BULGARS Map p281

☎ 212-521 1121; Mürsel Paşa Caddesi 85, Fener; ferry from Eminönü, bus 99, 99A, 36CE, 44B & 399B/C/D from Eminönü, bus 55T from Taksim Square (Fener)

These days we're accustomed to kit homes and assemble-yourself furniture from Ikea, but back in 1871, when this Gothic Revival cast-iron church was constructed from pieces shipped down the Danube and across the Black Sea from Vienna on 100 barges, the idea was novel to say the least.

It's hard to say which is the more unusual: the building and its interior fittings – all made completely of cast iron – or the history of its congregation.

During the 19th century, ethnic nationalism swept through the Ottoman Empire. Each of the empire's many ethnic groups wanted to rule its own affairs. Groups identified themselves on the basis of language, religion and racial heritage. This sometimes led to problems, as with the Bulgars.

Originally a Turkic-speaking people, the Bulgars came from the Volga in about AD 680 and overwhelmed the Slavic peoples living

Transport

Ferries travelling up the Golden Horn leave from Üsküdar and travel via Eminönü, Kasımpaşa, Fener, Balat and a few other stops until they reach Eyüp. The first ferries leave Eminönü at 7.20am, 8.25am and 9.15am, then hourly until 6.15pm, 6.55pm and 8pm. Going the other way, the first from Eyüp leaves at 7.15am, then 8am, 9am and 9.50am, then hourly until 3.50pm, then 5.05pm, 5.50pm, 6.50pm and 7.30pm. There are also buses to Eyüp from Eminönü and Taksim that journey just inland from the shoreline.

Fatih and Edirnekapı are best reached by bus from Taksim, Beyazıt or Eminönü.

in what is today Bulgaria. They adopted the Slavic language and customs, and founded an empire that threatened the power of Byzantium. In the 9th century they were converted to Christianity.

The Orthodox Patriarch, head of the Eastern church in the Ottoman Empire, was an ethnic Greek; in order to retain as much power as possible, the patriarch was opposed to any ethnic divisions within the Orthodox church. He put pressure on the sultan not to allow the Bulgarians, Macedonians and Romanians to establish their own religious groups.

The pressures of nationalism became too great, however, and the sultan was finally forced to recognise some sort of religious autonomy for the Bulgars. He established not a Bulgarian patriarchate, but an 'exarchate', with a leader supposedly of lesser rank, yet independent of the Greek Orthodox patriarch. In this way the Bulgarians would achieve their desired ethnic recognition and would get out from under the dominance of the Greeks, but the Greek Patriarch would allegedly suffer no diminution of his glory or power. St Stephen's functioned as the main church of the Bulgarian exarch.

Architectural historians believe that the cast-iron building, based on a design by the Ottoman architect Housep Aznavour (1853–1935), replaced an earlier timber church on the site. Its interior, which features screens, a balcony and columns all cast from iron, is extremely beautiful, with the gilded iron glinting in the hazy light that filters in through stained-glass windows.

If the church isn't open, see if you can find the caretaker who lives on the grounds – he's usually happy to open the gate and let you in if you tip (say, €2.50).

ECUMENICAL ORTHODOX PATRIARCHATE Map p281

Patrikhane; ☎ 212-531 9670/6; Sadrazam Ali Paşa Caddesi, Fener; ☺ 9am-4pm; ferry from Eminönü, bus 99, 99A, 36CE, 44B & 399B/C/D from Eminönü, bus 55T from Taksim Square (Fener)

The Ecumenical patriarch is a ceremonial head of the Orthodox Church, though most of the churches in Greece, Cyprus, Russia and other countries have their own patriarchs or archbishops who are independent of İstanbul. Nevertheless, the symbolic importance of the patriarchate, here in the city that saw the great era of Byzantine and Orthodox influence, is considerable. The patriarchate has been located in this district since 1601.

To the Turkish government, the patriarch is a Turkish citizen of Greek descent nominated by the church and appointed by the government as an official in the Directorate of Religious Affairs. In this capacity he is the religious leader of the country's Orthodox citizens and is known officially as the Greek Patriarch of Fener (Fener Rum Patriği). The relationship of the patriarchate and the wider Turkish community has been strained in the past, no more so than when Patriarch Gregory V was hanged for treason after inciting Greeks to overthrow Ottoman rule at the start of the Greek War of Independence (1821–32). The lingering antagonism over this and the Greek occupation of parts of Turkey in the 1920s no doubt explains the elaborate security around the patriarchate, including a security checkpoint at the main entrance.

The **Church of St George** within the patriarchate compound is a modest structure built in 1720. Its main glory is the ornate patriarchal throne that is thought to date from the last years of Byzantium. In 1941 a disastrous fire destroyed many of the buildings but spared the church.

EYÜP SULTAN CAMİİ & TOMB
Map pp276-7

Mosque of the Great Eyüp; Camii Kebir Sokak, Eyüp; admission by donation; ☺ tomb 9.30am-4.30pm; ferry Üsküdar & Eminönü (opposite for times), bus 55ET, 55T from Taksim Square or 99, 99A, 36CE, 44B & 399B/C/D from Eminönü (Eyüp)

This mosque complex occupies what is reputedly the burial place of Ayoub al-Ansari (Eyüp Ensari in Turkish), a friend of the Prophet's and a revered member of Islam's early leadership. Eyüp fell in battle outside the walls of Constantinople while carrying the banner of Islam during the Arab assault and siege of the city from 674 to 678. He was buried outside the walls and, ironically, his tomb later came to be venerated by the Byzantine inhabitants of the city.

When Mehmet the Conqueror besieged Constantinople in 1453, he built a grander and more fitting tomb. The mosque that he built on the site became the place where the Ottoman princes came for the Turkish equivalent of coronation: to gird the Sword of Osman, signifying

Neighbourhoods – Western Districts

Detail, Church of St Stephen of the Bulgars (opposite)

Maşallah!

If you visit Eyüp on a Sunday, you will usually see young boys in white suits being carried by their proud fathers and followed by a circle of relatives. These apprehensive yet excited young chaps are about to undergo one of the most important Muslim rites – circumcision (sünnet). Their white suit is supplemented with a spangled hat and red satin sash emblazoned with the word Maşallah (What wonders God has willed!).

Circumcision, or the surgical removal of the foreskin on the penis, is performed on a Turkish Muslim lad when he is between seven and 10 years old, and marks his formal admission into the faith.

On the day of the operation the boy is dressed in the special suit, visits relatives and friends, and leads a parade – formerly on horseback, now in cars – around his neighbourhood or city, attended by musicians and merrymakers.

The simple operation, performed in a hospital or in a clinic during the afternoon, is followed by a celebration with music and feasting. The newly circumcised boy attends, resting in bed, as his friends and relatives bring him special gifts and congratulate him on having entered manhood.

their power and their title as padişah (king of kings), or sultan. In 1766 Mehmet's building was levelled by an earthquake; a new mosque was built on the site by Sultan Selim III in 1800.

From the plaza outside the complex, enter the great doorway to a large courtyard, then to a smaller court shaded by a huge ancient plane tree. Note the wealth of brilliant İznik tilework on the walls. To the left, behind the tiles and gilded grillework, is Eyüp's tomb, rich with silver, gold, crystal chandeliers and coloured tiles. To the right is the mosque.

Be careful to observe the Islamic proprieties when visiting, as this is an extremely sacred place for Muslims – ranking fourth after the big three: Mecca, Medina and Jerusalem.

We suggest you avoid visiting on Friday or on other Muslim holy days. During your visit you may see boys dressed up in white satin suits with spangled caps and red sashes emblazoned with the word 'Maşallah'. These lads are on the way to their circumcision and have made a stop beforehand at this holy place.

After visiting the mosque, many visitors head north up the hill to **Pierre Loti Café**, where the famous French novelist is said to have come for inspiration. Loti loved İstanbul, its decadent grandeur and the late-medieval customs of a society in decline. When he sat in this café,

under a shady grapevine sipping tea, he saw a Golden Horn busy with caïques, schooners and a few steam vessels. The water in the Golden Horn was still clean enough to swim in and the vicinity of the café was given over to pasture. The café that today bears his name has no connection to Loti, but it occupies a similar spot and offers views similar to the ones he must have enjoyed. It's in a warren of streets on a promontory surrounded by the **Eyüp Sultan Mezarlığı** (Cemetery of the Great Eyüp). Many important people, including lots of grand viziers, are buried here.

The surest way to find the café is to walk out of the mosque complex to the plaza, turn right, and walk around the mosque complex (keeping it on your right) to the north side of the mosque until you see a cobbled path going uphill into the cemetery marked by a small marble sign, 'Maraşal Fevzi Çakmak'. Hike up the steep hill for 15 minutes to reach the café. If you take a taxi, it will follow a completely different route because of one-way streets. The café is open from 8am to midnight daily and serves drinks only.

FATİH CAMİİ Map pp282-3
Mosque of the Conqueror; Fevzi Paşa Caddesi;
⏰ **tombs 9.30am-4.30pm; bus 28, 36KE & 86 from Eminönü, bus 87 from Taksim Square, bus 39 from Beyazıt (Fatih)**

The Fatih was the first great imperial mosque built in İstanbul following the Conquest. For its location, Mehmet the Conqueror chose the hilltop site of the ruined Church of the Apostles, burial place of Constantine and other Byzantine emperors. The mosque complex, finished in 1470, was enormous, set in extensive grounds, and included in its külliye 15 charitable establishments, such as religious schools, a hospice for travellers and a caravanserai. Unfortunately, the mosque you see today is not the one Mehmet built. The original stood for nearly 300 years before toppling in an earthquake in 1766. Though rebuilt, it was destroyed by fire in 1782. The present mosque dates from the reign of Abdül Hamit I and is on a completely different plan. Though traces of Mehmet's mosque remain – the courtyard and its main entrance portal – the interior of the Fatih, with its ugly drinking fountain, is relatively unimpressive.

Directly behind the mosque are the tombs of Mehmet the Conqueror and his wife Gülbahar. Confusingly, Mehmet isn't buried here, but rather under the mimber in the mosque. Muslims consider Mehmet's tomb a very holy site. It's inevitably filled with worshippers.

The grassed outer courtyard of the mosque is a favourite place for locals to congregate and for families to picnic, especially on Sunday. On Wednesday both the courtyard and the surrounding streets host a weekly market selling fresh produce and clothing.

FETHİYE CAMİİ Map p281

Mosque of Victory; Fethiye Kapısı; Ferry from Eminönü, bus 99, 99A, 36CE, 44B & 399B/C/D from Eminönü, bus 55T from Taksim Square (Fener)

The Fethiye Camii was built in the 12th century as the Church of the Theotokos Pammakaristos or Church of the Joyous Mother of God. It is usually closed so if you want to enter you'll need to organise a time with the **caretaker at Aya Sofya** (☎ 212-522 0989).

The original monastery church was added to several over the centuries before being converted to a mosque in 1573 to commemorate Sultan Murat III's victories in Georgia and Azerbaijan. Before its conversion it served as the headquarters of the Ecumenical Orthodox Patriarch (1456–1568); not long after the conquest of the city Mehmet the Conqueror visited to discuss theological questions with Patriarch Gennadios. They talked in the side chapel known as the parecclesion, which has been restored to its former Byzantine splendour and functions as a museum; the rest of the building remains a mosque. Though not as splendid as those in the nearby Kariye Müzesi, the build-ing's Byzantine mosaics have been beautifully restored and are well worth seeing, particularly the Pantocrator and 12 Prophets adorning the dome, and the Christ Hyperagathos with the Virgin and St John the Baptist in the apse.

KARİYE MÜZESİ Map p281

Chora Church; ☎ 212-631 9241; Kariye Camii Sokak, Edirnekapı; admission €5.50; ⊙ 9am-4.30pm Thu-Tue; bus 28, 36KE & 86 from Eminönü, bus 87 from Taksim Square (Edirnekapı)

This building was once named Chora Church, or the Church of the Holy Saviour Outside the Walls. 'Chora' literally means 'Country' and the first church on this site was indeed outside the city walls built by Constantine the Great. But the Church of the Holy Saviour was soon engulfed by Byzantine urban sprawl and enclosed within the walls built by the Emperor Theodosius II in 413, less than 100 years after Constantine. So it was only in the country for about 80 years and has been in the city for nearly 1600!

It was not only the environs of the church that changed. For four centuries the building served as a mosque (Kariye Camii), but it's now a museum. What you see today is not the original church-outside the-walls. Rather, this one was built in the late 11th century, with reworking in the succeeding centuries. Virtually all of the interior decoration – the famous mosaics and the less-renowned but equally striking frescoes –

Kariye Müzesi (above)

dates from 1312 and was funded by Theodore Metochites, a man of letters who was auditor of the Treasury under Andronikos II (between 1282 and 1328). One of the museum's most wonderful mosaics (map item 48), found above the door to the nave in the inner narthex, depicts Theodore offering the church to Christ.

The mosaics, which depict the lives of Christ and Mary, are stunning. See the plan below. Look out for the Khalke Jesus (map item J33), which shows Christ and Mary with two donors – Prince Isaac Komnenos and Melane, daughter of Mikhael Palaiologos VIII. This is under the right dome in the inner narthex. On the dome itself is a stunning depiction of Jesus and his ancestors (the Genealogy of Christ; map item 27). On the narthex's left dome is a serenely beautiful mosaic of Mary and the Child Jesus surrounded by her ancestors (map item G34).

In the nave are three mosaics: of Christ (map item 50c), of Mary and the child Jesus (map item 50b) and of the Dormition (Assumption; map item 50a) of the Blessed Virgin – turn around to see this, it's over the main door you just entered. The 'infant' being held by Jesus is actually Mary's soul.

To the right of the nave is the parecclesion, a side chapel built to hold the tombs of the church's founder and his relatives, close friends and associates. It is decorated with frescoes that deal with the themes of death and resurrection, depicting scenes taken from the Old Testament. The striking painting in the apse known as the Anastasis (map item L) shows a powerful Christ raising Adam and Eve out of their sarcophagi, with saints and kings in attendance. The gates of hell are shown under Christ's feet. Less majestic but no less beautiful are the frescoes (map item U) adorning the dome, which show Mary and 12 attendant angels.

Though no one knows for certain, it is thought that the frescoes were painted by the same masters who created the mosaics. Theirs is an extraordinary accomplishment, as the paintings, with their sophisticated use of perspective and exquisitely portrayed facial expressions, rival those painted by the Italian master Giotto, the painter who more than any other ushered in the Italian Renaissance.

Between 1948 and 1959 the decoration was carefully restored under the auspices of the Byzantine Society of America. Plaster and whitewash covering the mosaics and frescoes was removed and the works were cleaned. Unfortunately, the mosaics seem to be in need

KARİYE MÜZESİ

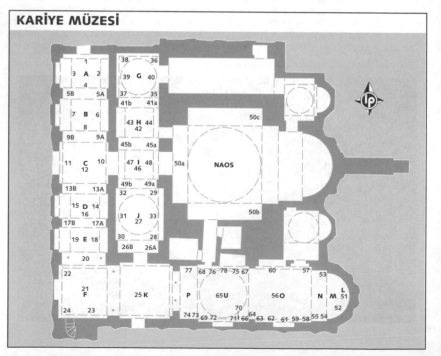

of further work today, with damp appearing under the Perspex covers on some of the outer narthex's examples.

This is one of the city's best museums and deserves an extended visit. On leaving, we highly recommend sampling the delectable Ottoman menu at the **Asitane restaurant** (p154), which is under the next-door **Kariye Oteli**. Alternatively, a quick snack (*tost* €2.20) or Turkish coffee (€1.60) can be enjoyed at the **Kariye Pembe Köşk** (p154) in the plaza overlooking the museum.

Finally, a plea: despite signs clearly prohibiting the use of flashes in the museum, many visitors wilfully ignore this rule. Please don't do the same – the future of these exquisite and delicate mosaics and frescoes, acknowledged to be among the most important surviving examples of Byzantine art in the world, is at stake!

MİHRİMAH SULTAN CAMİİ Map p281
Ali Kuşçu Sokak, Edirnekapı; bus 28, 36KE & 86 from Eminönü, bus 87 from Taksim Square (Edirnekapı)
The great Sinan put his stamp on the entire city at this mosque, constructed in the 1560s next to the Edirnekapı section of Theodosius'

great wall, is one of his best works. Commissioned by Süleyman the Magnificent's favourite daughter, Mihrimah, it was undergoing major restoration at the time of research. The mosque is noted for its delicate stained-glass windows and its large interior space, made particularly light by its 19 windows in each arched tympanum. The mosque occupies the highest point in the city and its dome and one slender minaret are major adornments to the city skyline; they are particularly prominent on the road from Edirne.

ST MARY OF THE MONGOLS Map p281
Tevkii Cafer Mektebi Sokak, Fener; ferry from Eminönü, bus 99, 99A, 36CE, 44B & 399B/C/D from Eminönü, bus 55T from Taksim Square (Fener)
History buffs will find a visit here more satisfying than those specifically interested in architecture, as this squat red-brick church is quite unprepossessing from the outside and an unfortunate exercise in ecclesiastical decorative overkill inside. Historically, though, is extremely significant, being the only Byzantine church in İstanbul which has not, at some

stage or another, been in Ottoman hands. It was consecrated in the 13th century and saved from conversion into a mosque by the personal decree of Mehmet the Conqueror. If you ring the bell on the outside gate you may attract the attention of the caretaker, who is usually happy to show visitors the church in exchange for a tip.

SULTAN SELIM CAMİİ Map p281

Mosque of Yavuz Selim; Yavuz Selim Caddesi; ☯ tomb 9.30am-4.30pm Tue-Sun; ferry from Eminönü, bus 99, 99A, 36CE, 44B & 399B/C/D from Eminönü, bus 55T from Taksim Square (Fener)

By all accounts the sultan to whom this mosque was dedicated (Süleyman the Magnificent's father, Selim I, known as 'the Grim') was a nasty piece of work. He is famous for having his father poisoned and for killing two of his brothers, six of his nephews and three of his own sons. Odd, then, that his mosque is one of the most loved in the city. The reason becomes clear when a visit reveals the mosque's position on a lawned terrace with spectacular views of the Golden Horn. Picnic spots don't come much better than this. The building itself, constructed in 1522, is a bit run-down, but is well used by local worshippers. Inside, its tilework and painted woodwork provide its most distinctive features.

TEKFUR SARAYI Map p281

Palace of the Sovereign, Palace of Constantine Porphyrogenitus; Hocaçakır Caddesi; bus 28, 36KE & 86 from Eminönü, bus 87 from Taksim Square (Edirnekapı)

Sacred buildings often endure because they continue to be used, even though they may be converted for use in another religion. Put simply, there's something a bit iffy about razing a place of worship and not too many people want to do it. No such squeamishness surrounds secular buildings such as palaces, though, and history shows that these are often torn down and rebuilt to cater to the tastes and needs of different generations. İstanbul is no different – the Byzantine palaces that once crowded Sultanahmet Square are all gone, so is the great Palace of Blachernae, which was also in this neighbourhood. Only the Tekfur Sarayı remains.

Though the building is only a shell these days, it is remarkably preserved considering its great age. Built in the late 13th or early 14th century and located close to the end of Theodosius' wall, it was a large three-storeyed palace that may have been an annex of the Palace of Blachernae. Later uses were not so regal: after the Conquest it functioned in turn as a menagerie for exotic wild animals, a brothel and a poorhouse for destitute Jews.

To see it, wander into the sportsground next door. The site itself is fenced.

Barbara Nadel's İstanbul

Çetin İkmen is a typical Turkish male. He smokes like a chimney, is unfailingly courteous to strangers and dotes on his children. Unlike the rest of his compatriots he also happens to be an Inspector in the İstanbul Police Department, a devotee of the brandy bottle and the possessor of special powers of divination passed down from his Albanian mother, who was known in her local neighbourhood of Scutari as being a witch. His sexy sidekick, Mehmet Suleyman, comes from a privileged Ottoman background, is as sensitive and intelligent as he is attractive, but is strangely unhappy despite possessing these palpable assets. Together, they form a successful but unorthodox crime-solving team gracing the pages of Barbara Nadel's wonderful series of İkmen crime novels.

Nadel is a British writer who knows İstanbul well and loves it with a passion. Her six İkman novels to date are all set in the city and conjure up its neighbourhoods with extraordinary colour and detail. In *Belshazzar's Daughter*, the first of the series, most of the action is in Balat and Beyoğlu; in *A Chemical Prison* (Nadel's favourite of all of the books) it's in the area around Topkapı Palace. The subsequent titles – *Arabesk, Deep Waters, Harem* – all lovingly evoke different areas of the city.

There is one part of the city that Nadel finds particularly fascinating – the old Jewish quarter of Balat. It featured in her first novel, reappears in her most recent title, *Petrified*, and is bound to pop up again, as her upcoming novel *(Deadly Web)* has İkman's much-loved daughter and ever-present character, Hulya, marrying a Jewish friend of the family and moving to Balat. When walking around the suburb, scenes from *Petrified* are immediately called to mind. The Church of St Stephen of the Bulgars where Russian villain Valery Rostov stages a fake drug drop to humiliate the police; the residential quarter around the Great School and the Church of St Mary of the Mongols where artist Melih Akdeniz and his family live; the junkyard near the rear of the Hotel Daphnis where Eren Akdeniz gives the police the slip – all of these sites are easy to identify and testify to Nadel's extensive on-the-ground research.

Nadel is setting the novel after *Deadly Web* in Cappadocia, but is on record as saying that İkman will be back on his usual patch after that. Fans of the novels and of the city will be greatly relieved to hear it.

THE WALLS

Since being built in the 5th century, Theodosius' city walls have been breached by hostile forces only twice. The first time was in the 13th century, when Byzantium's 'allies', the armies of the Fourth Crusade, broke through and pillaged the town, deposing the emperor and setting up a king of their own. The second time was in 1453 under Mehmet the Conqueror. Even though Mehmet was ultimately successful, he was continually frustrated during the siege as the walls admirably withstood even the heaviest bombardments by the largest cannon then in existence.

The walls were kept defensible and in good repair until about a century ago, when the development of mighty naval guns made such expense for security purposes pointless: If İstanbul was going to fall, it would fall to ships firing from the Bosphorus, not to soldiers advancing on the land walls.

During the late 1980s, the city started to rebuild the major gates and walls. Debates raged in the Turkish newspapers over the style of the reconstruction. Some said the restorations were too theatrical, with no basis in accepted conservation practice, while others said that if the walls never actually did look like that, perhaps they should have. The gates that have been completed include the Topkapı (Cannon), Mevlanakapı and Belgratkapı. Sights along the walls include the Marble Tower, the ruins of a small Byzantine imperial seaside villa on the Sea of Marmara; Yedikule fortress (below); and **Tekfur Sarayı** (opposite).

It's possible to spend a day walking on top of or beside the walls all the way from Yedikule to Ayvansaray on the Golden Horn (6.5km). Be warned, though, that the walls are in a bad condition in many spots and go through some less-than-salubrious neighbourhoods. Don't consider doing this walk by yourself – there are packs of dogs outside the municipal dog pound up the hill from the start of the walls at the Marble Tower; and vagrants living in the wall's cavities along its length who have been known to rob and assault passers-by.

Transport

Yedikule is a long way from most other sights in İstanbul and involves a special trip. Situated where the great city walls meet the Sea of Marmara, it's accessible by cheap train from Sirkeci. Take any suburban train (banliyö tren) and hop off at Yedikule, which is the fifth stop – it's a 15-minute trip and will cost a mere €0.50. Turn left as you come out of the station and walk about 500m to the entrance of the castle. You can also take bus 80 (Yedikule) from Eminönü, bus 80B from Beyazıt or bus 80T from Taksim. These don't run often (approximately every 40 minutes). The bus stop is on the opposite side of the small park in front of the castle.

YEDİKULE HISARI MÜZESİ Map pp276-7

Fortress of the Seven Towers; ☎ 212-585 8933; Kule Meydanı 4, Yedikule; train from Sirkeci to Yedikule station or bus 80 from Eminönü, bus 80B from Beyazıt or bus 80T from Taksim

If you arrived in İstanbul by train from Europe, or if you rode in from the airport along the seashore, you would have already had a glance at this fortress, which looms over the southern approaches to the city. One of the city's major landmarks, it has a history as impressive as its massive structure.

In the late 4th century Theodosius I built a triumphal arch here. When the next Theodosius (r 408–50) built his great land walls, he incorporated the arch in the structure. Four of the fortress' seven towers were built as part of Theodosius II's walls; the other three, which are inside the walls, were added by Mehmet the Conqueror. Under the Byzantines, the great arch became known as the **Porta Aurea** (Golden Gate), and was used for triumphal state processions into and out of the city. For a time its gates were indeed plated with gold. The doorway was sealed in the late Byzantine period.

In Ottoman times the fortress was used for defence, as a repository for the Imperial Treasury, a prison and a place of execution. In times of war, ambassadors of 'enemy' countries were thrown in prisons; for foreign ambassadors to the Sublime Porte, Yedikule was that prison. Latin and German inscriptions still visible in the Ambassadors' Tower bring the place's eerie history to light. It was also here that Sultan Osman II, a 17-year-old youth, was executed in 1622 during a revolt of the janissary corps. The kaftan he was wearing when he was murdered is now on display in Topkapı Palace's costumes collection.

The spectacular views from the battlements are the highlight of a visit here. The fortress was being restored at the time of research and was closed to visitors. When it re-opens there will be an entrance charge and dedicated opening hours.

NORTH OF THE GOLDEN HORN

Eating p155; Shopping p194; Sleeping p210

Across the Galata Bridge from Eminönü is Beyoğlu, old Pera. The main artery of Beyoğlu starts at its busy nerve centre, Taksim Square, and makes its way down İstiklal Caddesi through Tünel and Karaköy to the Galata Bridge. Or you can walk across the Galata Bridge from Eminönü and up the steep hill through Karaköy and Tünel to İstiklal Caddesi and on to Taksim Square.

Beyoğlu (*bey*-oh-loo), the 'new' or 'European' section of İstanbul on the northern side of the Golden Horn, is not really new. There was a settlement on the northern shore of the Golden Horn, near Karaköy Square (Karaköy Meydanı), before the birth of Christ. By the time of Theodosius II (r 408–50), the settlement was large enough to become an official suburb of Constantinople. Theodosius built a fortress here, no doubt to complete the defence system of his great land walls, and called it Galata, as the suburb was then the home of many Galatians, who used it as a trading base.

In the 19th century, new ideas brought from Europe by traders and diplomats walked into Ottoman daily life down the streets of Pera and Galata. The Europeans who lived in Pera imported new fashions, machines, arts and manners to the city. This part of town had telephones, underground trains (Tünel), tramways, electric light and modern municipal government. There were even European-style patisseries and shopping arcades. In contrast, Old İstanbul (Stamboul), on the south bank of the Golden Horn, kept its oriental bazaars, great mosques, draughty palaces, narrow streets and traditional values, and seemed almost to be living in the Middle Ages when compared with its sophisticated neighbour.

Eventually the sultans followed Pera's lead and the upper classes followed the sultans. From the reign of Abdül Mecit (r 1839–61) onwards, no sultan lived in Mehmet the Conqueror's palace at Topkapı. Rather, they built opulent European-style palaces in Pera and along the shores of the Bosphorus to the north.

Beyoğlu holds the architectural evidence of the Ottoman Empire's frantic attempts to modernise and reform itself, and the evidence of the European powers' attempts to undermine and subvert it. As the Ottomans struggled to keep their sprawling, ramshackle empire together, the European diplomats in the great embassies of Pera were jockeying for domination of the entire Middle East. They wanted to control its holy places, its sea lanes through the Suez Canal to India and especially its oil, already important at that time.

In this book, we have divided Pera into two sections: the first covers the areas of Karaköy (old Galata) and Tünel; and the second covers Pera's grand boulevard, İstiklal Caddesi (p120) and its surrounds. Nearby suburbs on the opposite side of Taksim Square and on the Bosphorus are covered in the neighbourhoods Taksim, Harbiye & Nişantaşı (p122) and Beşiktaş & Ortaköy (p123).

BEYOĞLU – GALATA BRIDGE TO İSTIKLAL CADDESİ

In order to avoid 'contamination' of their way of life, both the later Byzantine emperors and the Ottoman sultans relegated Genoese traders to offices and residences in Galata, now called Karaköy. The traders built a triangular-shaped fortification that stretched from a point near the Galata Bridge, over to where the Atatürk Bridge is today, and up to a higher point on the slope, where they built the Galata Tower, one of the major adornments to today's city skyline.

From the 16th century onwards, Galata had a largely Jewish population, hence the number of synagogues in the neighbourhood. In the 19th century, European émigrés arrived and built grandiose churches, schools and bank buildings – all reminders of the time when most of the empire's bankers and businesspeople were non-Muslims.

By the end of the last century, though, Galata developed a reputation as being an unsavoury neighbourhood. The city's largest municipal brothel was here, as well as drinking dens, vagrants and street prostitution. Times have changed, though, and these days the inexorable process of gentrification is under way, with tatty but grand apartment buildings being restored, and the city's artistic and student communities frequenting its bars, cafés and clubs, working in studios and living in its apartment blocks. Some commercial offices and banks, as well as small traders, also remain.

Orientation

At the Beyoğlu end of the Galata Bridge, you'll find the busy ferry and shipping docks, a small fish market and the docks for Mediterranean cruise ships. At the Karaköy end of the Galata Bridge there are busy bus stops, *dolmuş* queues and the lower station of the Tünel, a short underground railway built by French engineers in 1875. Said to be the shortest and oldest underground railway in Europe, the Tünel allowed European merchants to get from their offices in Galata to their homes in Pera without hiking up the steep hillside. The decorative tiles and murals at its two stations are certainly reminiscent of Pera in its heyday. The Tünel gives its name to the suburb surrounding its upper stop.

To the east of Karaköy is Tophane, home to the waterside Nusretiye Camii and the city's most popular pocket of nargileh cafés. Frantically busy Necatibey Caddesi merges into Kemeraltı Caddesi just west of Tophane, then into Yüzbaşı Sabahattin Evren Caddesi and finally Tersane Caddesi before meeting the Atatürk Bridge.

Transport

Galata's own underground railway only travels one stop, from Yüzbaşı Sabahattin Evren Caddesi in Karaköy to Tünel Square at the foot of İstiklal Caddesi. The service runs every five or 10 minutes from 7am to 10pm daily (from 7.30am on Sunday) and the fare is €0.35. Akbil (p239) can be used. Those who are unfit or disabled should seriously consider taking the Tünel rather than attempting the steep walk from the bridge up to İstiklal Caddesi.

Buses going south from Taksim Square stop at Karaköy, including the convenient T4 bus that runs to and from Sultanahmet. There are ferry services to and from Üsküdar and Kadıköy leaving from west (Üsküdar) and east (Kadıköy) of the Galata Bridge.

ARAP CAMİİ Map pp284-6

Arab Mosque; Galata Mahkemesi Sokak, Karaköy; ferry Karaköy, bus T4 from Sultanahmet or Taksim Square (Karaköy)

This mosque is the only surviving place of worship built by the Genoese; it was the largest of the Latin churches in the city. Dating from 1337, it was converted to a mosque by Spanish Moors in the 16th century. It has a simple plan – long hall, tall square belfry-cum-minaret – with ornate flourishes such as the galleries added in the 20th century. Look for an attendant if the mosque is locked; he may be willing to show you its interior in exchange for a tip.

AZAPKAPI SOKOLLU MEHMET PAŞA CAMİİ & SEBIL Map pp284-6

Tersane Caddesi, Karaköy; ferry Karaköy, bus T4 from Sultanahmet or Taksim Square (Karaköy)

This pretty mosque, designed by Sinan and built in 1577, is unusual in that it and the minaret are raised on a platform. Like Sinan's Rüstem Paşa Camii over the Golden Horn (also on a raised platform), it was commissioned by Sokollu Mehmet Paşa, a grand vizier of Süleyman the Magnificent. Today it's overshadowed by the approach to Atatürk Bridge and seems

to almost shrink back from the traffic mayhem of Tersane Caddesi. Still, it's well worth a visit, particularly for its fine marble mihrab and *mimber*. Look for the attendant if the mosque is locked; a tip is expected. Don't miss the nearby rococo fountain *(sebil)* built by Saliha Valide Hatun, mother of Mahmut I.

CHRIST CHURCH Map pp284-6

☎ 212-241 5616; Serdarı Ekrem Sokak 82-84, Tünel; ☽ prayer times 9-10am & 6-7pm, 10am Sun for communion; ferry Karaköy, bus T4 from Sultanahmet or Taksim Square (Karaköy)

Designed by CE Street (who also did London's Law Courts), the cornerstone of this Anglican church was laid in 1858 by Lord Stratford de Redcliffe, known as 'The Great Elchi' (*elçi*,

Beyoğlu Top Five

- İstiklal Caddesi (p120)
- Mevlevi Monastery (p118)
- Galata Tower (p118)
- Çiçek Pasajı (p120)
- Azapkapı Sokollu Mehmet Paşa Camii & Sebil (left)

meaning ambassador) because of his paramount influence in mid-19th-century Ottoman affairs. The church, dedicated in 1868 as the Crimean Memorial Church, is the largest of the city's Protestant churches. It was restored and renamed in the mid-1990s.

CHURCH OF SS PETER & PAUL
Map pp284-6

SS Pierre et Paul; ☎ 212-249 2385; Galata Kulesi Sokak 44, Karaköy; ۞ mass 7.30am daily & 11am Sun (in Italian); ferry Karaköy, bus T4 from Sultanahmet or Taksim Square (Karaköy)

Tucked away in one of the steep streets below Galata Tower you'll find the small grey-and-white doorway to the courtyard of the Church of SS Peter and Paul. A Dominican church originally stood on this site, but the building you see today dates from the mid-19th century. It's the work of the Fossati brothers who also designed the Dutch and Russian consulate buildings (both in Beyoğlu). Like many other Latin churches in the city, its courtyard design reflects the Ottoman ruling that Latin churches could not be built directly fronting onto a road or on top of a hill (the Church of St Mary Draperis on İstiklal Caddesi is another example of this). The church backs onto a section of the Genoese fortifications. It's not open very often – ring the bell and try your luck.

GALATA TOWER Map pp284-6

Galata Kulesi; Galata Meydanı, Karaköy; admission €3.80; ۞ 9am-8pm; ferry Karaköy, bus T4 from Sultanahmet or Taksim Square (Karaköy)

The cylindrical Galata Tower, originally constructed in 1348, was the high point in the Genoese fortifications of Galata, and has been rebuilt many times. It has survived a number of earthquakes, as well as the demolition of the rest of the Genoese walls in the mid-19th century. It now holds a forgettable restaurant/nightclub that smells of school dinners and hosts busloads of package-tour travellers who have been duped into thinking that this is the best spot to trip the İstanbul light fantastic. Guests dress up as sultans and sultanas and are entertained by a cabaret singer and belly dancer. If you're in a masochistic mood, the number for reservations is ☎ 212-293 8180. Fortunately there's a pleasant **cafeteria** (tea €0.75, beer €2.50) on the 8th floor where you can enjoy a drink. There's also a vertiginous **panorama balcony** offering spectacular 360° views of the city.

The paved **public square** surrounding the tower was created by the municipality as part

Galata Tower (below)

of the ongoing Beyoğlu Beautification Project and it's been a big hit with locals of all ages, who gather each day to play soccer or backgammon, drink tea, buy food from the street vendors and swap local news.

KAMONDO STAIRS & SCHNEIDERTEMPEL ART CENTRE
Map pp284-6

ferry Karaköy, bus T4 from Sultanahmet or Taksim Square (Karaköy)

The curvaceous 18th-century Kamondo Stairs, one of Beyoğlu's most distinctive pieces of urban design, run south from Kart Çınar Sokak. Around the corner from the stairs you'll find the **Schneidertempel Art Centre** (p181). This art gallery, which is housed in a modest former synagogue, hosts shows of Jewish art, usually contemporary and local in origin.

MEVLEVİ MONASTERY Map pp284-6

Museum of Court Literature, Divan Edebiyatı Müzesi; ☎ 212-245 4141; Galipdede Caddesi 15, Tünel; admission €0.55; ۞ 9.30am-4.30pm Wed-Mon; ferry Karaköy, bus T4 from Sultanahmet or Taksim Square (Karaköy), Tünel from Karaköy

If you thought the Hare Krishnas or the Harlem congregations were the only religious orders to celebrate their faith through music and movement, think again. Those sultans of spiritual spin known as the Whirling Dervishes have been twirling their way to a higher plane ever since the 13th century and show no sign of slowing down soon.

The Mevlevi *tarikat* (order), founded in Konya during the 13th century, flourished throughout the Ottoman Empire. Like several other orders, the Mevlevis stressed the unity of humankind before God regardless of creed.

The Whirling Dervishes took their name from the great Sufi mystic and poet, Celaleddin Rumi (1207–73), called Mevlana (Our Leader) by his disciples. Sufis seek mystical communion with God through various means. For Mevlana, it was through a *sema* (ceremony) involving chants, prayers, music and a whirling dance. The whirling induced a trancelike state that made it easier for the mystic to seek spiritual union with God.

Dervish orders were banned in the early days of the Turkish republic because of their ultraconservative religious politics. Although the ban has been lifted, only a handful of functioning *tekkesi* (dervish lodges) remain in İstanbul, including this one. Konya remains the heart of the Mevlevi order. For more information check www.emav.org.

The museum was originally a *Mevlevihanesi* (Whirling Dervish hall) and a meeting place for Mevlevi (whirling) dervishes. The modest *tekke* was restored between 1967 and 1972, but the first building here was erected by a high officer in the court of Sultan Beyazıt II in 1491. Its first *şeyh* (sheik) was Mohammed Şemai Sultan Divani, a grandson of the great Mevlana. The building burned in 1766, but was repaired that same year by Sultan Mustafa III.

Nowadays this former monastery has become a slightly run-down compound with overgrown gardens and shady nooks. As you approach the *tekke*, notice the graveyard on the left and its stones with graceful Ottoman inscriptions. The shapes atop the stones reflect the headgear of the deceased, each hat denoting a different religious rank. The tomb of Galip Dede, the 17th-century Sufi poet who the street was named after, is here. Note also the tomb of the sheik by the entrance passage and the ablutions fountain.

Inside the *tekke* the central area was for the whirling *sema*, while the galleries above were for visitors. Separate areas were set aside for the orchestra and for female visitors (who were concealed behind the lattices). These days the upstairs area is only for the musicians who play during the ceremony. In the display cases surrounding the central area, there are also exhibits of Mevlevi calligraphy, writing and musical instruments.

NEVE SHALOM SYNAGOGUE
Map pp284-6

☎ 212-293 7566; Büyük Hendek Caddesi 61, Karaköy; ferry Karaköy, bus T4 from Sultanahmet or Taksim Square (Karaköy)

During the 19th century, Galata had a large Sephardic Jewish population and a number of synagogues. Most of this community has now moved to other residential areas in the city, but the synagogues remain. Tragically, this building in particular seems to have become a target for anti-Jewish extremists and it has suffered two attacks in recent decades – a brutal massacre by Arab gunmen during the summer of 1986 and a 2003 car bomb attack carried out by a motley group of Turkish Muslims inspired by Osama bin Laden, which killed 23, injured over 300 and caused extensive damage to the building. It's a depressing testament to the intolerance that all-too-often afflicts our world.

Seeing the Dervishes Whirl

Even in Ottoman times, Galata's *Mevlevihanesi* was open to all who wished to witness the *sema*, including foreign, non-Muslim visitors. Though banned for a short period in the 1920s by Atatürk, the tradition remained strong and continues today. It is a highlight for many visitors to the city.

The dervishes whirl at 5pm every Sunday from May to October, and at 3pm from November to April. The performance (adult/student €11.10/8.30) lasts for 90 minutes, starting with a live performance of Sufi music. It's a good idea to buy tickets from the monastery a few days beforehand as the shows get booked up. Make sure you arrive early and enter the *tekke* as soon as the door is opened so that you can get a seat. The best seats are those near the rear windows, on the opposite side to the entrance. There is also a performance in the exhibition hall on platform 1 at Sirkeci Railway Station near Sultanahmet at 7.30pm every Sunday, Wednesday and Friday. Phone ☎ 212-458 8834 for information and to make bookings.

Remember that the ceremony is a religious one – by whirling, the adherents believe that they are attaining a higher union with God – so don't talk, leave your seat or take flash photographs while the dervishes are spinning.

BEYOĞLU – ON & AROUND İSTİKLAL CADDESİ

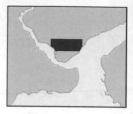

İstiklal Caddesi (Independence Ave) was formerly the Grande Rue de Pera. Home to the city's smartest shops, several large embassies and churches, many impressive residential buildings and a scattering of fashionable teashops and restaurants, it was *the* place to be seen in European İstanbul. However, all this changed after independence, as the glamorous shops and restaurants closed, the grand buildings became dilapidated and the surrounds took on a decidedly sleazy air. Fortunately, the new millennium has brought about a rebirth, and the boulevard is once again crowded with throngs of locals who come to eat in the atmosphere-laden restaurants, drink in the bars and clubs that line the side streets and browse in the hundreds of shops crammed along its length. This *Zeitgeist* can be attributed to the inspired Beyoğlu Beautification Project, an initiative that has been steered by the municipality. This initiative has led to the street becoming a pedestrian thoroughfare, security being a focus, buildings being restored and awnings and street signage conforming to rigid urban design specifications (all shop signs are in gold, for instance).

Orientation

İstiklal Caddesi stretches between Tünel and Taksim Squares. To the northwest of Tünel is the area known as Asmalımescit, filled with meyhanes, stylish Western-style brasseries and art galleries. Tepebaşı, the pocket that is home to the famous Pera Palas Oteli (Pera Palace Hotel), is behind Asmalımescit.

Midway along the boulevard is Galatasaray Square, occupied since 1868 by its namesake, the Galatasaray Lycée. This school was established by Sultan Abdül Aziz, who wanted a place where students could listen to lectures in both Turkish and French. Today it's a prestigious public school. On the opposite side of the street are the Çiçek Pasajı (Flower Passage), busy Balık Pazar (fish market) and Nevizade Sokak, the most famous restaurant strip in the city.

To the east and south of the lycée are the areas known as Çukurcuma and Cihangir. Çukurcuma is where you'll find many of the city's best antique shops and Cihangir is an upmarket residential area where trendy bars and cafés are starting to sprout.

ÇİÇEK PASAJI Map pp284-6
Bus T4 from Sultanahmet to Taksim Square

Back in the days when the *Orient Express* was rolling into Old Stamboul and promenading down İstiklal Caddesi was the fashionable thing to do (how little things change…), the Cité de Pera building was the most glamorous address in town. Built in 1876 and decorated in Second Empire style, it housed a shopping arcade as well as apartments. As Pera declined, so too did the building, its stylish shops giving way to cheap restaurant-taverns, where in good weather beer barrels were rolled out onto the pavement, marble slabs were balanced on top, wooden stools were arranged and enthusiastic revellers caroused the night away. Renamed Çiçek Pasajı (Flower Passage), it continued in this vein until the late 1970s, when parts of the building collapsed. When it was reconstructed, the passage was 'beautified'. That is, its makeshift barrel heads and stools were replaced with comfortable and solid wooden tables and benches, and its broken pavement was covered with smooth tiles. The passage also acquired a glass canopy to protect pedestrians from foul weather.

Transport

A quaint antique tram rattles its way up and down İstiklal Caddesi daily, beginning its journey just outside the Tünel station and stopping once at Galatasaray Square before ending at Taksim Square. Tickets are not available on board – you must use an Akbil or purchase a ticket (€0.35) from the Tünel station.

Regular buses run to and from Eminönü, and the T4 bus travels to Taksim Square from Sultanahmet and back again every 30 minutes (approx) from 7.15am to 10pm.

Making its Markiz

In Pera's heyday, there was no more glamorous spot to be seen than Patisserie Lebon in the Grand Rue de Pera (now İstiklal Caddesi). *The* place to enjoy gateaux and gossip, it was favoured by the city's European elite, who dressed to kill when they popped in for afternoon tea. Noting this, tailors, furriers and milliners opened shops in the adjoining Passage Orientale and did a brisk trade, making it the city's most exclusive retail precinct.

Part of the patisserie's attraction was its gorgeous Art-Nouveau interior. Four large tiled wall panels had been designed around the theme of the four seasons by Alexandre Vallaury, the architect of the Pera Palas Oteli, and were created in France. Unfortunately, only two (Autumn and Spring) survived the trip from France – they have adorned the walls ever since. With chandeliers, fragile china, gleaming wooden furniture and decorative tiled floor, the place was as stylish as its clientele.

In 1940 the Lebon was taken over by Avedis Çakır, who renamed it Patisserie Markiz. It continued to trade until the 1960s, when Pera's decline and a lack of customers led to its closure. Fortunately, closure didn't mean destruction – the building was boarded up and left just as it had been, fittings and all. In the 1970s, local artists and writers lobbied the authorities to have the patisserie and passage added to the country's register of historical buildings; this occurred in 1977, ensuring the entire building's preservation.

In late 2003 the patisserie and the passage re-opened as the Passage and Patisserie Markiz. Exclusive European labels feature in the shops and there are cafés, a brasserie and a bar along its super-stylish length. Best of all, the **patisserie** (p157) fronting İstiklal Caddesi has been magnificently restored and is once again serving delicious gateaux and tea to İstanbul's elite. Long may it continue to do so!

These days its raffish charm is nearly gone and locals in the know bypass the touts and the mediocre food on offer here and make their way behind the passage to İstanbul's most colourful and popular eating precinct, **Nevizade Sokak** (p158).

Next to the Çiçek Pasajı you'll find Sahne Sokak, the heart of Beyoğlu's **Balık Pazar** (Fish Market), where small stands sell *midye* (skewered mussels) fried in hot oil (get a skewer that's been freshly cooked). You'll also find stalls selling fruit, vegetables, pickles and other produce here.

At 24A Sahne Sokak, look for the gigantic black doors to the courtyard of the **Üç Horan Ermeni Kilisesi** (Armenian Church of Three Altars). Visitors can enter the church providing the doors are open. Opposite the church are the neoclassical **Avrupa Pasajı** (European Passage or *Aynalı Pasajı* – Arcade of Mirrors), a small gallery with marble paving and shops selling tourist wares and some antique goods, and **Aslıhan Pasajı**, an arcade jampacked with second-hand book and record stalls.

PERA PALAS OTELİ Map pp284-6
Pera Palace Hotel; Meşrutiyet Caddesi 98-100,
Tepebaşı; bus T4 from Sultanahmet to Taksim Square
The **Pera Palas** (p211) was built by Georges Nagelmackers, the Belgian entrepreneur who founded the *Compagnie Internationale des Wagons-Lits et Grands Express Européens* in 1868. Nagelmackers, who had succeeded in linking Paris and Constantinople by luxury

train with his famed *Orient Express*, found that once he had transported his esteemed passengers to the Ottoman imperial capital, there was no suitable place for them to stay. What was Nagelmackers to do? Why, build a new luxury hotel of course!

The hotel opened in 1892 and advertised itself as having 'a thoroughly healthy situation, being high up and isolated on all four sides', and 'overlooking the Golden Horn and the whole panorama of Stamboul'. Numbered among its guests were Agatha Christie, who supposedly wrote *Murder on the Orient Express* in Room 411; Mata Hari, who no doubt frequented the elegant bar with its lovely stained-glass windows and excellent eavesdropping opportunities; and Greta Garbo, who probably enjoyed her own company in one of the spacious suites.

Though it's looking a bit worn these days, the Pera Palas is a living memory of what life was like in İstanbul a century ago. Hotel staff are happy to show visitors Room 101, where the legendary Atatürk often stayed. It has been preserved as a museum, so if you're keen to see mementos of the great leader, such as his slippers and silk pyjamas, this is the place to do it. Also worth a gawk are the superb restaurant areas, with their soaring ceilings, chandeliers and rich furnishings – and let's not forget the gilded birdcage lift. It's worth having a coffee at the patisserie or a drink at the bar to take in the hotel's atmosphere.

TAKSİM, HARBİYE & NİŞANTAŞI

If you're a dab hand at air-kissing and striking attitudes over a caffe latte, these are the suburbs for you. Whether you're after İstanbul's hippest hotel, most expensive designer clothes shops or most indulgent beauty parlours, you'll find what you want in these leafy and exclusive suburbs.

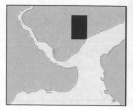

Orientation

To the south of Taksim Square is the landmark Marmara Hotel. To the north is the Taksim Gezi Yeri (Taksim Parkı or Promenade), with the Ceylan InterContinental İstanbul hotel at its northern end.

From Taksim Square, busy Cumhuriyet Caddesi (Republic Ave) leads north past banks, travel agencies, airline offices, nightclubs and luxury hotels to the upmarket districts of Harbiye and Nişantaşı. Harbiye is home to the Turkish war college and its military museum, and Nişantaşı is an upmarket shopping district that incorporates Teşvikiye Caddesi and so is often referred to as Teşvikiye around that spot.

ASKERI MÜZESI Map p287

Military Museum; ☎ 212-233 2720; Vali Konağı Caddesi, Harbiye; adult/student €1.10/0.40, camera €2.20, video €4.40; ⏱ 9am-5pm Wed-Sun; any bus travelling north up Cumhuriyet Caddesi from Taksim Square, bus 66, 70FE, 70KE, 74 or 74A from Eminönü

For a rousing museum experience, present yourself at this splendid institution located 1km north of Taksim in Harbiye. Try to visit in the afternoon so that you can enjoy the concert given by the Mehter, the medieval Ottoman Military Band, which occurs between 3pm and 4pm daily.

The large museum is spread over two floors. On the ground floor are displays of weapons, a 'martyrs' gallery (şehit galerisi) with artefacts from fallen Turkish soldiers of many wars, displays of Turkish military uniforms through the ages, and glass cases holding battle standards, both Turkish and captured. These include Byzantine, Greek, British, Austro-Hungarian, Italian and Imperial Russian standards. Perhaps the most interesting of the exhibits are the im-

perial pavilions (sayebanlar). These luxurious cloth shelters, heavily worked with fine silver and gold thread, jewels, precious silks and elegant tracery, were the battle headquarters for sultans during the summer campaign season.

Also on show are a portion of the great chain that the Byzantines stretched across the mouth of the Golden Horn to keep out the sultan's ships during the battle for Constantinople in 1453; and a tapestry woven by Ottoman sailors (who must have had lots of time on their hands) showing the flags of all of the world's important maritime nations.

The upper floor has more imperial pavilions and a room devoted to Atatürk, who was, of course, a famous Ottoman general before he became founder and commander-in-chief of the republican army, and first president of the Turkish Republic. This floor is where you really feel the spirit of the Ottoman Empire. It has exhibits of armour (including cavalry), uniforms, field furniture made out of weapons (eg chairs with rifles for legs), and a Türk-Alman Dostluk Köşesi (Turco-German Friendship Corner) with mementos of Turkish and German military collaboration before and during WWI.

Outside the museum, to the east of the building, you'll find cannons, including Gatling guns cast in Vienna, bearing the sultan's monogram. More of the Golden Horn's great chain is here as well.

Perhaps the best reason to visit this museum is to view the short concert by the Mehter. According to historians, the Mehter was the world's first true military band. Its purpose was not to make pretty music for dancing, but to precede the conquering Ottoman paşas (governor) into vanquished towns, impressing upon the defeated populace their new,

Transport

Under the northern end of Taksim Parkı is the terminal of a metro line linking Taksim to the business and residential districts of Şişli, Etiler and Levent. An extension to this line is currently being built that will see it extend south to the seabus terminal at Yenikapı and north to Maslak.

Innumerable buses run north from Taksim Square up Cumhuriyet Caddesi to the junction of Halaskargazi and Vali Konaği Caddesis on the border of Harbiye and Nişantaşı. Buses from Eminönü also stop at this intersection.

subordinate status. Children in particular will love watching them march with their steady, measured pace, then turning all together to face the left side of the line of march, then the right side.

The easiest way to get to the museum is to walk up Cumhuriyet Caddesi from Taksim Square. This will take around 15 minutes.

TAKSİM SQUARE Map p287
Bus T4 from Sultanahmet, buses from Eminönü, bus 61B from Beyazıt

The symbolic heart of modern İstanbul, this busy square is named after the stone reservoir on its western side, once part of the city's old water-conduit system. The main water line from the Belgrade Forest, north of the city, was laid to this point in 1732 by Sultan Mahmut I (r 1730–54). Branch lines then led from the *taksim* to other parts of the city.

Hardly a triumph of urban design, the square is a bit of a mess, with a chaotic bus terminus on one side, a slightly pathetic garden laid out in its centre and the tracks of the İstiklal Caddesi tram circumnavigating it. With the construction of a new metro line and station currently under way, it's even more chaotic than usual, though this doesn't prevent

locals nominating it as a favoured meeting point and making the terrace of the nearby Pizza Hut, which affords views over it, one of the most popular fast-food stops in the city. The government and municipality often organise for official events – usually related to the police or military – to be held here. During such events it's not unusual to see tanks and riot police surrounding the square and police sharpshooters atop nearby buildings – scary stuff indeed.

The prominent modern building at the eastern end of the plaza is the **Atatürk Cultural Centre** (Atatürk Kültür Merkezi, sometimes called the Opera House; p177). In the summertime, during the International İstanbul Music Festival, tickets for the various concerts are on sale in the ticket kiosks here, and numerous performances are staged in the centre's halls.

At the western end of the square is the **Cumhuriyet Anıtı** (Republic Monument), created by Canonica, an Italian sculptor, in 1928. It features Atatürk, his assistant and successor, İsmet İnönü, and other revolutionary leaders. The monument's purpose was not only to commemorate revolutionary heroes, but also to break down the Ottoman-Islamic prohibition against the making of 'graven images'.

BEŞİKTAŞ & ORTAKÖY

As well as being a major transport hub and the home of one of the 'Big Three' football teams, Beşiktaş has the largest concentration of Ottoman pleasure palaces and pavilions in İstanbul. French writer, Pierre Loti, described the shoreline here as a '...line of palaces white as snow, placed at the edge of the sea on marble docks' and the description is still as accurate as it is evocative. Nearby Ortaköy is nowhere near as grand, but has considerable charm, particularly on warm summer nights when its main square is crowded with locals dining at the fish restaurants or enjoying an after-dinner coffee and ice cream by the water. Later in the evening, the clubbing set hit the nearby super-venues on the Bosphorus or pop into the many small bars and clubs in the cobbled lanes around the square.

Orientation

The major roads leading to Beşiktaş and Ortaköy are İnönü Caddesi from Taksim, Maçka and Spor Caddesis from Nişantaşı and Necatibey Caddesi from Galata. The narrow road that follows the Bosphorus from Dolmabahçe Palace starts as Dolmabahçe Caddesi, then becomes in turn Beşiktaş Caddesi, Çırağan Caddesi and Muallim Naci Caddesi. At night and on weekends this road is packed with traffic, and sets off many a local road-rage incident. As a result, many people choose to catch a ferry or bus to Beşiktaş and walk the kilometre or so to Ortaköy rather than driving or catching a taxi.

Beşiktaş & Ortaköy Top Five

- Yıldız Parkı (p127)
- Dolmabahçe Palace (p124)
- Ihlamur Kasrı (p126)
- Deniz Müzesi (p124)
- Ortaköy Camii (p127)

Transport

Bus routes come here from both Eminönü and Taksim Square. Bus 56 from Sultanahmet to Esentepe stops at Beşiktaş and Dolmabahçe, but doesn't go past Çırağan, Yıldız or Ortaköy. The T4 bus from Sultanahmet stops outside Dolmabahçe en route for Taksim Square.

The Beşiktaş ferry terminal and bus station are just near the Deniz Müzesi. Ferries run to and from Kadıköy and Üsküdar but not Eminönü.

ÇIRAĞAN SARAYI Map p288

Çırağan Palace; Çırağan Caddesi 84, Beşiktaş; bus DT1/2, 40 & 40T from Taksim Square, bus 57UL from Beşiktaş, bus 25E & 30D from Eminönü (Yahya Efendi)

Not satisfied with the architectural exertions of his predecessor at Dolmabahçe, Sultan Abdül Aziz (r 1861–76) built his own grand residence at Çırağan, on the Bosphorus shore only 1.5km away from Dolmabahçe. The architect was Nikoğos Balyan, one of the designers of Dolmabahçe and here he created an interesting building melding European neoclassical with Ottoman and Moorish styles.

Abdül Aziz's extravagance may have been one of the reasons why he was deposed in 1876, to be replaced by his mentally unstable and alcoholic nephew, Murat. Abdül Aziz later died in Çırağan under mysterious circumstances, probably suicide. Murat was in turn swiftly deposed by Abdül Hamit II, who kept his predecessor and brother a virtual prisoner in Çırağan. Murat died in the palace in 1904. In 1909 it became the seat of the Ottoman Chamber of Deputies and Senate, but in 1910 it was destroyed by fire under suspicious circumstances.

Parts of the palace have been restored (the interior in lurid lollypop colours) to house sections of the ritzy Çırağan Palace Hotel Kempinski, which opened in 1986.

DENİZ MÜZESİ Map p288

Naval Museum; ☎ 212-261 0040; cnr Cezayir & Beşiktaş Caddesis, Beşiktaş; admission €1.20; ☒ 9am-12.30pm & 1.30-5pm Fri-Tue; bus 56 from Sultanahmet, bus 22E, 25E, 28 & 30D from Eminönü, bus DT1/2, 40 & 40T from Taksim Square (Beşiktaş)

Though this museum is picturesquely situated on the Bosphorus shore, most landlubbers (including us) find it just a tad dull. Still, those of the naval persuasion will no doubt feel like dropping an anchor here for an hour or so.

Though the Ottoman Empire is most remembered for its conquests on land, its maritime power was equally impressive. During the reign of Süleyman the Magnificent (r 1520–66), the eastern Mediterranean was virtually an Ottoman recreational lake. The sultan's navies cut a swathe in the Indian Ocean as well. Sea power was instrumental in the conquests of the Aegean coasts and islands, Egypt and North Africa. Discipline, well-organised supply and good ship design contributed to Ottoman victories.

The museum's prize exhibits are the sleek and swift imperial caïques (long, thin rowboats) in which the sultan would speed up and down the Bosphorus from palace to palace. These boats are over 30m in length but only 2m wide. With 13 banks of oars, the caïques were the speed boats of their day. Those with latticework screens were for the imperial women. These days, modern-day replicas of the caïques ply the waters between Dolmabahçe and Beylerbeyi Palaces on weekends.

You may also be curious to see a replica of the *Map of Piri Reis*, an early Ottoman map (1513), which purports to show the coasts and continents of the New World. It's assumed that Piri Reis (Captain Piri) got hold of the work of Columbus for his map. The original map is in Topkapı Palace.

There's an outdoor display of cannons (including Selim the Grim's 21-tonne monster) and a statue of Barbaros Hayrettin Paşa (1483–1546), the famous Turkish admiral known also as Barbarossa who conquered North Africa for Süleyman the Magnificent. The admiral's tomb, designed by Sinan, is in the square opposite the museum.

DOLMABAHÇE PALACE Map p288

Dolmabahçe Sarayı; ☎ 212-236 9000; Dolmabahçe Caddesi, Beşiktaş; camera €3.30, video €5, for admission to Selamlık & Harem see following entries; ☒ 9am-4pm Tue, Wed & Fri-Sun; bus T4 & 56 from Sultanahmet, bus 22E & 28 from Eminönü, bus 256, DT2 & 40 from Taksim Square (İnönü Stadium)

These days it's fashionable for architects and critics influenced by the less-is-more aesthetic of the Bauhaus masters to sneer at buildings such as Dolmabahçe. The crowds that throng to this imperial pleasure palace with its neoclassical exterior and over-the-top interior fit out clearly don't share their disdain, though.

More rather than less was certainly the philosophy of Sultan Abdül Mecit, who, deciding that it was time to give the lie to talk of Ottoman military and financial decline, decided to move from Topkapı to a lavish new palace on the shores of the Bosphorus. For a site he chose the *dolma bahçe* (filled-in garden) where his predecessor Sultan Ahmet I (1607–17) had filled in a little cove in order to build an imperial pleasure kiosk surrounded by gardens. Other wooden buildings succeeded the original kiosk, but all burned to the ground in 1814. In 1843 Abdül Mecit commissioned imperial architects Nikoğos and Garabed Balyan to construct an Ottoman-European palace that would impress everyone who set eyes on it. Traditional Ottoman palace architecture was eschewed – there are no pavilions here and the palace turns its back to the splendid view rather than celebrating it. The designer of the Paris Opera was brought in to do the interiors, which perhaps explains their exaggerated theatricality. Construction was finally completed in 1856. Though it had the wow factor in spades, Abdül Mecit's project also did more to precipitate the empire's bankruptcy than to dispel rumours of it, and signalled the beginning of the end for the Osmanli dynasty. During the early years of the republic, Atatürk used the palace as his İstanbul base. He died here in 1938.

The palace, which is set in well-tended gardens and entered via its ornate imperial gate, is divided into two sections, the **Selamlık** (Ceremonial Suites) and the **Harem-Cariyeler** (Harem and Concubines' Quarters). You must take a guided tour to see either section. Only 1500 people are allowed into each section each day, so it's not a bad idea to reserve your space on a tour in advance. If you have only enough time for one tour, be sure to make it the Selamlık. Tours are in English and Turkish; French and German guides are sometimes available. In busy periods the tours leave every five minutes; during quiet times every 25 minutes is more likely. For more details see the following two entries.

The tourist entrance to the palace is near the ornate clock tower, built by Sultan Abdül Hamit II between 1890 and 1894. There is an outdoor café near here with premium Bosphorus views. Watch out at the ticket box – when we were there two customers in a row were short-changed. If you are keen to visit **Beylerbeyi Sarayı** (p217) on the Asian shore after your Dolmabahçe tour it is sometimes possible to cross the water in a replica of one of the imperial caïques for €20. For information contact ☎ 212-296 5240.

Finally, don't set your watch by any of the palace clocks, all of which are stopped at 9.05am, the moment at which Kemal Atatürk died in Dolmabahçe on 10 November 1938. When touring the harem you will be shown the small bedroom he used during his last days. Each year on 10 November, at 9.05am, the country observes a moment of silence in commemoration of the great leader.

Entrance, Dolmabahçe Palace (opposite)

DOLMABAHÇE SELAMLIK Map p288

Dolmabahçe Caddesi, Beşiktaş; admission Selamlık only €6.60, Selamlık & Harem-Cariyeler €8.80, 1-hr tour

The tour starts by passing through opulent salons and halls to a room with glass cabinets displaying gaudy crystal, gold and silver tea sets. After visiting the palace mosque and ablutions room, things really start to get extravagant at the staircase, with a French crystal balustrade made by Baccarat. Here the Bohemian chandelier weighs close to 1000kg. The hallway at the top of the stairs has two Russian bearskins, a 2000kg chandelier and candelabras standing about 3m tall. Off this is a reception hall featuring ornate gilt ceiling and walls. These and the enormous carpet from Iran must have impressed the official visitors who came here to be received by the sultan.

If your eyes are popping out of your head, you haven't seen anything yet; the tour continues past exquisite parquetry floors, Sèvres vases and Czechoslovakian meringue-like tiled fireplaces, through an exquisite *hamam* and past more monster candelabras. But even these extravagances are a mere prelude to the magnificent Imperial Ceremonial Hall, or Throne Room. Used in 1877 for the first meeting of the Ottoman Chamber of Deputies, this lavishly painted hall comes complete with a chandelier made of Irish glass that weighs over 4000kg – the tour guides here maintain that it is the largest in the world. There are grated windows, from which the resident women could watch the goings-on, and gilt on every available surface. The hall was designed to hold 2500 dignitaries and other guests.

At the end of your tour, make sure you visit the Crystal Palace, with its fairytale-like conservatory featuring etched glass windows, crystal fountain and myriad chandeliers. There's even a crystal piano and chair. It's easy to imagine Hans Christian Andersen's *Snow Queen* holding court in such a place. You'll find it next to the aviary on the street side of the palace.

DOLMABAHÇE HAREM-CARİYELER

Map p288

Dolmabahçe Caddesi, Beşiktaş; admission Harem-Cariyeler only €4.40, Selamlık & Harem-Cariyeler €8.80; 30-min tour

The pink building houses the Harem and Concubines' Quarters, which are not as lavish as the Selamlık but still worth touring. Though relatively cramped and plain by Dolmabahçe standards (which isn't saying much), they have

some bizarre features, including the huge ornate bed used by Sultan Abdül Aziz, who was known by his subjects as Güresçi (the Wrestler) due to his great size, considerable strength and predilection for the sport.

The tour passes through a post-circumcision resting hall, a couple of *hamams* and the Blue Hall, the sultan's reception hall in the harem. Note the hand-painted ceilings throughout and the amazing wallpaper in Atatürk's bedroom.

IHLAMUR KASRI Map p288

Kiosk of the Linden Tree; ☎ 212-259 5086; Ihlamer-Teşvikiye Yolu, Beşiktaş; admission Tue & Wed €1.10, Fri-Sun €0.75; ☾ 9.30am-5pm Tue & Wed, Fri-Sun Mar-Sep, 9am-3pm Tue & Wed, Fri-Sun Oct-Feb; bus 56 from Sultanahmet, bus 22E, 25E, 28 & 30D from Eminönü, bus DT1/2, 40 & 40T from Taksim Square (Beşiktaş)

Sheltered in a narrow valley about 1.2km inland and to the north of the Deniz Müzesi is a park containing the two pavilions of the Ihlamur Kasrı. If you've just witnessed the aesthetic excesses of Dolmabahçe Palace you may want to give this place a miss, because it's more of the same, having been built by one of the same architects, Nikoğos Balyan. Like Dolmabahçe, it can only be viewed on a guided tour. This tour is included in the modest entry fee, though.

Ortaköy Camii (opposite)

Try to imagine what it must have been like when these two miniature hunting palaces stood here alone, in the midst of a forest. Near the entry gate the park is open and formal, with grassy lawns, ornamental trees and a quiet pool.

Look across the pool to find the **Merasim Köşkü** (Sultan's Kiosk) built on the orders of Sultan Abdül Mecit between 1849 and 1855.

Up the marble stairway and through the ornate door is the Hall of Mirrors, with crystal from Bohemia and vases from France. The music room, to the right of the entrance, has precious Hereke fabrics on the chairs and an enamelled coal-grate fireplace painted with flowers. The main appliance in the Imperial Water Closet is of the traditional flat Turkish type, demonstrating that in here even the sultan was dethroned. The room to the left of the entrance was a reception salon.

The **Maiyet Köşkü**, or Retinue Kiosk, was for the sultan's suite of attendants, guests or harem. Make yourself welcome too: it's now a teahouse serving tea, coffee and snacks.

İSTANBUL MUSEUM OF PAINTING & SCULPTURE Map p288

Resim ve Heykel Müzesi; ☎ 212-261 4298; Dolmabahçe Caddesi, Beşiktaş; admission free; ⏱ 10.30am-4.30pm Wed-Sun; bus 56 from Sultanahmet, bus 22E, 25E, 28 & 30D from Eminönü, bus DT1/2, 40 & 40T from Taksim Square (Beşiktaş)

Established by Atatürk in 1937 in a building that was originally the Crown Prince Pavilion of Dolmabahçe Palace, this museum holds over 2500 paintings and 550 sculptures from the early 19th century onwards.

ORTAKÖY CAMİİ Map p288

Büyük Mecidiye Camii, Ortaköy; bus DT1/2, 40, 40T from Taksim Square, bus 25E from Eminönü

Right on the water's edge, this mosque (a strange mix of baroque and neoclassical influences), is the work of Nikoğos Balyan, one of the architects of Dolmabahçe Palace. It was built for Sultan Abdül Mecit III between 1853 and 1855. With the super-modern Bosphorus Bridge now looming behind it, the mosque provides a fabulous photo opportunity for those wanting to illustrate İstanbul's 'old meets new' character. Within the mosque hang several masterful examples of Arabic calligraphy executed by the sultan, who was an accomplished calligrapher.

The mosque fronts onto Ortaköy Square, home to a pretty fountain, and popular waterfront cafés and restaurants.

YILDIZ PARKI Map p288

Yıldız Park; ☎ 212-261 8460; Çırağan Caddesi; admission free; ⏱ 9am-6pm summer, 9am-5.30pm winter; bus DT1/2, 40 & 40T from Taksim Square, bus 57UL from Beşiktaş, bus 25E & 30D from Eminönü

Sultan Abdül Hamit II (r 1876–1909) didn't allow himself to be upstaged by his predecessors. He built his own fancy palace by adding considerably to the structures built by earlier sultans in Yıldız Parkı, continuing the Ottoman tradition of palace pavilions that had been employed so wonderfully at Topkapı. It was to be the last sultan's palace built in İstanbul.

The park began life as the imperial reserve for the Çırağan Sarayı, but when Abdül Hamit built Yıldız Şale, largest of the park's surviving structures, the park then served that palace and was planted with rare and exotic trees, shrubs and flowers. It also gained carefully tended paths and superior electric lighting and drainage systems. The landscape designer, G Le Roi, was French.

The park, with its kiosks, had become derelict, but was beautifully restored by the Turkish Touring & Automobile Association (Turing) in the 1980s, under lease from the city government. In 1994 the newly elected city government declined to renew the lease and took over operation of the park. Today it's a pretty, leafy retreat alive with birds and picnickers.

Near the top of the hill (to the left of the road if you enter by the Çırağan Caddesi entrance) you'll see the **Çadır Köşkü**. Built between 1865 and 1870, the ornate kiosk is nestled beside a small lake and now functions as a café.

To the right (north) as you go up the hill from the entrance are two greenhouses hidden by vegetation, the **Kış Bahçesi** (Winter Garden) and the **Yeşil Sera** (Green Nursery).

Around 500m past the turn-off to Yıldız Şale (see following) you'll come to the **Malta Köşkü**. Built in 1870, it was where Abdül Hamit imprisoned the deposed Murat V and his family. With its views of the Bosphorus, the terrace here makes a great place for a light lunch.

If you continue walking past the Malta Köşkü for 10 minutes you'll arrive at the **Yıldız Porselen Fabrikası** (Yıldız Porcelain Factory; ☎ 212-260 2370; ⏱ 9am-5pm Mon-Fri). The factory is housed in a wonderful building designed by Italian architect Raimondo D'Aronco, who was to introduce Art Nouveau into İstanbul. Constructed to manufacture dinner services for the palace, it still operates and is open to visitors. There's a small ceramics shop at the entrance.

If you come to the park by taxi, have it take you up the steep slope to Yıldız Şale. You can visit the other kiosks on the walk down. (A taxi from Taksim Square to the top of the hill should cost around €3.)

YILDIZ ŞALE Map p288

Yıldız Chalet Museum; ☎ 212-259 4570; admission €1.70; ◷ 9.30am-5pm summer, 9.30-4pm winter Tue-Wed & Fri-Sun

In the park at the top of the hill, enclosed by a lofty wall, is the Yıldız Şale, a 'guesthouse' built in 1875 and expanded in 1889 and 1898 by Abdül Hamit – both times for the use of Kaiser Wilhelm II of Germany during state visits. As you enter the palace, a guide will approach and give you the half-hour tour, which is required. The chalet isn't as plush as Dolmabahçe, but it's less crowded, so you get more time to ask questions and to feast your eyes on the exhibits.

It would seem the kaiser had enough space to move in, as the chalet has 64 rooms. After his imperial guest departed, the sultan became quite attached to his 'rustic' creation and decided to live here himself, forsaking the palaces on the Bosphorus shore.

Abdül Hamit was paranoid, and for good reason. When eventually deposed, he left this wooden palace in April 1909 and boarded a train that took him to house arrest in Ottoman Salonika (today Thessaloniki, Greece). He was later allowed by the Young Turks' government to return to İstanbul and live out his years in Beylerbeyi Sarayı, on the Asian shore of the Bosphorus.

Yıldız Şale was to be associated with more dolorous history. The last sultan of the Ottoman Empire, Mehmet V (Vahideddin), lived here until, on 11 November 1922, he and his retinue, accompanied by trunks full of jewels, gold and antiques, boarded two British Red Cross ambulances for a secret journey to the naval dockyard at Tophane. There they boarded the British battleship HMS *Malaya* for a trip into exile, ending the Ottoman Empire forever. On the way to the quay one of the tyres on the sultan's ambulance went flat; while it was being changed the 'Shadow of God on Earth' quaked, fearing he might be discovered.

In the republican era, the Yıldız Şale has served as a guesthouse for visiting heads of state, including Charles de Gaulle, Pope Paul VI and the Empress Soraya of Iran.

The first room on the tour was used by Abdül Hamit's mother for her religious devotions; the second was her guest reception room with a very fine mosaic tabletop. Then comes a women's resting room and afterwards a tearoom with furniture marked with a gold star on a blue background, which reminds one that this is the 'star' (*yıldız*) chalet.

During the 1898 works the chalet was expanded, and the older section became the harem (with steel doors), while the new section functioned as the *selamlık*. In the *selamlık* are a bathroom with tiles from the Yıldız Porcelain Factory and several reception rooms, one of which has furniture made by Abdül Hamit himself. The grand hall of the *selamlık* is vast, its floor covered by a 7½-tonne Hereke carpet woven just for this room. The rug is so huge that it had to be brought in through the far (north) wall before the building was finished.

HASKÖY

Hasköy was for centuries a small, predominantly Jewish village. In the Ottoman period it also became home to a naval shipyard and a sultan's hunting ground. Today, Hasköy's main claims to fame are two very different tourist attractions, namely a splendid industrial museum and the rarely visited imperial pleasure palace. There's also a bizarre architectural theme park in the neighbouring suburb of Sütlüce.

Orientation

Hasköy is located on the Golden Horn approximately 6km northwest of Karaköy. Heading north towards Sütlüce, its main road, Hasköy Caddesi, becomes Kumbarahane Caddesi before becoming Karaağaç Caddesi. At the time of research, the filthy and overgrown stretch of grass on the bank of the Golden Horn between the Rahmi M Koç museum and Miniaturk was undergoing re-landscaping as part of its transformation into a public park.

Transport

Though a ferry from Üsküdar (via Eminönü) stops at Sütlüce, it doesn't make a stop at Hasköy. The closest stop to the Rahmi M Koç Museum is the Sütlüce stop, while the Kasımpaşa stop is closest to Aynalıkavak Kasrı. Ferries leave Eminönü between 7.20am and 8pm every hour (approximately).

There are buses from Eminönü and Taksim Square to Hasköy and Sütlüce.

AYNALIKAVAK KASRI Map pp276-7

Tersane Sarayı; ☎ 212-250 4094; admission €1.10; ☉ 9am-4pm Tue & Wed, Fri-Sun; bus 47, 47C/E from Eminönü, bus 54HT from Taksim Square (Hasköy)

Centuries ago an imperial naval arsenal was set at Kasımpaşa, southeast of Hasköy, and near it a shipyard (tersane), which gave its name to several imperial hunting lodges and pleasure kiosks at Hasköy – the Tersane Sarayı, more commonly known as Aynalıkavak Kasrı, the Palace of Mirrors.

İstanbul's kasrs (imperial lodges) are less outwardly impressive than its many palaces. Designed on a more human scale, they were built not to impress visitors but to please the monarchs themselves.

A wooden kasr was built on this site by Sultan Ahmet III (r 1703–30) and restored by Selim III (r 1789–1807). The palace and gardens are mostly the work of Sultan Mahmut II (r 1808–39). With its Tulip Period decoration and Ottoman furnishings, the pavilion is a splendid if dusty place that gives a vivid impression of the lifestyle of the Ottoman ruling class at the turn of the 19th century, when Hasköy was a thriving Jewish neighbourhood. Some rooms are furnished in Eastern style, others in European style.

Selim III composed poetry and music in one of the eastern rooms; futon-like beds were tucked away into cabinets during the day. The waiting room (bekleme salonu) has the only extant Tulip Period ceiling in the city. One of the European rooms is filled with sumptuous mother-of-pearl furniture. There's also the small **Museum of Turkish Musical Instruments** on the lower level.

The easiest way to Aynalıkavak is by taxi (€3 from Beyoğlu). Tell the driver to take you to Hasköy police station (polis karakolu) or to the athletic facilities (Şükrü Urcan Spor Tesisleri), which are well known. Just southeast of the police station, along Kasımpaşa–Hasköy Yolu, is Aynalıkavak Kasrı. Alternatively, alight at the bus stop at Hasköy and ask for directions.

MINIATURK Map pp276-7

☎ 212-222 2882; www.miniaturk.com; Imrahor Caddesi, Sütlüce; adult/child or student €2.70/1.60; ☉ 9am-6pm; bus 47C/E from Eminönü (Miniaturk)

We're can't explain why this new museum has been such a hit with locals. Marketed as a miniature park that showcases 'all times and locations of Anatolia at the same place at the same time', it's a bizarre, tiny town stocked with models of Turkey's great buildings – everything from the Celsus Library at Ephesus to Atatürk International Airport – set in manicured lawns dotted with fake rocks blasting a distorted recording of the national anthem. Children aren't interested in the models but love the miniature train that traverses the paths and the playground equipment. It's tacky and only really interesting as a demonstration of how greatly Turks revere their heritage, even when kitsch coated.

At the time of research, a path along the Golden Horn linking Miniaturk and the Rahmi M Koç Industrial Museum was being mooted. When this is built, it should take 20 minutes to walk between the two.

RAHMİ M KOÇ MÜZESİ Map pp276-7

Rahmi M Koç Industrial Museum; ☎ 212-256 7153; Hasköy Caddesi 27; adult/child or student €2.70/0.75, submarine adult/child or student €1.30/0.50; ☉ 10am-5pm Tue-Fri, 10am-7pm Sat & Sun; bus 47, 47C/E from Eminönü, bus 54HT from Taksim Square (Kasımpaşa)

This museum was founded by the head of the Koç industrial group, one of Turkey's most prominent conglomerates, to exhibit artefacts from İstanbul's industrial past. Its collection is highly eclectic, giving the impression of being a grab-bag of cool stuff collected over the decades or donated to the museum by individuals, organizations or companies who don't know what else to do with it. This might sound like we're damning the place with faint praise, but this is far from the case. In fact, this is a corker of a museum that children in particular will love.

The museum is in two parts: a new building on the Golden Horn side of the road and a superbly restored and converted Byzantine stone building opposite. Exhibits are largely concerned with forms of transport: Bosphorus ferry parts and machinery; a horse-drawn tram; an Amphicar (half car, half boat) that crossed the English Channel in 1962; Sultan Abdül Aziz's ornate railway coach with its duck-egg-blue stain upholstery; cars (everything from ugly Turkish Anadol models to fabulous pink Cadillacs); a 1960 Messerschmitt; and even much of the

Neighbourhoods – Hasköy

fuselage of 'Hadley's Harem', a US B-24D Liberator bomber that crashed off Antalya in August 1943. Other exhibits look at how appliances and electronic devices work – the exhibition of how whitegoods work is particularly fascinating.

Unlike most of the city's museums, wheelchair access is offered throughout the complex. What's more excellent interpretive panels in Turkish and English are provided. A guide can be organised to take you on a private tour (€16.60) and experts demonstrate how the machines work twice a day (11am and 5pm). There are buttons galore to push, two excellent places to eat – namely, **Halal** (p160) and **Café du Levant** (p160) – and a convivial bar. The submarine exhibit, from which children under eight years of age are barred, requires an extra ticket.

The museum is near the northern end of the old Galata Bridge (near where Hasköy Caddesi changes into Kumbarahane Caddesi) about 1km northwest of Aynalıkavak Kasrı. A taxi from Beyoğlu will cost around €3.

THE ASIAN SHORE

Eating p162

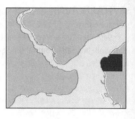

The Asian shore starts south of the city along the Sea of Marmara, where urban sprawl has taken over, with suburb after suburb being established to accommodate the city's ever-expanding population. Kadıköy was the first of these suburbs (it was actually established before Byzantium) and it is the only one that makes a serious claim on the traveller's time. North of Kadıköy is the fascinating suburb of Üsküdar and further north again is a trail of suburbs and villages dotted along the length of the Bosphorus and ending at the Black Sea.

The trip to Üsküdar or Kadıköy by ferry from Eminönü is a lovely way to start the day and is highly recommended.

Buses 12A and 12H run between Kadıköy and Üsküdar approximately every 20 minutes from 5.50am to 11.35pm. They leave from the bus station to the left as you exit the Kadıköy ferry terminal and from Demokrasi Meydanı in Üsküdar.

ÜSKÜDAR

Üsküdar (pronounced: *ooh*-skoo-dar) is the Turkish form of the Byzantine name, Scutari, which dates from the 12th century. It comes from the imperial palace of Scutarion, once located on the point of land near Kız Külesi. The first colonists lived in Chalcedon (modern-day Kadıköy), to the south, and Chrysopolis (now Üsküdar) became its first major suburb; both towns existed about two decades before Byzantium was founded. The harbour at Chrysopolis was superior to that of Chalcedon so that, as Byzantium blossomed, Chrysopolis outgrew Chalcedon to become the largest suburb on the Asian shore. Unwalled and therefore vulnerable, it became part of the Ottoman Empire at least 100 years before the Conquest of 1453.

Judging that Scutari was the closest point in İstanbul to Mecca, many powerful Ottoman figures built mosques here to assist their passage to Paradise. Every year during the Empire a big caravan left from here en route to Mecca and Medina for the Haj, further emphasising its reputation for piety.

Even today, Üsküdar is one of İstanbul's more conservative suburbs. Home to many migrants from rural Anatolia, the mosques are busier here, the families are larger and the headscarf is more obvious than elsewhere in the city. It's a fascinating place to explore.

Orientation

Üsküdar's many mosques and religious buildings are littered throughout the suburb. The main streets radiate from the central square, Demokrasi Meydani, where the ferry terminal and bus stations are located. The nearby suburbs of Harem and Kadıköy are to the south. *Dolmuşes* to Harem travel along the main waterside road, Sahil Yolu, and buses to Kadıköy take Selámi Ali Effendi Caddesi through the hills above town. Upmarket residential suburbs and two public parks, Büyük Çamlıca and Küçük Çamlıca, are located on these hills.

Transport

If you're making your way from Sultanahmet to Üsküdar, hop on the ferry from Eminönü (dock 1), which runs every 15 to 30 minutes (depending on the time of day) between 6.35am and 11pm.

A ferry service also operates between Beşiktaş (catch it from beside the Deniz Müzesi) and Üsküdar. Ferries start at 6.30am and run every 30 minutes until 10.30pm. From nearby Kabataş, just south of Dolmabahçe Palace, ferries run to Üsküdar every 30 minutes from 7.15am until 9.15am; they also run every 30 minutes from 4.15pm until 8.15pm.

Peak-hour ferries also run from just west of the Galata Bridge (near the small fish market) at Karaköy. These leave at 7.35am, 8.20am, 8.55am, 9.35am, 4.55pm, 5.35pm, 6.10pm and 7pm.

Buses and *dolmuşes* also run to and from Taksim Square.

ATIK VALİDE CAMİİ Map p289

Tabaklar Camii Sokak; ferry from Eminönü or Beşiktaş

This is one of the grandest of Sinan's İstanbul mosques, second only to his Süleymaniye. Experts rate it as one of the most important Ottoman mosque complexes in the country. It was built in 1583 for Valide Sultan Nurbanu, wife of Selim II and mother of Murat III. Nurbanu had been captured by Turks on the Aegean island of Paros when she was 12 years old, ending up as a slave in Topkapı. The poor woman had a lot to bear – first being kidnapped and then taking the fancy of Selim the Sot – but she was his favourite concubine and became a very clever player in Ottoman political life. The Kandınlar Sultanatı (Rule of the Women) under which a succession of powerful women influenced the decisions made by their sultan husbands and sons began with her. Murat adored his mother and on her death commissioned Sinan to build this monument to her on Üsküdar's highest hill. Like the Süleymaniye, it has an impressive courtyard (closed for renovation at the time of research) and interior galleries. The tile-adorned mihrab is particularly attractive.

BÜYÜK ÇAMLICA

☎ 216-443 2198; Turistik Çamlıca Caddesi; admission free; ☽ 9am-11pm; ferry from Eminönü or Beşiktaş

The term megalopolis is bandied about a fair bit to describe İstanbul, but it's only when you come to a spot like this that it becomes meaningful. Larger than many sovereign states, the city sprawls further than the eye can see, even

when afforded this bird's eye view. And what a view it is! A hilltop park with a crown of pine trees, Büyük Çamlıca is the highest point in the city and can be seen from miles away (you'll see it as you ferry down the Bosphorus, for example). It's beloved by İstanbullus, who flock here to relax, picnic in the pretty gardens, eat at the **Çamlıca Restaurant** (p162) and gaze upon their fine city. From the terraces you'll see the minaret-filled skyline of Old İstanbul, as well as the Bosphorus winding its way to the Black Sea.

Once favoured by Sultan Mahmut II (r 1808–39), by the late 1970s the park was a muddy and unkempt car park threatened by illegal and unplanned construction. In 1980 the municipal government leased the land to the Turing group, which landscaped the hilltop and built a restaurant such as Mahmut might have enjoyed. The municipal government took over management of the park in 1995.

To reach the hilltop from Üsküdar's main square, you can take a taxi (€4.40) all the way to the summit, or a *dolmuş* most of the way. For the latter, walk to the *dolmuş* ranks in front of the İskele Camii, take a *dolmuş* headed for Ümraniye and ask for Büyük Çamlıca. The *dolmuş* will pass the entrance to Küçük Çamlıca and drop you off shortly thereafter in a district called Kısıklı. The walk uphill (pleasant but no great views) following the signs to the summit takes from 30 to 40 minutes.

ÇİNİLİ CAMİİ Map p289

Tiled Mosque; Çinili Mescit Sokak; ferry from Eminönü or Beşiktaş

This little mosque is unprepossessing from the outside, but boy oh boy – wait till you see the interior! It is brilliant with İznik faïence, the bequest of Mahpeyker Kösem (1640), wife of Sultan Ahmet I (r 1603–17) and mother of sultans Murat IV (r 1623–40) and İbrahim (r 1640–48).

You'll find the mosque in a neighbourhood called Tabaklar, up the hillside away from Üsküdar's main square. It can be tricky to find on your own (a 30-minute walk); a taxi will cost no more than €2 and is well worth the price.

FLORENCE NIGHTINGALE MUSEUM

Map pp276-7

Selimiye Army Barracks, Nci Ordu Komutanliği 1; admission free; ☽ Mon-Fri 9am-5pm ferry from Eminönü or Beşiktaş & then dolmuş or taxi

The experience of visiting the Selimiye Army Barracks, where this museum is housed, is even better than the museum itself. The barracks, built by Mahmut II in 1828 on the site of a barracks originally built by Selim III in 1799 and extended by Abdül Mecit I in 1842 and 1853, is the headquarters of the Turkish First Army, the largest division in the country, and is an extremely handsome building, with 2.5km of corridors, 300 rooms and 300 windows. During the Crimean War (1853–56) the barracks became a military hospital where the famous lady with the lamp and 38 nursing students worked. It was here that Nightingale put in practice the innovative nursing methods that history has remembered her for. Though they seem common-sensical from a modern perspective, it is hard to overstate how radical they seemed at the time. It really is amazing to hear that before she arrived, the mortality rate was 70% of patients and when she left it had dropped to 5%.

The museum is spread over three levels in the northwest tower of the barracks. Downstairs there is a display charting the history of the First Army and concentrating on the Crimean War. On the two upstairs levels you see Nightingale's personal quarters, including her surgery room with original furnishings (including two lamps) and her living room, with extraordinary views across to Old İstanbul. Here there are exhibits such as an original letter explaining how the lady herself defined being a good nurse.

To visit, you need to fax (☎ 216-553 1009) a letter requesting to visit and nominating a time. Include a photocopy of your passport photo page. Do this 48 hours before you wish to visit and make sure you include your telephone number in İstanbul so that someone can respond to your request. The recruits who vet your papers at the entrance show you from the security check to the museum, and take you on a guided tour are almost all young conscripts counting down the days until their military service is finished. They may not all speak English (although the tour is always in that language) but they are without exception charming and helpful. Their mothers would be proud!

The museum is about half way between Üsküdar and Kadıköy, near the fairytale-like clock towers of the TC Marmara University. To get here, catch a dolmuş from outside the ferry terminals in Üsküdar to Harem and ask locals to point you towards the Selimiye Kışlası Harem Kapısı (the barracks' Harem Gate), a short walk away. A taxi from the ferry shouldn't cost more than €3.50.

İSKELE CAMİİ Map p289
Dock Mosque; Demokrasi Meydanı; ferry from Eminönü or Beşiktaş

Sometimes called the Mihrimah Sultan Camii, this mosque was built in 1547 and 1548 by Sinan for Süleyman the Magnificent's daughter. Though imposing on the outside, it's a bit claustrophobic and dull inside. You'll find it northeast of the Demokrasi Meydanı (main square).

KIZ KULESİ Map p289
Maiden's or Leander's Tower; ☎ 216-342 4747;
◷ noon-7pm Tue-Sun; ferry from Eminönü or Beşiktaş

İstanbul is a maritime city, so it's appropriate that the Kız Kulesi, one of its most distinctive landmarks, is on the water. Arriving at Üsküdar by ferry, you'll notice the squat tower on a tiny island to the south, just off the Asian mainland. In ancient times a predecessor of the current 18th-century structure functioned as a tollbooth and defence point; the Bosphorus could be closed off by means of a chain stretching from here to Seraglio Point. Some think its ancient pedigree goes back even further, calling it Leander's Tower after the tragic youth who drowned after attempting to swim across a strait to Europe to visit his lover, Hero. The object of his desire, who held a torch aloft from a tower to guide his way, was so distraught when he died that she plunged to her death from the tower. Though the European shore and a tower are here, it was the strait of the Hellespont (Dardanelles), 340km away, that Leander swam. More recently, the tower featured in the 1999 Bond film The World is Not Enough.

The tower is subject to the usual legend: oracle says maiden will die by snakebite; concerned father puts maiden in snake-proof tower; fruit vendor comes by boat, sells basket of fruit (complete with snake) to maiden, who is bitten and proves the oracle correct. The legend seems to crop up wherever there are offshore towers and maidens, and then we have to repeat it in guidebooks!

The tower is open to the public during the day as a café. At night it functions as a pricey restaurant (◷ 8.30pm-1am Tue-Sun) serving a set menu. Small boats run from Salacak to the tower every 15 minutes from noon to late at night Tuesday to Sunday for €2.70 return. There are also boats from Ortaköy at 11.30am, 1.30pm and 5.30pm (€3.30); guests booking for dinner can catch a boat from Kabataş at 8.30pm, returning at 11.15pm and 12.15am.

MİMAR SİNAN ÇARŞISI Map p289
Hakimiyet-i Milliye Caddesi; admission free;
9am-6pm; ferry from Eminönü or Beşiktaş

Built by Nurbanu Sultan, mother of Sultan Murat III, between 1574 and 1583, this *hamam* is thought to have been the first designed by Sinan. Having fallen into ruins, part of it was torn down to accommodate construction of the avenue; the remaining half was restored in 1966 and is now cramped and crowded with shops.

The area around here is noted for its antique shops – particularly on Büyük Hamam Sokak.

ŞEMSİ PAŞA CAMİİ Map p289
Sahil Yolu; ferry from Eminönü or Beşiktaş

This charming mosque right on the waterfront was designed by Sinan and built in 1580 for grand vizier Şemsi Paşa. It is modest in size and decoration – reflecting the fact that its benefactor only occupied the position of grand vizier for a couple of months under Süleyman the Magnificent. Its *medrese* has been stylishly converted into a library. The tomb of Şemsi Paşa, which has an opening into the mosque, is minded by a very friendly attendant, who is happy to show visitors throughout the complex for a small tip.

In the vicinity you'll find the Şemsipaşa Çay Bahçesi and bobbing boat restaurants selling fresh fish sandwiches, both great places to recover from a hectic schedule of Üsküdar mosque viewing.

YENİ VALİDE CAMİİ Map p289
New Queen Mother's Mosque; Demokrasi Meydanı;
ferry from Eminönü or Beşiktaş

Unusual because of the striking 'birdcage' tomb in its overgrown garden, the Yeni Valide Camii was built by Sultan Ahmet III between 1708 and 1710 for his mother, Gülnuş Emetullah. After being captured as a child on Crete and brought to Topkapı, Gülnuş became the favourite concubine of Mehmet IV, and bore him two sons who would become sultan: Mustafa II and his younger brother, Ahmet. Built late in the period of classical Ottoman architecture, it lacks the architectural distinction of many of the suburb's other mosques. The odd wooden additions to the side that faces Demokrasi Meydanı were added as the entrance to the imperial loge.

Kız Kulesi (opposite)

KADIKÖY

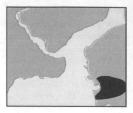

Legend has it that the first colonists established themselves at Chalcedon, now modern Kadıköy. Byzas, bearing the oracle's message to found a colony 'Opposite the blind', thought the Chalcedonites blind to the advantages of Seraglio Point (Seray Burnu) as a town site, and founded Byzantium on the European shore.

Though there's nothing to show of these historic beginnings and few headline sights, Kadıköy is a neighbourhood well worth visiting. There's fabulous fresh produce available in the market precinct near the ferry terminal; cafés and bars galore around Kadife Sokak (also home to the Rexx Cinema, one of the venues for the International İstanbul Film Festival); and one of the city's largest street markets, the Salı Pazarı (p199).

The two ferry docks – Eminönü and Karaköy & Kızıl Adalar – face a plaza along the south side of Kadıköy's small harbour. To the north is Haydarpaşa Train Station, a 15-minute walk from the ferry terminals. In the early 20th century, when Kaiser Wilhelm of Germany was trying to charm the sultan into economic and military cooperation, he presented the station as a small token of his respect. Resembling a German castle, the neoclassical exterior is a prominent part of Kadıköy's skyline as you approach by ferry. It also has a very pretty, small ferry terminal.

Kadıköy's main street, Söğütlüçeşme Caddesi, runs eastward from the docks into Kadıköy proper; another main road, Serasker Caddesi, runs parallel to it. Busy Bahariye Caddesi runs perpendicular to both of them, around 300m inland, and continues on to the posh residential suburb of Moda.

Near the street market is Rüştü Saraçoğlu Stadium (the home of Fenerbahçe Football Club), and further on from this is the glamorous shopping and café precinct of Bağdat Caddesi, İstanbul's very own Rodeo Drive.

TURKBALON

☎ 0216-347 0405; www.turkbalon.com; €9.50;
☘ summer 8am-1am, winter 9am-midnight

To see İstanbul from the air, head south along the waterfront until you come to the tethered Turkbalon , which will carry you 200m into the air to give you a 360-degree panorama of the city. Weather permitting, of course.

Transport

If you're coming from Sultanahmet, hop on the ferry from Eminönü (dock 2), which runs every 15 to 25 minutes (depending on the time of day) between 7.30am and 10.35pm.

A ferry service also operates from Beşiktaş (catch it from beside the Deniz Müzesi), starting at 7.15am, running every half-hour until 10.45pm.

From the ferry terminal at Karaköy (east of the Galata Bridge) a service runs from 6.10am every 10 to 30 minutes (depending on the time of day) until 11pm. At least half of these stop at Haydarpaşa, İstanbul's terminal for trains to Anatolia and destinations in Asia.

Buses and dolmuşes also run to and from Taksim Square.

Walking Tours

Walking Tours

İstanbul has so much to do and see that it's often difficult to choose between visiting a world-class museum, peering into a dimly lit mosque, feasting on a local specialty or sharing a leisurely game of backgammon with a local character or two. Wrap up all of these things into one package and walk from one to the other and you've got the perfect way to spend a day – one of our walking tours. These are designed to help architecture buffs find buildings of note around every corner, encourage history fiends to delve into the many layers of this ancient city and prompt curious souls to wander down secret laneways, into local cafés and around character-laden neighbourhoods. Grab a pair of comfortable shoes (the city's cobbled streets can be hard on your feet) and set off!

BYZANTINE SULTANAHMET

The Great Byzantine Palace crowned the top of the city's first hill for over 1500 years, and though it's no longer here there are plenty of other Byzantine glories in the surrounding area to discover.

Start the day at the **Great Palace Mosaic Museum 1** (p86), which features remnants of an enormous mosaic pavement thought to have been part of the palace. You'll exit into the Arasta Bazaar, a row of shops originally built to provide revenue for the upkeep of the Blue Mosque (Sultan Ahmet Camii). Dodge the touts trying to lure you into their carpet shops and move on to İstanbul's most beautiful building, **Aya Sofya 2** (p79). After spending an hour marvelling at its harmonious proportions, majestic dome and exquisite mosaics, tear yourself away

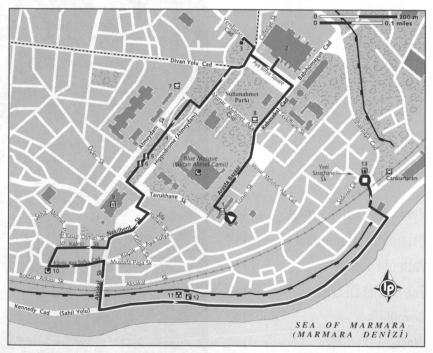

and cross the road to visit another grand structure erected by Justinian, the **Basilica Cistern 3** (Yerebatan Sarnıçı, p83). Emerging from its watery depths, head towards the **Hippodrome 4** (Atmeydanı, p86), where rival chariot teams raced in Byzantine times and Emperor Theodosius erected the Egyptian **Obelisk of Theodosius 5** (p86) that is still here 1600 years later. Fortunately, it's in better condition than Constantine the Great's sad-looking **Spiral Column 6** (p86), which lost its crown of serpents' heads in the eighteenth century.

After a tea break at the nearby **Sultan Sofrası 7** (p165) or the **Derviş Aile Çay Bahçesi 8** (p164), turn left at the end of the Hippodrome, then right, left and right again onto Nakilbent Sokak. You'll see the filled-in arches of the Byzantine **Sphendoneh 9** on your right, with a small bare park in front of it. This building originally supported the southern end of the Hippodrome. Turn left onto Aksakal Sokak and right onto Kaleci Sokak and you'll see an old *hamam*

İstanbul Archaeology Museums (p88)

(Turkish steam bath) called Çardaklı Hamamı at the intersection with Şehit Mehmet Paşa Sokak; turn left to find the **Küçük Aya Sofya Camii 10** (p89), a church built by Justinian and Theodora sometime between 527 and 536, just before Justinian built Aya Sofya. After admiring the church (which is now a mosque) and its attractive *medrese* (Islamic theological school), exit the complex, turn right onto Küçük Aya Sofya Caddesi and right onto Aksakal Sokak. Head south towards the Sea of Marmara, pass under the train line and turn left (east) at busy Kennedy Caddesi (Sahil Yolu). After about 200m you'll come to the remains of the **Bucoleon Palace 11**, built by Theophilos (c AD 830). One of the buildings of the Great Byzantine Palace, this is the only part of the complex left standing. The building jutting out to the east of the Bucoleon Palace was the **Pharos lighthouse 12**. End the tour at the friendly restaurant **Yeni Yıldız 13** (p152) just next to the Cankurtaran Railway Station, where you can enjoy lunch, dinner or a cup of tea and a game of backgammon.

Walk Facts

Start Great Palace Mosaic Museum, Sultanahmet.
End Yeni Yıldız, Sultanahmet.
Distance 1.5km.
Time 4 hours.
Fuel stops Sultan Sofrası, Derviş Aile Çay Bahçesi, Yeni Yıldız.

OTTOMAN SULTANAHMET

In 1453, Mehmet the Conqueror barged into Constantinople and made it the capital of one of the greatest empires the world has ever known. This tour will give you a taste of the empire's remarkable buildings and treasures.

Start at the **İstanbul Archaeology Museums 1** (p88). The complex has three buildings, one of which – the Tiled Kiosk of Sultan Mehmet the Conqueror – was constructed in 1472 not long after the Conquest. You'll need at least 90 minutes to view the collections in the museum's three buildings. On exiting, head right and down the hill to **Gülhane Parkı 2** (p86), once the palace park of Topkapı. At the far (north) end of the park, up the hill, is a series of terraces with a tea garden, the **Set Üstü Çay Bahçesi 3**, that has superb views over the Bosphorus.

Retrace your steps and leave the park by the south end. As you exit look to your right to see a bulbous little kiosk built into the park walls at the next street corner. This is the

Walk Facts

Start İstanbul Archaeology Museums, Sultanahmet.
End Sokollu Mehmet Paşa Camii, Sultanahmet.
Distance 2.3km.
Time 6 hours.
Fuel stops Set Üstü Çay Bahçesi, Café Meşale.

Alay Köşkü 4 (Parade Kiosk). The sultan would sit here and watch the periodic Ottoman parades of troops and trade guilds held to commemorate great holidays and military victories. Across the street from the Alay Köşkü (not quite visible from the Gülhane Parkı gate) is the famous **Sublime Porte 5**, a fantastical rococo gate leading into the precincts of what was once the grand vizierate, or Ottoman prime ministry. Rather than following the tram up Alemdar Caddesi, turn left into the steep and extremely picturesque **Soğukçeşme Sokak 6** (p90), a street of Ottoman wooden houses that runs between the Topkapı Palace (Topkapı Sarayı) walls and Aya Sofya. Just off Soğukçeşme Sokak you'll find the **Caferağa Medresesi 7** (p85) designed by court architect Sinan in 1560 on the orders of Cafer Ağa, the chief black eunuch. Walk back to Soğukçeşme Sokak and turn right. After a short walk you'll come to the elegant **Fountain of Sultan Ahmet III 8** (p91) outside the main entrance to Topkapı Palace, where you should turn right into Babıhümayun Caddesi. Follow the street until you come to Aya Sofya Square and turn to your right again; just past the corner on the opposite side to Aya Sofya itself is the **Baths of Lady Hürrem 9** (p83), a *hamam* commissioned

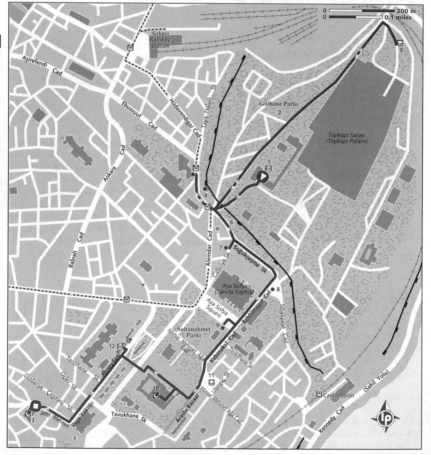

by Süleyman the Magnificent for his wife Roxelana. Now a government-run carpet shop, it's part of Sinan's prodigious oeuvre. After wandering through the baths, make your way to the building that has graced more postcards than any other: the sexily curvaceous **Blue Mosque 10** (p84). If a lunch stop is called for at this point, think about trying the nearby **Café Meşale 11** (p164).

Next, check out the excellent collection of rugs at the **Museum of Turkish & Islamic Arts 12** (p89), housed in what was the Palace of İbrahim Paşa. Your final stop for the day, the **Sokollu Mehmet Paşa Camii 13** (p90), is only a short walk away.

PATH OF EMPIRES

Divan Yolu, the main thoroughfare of the old city, was laid out by Roman engineers to connect the city with Roman roads heading west. In this tour you will set off in their footsteps and finish at one of the most magnificent of all Ottoman buildings, the Süleymaniye Camii.

Hit the road opposite the Sultanahmet

<table>
<tr><td colspan="2">**Walk Facts**</td></tr>
<tr><td>**Start** Milion, Divan Yolu.</td></tr>
<tr><td>**End** Süleymaniye Camii, Süleymaniye.</td></tr>
<tr><td>**Distance** 1.5km.</td></tr>
<tr><td>**Time** 5 hours.</td></tr>
<tr><td>**Fuel stops** İlesam Lokalı, Dârüzziyafe, Lale Bahçesi.</td></tr>
</table>

tram stop, at the **Milion 1**, the great marble milestone from which all distances in Byzantium were measured. You'll find it in the south side of the park near the Basilica Cistern. Head west along Divan Yolu to the little **Firuz Ağa Camii 2**, built in 1491 during the reign of Beyazıt II (r 1481–1512). Just behind Firuz Ağa Camii is the 5th-century **Palace of Antiochus 3**, now mere ruined foundations. Further along Divan Yolu, turn left into Klodfarer Caddesi, named after the Turcophile French novelist Claude Farrère. This leads to a small park, beneath which lies the 4th-century **Binbirdirek Cistern 4** (p84). Back on Divan Yolu, you'll see an impressive enclosure right at the corner of Babıali Caddesi which is filled with **tombs 5**

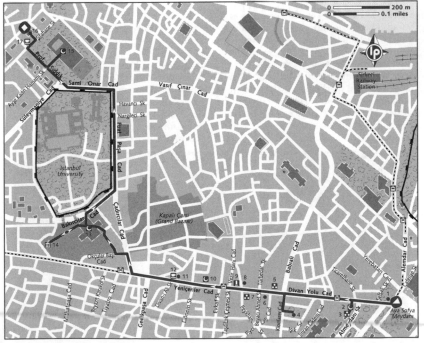

of the Ottoman high and mighty, including several sultans. The first to be built was for Sultan Mahmut II (r 1808–39), the reforming emperor who wiped out the janissaries and revamped the Ottoman army. Several of Mahmut's successors, including sultans Abdül Aziz (r 1861–76) and Abdül Hamit II (r 1876–1909), are buried here as well.

Exit the tombs and cross the road to find the small stone **Köprülü library 6** built by the Köprülü family in 1659 as part of a *külliye* (mosque complex). Stroll a bit further along Divan Yolu and into the Çemberlitaş district, where Divan Yolu changes name to Yeniçeriler Caddesi. On the left are some more buildings from the Köprülü *külliyesi*. The **tomb 7** is that of Köprülü Mehmet Paşa (1575–1661) and the octagonal mosque, on the corner, was a lecture and study room. Across the street, that strange building with a row of street-front shops is actually an ancient Turkish bath, the **Çemberlitaş Hamamı 8** (p172).

The derelict column rising up from the pigeon-packed plaza close by is, surprisingly, one of İstanbul's most ancient and revered monuments, **Çemberlitaş 9** (p85), the Banded Stone or Burnt Column. A bit further on is the **Atik Ali Paşa Camii 10**, built in 1496 by a eunuch and grand vizier of Beyazıt II. It's one of the oldest mosques in the city. Beyond Atik Ali Paşa Camii on the right (north) side is the **Koca Sinan Paşa Medresesi 11**, resting place of Grand Vezir Koca Sinan Paşa. His tomb is finely carved, complete with coloured stonework. After you've seen the tomb, head past the cemetery and to the right, where you'll find the quiet gardens of the **İlesam Lokalı 12** (p166), a great place to enjoy a tea and nargileh.

Continue along Yeniçeriler Caddesi until you see the **Beyazıt Camii 13** (p102) on your right. Its *medrese* is now the **Museum of Turkish Calligraphic Art 14** (p104). After exiting the mosque towards İstanbul University, go to the right and head up Fuat Paşa Caddesi, following the university's walls. Turn left up Prof Sıddık Sami Onar Caddesi and you will come to one of the most majestic of all Ottoman mosques and the last stop on this tour, the **Süleymaniye Camii 15** (p106).

After visiting the mosque, consider enjoying a tea or coffee at **Dârüzziyafe 16**, a restaurant in the mosque's *külliye* (don't eat here, as in our experience the food's poor) or the nearby **Lale Bahçesi 17** (p166).

THE BAZAAR DISTRICT

A walk in this vibrant part of the old city will take you through İstanbul's most famous bazaars, past ancient *hans* (caravanserais), along bustling shopping streets and into exquisite mosques.

Set off from the **Nuruosmaniye Camii 1** (p104) outside the **Grand Bazaar 2** (Kapalı Çarşı, p102). From the mosque's courtyard you will notice **Nuruosmaniye Kapısı 3**, one of several doorways into the ancient marketplace. The gold emblem above the doorway is the Ottoman armorial emblem with the sultan's monogram. Enter the bazaar and walk down glittering **Kalpakçılarbaşı Caddesi 4**. Pop into the **Sandal Bedesten 5**, a rectangular hall with a domed roof supported by 12 large pillars – this was once the city's auction place for used and antique goods. Back on

Spice Bazaar (p106)

Walk Facts

Start Nuruosmaniye Camii, Beyazıt.
End Galata Bridge, Eminönü.
Distance 1.7km.
Time 5 hours.
Fuel stops Şark Kahvesi, Havuzlu Restaurant.

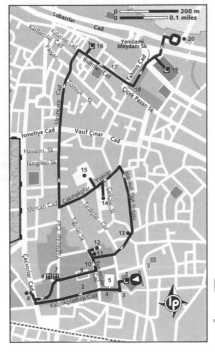

Kalpakçılarbaşı Caddesi head west, exit the bazaar at the end of Kalpakçılarbaşı Caddesi and once outside, turn right onto Çadırcılar Caddesi, then left through a doorway to the **Sahaflar Çarşısı 6** (Old Book Bazaar, p102). After having a browse, head back into the Grand Bazaar and take a break at **Şark Kahvesi 7** (p166) or **Havuzlu Restaurant 8** (p153).

When you're ready to set off again, make your way to the **Old Bazaar 9** (İç Bedesten, p102), at the centre of the market, which dates from Mehmet the Conqueror's time. Exit the Old Bazaar via its eastern doorway to **Kuyumcular Caddesi 10** (Jewellers St), aglitter with gold and gems. Turn left to find the crooked **Oriental Kiosk 11**, which was built as a coffee house. Continue north, up Acı Çeşme Sokak as far as the right turn, into the gorgeous, pink **Zincirli Han 12** – the first of three *hans* you'll see on this walk.

It's now time to head out, via Mahmut Paşa Kapısı, into the streets where locals shop. Along cobbled Mahmut Paşa Yokuşu spruikers fill most of the roadway, and the good-natured throng of shoppers elbow-jostle and lurch through the maze, frequently parting (under duress) to allow an overloaded pick-up truck to squeeze through. Head downhill. You'll soon pass the **Mahmut Paşa Hamamı 13** on the left. Built in 1476, it's one of the oldest *hamams* in the city. Today it houses clothing shops and a clean public toilet. Walk another 250m, and then turn left into Çakmakçılar Yokuşu. The large blue doors just after the first street on the left hide one of İstanbul's Ottoman baroque caravanserais, the **Büyük Yeni Han 14** (Big New Caravanserai). The nearby **Büyük Valide Han 15**, the biggest in İstanbul, was built in 1651 by Sultan İbrahim's mother. To find it, continue another 150m up Çakmakçılar Yokuşu and you'll see the entrance on the right. Pass through the first small courtyard and stand in the gateway of the huge courtyard; you should see steps on either side leading to the grimy 1st floor.

Back on Çakmakçılar Yokuşu, turn right into Uzunçarşı Caddesi (Longmarket St) to continue your walk. Uzunçarşı Caddesi lives up to its name, being one long market of woodturners' shops, luggage merchants, shops selling guns and hunting equipment, plastic toys, freshly baked sesame rolls *(simits)*, backgammon sets and more. At the foot of the hill, Uzunçarşı Caddesi runs straight to the small, exquisite **Rüstem Paşa Camii 16** (p105). Going southeast from the Rüstem Paşa Camii is **Hasırcılar Caddesi 17** (Mat-Makers' St). Shops along here sell spices, nuts, condiments, knives, bowls and tea. The colours, smells, sights and sounds make this one of the liveliest and most interesting streets in the city.

A 10-minute stroll to the east brings you to the **Spice Bazaar 18** (Mısır Çarşısı, p106). After indulging in its olfactory delights, maybe even sampling some of the *lokum* (Turkish delight) on offer, walk from the waterside exit across the square to the **Yeni Camii 19** (New Mosque, p99). Your last stop of the day is the **Galata Bridge 20** (Galata Köprüsü, p101), from where you may want to walk over to Beyoğlu and enjoy a drink or dinner in one of the suburb's many bars, cafés or restaurants.

BEYOĞLU

This full-day walk starts from Beyoğlu's busy nerve centre, **Taksim Square 1** (p123) and works its way down the former Rue de Pera, now called İstiklal Caddesi, the city's most famous shopping and entertainment strip, to end at Karaköy.

Walk Facts

Start Taksim Square, Taksim.
End Azapkapı Sokollu Mehmet Paşa Camii, Karaköy.
Distance 2.2km.
Time 6 hours.
Fuel stops Patisserie Markiz.

Just out of Taksim Square, the first building on the right of İstiklal Caddesi is the former French plague hospital (1719), now the **French Consulate General 2**. Walk down towards Galatasaray Square, which has as its most prominent feature the **Galatasaray Lycée 3** (p120). Just before you reach the square, turn right into the **Çiçek Pasajı 4** (Flower Passage, p120) and make your way through it into the **Balık Pazar 5** (Fish Market). Turn left into the **Avrupa Pasajı 6** (European Passage) and into Meşrutiyet Caddesi. On the corner in front of you is the **British Consulate General 7**, an Italian *palazzo* built in 1845 to plans by Sir Charles Barry, architect of London's Houses of Parliament. The consulate was bombed in 2003, but is being restored.

If you head further up Meşrutiyet Caddesi, you'll make your way down to the famous hotel **Pera Palas Oteli 8** (p121). Just past the British Consulate General, watch for an iron gate

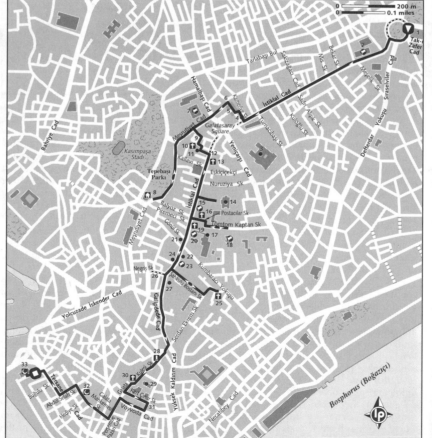

Tünel Square (p155)

and a small passage on the left, leading into a little stone courtyard, the **Hacopulo Pasajı 9**, with a derelict lamppost in the centre. Enter the courtyard, turn right up the stairs and you'll discover the Greek Orthodox **Church of Panaya Isodyon 10**. Go down the stairs to the east of the church (not the stairs you came up), turn right and just past the church property on the right-hand side you will see the entrance to the **Rejans Lokantası 11** (Regency Restaurant). Founded by three White Russian dancing girls who fled the Russian Revolution, the restaurant is still operated by their Russian-speaking descendants, who ply cashed-up guests with flavoured vodka and caviar. Go down the steps, turn right and then left along the narrow alley called **Olivia Han Pasajı 12**, which brings you back to İstiklal Caddesi. Turn right and continue walking. You'll soon notice a large Italian Gothic church behind a fence on the left-hand side of the road. This is the Franciscan **Church of San Antonio di Padua 13**, founded here in 1725; the present red-brick building dates from 1913. The third street, past the church, Muammer Karaca Sokak, ends at the gates of the **Palais de France 14**, once the French embassy to the Ottoman sultan. The grounds are extensive and include the chapel of St Louis of the French, founded here in 1581, though the present chapel building dates from the 1830s.

Back on İstiklal Caddesi, you'll soon come to the pretty **Netherlands Consulate General 15**, built in 1855 by the Swiss Fossati brothers, formerly architects to the Russian tsar. Past the consulate, turn left down the hill into Postacılar Sokak. The **Dutch Chapel 16**, on the left, is now the home of the Union Church of İstanbul. The narrow street turns right, bringing you face to face with the **former Spanish embassy 17**. The little chapel, which was founded in 1670, is still in use. The street then bends left and changes names to become Tomtom Kaptan Sokak. At the foot of the slope, on the right, is the **Palazzo di Venezia 18**, once the embassy for Venice, now the Italian consulate. Backtrack to İstiklal Caddesi, where the **Church of St Mary Draperis 19**, built in 1904, is behind an iron fence on the left and down a flight of steps. It occupies the site of its previous building, destroyed by fire in 1870. During the Ottoman period, there was a law that prevented non-Muslim spires from appearing on the city skyline – no doubt the reason for this 'sunken' location. Past the church, still on the left-hand side, is the grand **Russian Consulate General 20**, built in 1837 to designs by the Fossati brothers. Opposite and a bit further on is the newly restored **Passage Markiz 21** (p121) with its famous patisserie. This is a perfect place to stop and enjoy a decadent cake and coffee. A bit further on from the Russian consulate is a wonderful, if dilapidated, building known as **Botter House 22**. Designed by Raimondo D'Aronco for the chief tailor to the imperial court of Sultan Abül Hamıt II, this was the first Art Nouveau building in Pera (as Beyoğlu was previously known). Next to it is the **Royal Swedish Consulate 23**. Across the street, the large pillared building called the **Narmanlı Han 24** served as the Russian embassy until the 1840s. Turn left downhill on Şahkulu Bostanı Sokak next to the Swedish Consulate. At the base of the slope turn left, then right, onto Serdarı Ekrem Sokak to find the Anglican sanctuary of **Christ Church 25** (p117).

Back up on İstiklal Caddesi, the road curves to the right into **Tünel Square 26.** Turn left into Galipdede Caddesi, which is lined with shops selling musical instruments, and you'll see on your left the **Mevlevi Monastery 27** (p118), home of İstanbul's Whirling Dervishes. Keep walking down Galipdede Caddesi until you come to the first cross street. Look right and you will see one of the city's major landmarks, the **Galata Tower 28** (p118).

From Galata Tower continue downhill on the street called Galata Kulesi Sokak. On the left you'll see the distinctive tower of İstanbul's Eye Hospital, the **former British Seaman's Hospital 29**, designed by Charles Holden and Percy Evans in 1904. On the right, you'll see the small blue-grey doorway to the courtyard of the **Church of SS Peter and Paul 30** (p118). Continue down Galata Kulesi Sokak and turn left into Kart Çınar Sokak; from here the sculptural **Kamondo Stairs 31** (p118) run south down to Voyvoda Caddesi (also called Bankalar Caddesi). This street was the heart of the banking centre during the days of the empire and many merchant banks still have headquarters or branches here. Turn right at Voyvoda Caddesi and walk for around 100m until you see Perşembe Pazarı Caddesi (Thursday Market St) on your left. Take this road and the first right, Galata Mahkemesi Sokak, will lead you to the **Arap Camii 32** (p117), designed by the great Sinan. Continue along Galata Mahkemesi Sokak to the intersection with Abdül Selah Sokak and then turn left and head to the end of the street to busy Tersane Caddesi. Walk right to find, after five minutes' walk, another of Sinan's works, the **Azapkapı Sokollu Mehmet Paşa Camii 33** (p117). This is where the walking tour ends.

WESTERN DISTRICTS

This part of the city is one of the least visited by visitors and that's a shame, because it's one of the most interesting. Buck the trend and kick off from the **Fatih Camii 1** (p110), built atop one of İstanbul's seven hills. The resting place of Mehmet the Conqueror, it is one of the most sacred places in the city for Muslims. From here walk 30 minutes or so north up busy Fevzi Paşa Caddesi past Vefa Stadyumu (Vefa Soccer Stadium) to Edirnekapı, one of

Kariye Müzesi (p111)

the gates in the city's ancient walls. To the left is the attractive **Mihrimah Sultan Camii 2** (p113). From here, cross the road and, still inside the walls, head north towards the Golden Horn (Haliç). You'll see signs pointing the way to the **Kariye Müzesi 3** (Chora Church, p111), one of the city's most magnificent museums.

After marvelling at the Byzantine mosaics and frescoes, consider stopping for lunch at the excellent **Asitane 4** (p154).

Having noshed on Ottoman delicacies, head west to the city walls, then north again and you'll soon come to the **Tekfur Sarayı 5** (Palace of Constantine Porphyrogenetus, p114). Retrace your steps to the Kariye Müzesi and turn left downhill on Neşler Sokak just past the Kariye Oteli. Turn left at

Walk Facts

Start Fatih Camii, Fatih.
End Church of St Stephen of the Bulgars, Fener.
Distance 6km.
Time 6 hours.
Fuel stops Asitane, Hotel Daphnis.

the bottom of the hill around a little pink mosque, then head straight on along a level street and uphill on Fethiye Caddesi. It will take you around 30 minutes to reach the top of the slope, turn left and arrive at the **Fethiye Camii 6** (Mosque of the Conquest, p111).

Backtrack to Fethiye Caddesi and walk southeast along shop-filled Manyasizade Caddesi for 10 minutes, then turn sharp left around the police station (*polis karakolu*) onto

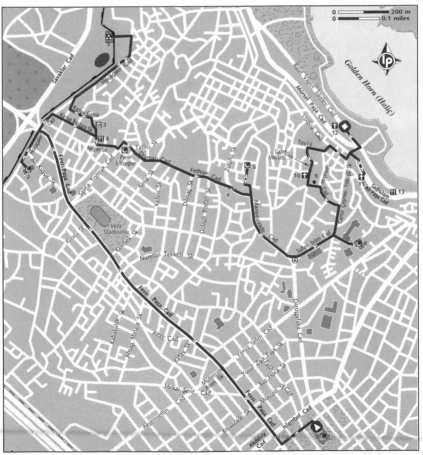

Sultan Selim Caddesi. Pass the huge, open Roman **Çukur Bostan 7** (Cistern of Aspar), built by a general in the Roman army in the AD 400s and now used as a sportsground. Just past the cistern you'll come to the **Sultan Selim Camii 8** (p114). After viewing the mosque and tomb and enjoying the views over the Golden Horn, exit the mosque compound and turn right, heading down Camcı Çeşme Yoküşü Sokak. Take the first street on the left, Mesnevihane Sokak and walk along it until you see a large red-brick tower ahead. This is the **Great School 9** (Greek Lycée of Fener), the oldest learning institution in İstanbul and founded long before the Conquest. The present building dates from 1881. Walk up and around the school to find the historic **St Mary of the Mongols 10** (p113).

Head left (downhill), take the first right and you'll see a flight of steps at the end of the lane. Walk down these, turn left and take the first right again. Continue through the Akçin Sokak intersection (you'll see the Golden Horn on your left) for another 500m or so along Sadrazam Ali Paşa Caddesi and you'll come to the **Ecumenical Orthodox Patriarchate 11** (p109). After you've seen the patriarchate compound, retrace your steps to Akçin Sokak and turn left on the main road, Balat Vapur İskelesi Caddesi. Head northwest, past the Women's Library, to what would have to be the city's most unusual building, the cast-iron **Church of St Stephen of the Bulgars 12** (p108), where this walk ends. The nearby **Hotel Daphnis 13** (p210) has a great little café serving meals, coffee and cake.

Eating

Eating

İstanbul is a food-lover's paradise. Teeming with affordable fast-food joints, cafés and restaurants, it leaves visitors spoiled for choice when it comes to choosing a venue. Best of all, it's proud of its national cuisine. And oh, what a great cuisine it is! The city's restaurants vie with each other to produce the best damn meze, the freshest possible seafood and the most succulent kebabs in town, all appreciated by legions of locals for whom eating out is a way of life and a true passion. There are other cuisines on offer (you can eat fusion dishes in Western-style brasseries and sample cuisines as diverse as Russian, Italian and Thai), but the best places to eat are the lokantas, meyhanes and Ottoman-style restaurants that the locals frequent.

Unfortunately, the area where most visitors to the city stay is also a wasteland when it comes to food. With the exception of Balıkçı Sabahattın, there are no top-class restaurants in Sultanahmet and only a few decent cheap eateries. Instead, visitors should cross the Galata Bridge and join the locals eating in Beyoğlu, Teşvikiye and Beşiktaş. Absolutely nothing can beat the enjoyment of spending a night in a meyhane on Nevizade Sokak or in the streets surrounding Asmalımescit Sokak (both in Beyoğlu), or dining at one of the swish restaurants down near the Bosphorus such as Vogue in Beşiktaş. There are other pockets of town worth investigating – Eminönü has the wonderful Hamdi Et Lokantası, Samatya is home to the best kebabs in town at Develi and Edirnekapı has the excellent Asitane – but on the whole you will be well served by making your way across the Galata Bridge every night. As the Turks say, *afıyet olsun! (bon appétit!)*.

Opening Hours

Most eateries in İstanbul are open for long hours every day of the week; occasionally they will close on a Sunday or Monday. Some lokantas and all börekçis and büfes open for early breakfasts; cafés open around 9am and serve into the night; and pidecis, kebapçıs, meyhanes, cafés and restaurants all open for lunch and dinner. Their average closing time will be 11pm, though many stay open later, particularly on Friday and Saturday evenings.

How Much?

You can spend a fortune or a pittance on a meal in İstanbul, but most visitors will spend something in between. The cheapest meals are those served in pidecis, kebapçıs and lokantas – it's quite usual for a meal to cost a mere two or three euros in these joints. A toasted sandwich or döner kebap and fresh juice in a büfe will usually cost even less. And one of the city's most famous meals – a delicious fish sandwich on the quay at Eminönü or Üsküdar – costs a bargain basement €0.80. Cafés are pricey in comparison, with a cappuccino costing as much as a lokanta meal in many instances. Restaurants where alcohol is served are in another league again: a meyhane meal will cost around €20 including alcohol and a meal in one of the swish Western-style eateries in town can cost up to double that.

In this chapter we've listed all places offering meals for less than €4 under a 'Cheap Eats' heading.

Booking Tables

İstanbullus like to eat out and they often book ahead, which means that you should, too. On Friday and Saturday nights it's very difficult to get a table anywhere popular if you haven't booked. Restaurants with views almost inevitably expect diners to reserve; if you want to ensure a table with a view, be very sure to specify this when you book.

Some of the more glamorous places in town will have more than one sitting in an evening. This means that you may be offered a table at 6pm or 10pm, and be told that there's nothing available in between. Fortunately this is quite uncommon.

Tipping

In all places where table service is given tipping is expected. Ten per cent is the norm. A few of the more touristy establishments include an extra service charge in the bill (look for the words *servis dahil*), but as is the case in many European countries you are usually expected to tip on top of this.

Self-Catering

İstanbul has many small supermarkets (eg Gima, Makro) sprinkled through the streets around Beyoğlu, with giant cousins (eg Migros) in the suburbs. These sell most of the items you will need if you plan to self-cater. Then there is the ubiquitous *bakkal* (corner shop), which stocks bread, milk, basic groceries and usually fruit and vegetables. Some of these also sell *süt* (fresh milk) – look for the term 'pasteurized' on the label and you'll know it's fresh rather than long-life.

The best places to purchase fresh produce are undoubtedly the street markets. Akbıyık Caddesi in Cankurtaran (near Sultanahmet) – backpacker central – has a street market all day Wednesday where a decent range of fruit, vegetables, eggs, pickles, cheese and olives can be purchased. Down in Eminönü, the streets around the Spice Bazaar (Mısır Çarşısı) sell fish, meats, vegetables, fruit, spices, sweets and much more. The best stuff is available at the street stalls on Tahmis Caddesi on the market's west wall. In Beyoğlu, the Balık Pazar (Fish Market) next to the Çiçek Pasajı on İstiklal Caddesi is a great, if expensive, little market. As well as its many fish stalls, it has small shops selling freshly baked bread, greengrocers selling a wide range of fruit and vegetables, and delicatessens (*şarküteri*) selling cheeses, dried meats such as pastrami (*pastırma*), pickled fish, olives, jams and preserves. You can even get imported goods such as French jams, Iranian caviar and English tea here. Larger produce markets are found opposite the ferry terminals in Kadıköy and Beşiktaş – Kadiköy is known for its delicatessens and bakeries, and Beşiktaş for its fruit and vegetable stalls. See the Shopping chapter (pp185–200) for reviews of fresh produce shops.

OLD İSTANBUL

SULTANAHMET

It really is a shame that the quality of food served up in Sultanahmet's eateries is so mediocre. With the exception of Balıkçı Sabahattin, we can't get too excited about any of the restaurants feeding the hordes of tourists staying in this area. Fortunately, there are a few decent köftecis, pidecis and kebapçıs around (p151), as well as the fabulous Çiğdem Pastanesi, one of the best places in town to enjoy a tea and honey-soaked baklava. Places close early and there is no food strip as such.

AMEDROS Map pp278-80 *Modern Turkish*
☎ 212-522 8356; Hoca Rüstem Sokak, off Divan Yolu Caddesi; mains €10; ✆ 9.30am-11pm
There always seems to be a golden glow over this restaurant. We're not sure whether it's down to the candle-lit tables, the warm terracotta tones of the interior or the aura emanating from the happy owners, who have ensured through their consummate professionalism that the place is constantly full of cashed-up tourists. We can't fault the atmosphere, love

the soft jazz on the sound system, admire the varied wine list and always enjoy watching the theatrical tableside serving of the house specialty 'testi kebab', but we wish the food was equally impressive. As it is, the menu is perfectly acceptable but a bit bland. The coffee is the best on this side of town.

ANTIQUE GALLERY
Map pp278-80 *Modern Turkish*
☎ 212-517 3750; Akbıyık Caddesi 40, Cankurtaran; mains €4.40-11; ✆ 9.30am-11pm
The hundreds of brightly coloured lamps on the ceiling beckon guests into this popular place on Akbıyık Caddesi, aka 'backpacker central'. Unfortunately, the décor's the only thing that's inspired, with the menu featuring Turkish staples that are of an acceptable standard but no more than that. There are a number of vegetarian options on offer.

BALIKÇI SABAHATTIN
Map pp278-80 *Seafood*
☎ 212-458 1824; Seyit Hasan Koyu Sokak 1, Cankurtaran; mains €19; ✆ noon-1am
The solid stream of chauffeur-driven limousines stopping outside Balıkçı Sabahattin is

testament to its enduring popularity with the city's establishment. The only top-notch restaurant in Sultanahmet (praise be!), it's set in a restored wooden Ottoman house tucked away in a ramshackle street just near the train line. The menu comprises a limited range of top-notch meze and good-quality fresh fish. In summer, grab a table in the garden with the politicians and industrialists, and try to guess whether the glamorous women at their tables are wives, daughters or mistresses. We know where we'd put our bets.

DUBB Map pp278-80 *Indian*
☎ 212-513 7308; İncili Çavuş Sokak, Alemdar; mains €8.30; ⏲ noon-3pm & 6-10.30pm
One of İstanbul's few Indian restaurants and the only one worthy of a recommendation, Dubb is a little piece of the Subcontinent slap-bang in the middle of Sultanahmet. It specialises in tandoori dishes (try the *chandi ki mohren* – cottage cheese and potato stuffed in green pepper and cooked in a clay oven, €7.50), but also serves the full complement of fragrant curries. The *thalis* (€12.50-13.60), which offer small serves of a number of dishes including dessert, are particularly popular. The newly opened outdoor terrace on the fourth floor offers fabulous views of **Aya Sofya** (p79) – request a table there when you book.

KONUK EVİ
Map pp278-80 *Garden Restaurant/Café*
☎ 212-517 6785; Soğukçeşme Sokak; mains €4.50-8.30; ⏲ noon-3.30pm, 6.30-10.30pm, closed winter
A secluded flower-filled garden and fairytale-like glass conservatory around the corner from **Topkapı Palace** (p91) is waiting just for you. Don't believe us? Walk down Soğukçeşme Sokak

and go through the gate opposite Ayasofya Pansiyonları and you'll find the Konuk Evi, one of the most relaxing places in the city to enjoy a quiet alfresco lunch. A toasted sandwich costs €2.80 and a cup of tea €1.70.

KONYALI Map pp278-80 *Turkish*
☎ 212-513 9696; Topkapı Palace; mains €9; ⏲ 10am-5pm
Fabulously positioned in the grounds of **Topkapı Palace** (p91) and emanating a charmingly down-at-heel Riviera feel, Konyalı is a perennial favourite. There are few more pleasant experiences than sitting in its glass pavilion or outdoor terrace, both of which overlook the Golden Horn and Sea of Marmara, while noshing on the *beğendili kebab* (lamb kebab with eggplant puree, €10.50). For something special, why not sample an Ottoman sherbet (€3) with your meal – you'll see their bright colours glinting from the large glass decanters on display. There's another branch on Ankara Caddesi opposite Sirkeci Railway Station.

MAGNAURA Map pp278-80 *Modern Turkish*
☎ 212-518 7622; Akbıyık Caddesi 27, Cankurtaran; mains €8; ⏲ 9.30am-11pm
If you loved the fussy and dried-herb-laden cuisine of London bistros c 1990, Magnaura is for you. Its interior is very pleasant – the restaurant equivalent of hotel 'Cankurtaran Modern', featuring a warm paint scheme, wooden boards and artfully placed Anatolian *objets d'art* – but the food doesn't live up to its surrounds. If you sit on the pleasant roof terrace (open mid-May) and stick to the most simple dishes, you'll enjoy your evening – particularly as in most cases it will only be a short saunter back to your hotel room.

Kumkapı

In Byzantine times, the fishers' harbour called Kontoscalion was due south of Beyazıt. The gate into the city from that port came to be called Kumkapı (Sand Gate) by the Turks. Though the gate is long gone, the district is still filled with fishermen, who moor their boats in a more modern version of the old harbour. And around this harbour cobbled laneways are filled with seafood restaurants and meyhanes. A few years ago the district was always packed with large groups of locals enjoying a boozy night on the town, but these days the attractions of Nevizade Sokak in Beyoğlu have caused its star to wane and its streets are only full of hawkers trying to lure passers-by into establishments that are rarely even half full. Still, the surrounds and the quality of the seafood in a few of the longer-standing eateries make it worth a visit when you're in town. On the Sea of Marmara just inside the Wall, it's a quick taxi ride from Sultanahmet. Alternatively, you can catch a train to Kumkapı Station from Sirkeci and walk north up Ördekli Bakkal Sokak (Grocer with a Duck St), or walk all the way down Tiyatro Caddesi from Beyazıt. When there, wander around and see which establishment takes your fancy. We usually gravitate towards **Kör Agop Restaurant** (☎ 212-517 2334; Ördekli Bakkal Sokak 7, Kumkapı; fish meze €3.40, fish €5.60; ⏲ 11am-2am), which was established in 1938 and has one of the best *fasıl* bands around. It also serves excellent fresh fish.

terranean touches. Try the thyme-marinated lamb wrapped in fried aubergine slices.

SERA RESTAURANT

Map pp278-80   *Modern Turkish*
☎ 212-638 1370; Hotel Armada, Ahırkapı Sokak, Cankurtaran; degustation menu €19; ⏰ 12.30-3pm & 7.30pm-midnight

The chef at the Sera came up with an inspired idea when he devised the Turkish degustation menu at this hotel restaurant. Six sampling courses of 'İstanbul cuisine' feature, and they are wonderfully complemented by the excellent wine list and lovely atmosphere. The outdoor terrace has a view of **Blue Mosque** (p84) and very comfortable seating; live Turkish music occasionally accompanies your dinner.

Cheap Eats

CENNET Map pp278-80   *Anatolian*
☎ 212-513 5098; Yeniçeriler Caddesi 90, Çemberlitaş; ⏰ 8am-11pm

Only the cheesy nightclubs offering 'live Turkish shows' come near to emulating the outrageous kitsch of this Anatolian restaurant. Set in part of the historic Çemberlitaş Hamamı, it encourages diners to don Ottoman costumes, recline 'Ottoman-style' and listen to 'Ottoman' musicians (noon to 9.30pm) while noshing on *gözleme* (Turkish pancake), the restaurant's specialty. Consider yourself warned.

ÇİĞDEM PASTANESİ

Map pp278-80   *Patisserie*
☎ 212-526 8859; Divan Yolu Caddesi 62A; ⏰ 8am-11pm

Customers have been ordering tea and baklava here since 1961. Çiğdem makes the best tea on Divan Yolu (€0.50), a cappuccino that could hold its head high on the Via Veneto in Rome (€1.90) and the most heavenly baklava imaginable. No wonder it's always crammed with students from nearby İstanbul University, and tourists who've heard of its fame and want a piece of the action.

DOY-DOY Map pp278-80   *Lokanta*
☎ 212-517 1588; Şifa Hamamı Sokak 13; mains €1.70; ⏰ 8am-11pm

The rooftop of this simple restaurant is always packed with backpackers sampling the extensive menu and being served by friendly waiters. Don't expect a gourmet experience.

Rami (below)

RAMİ Map pp278-80   *Ottoman*
☎ 212-517 6593; Utangaç Sokak 6, Cankurtaran; mains €13.30; ⏰ noon-midnight

This restored Ottoman house has several quaint dining rooms that are decorated with impressionist-style paintings by Turkish painter Rami Uluer (1913-80), but the favoured spot for dinner is the rooftop terrace, which has a full view of the **Blue Mosque** (Sultan Ahmet Camii; p84). Make sure you request a table there when you book. Ottoman specialities such as *hünkâr beğendi* (grilled lamb and rich aubergine puree) or *kağıt kebap* (lamb and vegetables cooked in a paper pouch) are served and, although they're not the best we've tasted, the view certainly compensates.

RUMELİ Map pp278-80   *Modern Turkish*
☎ 212-512 0008; Ticarethane Sokak 8, off Divan Yolu Caddesi; mains €7.20; ⏰ 9am-midnight

Over the years Rumeli has built a reputation as the most stylish restaurant in this part of town (which isn't, of course, saying too much). The attractively rustic interior is particularly pleasant in cooler weather, when an open fire warms guests; in summer it's best to bag a streetside table. Food is Turkish with Medi-

HAFİZ MUSTAFA ŞEKERLEMELERİ

Map pp278-80   *Patisserie/Börekçi*

☎ 212-526 5627; Hamidiye Caddesi 84-86, Eminönü;
🕙 8am-9pm Mon-Sat, 9am-9pm Sun

If you walk up the steep staircase at the rear of this excellent börek, pastry and Turkish-delight shop, you'll find a tiny café secreted under the roof. Here locals eat all-day snacks of melt-in-your-mouth cheese börek, peppery *ispanaklı börek* (spinach börek) and delicious biscuits and sweet pastries, all washed down with tea and coffee. Breakfast will set you back a mere €1 or so.

KARADENİZ AİLE PİDE VE KEBAP
SALONU Map pp278-80   *Pideci & Kebapçı*

☎ 212-528 6290; Hacı Tahsınbery Sokak 1, off Divan Yolu Caddesi; 🕙 7am-11pm

This tiny place serves super-fresh soup, kebabs and *pide*. If you sit downstairs, you can watch the cooks making your food; upstairs there's a family salon. The *pide* (€1.70-2.50) are excellent and the *İskender kebaps* (€2.50) go down a treat. Recommended.

LALE RESTAURANT Map pp278-80   *Lokanta*

Pudding Shop; ☎ 212-522 2970; Divan Yolu Caddesi 6; mains €1.70; 🕙 7am-11pm

It's a long time since the Pudding Shop served up fare to the hippies who made it famous, but its fame still drags in backpackers travelling in their parents' footsteps, who choose from the large spread of stodgy dishes on offer.

TARİHİ SULTANAHMET KÖFTECİSİ
SELİM USTA Map pp278-80   *Köfteci*

☎ 212-511 3960; Divan Yolu Caddesi 4;
🕙 9am-11pm

You'll feel as if you're dining in a bathroom when you eat at this no-frills, no-menu place. Famous for its delicious *köfte* (meatballs) served with bread and salad, it's always packed to the rafters with hungry locals grabbing a cheap snack.

YENİ YILDIZ

Map pp278-80   *Pideci & Kebapçı*

☎ 212-518 1257; Cankurtaran Meydanı 18, Cankurtaran; 🕙 7am-11pm

Not many tourists make their way down the cobbled streets below the Cankurtaran hotel strip, but if they were to walk down to the train line they'd find Yeni Yıldız, one of the best local eateries in this part of town. A large place with indoor and outdoor seating, it's inevitably filled with locals who spend the afternoon sitting under the trees and vine-covered awning, drinking tea, playing backgammon and sampling the cheap and tasty food on offer. At night, groups of young people claim the seats and order dinner, followed by coffee and a nargileh (water pipe). *Patlıcanlı kebab* (aubergine kebab) costs €2.80 and *pide* range from €1.90 to €2.20.

Top Five Old İstanbul Eats

- Balıkçı Sabahattin (p149)
- Hamdi Et Lokantası (opposite)
- Havuzlu Restaurant (opposite)
- Develi (p154)
- Asitane (p154)

THE BAZAAR DISTRICT

Generations of shoppers have worked up an appetite around the Grand Bazaar, and fortunately there have always been eateries to meet this need. These days, Western-style places such as Fez Café vie with traditional eateries such as Havuzlu to keep tourists and locals well fed at lunchtime. Down near the water there aren't too many choices. If you don't want to spend a fortune for a lunch at the touristy Pandeli, a delicious fish sandwich on the quay at Eminönü should hit the spot. At night, the only sensible options are on the roof at Hamdi Et Lokantası or below the bridge at New Galata.

CAFÉ SULTAN Map p103   *Café*

☎ 212-527 0145; Halıcılar Caddesi 44-46, Grand Bazaar; 🕙 8.30am-7pm Mon-Sat

Offering very similar fare to its next-door neighbour Fez Café, this small place is cheaper (Turkish coffee is €1.70 as opposed to €2 at Fez) and its waiters have a little less attitude. It's a pleasant place to rest from your shopping exertions.

COLHETI CAFÉ & RESTAURANT

Map p103   *Turkish*

☎ 212-512 5094; Sandal Bedesteni 36, Grand Bazaar; 🕙 9am-6.30pm Mon-Sat

This café is set up in the former auction hall (Sandal Bedesteni) of the bazaar; sit here for lunch and the historic atmosphere will flavour your meal. Guests sit in comfortable cane chairs and enjoy tasty *döner kebaps* (€4.10), sandwiches (€2.80) and salads (€3.90-4.50). The best thing about the place is that it's licensed. A beer costs €2.30.

FEZ CAFÉ Map p103 — Café
☎ 212-527 3684; Halıcılar Caddesi 62, Grand Bazaar; ⏱ 8.30am-7pm Mon-Sat

Set in a rough-stone den, the very popular Fez is a modern Western-style café on one of the bazaar's most atmospheric streets. You'll certainly pay a premium to sit at the flower-adorned tables – this place is pricey. Sandwiches cost €3-3.90 and salads €4.50-5.50. There's a wide range of herbal teas (€3.60 for a two-cup bodum) on offer.

HAMDİ ET LOKANTASI
Map pp282-3 — Turkish
Hamdi Restaurant; ☎ 212-528 0390; Kalçın Sokak 17, off Tahmis Caddesi, Eminönü; kebabs €4.70; ⏱ noon-11pm

It's a hard call to make in a city with as many fabulous eateries as İstanbul, but if forced to choose our favourite Turkish restaurant it would have to be Hamdi. Its setting (on a rooftop with panoramic views across to Galata, down the Golden Horn and back to the Old İstanbul skyline) is simply spectacular, and its food is among the best in town. Try the hayari (yogurt with roasted eggplant and garlic), the içli köfte (meatballs rolled in bulgur) and the fıstıklı kebab (lamb kebab with pistachios) and you'll see what we mean. Any place this good is always going to be busy, so make sure you book, and don't forget to request a rooftop table with a view (outside if the weather is hot). Enter through the ground-floor baklava shop.

HAVUZLU RESTAURANT
Map p103 — Lokanta
☎ 212-527 3346; Gani Çelebi Sokak 3, Grand Bazaar; mains €4; ⏱ 8am-7pm Mon-Sat

There are few more pleasant experiences than parking your shopping bags and enjoying a meal at the best eatery at the Grand Bazaar (Kapalı Çarşı; p102). A lovely space with a vaulted ceiling, pale lemon walls and an ornate central light fitting, Havuzlu serves up excellent fare to hungry hordes of tourists and shopkeepers. Try the spinach and yogurt dish or the damn fine İskender kebap (€4.40), and don't even think of leaving without sampling the delights of the figs stuffed with walnuts and served with kaymak (clotted cream). Yum.

NEW GALATA Map pp282-3 — Meyhane
☎ 212-292 6215; Galata Bridge, Karaköy; ⏱ midday-2am

It may be a shameless tourist trap, but there's really something quite endearing about New Galata. Located underneath the Galata Bridge (Galata Köprüsü; p101), its outdoor tables look out over Topkapı Palace (p91) and Seraglio Point – views don't get much better than this! Food is the standard meyhane fare, with prices inflated to reflect New Galata's tourist-attraction status. The live fasıl music is performed enthusiastically and the waiters know their stuff. You could do worse than spend a night here.

PANDELİ Map pp282-3 — Turkish
☎ 212-522 5534; Spice Bazaar 1, Eminönü Meydani, Eminönü; meze €3.30, mains €6.60-10; ⏱ noon-3.30pm Mon-Sat

What a shame that the food and service at this İstanbul institution don't live up to the beautiful surroundings. Billing itself as 'the World-Famous Turkish Restaurant', Pandeli's lack of modesty is only surpassed by the breathtaking rudeness of its waiters and the disappointing standard of its food. Three salons, encrusted with stunning turquoise glazed İznik tiles and furnished with chandeliers and richly upholstered banquettes, are perched above the main waterside entrance to the Spice Bazaar (p106); climb the stone stairs to enter the restaurant. Once inside, we recommend the patlıcan böreği (eggplant pie) but not much else. One of the most annoying things about eating here is the attitude of the waiters: don't let them pressure you into ordering the pricey special appetiser plate or the seafood dishes unless you really do want them. Additionally, beware of the fava bean and eggplant salads on the table: you will be charged for these unless you send them back. You will also have to pay a cover charge.

ZEYREKHANE Map pp282-3 — Turkish
☎ 212-532 2778; İbadethane Arkası Sokak 10, Zeyrek; mains €10.50; ⏱ 9am-midnight Tue-Sun

This restaurant behind the Zeyrek Camii (p107) has an outdoor garden with cushioned couches on which you can recline and soak up the superb view of the Süleymaniye Camii (p106) and the Golden Horn. It serves tasty mains (fancy quail kebab served with eggplant?) as well as snacks. In winter it's possible to order the strange local drink boza, a grain-based beverage.

Cheap Eats

CAFÉ HOME-MADE

Map pp282-3 *Anatolian*

☎ 212-514 2721; Hüdavendigar Caddesi 48, Sirkeci; ⏱ 8am-11pm

Sit and watch trams rattle up and down busy Hüdavendigar Caddesi from the floor-to-ceiling windows of this cute eatery. The Anatolian decoration is simple but stylish, the food is cheap and alcohol is available – not a combination seen too often around Old İstanbul. A woman in traditional costume will make you a *beyaz peynirli gözleme* (cheese pancake, €1.60) or the chef in the kitchen can whip up a quick kebab (€6) or *mantı* (Turkish ravioli, €3.80). The food is acceptable rather than inspired.

KANAAT LOKANTASI

Map pp282-3 *Lokanta*

Prof. Sıddık Sokak, Süleymaniye; mains €2

This popular local lokanta in the former *medrese* (Muslim seminary) of the Süleymaniye Camii serves up *İskender kebab* (€3.90) and fava dishes to hordes of hungry locals from the theological college and nearby commercial areas.

Fish Sandwiches

The cheapest way to enjoy fresh fish from the waters round İstanbul is to buy a fish sandwich from a boatman. Go to either the Eminönü end of the Galata Bridge or to the right of the ferry terminal at Üsküdar and you'll see bobbing boats tied to the quay. In each boat men tend a cooker loaded with fish fillets. The quick-cooked fish is slid into a slit quarter-loaf of bread and costs about €0.80. Delicious!

WESTERN DISTRICTS

There aren't too many eateries of note in this area, but it is home to one of the city's best restaurants, Asitane. The suburbs here are quiet at night, so you're probably best off sampling Asitane's delights at lunch after visiting the Kariye Müzesi.

ASİTANE Map p281 *Ottoman*

☎ 212-635 7979; Kariye Oteli, Kariye Camii Sokak 18, Kariye-i Atik; mains €8.90; ⏱ 8am-11pm

It's not often that you'll get the opportunity to sample Ottoman dishes devised especially for a sixteenth-century royal circumcision feast, but this is what's on offer at this popular restaurant. The food is magnificent – try the *vişne yalanci*

The Best Kebabs in Town

It's been serving up kebabs to hungry locals since 1912, so Develi (☎ 212-529 0833; Gümüşyüzük Sokak 7, Samatya; mains €7.50; ⏱ noon-midnight) really knows what it's doing when it comes to the national dish. Near the Wall at Samatya, the five floors (including a roof terrace) of this restaurant are always full of happy punters enjoying the flavours of southeastern Anatolia. Try the *çiğ köfte* (raw ground lamb, *bulgur*, onions and spices) and the *fıstıklı* (pistachio) *kebab* and you'll feel happy too. To get there, catch a taxi along Kennedy Caddesi from Sultanahmet or the train from Sirkeci Railway Station (get off at Mustafa Paşa Station). You'll find Develi inland from the station on a plaza filled with parked cars. There are other branches in Etiler and Kalamış.

dolmasi (vine leaves stuffed with morello cherries, €4.50) and *yufkada kuzu incik marmarina'li* (baked lamb with pureed spinach and cheese on a plate of flaky pastry, €8.90); we're sure that Süleyman the Magnificent would have approved of them as much as we did. The surrounds are modern and elegant, featuring a pale-lemon colour scheme, comfortable seating, pristine napery and an outdoor courtyard for summer dining. Vegetarians are well catered for. Definitely one of the city's most impressive dining experiences.

HOTEL DAPHNIS

Map p281 *Modern Turkish*

☎ 212-531 4858; Sadrazam Ali Paşa Caddesi 26, Fener; pasta €2.80, grills €4.50; ⏱ noon-10pm Tue-Sun

Most of the cars zoom along frantic Sadrazam Ali Paşa Caddesi, but the occasional one stops so that its occupants can occupy the banquettes in this small hotel brasserie. Large streetside windows look over to the Golden Horn and ensure a light space that complements the simple menu on offer (mainly pasta dishes and grills). Regulars usually elect to finish their meal with the rich chocolate cake topped with slivers of caramelised orange (€2.50).

Cheap Eats

KARİYE PEMBE KÖŞK

Map p281 *Turkish Café*

☎ 212-635 8586; Kariye Müzesi Meydanı, Kariye-i Atik; ⏱ 7am-midnight

If you choose to have a quick snack after visiting the **Kariye Müzesi** (p111) rather than indulge

Ottoman-style at Asitane, this outdoor café is one of the few nearby choices. A *tost* (toasted sandwich) will set you back €2.20 and a cappuccino €1.70.

NORTH OF THE GOLDEN HORN
BEYOĞLU – GALATA BRIDGE TO İSTİKLAL CADDESİ

This part of town once had a very unsavoury reputation, but it's rapidly gentrifying and we won't be at all surprised if loads of eateries open around here over the next couple of years. It's still reasonably quiet at night, so be a bit careful walking around after dark. During the day it's filled with small börekçis serving local workers and residents. The area around Tünel Square is littered with groovy coffee shops.

Kaffeehaus (below)

GALATA HOUSE Map pp284-6 *Georgian*
☎ 212-245 1861; Galata Kulesi Sokak 61, Karaköy; mains €7.20; ☺ noon-midnight Tue-Sun

This would have to be one of the most eccentric restaurants in town. Run by the utterly charming husband-and-wife team of Nadire and Mete Göktuğ, it is housed in the Old British Jail, just down from **Galata Tower** (p118). The jail functioned from 1904 to 1919, and has been sympathetically but comfortably restored by Mete, who is one of İstanbul's most prominent heritage architects. Nadire uses recipes handed down from her Georgian mother to concoct great comfort food – the *hingali* (meat-filled dumplings in tomato sauce) are absolutely delicious. She also plays the piano for guests.

KAFFEEHAUS Map pp284-6 *Café*
☎ 212-245 4028; Tünel Meydanı 4, Tünel; ☺ 9am-9pm

One of the most stylish cafés in the city, Kaffeehaus is popular with the local arty set, who monopolise its tables for long breakfasts every day of the week. In warmer weather the front of the space opens to Tünel Square and provides great people-watching opportunities; when it's cooler the velvet-upholstered armchairs are perfect for drinking coffee and reading the paper. Breakfasts are really good – the *menemen*, a strange-looking concoction of

eggs with onions, tomato, peppers and white cheese, is delicious – and the two-course daily lunch specials offer excellent value (€3.90-5). A caffe latte costs €2.30.

Cheap Eats
GÜNEY RESTAURANT
Map pp284-6 *Lokanta*
☎ 212-249 0393; Kuledibi Şah Kapısı 6, Tünel; mains €1.90-3.30; ☺ 7am-10pm Mon-Sat

You'll be lucky if you can fight your way through the crowds of hungry locals to claim a lunchtime table at this bustling eatery directly opposite **Galata Tower** (p118). Friendly waiters will set you up with a basket of fresh bread and point you towards the array of meze and hot dishes on offer. You'll be sure to enjoy whatever you choose and will feel happy indeed when you pay the modest bill. It's also a great place to grab a hearty bowl of *çorba* (soup) for breakfast (€1.10).

Top Five Cafés
- **Kaffeehaus** (left)
- **Patisserie Markiz** (p157)
- **Şimdi** (p158)
- **Çiğdem Pastanesi** (p151)
- **İnci Pastanesi** (p159)

BEYOĞLU – ON & AROUND İSTİKLAL CADDESİ

The streets around Asmalımescit Sokak, with their raft of good-quality meyhanes packing the crowds in every Friday and Saturday night, are giving the famous Nevizade Sokak a run for its money these days, but they're not the only establishments off İstiklal doing well. This is without doubt the best neighbourhood in town in which to eat, drink and be merry. You would be mad if you didn't make your way here at least once during your visit. It's a great place to come during the day, too – particularly on the weekend.

5 KAT Map pp284-6 *Modern European*
☎ 212-293 3774; Soğancı Sokak 7/5, Cihangir; mains €9-11; ⊗ 11am-2am

If you want views with your meal, this bohemian place is certainly worth considering. It's amazing how good a meal can taste when it's eaten while watching the sun set over the Bosphorus. A large and varied menu is served in a dining space resembling a baroque boudoir – make sure you specify a table next to the window or on the outdoor roof terrace when you book. The chicken marbella (chicken pieces with prunes and olives served with pilaf) and the home-made pasta dishes (€8) go down a treat. There is an extensive wine list (mainly local) and the bar staff know how to mix a good pre-dinner cocktail.

BONCUK RESTAURANT
Map pp284-6 *Meyhane*
☎ 212-243 1219; Nevizade Sokak 19; meze €2.30-3.40, fish €3.30-8; ⊗ noon-2am

Armenian specialities differentiate Boncuk from its Nevizade neighbours. Try the excellent *topik* (meze made with chickpeas, pistachios, onion, flour, currants, cumin and salt) and the very tasty börek. To ensure that you get a table on the street, where all the action is, get there very early or ring ahead and book.

CAFÉ-BRASSERIE MARKİZ
Map pp284-6 *Modern European*
☎ 212-245 8394; İstiklal Caddesi 360-2/1, Asmalımescit; ⊗ noon-11.30pm

Located on the floor above the Patisserie Markiz, this new brasserie serves up dishes that sound a little better than they taste. That said, the Markiz salad (€7.20), with its mixture of spinach leaves, pomegranate, Roquefort, bacon, poppy-seed *grissini* and lemon sauce has a fair few fans around town, and the dining space, which looks out over İstiklal Caddesi, is one of the most elegant in the city. Best of all, its desserts come from the sublime patisserie downstairs.

FLAMM Map pp284-6 *Modern European*
☎ 212-245 7604; Sofyali Sokak 16/1, Asmalımescit; mains €8; ⊗ 11am-midnight

A newcomer to the bustling Asmalımescit scene, Flamm's stylish interior, attentive service and excellent food should ensure that it becomes a permanent fixture. The exposed brick walls are the only rustic touch – the rest of the fittings are super elegant and ensure a comfortable dining experience. You can sit inside or opt for candle-lit tables out on the street – both are good spots to enjoy the *al dente* linguine with fresh seafood (€7.80) or the best crème brûlée in town (€4).

HACI ABDULLAH
Map pp284-6 *Lokanta*
☎ 212-293 8561; Sakızağacı Caddesi 17; meze €3.30, mains €6; ⊗ 11am-10pm

Just contemplating the sensational *imam bayildi* at Hacı Abdullah's makes our tastebuds go into overdrive. This İstanbul institution (it was established in 1888) is probably the best lokanta in the city and is one of the essential gastronomic stops you should make when in town. You'll find all the traditional favourites, as well as a wide selection of desserts, including home-bottled fruit compote and a damn fine *künefe* (shredded wheat pastry with pistachios, honey and sugar). The elegant surrounds feature bottle upon bottle of pickled vegetables and comfortable banquette seating. No alcohol is served.

HACI BABA Map pp284-6 *Lokanta*
☎ 212-244 1886; İstiklal Caddesi 49; meze €2.80, mains €4.40; ⊗ noon-midnight

A long-term favourite with businessmen, as well as ladies spending a day shopping on İstiklal, Hacı Baba isn't quite as old as its nearby rival, Hacı Abdullah (it was established in 1921), but its food and surrounds are just as impressive. There are a large non-smoking section overlooking the main strip and a vine-garlanded terrace for alfresco dining. Best of all is the fact that you can order a beer, raki or wine with your meal.

KREPENDEKİ İMROZ RESTAURANT

Map pp284-6   *Meyhane*

☎ 212-249 9073; Nevizade Sokak 24;
meze €2.30-3.40; ☽ noon-midnight

The minute you see the waiters heaving around their enormous meze-laden trays in this popular meyhane you'll know you've made the right dinner choice. With outdoor tables on both sides of the street, you'll also have a slightly better chance of scoring a spot in the middle of the action – to make sure, ring ahead and book. The food is typical of the island of Gökceada (İmroz) and is top-class; those in the know always include the octopus salad and pickled anchovies (€3.30) in their meze choices.

LEB-İ DERYA

Map pp284-6   *Modern International*

☎ 212-293 4989; Kumbaracı Yokuşu 115/7;
☽ 11-4am

It may be the best bar in the city, but this is a damn fine restaurant, too. As it serves all day, we think nothing of kicking off with a late house breakfast (€8.90), which includes all-you-can-drink tea, progressing to a lunch of the Leb-i Derya Burger and spiced fries (€9), and finishing off the day with a dinner finale of the 'Special Turkish Dessert', a strange but compelling concoction of milk and chicken pieces served with ice cream and topped with bitter almond (€4.50). We never get bored, as the spectacular views over the Bosphorus and friendly crowd suit us down to the ground. Make sure you book.

LOKAL

Map pp284-6   *Modern International*

☎ 212-245 5743; Müeyyet Sokak 9, off İstiklal
Caddesi, Tünel; pasta €5, noodles €6, mains €7;
☽ noon-10.30pm Sun-Thu, noon-11.30pm Fri & Sat

Funksters, come on down! This quirky establishment just off İstiklal Caddesi has only seven tables inside and five outside, and these are always full of bright young things ordering from the eclectic menu. Some of the cooks are Asian and this is reflected in the number of curries that feature – try the Thai green chicken curry with its creamy coconut base and fragrant herbs (€7) or the succulent tandoori lamb chops (€6.60). The city's gay community flocks to the Sunday brunch, which features delicious 'Eggs a la Turka' (eggs with hollandaise, grilled sausage and toast, €5.50).

LOKANTA

Map pp284-6   *Modern Mediterranean*

☎ 212-245 6070; Meşrutiyet Caddesi 149/1, Tepebaşı;
☽ noon-11.30pm Mon-Sat

You'd be forgiven for thinking that you're in a city other than İstanbul when you enter Lokanta. A huge high-ceilinged space with exposed brick walls and a long bar illuminated with red lights, the interior is theatrical but the food is reassuringly down to earth – and truly excellent. The menu would be equally at home in London or New York: the pizza with caramelised onions and chèvre (€10) goes down a treat, as does the *tuna au poivre* (rare tuna served with garlic-roasted potatoes and a sauce of cracked black pepper, €11). If you leave without sampling the espresso chocolate soufflé (€3.30), we'll be most disappointed.

NATURE & PEACE

Map pp284-6   *Vegetarian*

☎ 212-252 8609; Büyükparmakkapı Sokak 21-23;
☽ 11am-midnight, closed Sunday during school
holidays

Why is it that so many vegetarian restaurants are stuck in a 1970s time warp when it comes to both décor and menu? Nature & Peace features the obligatory wooden floorboards, dried corn cobs and poo-brown walls, and serves up vegetarian dishes with loads of lentils, as well as the occasional more-expensive dish for carnivores. There are a few vegan choices on offer. You'll be offered the set menu of main soup and salad for €7; if you don't want to pay this much, ask for the pink 'lunch menu', which is much cheaper (dishes €3.40).

NEY'LE MEY'LE   Map pp284-6   *Meyhane*

☎ 212-249 8103; Nevizade Sokak 12; meze €1.10-
1.60, fish €3.90-8; ☽ 10-2am

On the busiest restaurant strip in town, Ney'le Mey'le serves up super cheap meze and delicious seafood – try the fried calamari (€3.90). Diners are crammed into two levels and can contemplate the interesting contemporary art on the walls between courses, though watching the passing parade along Nevizade is even better. The fava bean–paste meze is sensational.

PATİSSERİE MARKİZ

Map pp284-6   *Patisserie*

☎ 212-245 8394; İstiklal Caddesi 360-2; ☽ 9am-10pm

If there's a heaven on earth, it just might be Markiz. Everything here is a work of art: the gloriously restored Art-Nouveau interior, the delectable cakes and pastries, and the starched aprons on the suitably glamorous waiting staff. Sipping a Turkish coffee (€2.80) and devouring a piece of the chocolate gateau (€3.90) here is absolutely our favourite afternoon activity when on this side of town.

REFİK Map pp284-6 *Meyhane*
☎ 212-245 7879; Sofyali Sokak 7, Asmalımescit; meze €2.30, fish €6.70; ✆ noon-midnight Mon-Sat, 6.30pm-midnight Sun

Refik is the original meyhane in the Asmalımescit area. It's a convivial place famous for its genial host, Refik Arslan, who will make you feel welcome the minute you set foot through the door. The tiled floor and wooden furniture provide a noisy setting in which to enjoy a meal featuring meze and fish. Try the excellent *cacık* (yogurt and mint salad). Mr Arslan bottles his own house wine (€11) – you'll be sure to drink a lot of it.

ŞİMDİ Map pp284-6 *Café*
☎ 212-252 5443; Asmalımescit Sokak 9, Asmalımescit; sandwiches & salads €4; ✆ 9am-midnight

Lolling on the couches at the front of this laid-back café is a great way to spend a few hours. On the ground floor of the recently renovated Atlas Apartments, Şimdi has amazing décor and features a three-storey atrium that ensures a relatively smoke-free environment (something almost impossible to find in this town of chain smokers). The breakfast meze is a great idea, staff know how to get the best out of the Faema coffee machine and the crowd is always interesting.

SOFYALI 9 Map pp284-6 *Meyhane*
☎ 212-245 0362; Sofyali Sokak 9, Tünel; meze €1.40, grills €4.20; ✆ noon-3pm, 7pm-midnight Mon-Sat

Tables here at Sofyali 9 are hot property on a Friday or Saturday night, and no wonder. This gem of a place serves up some of the best meyhane food in all İstanbul, and does so in surroundings that are as welcoming as they are attractive. It's a bit like eating in a close friend's home, except here you're offered a large array of meze and a wealth of grills and fresh fried fish along with the bonhomie. The *köpeoğlu* (eggplant and tomato with yogurt and garlic) is the best we've ever had and the *kaşaril börek* (cheese pastries) have to be tasted to be believed. Regulars swear by the *Anavut ciğeri* (Albanian fried liver, €2.80). Do yourself a favour: go.

YAKUP 2 Map pp284-6 *Meyhane*
☎ 212-249 2925; Asmalımescit Caddesi 35/37, Asmalımescit; meze €1.90-4.40, grills €6; ✆ noon-2am, closed Sun Jun-Sep

This bohemian haunt is a great place to spend a night on the town. Inevitably full of large groups of liquored-up locals, it serves a wide range of good-quality meze, grills and fish. The nicotine-yellow walls covered in posters are testament to the fact that patrons here smoke as much as they eat and talk – it's most definitely not the place to come if you're feeling like a restrained night.

ZARİFİ Map pp284-6 *Greek/Armenian*
☎ 212-293 5480; Çukurlu Çeşme Sokak 13; mains €9.50; ✆ 8pm-1am Sun-Thu, 8pm-4am Fri & Sat

This stylish place dubs its cold meze 'Pera cuisine' and we have to say that it's particularly tasty. In fact, the honeyed aubergine and the *topik* are among the best we've ever eaten. Unfortunately, the hot appetizers and strange *saghanakis* dishes didn't reach the same heights. And the Phoenician kebab (mixed kebab with orange peel and parched spinach mash) was, um, interesting. Still, large

Nevizade Sokak: The Biggest Party in Town

If you only have one night out on the town when you visit İstanbul, make sure you spend it at one of the meyhanes on Nevizade Sokak in Beyoğlu. Buried in the maze of narrow streets behind the historic Çiçek Pasaji (Flower Passage) on İstiklal Caddesi, this is the most famous eating precinct in the city and is certainly the most atmospheric. On any night of the week its taverns will be full of chattering locals sampling the dizzying array of meze and fresh fried fish on offer, washed down with a never-ending supply of raki. Vendors wander from table to table selling fresh almonds and at some places small groups of musicians entertain diners with fasıl music and wisecracks in return for tips (anything less than €10 per group or couple is considered niggardly, so make sure you proffer this when the musicians come to your table). The whole experience is enormous fun. Our favourite meyhanes are Krependeki İmroz (p157), Boncuk (p156) and Ney'le Mey'le (p157), but the food is pretty similar at every joint. On Friday and Saturday summer evenings the street literally heaves with people looking for a table, grabbing a drink at one of the bars along the strip or just wandering past. You'd be mad if you didn't join them.

groups of forty-somethings love to come and listen to the very loud live band (starts 9.30pm) while they're eating and throwing back the raki.

ZENCEFİL NATURE & PEACE
Map pp284-6   *Vegetarian*
☎ 212-243 8234; Kurabiye Sokak 8; mains €4.40; ⊗ 10am-10.30pm Tue-Sun
This vegetarian café is so popular it has just moved into a new, larger building opposite its former home. We're not surprised that it's got a loyal following, as the interior is comfortable and stylish, with a lovely glassed courtyard and a funky candy-pink and lime-green colour scheme, and the food is fresh and varied. Bread is home made and there's a wide range of herbal teas. It's homespun without being hippy and we heartily approve.

Cheap Eats
BİR KAHVE Map pp284-6   *Café*
☎ 212-293 6660; Mis Sokak 6/1, off İstiklal Caddesi; ⊗ 11am-midnight Mon-Sat
Pull up a seat next to the resident one-eyed cat, grab a magazine from the rack and order a coffee – it's what all the regulars at this tiny first-floor café do. An oasis of calm off busy İstiklal Caddesi, Bir Kahve serves up basic dishes such as *ev mantisi* (home-made Turkish ravioli, €2.30) and house specialities such as the decadent chocolate brownie (€2.20). An espresso costs €1.40.

CAFÉ DE FLORE Map pp284-6   *Café*
☎ 212-334 8734; İstiklal Caddesi 8; ⊗ 9am-9pm
In the basement of the Institute Française d'İstanbul in the grounds of the French Consulate, this café offers delicious, light snacks for very reasonable prices. There is an inside section with sand-yellow walls, a TV screening French-language programmes and a courtyard that is packed with stylish French café furniture. The menu is 'combo style' (tea and quiche €2.20, baguette and coffee €2). This is a great place for breakfast (coffee and croissant €1.70).

İNCİ PASTANESİ Map pp284-6   *Patisserie*
İstiklal Caddesi 124, Beyoğlu; ⊗ 9am-9pm
A Beyoğlu institution, İnci is famous throughout the city for its delicious profiteroles. You'll have to fight through the crowds to reach the counter at this tiny shop, but believe us, it's worth the effort!

KONAK Map pp284-6   *Pideci & Kebapçı*
☎ 212-244 4281; İstiklal Caddesi 259; ⊗ 9am-9pm
The waiters run rather than walk at this frantically busy place on İstiklal Caddesi. You'll understand why they're so busy as soon as you taste the sensational *İskender kebap* (€3.40), the excellent *yoğurtlu kebab* (€3.40) and the melt-in-your-mouth *pide* (€2.80). The setting is a cut above, too, with ornate gilded ceiling, chandeliers and banquettes covered in rich brocade. There's another branch near Tünel Square.

MUSA USTA ADANA KEBAP SALONU
Map pp284-6   *Kebapçı*
☎ 212-245 2932; Küçük Parmakkapı Sokak 14, off İstiklal Caddesi; mains €1.50; ⊗ noon–1am
Three floors of old-fashioned atmosphere, plus excellent food, have kept this place in business for years. Sit around the downstairs *ocakbaşı* and watch your meat grilled to perfection or grab a table on the outdoor terraces upstairs. It's possible to get a drink here, which is unusual for a kebapçı, and probably a factor contributing to the place's popularity with local students and arty types (the dirt-cheap prices no doubt contribute, too).

OTANTİK
Map pp284-6   *Anatolian*
☎ 212-293 8451; İstiklal Caddesi 170; mains €3; ⊗ 11am-10pm
The Beyoğlu branch of this popular chain looks like a tourist trap from the front, but it's worth ignoring the cheesy sight of the women in traditional Anatolian costume making crispy *gözleme* (€1.10-1.60) in the window and coming inside, because the place is always full of locals enjoying the cheap and tasty dishes on offer.

SARAY Map pp284-6   *Café*
☎ 212-292 3434; İstiklal Caddesi 102; ⊗ 8am-11pm
A *muhallebici* that's been serving puddings to appreciative sweet-tooths since 1935, Saray is still going strong. Pop in for a Turkish breakfast (€2.20) in the morning or a *fırın sütlaç* (rice pudding, €1.30) and tea (€0.50) in the afternoon.

Top Five Beyoğlu Meyhanes
- **Sofyali 9** (opposite)
- **Krependeki İmroz Restaurant** (p157)
- **Boncuk Restaurant** (p156)
- **Refik** (opposite)
- **Yakup 2** (opposite)

Eating – Beyoğlu – On & Around İstiklal Caddesi

TAKSİM, HARBİYE & NİŞANTAŞI

These suburbs are where the moneyed elite choose to eat and drink. If you make your way here, you should book, dress up and be prepared for an expensive meal by local standards. You'll find the quality of food and service high, and the people-watching opportunities endless. Nişantaşı is particularly well-endowed with glamorous cafés, particularly around Abdi İpekçi Caddesi.

Top Five Restaurant Views

- **Vogue** (opposite)
- **5 Kat** (p156)
- **Hamdi Et Lokantası** (p153)
- **Rami** (p151)
- **Konyalı** (p150)

BANYAN: FOOD FOR THE SOUL

Map p287   *Asian*
☎ 212-219 6011; Abdi İpekçi Caddesi 40-3, Nişantaşı; mains €9; ☉ 11am-11pm

Like many of the Nişantaşı joints most of the action here is out on street tables in summer. This is a shame, because the interior of this restaurant provides a lovely setting for a meal. The dark wood floor and neutral and olive-green tones of the napery and upholstery are topped up with touches such as a bonsai tree on every table. The menu travels around Asia, featuring Thai, Japanese and Chinese dishes. There is even the occasional fusion number: why not try the grilled vegetables and warm goat's cheese with pea *paratha* and green mandarin and ginger-infused olive oil and see if it works for you?

BRASSERIE NİŞANTAŞI

Map p287   *Modern European*
☎ 212-343 0443; Abdi İpekçi Caddesi 23, Nişantaşı; mains €12; ☉ 10am-1am Mon-Sat, noon-1am Sun

We're not sure if this glamorous newcomer is best described as a bar, café or restaurant, but we're absolutely convinced that it's a place to be seen. Join the beautiful people for dinner and sample the delights of dishes such as rump steak with Béarnaise sauce, or pop in for a late-night treat of panacotta with raspberry coulis. Mornings are worth a visit, too, with a Turkish breakfast costing €5.50. Everything is top quality.

CHANGA Map p287   *Modern European*
☎ 212-249 1348; Sıraselviler Caddesi 87/1, Taksim; mains €14; ☉ 6pm-1am Mon-Sat

İstanbul's most controversial eatery has fans and detractors. At issue is its handling of fusion dishes: do they work? Try the wasabi and salmon tortellini with grilled porcini and creamed lemon-grass sauce and see what you think. One dish that no-one would question is the soft meringue of strawberries and fresh cheese with strawberry-raspberry sauce – delicious. The décor is stark moderne, featuring Eames chairs and a stylish bar, with the quirky touch of a glass floor looking down on the kitchen. The wine list is superb. You'll find the entrance directly opposite the **Vardar Palace Hotel** (p214).

BEŞİKTAŞ & ORTAKÖY

Vogue, one of the city's best restaurants, is housed on the top floor of a gleaming office block located in a residential strip in Beşiktaş. The cafés, bars and restaurants around the waterside road Iskele Square in Ortaköy, on the other hand, form a bustling entertainment precinct that's particularly busy on Friday and Saturday evenings.

A Taste of Europe on the Golden Horn

Hasköy's not a suburb that offers a lot for the tourist, but oddly enough two of the city's better European restaurants are located here, both in the grounds of the **Rahmi M Koç Müzesi** (Map pp276-7).

Café du Levant (☎ 212-297 6644; Hasköy Caddesi 27, Hasköy; mains €11-13; ☉ 10am-10pm Tue-Sun) If you feel like bursting into a rendition of an Edith Piaf number the minute you walk into this bistro we won't be at all surprised. The menu is as Gallic as the setting, which features stained-glass ceiling, tiled floors, French posters from the 1930s and wooden dining booths. Try the duck *confit* (€11) and crème brûlée (€6.70).

Halal (☎ 212-297 6644; Hasköy Caddesi 27, Hasköy; mains €11-19; ☉ 10am-midnight Tue-Sun) Whether you choose to sit on the outdoor terrace and look over the Golden Horn to Balat or claim a table in the comfortable dining room with its artfully displayed maritime memorabilia, you'll enjoy the Halal experience. While full meals are expensive, it's also possible to order from a cheaper café menu (sandwiches €4.10-5.20) – the view comes with either option.

ÇINAR Map p288   *Meyhane*

☎ 212-261 5818; Iskele Square 42, Ortaköy; meze €3.30, mains €8; ⏲ noon-2am

This is our favourite Ortaköy waterside restaurant. With loads of outdoor tables and waiters running around with loaded trays, it's like a busy French brasserie. The views over the water and of the bustling square are great, and the food is quite good, too. Seafood mezes feature and you can choose your own fish for mains. The perfect place to spend a summer's evening.

İLHAMİ'NİN YERİ Map p288   *Meyhane*

İlhami's Place; ☎ 212-260 8080, Osmanzade Sokak 6; meze €1.90-4.40, mains €5-8; ⏲ noon-1am

This is one of the last true meyhanes with live fasıl music in the area. A white-tableclothed affair specialising in seafood, it also serves up flavourful meze and meat dishes. The musicians usually play nightly from 8pm onwards.

MADO Map p288   *Ice-Cream Parlour*

☎ 212-227 3876; Iskele Square, Ortaköy; ice-cream sundae €3; ⏲ 7am-2am

Next to Çınar, this branch of the popular ice-cream chain is packed on weekends, when locals stop by after checking out the flea market. The views are great and the people-watching opportunities unrivalled. Oh, and the ice cream goes down a treat. A coffee costs €2. There are also Mado branches in **Teşvikiye** (☎ 212-261 0322; cnr Teşvikiye Caddesi & Atiye Sokak) and **Beyoğlu** (☎ 212-244 1781; 188 İstiklal Caddesi).

Top Five Dining Experiences

- Eating sushi with the beautiful people at **Vogue** (below).
- Ordering the *imam bayıldı* at **Haci Abdullah** (p156).
- Soaking up the scene and scoffing the Mediterranean morsels at **Lokanta** (p157).
- Sampling the magnificent mezes at **Sofyali 9** (p158).
- Kicking up our heels at any of the joints along **Nevizade Sokak** (p158).

VOGUE Map p288   *Modern European*

☎ 212-227 4404; BJK Plaza, A Blok Kat 13, Spor Caddesi, Akaretler, Beşiktaş; mains €16; ⏲ noon-midnight Mon-Sat, noon-11pm Sun

Grace Jones purrs on the sound system, trained Japanese sushi chefs perform wonders with a sliver of tuna and well-trained waiters make sense of a large and thoughtful wine list. This is Vogue and we love it to bits. The food is as sensational as the views over the Bosphorus – try the grilled sea bass with spinach tart, grilled potato and preserved lemon sauce or the roasted duck with caramelised quince and dried fig sauce. If you feel like eating Japanese, the sushi is so fresh it's almost jumping off the plate. You'll be in the company of a forty-something crowd and should make sure your credit card has leverage. Ask for a table on the terrace.

Eating – Beşiktaş & Ortaköy

Vogue (above)

Eating in Kadıköy

Kadıköy is home to one of the city's best fresh produce markets, a sign that locals here take their food seriously. It's a good place to visit for a rustic lunch, or for a casual early dinner after enjoying the ferry trip from Eminönü. We suggest trying these three simple places.

Café Antre (☎ 216-418 1219; Miralay Nazım Sokak 10, Kadıköy; burgers & pastas €3-5.50; ☼ 10am-10pm Sun-Thu, 10am-11pm Fri & Sat) If you're homesick and missing the coffee at your favourite café, this popular student hang-out is a good substitute. Occupying both floors of a converted house in a street parallel (sea side) to busy Bahariye Caddesi, it serves Lavazza coffee and fresh brownies (€2.50), as well as burgers and pasta. A caffe latte costs €2.20.

Denizati (☎ 216-414 7643; Tarihi Kadıköy İskelesi Üstü, Kadıköy; mains €2.80-5.50; ☼ 8am-1am) The terrace overlooking the water, cosy indoor space and live music (acoustic folk/pop) make Denizati a favourite spot for young local couples to come on dates. The food's nothing special – a predictable mix of pasta, omelettes and salads – but the atmosphere is undeniably welcoming. You'll find it in a building to the right as you exit the ferry terminal.

Otantik Anadolu Yemekleri (☎ 216-330 7144; Muvakkithane Caddesi 62-64, Kadıköy; mains €3; ☼ 8am-10pm Wed, 11am-10pm Thu-Tue) The original branch of a popular chain, this is a great place to grab a cheap and extremely tasty meal when checking out the excellent fresh-produce market in Kadıköy. Two women in traditional Anatolian costume make crispy *gözleme* (€1.10-1.60) in the window; staff in no doubt more orthodox cooking attire cook up dishes such as *mantı* (traditional ravioli, €2.20) in the kitchen. You'll find it in one of the main streets in the produce market, opposite the ferry terminal and slightly to the right.

THE ASIAN SHORE
ÜSKÜDAR

One of the city's most conservative areas, Üsküdar is not the place to come if you're looking for a boozy night on the town. During the day, the streets around the ferry terminal are filled with unremarkable kebab joints and cafés.

Cheap Eats
ÇAMLICA RESTAURANT
Map p289　　　　　　　　　　　　　　　　　*Café*
Küçük Çamlıca Köşkleri; ☎ 216-443 2199; Büyük
Çamlıca; ☼ 9am-midnight

Should you take the time to visit Uskudar, this charming kiosk on the hill is just the right place to savour a coffee or a snack. Marble floors are covered by rugs with small stools clustered around brass tray tables. In winter there's a log fire, and in summer the windows looking out over the park provide an attractively airy feel. Tea costs a mere €0.30, cakes are €0.80, breakfast is €2.20 and grills are around €2.20.

Drinking

Drinking

It may be the biggest city in an officially Muslim country, but İstanbul's population likes nothing more than a drink or three. If the raki-soaked atmosphere in the city's meyhanes isn't a clear enough indicator, a foray into Beyoğlu's thriving bar scene will confirm it. If you're up for a drink, we suggest you go out on the town on a Thursday, Friday or Saturday night. Alternatively, you could check out the alcohol-free, atmosphere-rich *çay bahçesi* (tea gardens) or *kahvehanes* (coffee houses) dotted around Old İstanbul and in Tophane over the Galata Bridge (Galata Köprüsü). These are great places to relax and sample a Turkish institution, the nargileh (water pipe), and a cup of *Türk kahvesi* (Turkish coffee) or *çay* (tea).

When ordering a nargileh, you'll need to specify what type of tobacco you would like. Most people opt for *elma* (when the tobacco has been soaked in apple juice, giving it a sweet flavour and scent), but it's possible to order it unadulterated (*tömbeki*). The water pipe will be brought to your table, hot coals will be placed in it to get it started and you will be given a disposable plastic mouthpiece to slip over the pipe's stem. Just draw back and you're off. Bliss!

OLD İSTANBUL

SULTANAHMET

Sadly, there are few pleasant bars in Sultanahmet. The joints along Akbıyık Caddesi are great for backpackers and unthinkable for everyone else. Don't despair, though. Why not substitute tobacco or caffeine for alcohol and visit one of the many atmospheric *çay bahçesis* or *kahvehanes* dotted around the neighbourhood?

CAFÉ MEŞALE
Map pp278-80   *Tea Garden/Coffee House*
☎ 212-518 9562; Arasta Bazaar, Utangaç Sokak, Cankurtaran; ☯ 24hr
Meşale, located in a sunken courtyard behind the **Blue Mosque** (p84) is a tourist trap *par excellence* but we still love it. Generations of backpackers have joined locals in claiming one of its cushioned benches under coloured lights and enjoying a tea (€0.70) and nargileh (€3.30). There is live Turkish music (5-11pm) and a weekend Whirling Dervish performance (8pm and 10pm).

CAĞALOĞLU HAMAMI PUB
Map pp278-80   *Bar*
☎ 212-522 5575; Kazım Ismail Gürkan Caddesi 34, Cağaloğlu; ☯ 10am-10pm
Not too many bars encourage you to take your clothes off (well, the ones that we go to don't), but this small bar in the city's most beautiful *hamam* does. Even if you don't want to take

your gear off, it's a great place to have a drink, as evidenced by the number of local men who seem to spend their entire day here.

CHEERS BAR Map pp278-80   *Bar*
☎ 0532-409 6369; Akbıyık Caddesi 20, Cankurtaran; ☯ 10am-2am
Slap-bang in the middle of backpacker central, this raucous bar is not for the faint-hearted. If you can imagine nothing better than sinking a skinful, listening to Men at Work's *Land Down Under* and bragging about how cheaply you're managing to live while on the road, this place is for you. The nearby **Backpackers Bar** (Map pp278-80) offers more of the same.

DERVİŞ AİLE ÇAY BAHÇESİ
Map pp278-80   *Tea Garden/Coffee House*
Dervish Family Tea Garden; Mimar Mehmet Ağa Caddesi, Cankurtaran; ☯ 9am-11pm, closed winter
The Derviş' paved courtyard, which is superbly located directly opposite the **Blue Mosque** (p84), beckons patrons with its comfortable cane chairs and shady trees. Efficient service, reasonable prices and peerless people-watching opportunities make it a great place for a leisurely tea, nargileh and game of backgammon.

KONUK EVİ
Map pp278-80   *Bar/Outdoor Café*
☎ 212-517 6785; Soğukçeşme Sokak; ☯ noon-3.30pm, 6.30-10.30pm, closed winter
Every visitor to İstanbul visits Topkapı, but only a few know that nearby there's an idyllic spot

to relax over a drink, coffee or food (p149). After a day tramping through the palace, walk down Soğukçeşme Sokak and go through the gate opposite **Ayasofya Pansiyonlari** (p203). Here you'll find a secluded garden in front of a restored Ottoman house – our favourite local spot for a drink on an early summer's evening. A beer costs €3.60.

ŞAH PUB & BAR Map pp278-80 *Bar*
☎ 212-519 5807; İncili Çavaş Sokak 11; ☺ 10am-3am
If you're looking for Sex on the Beach or a Long Slow Screw Against the Wall (the cocktails, of course), this is the place for you. It's vaguely sleazy, but there aren't too many options around here. The small alleyway entrance is often full of backpackers enjoying a beer (€1.90) and nargileh (€4.20).

SULTAN PUB Map pp278-80 *Bar*
☎ 212-528 1719; Divan Yolu Caddesi 2; ☺ 9.30am-1am
Sultanahmet's version of Ye Olde English Pub, the Sultan has been around for years and continues to attract the crowds due to its peerless position close to **Aya Sofya** (p79), the **Blue Mosque** (p84) and the **Basilica Cistern** (p83). The pub grub is what you would expect from a place like this (le stodge), but the outdoor tables are a great spot to watch the world go by and the beer is served in iced glasses just the way we like it.

SULTAN SOFRASI
Map pp278-80 *Turkish Café*
Café Sultan; ☎ 212-518 1526; Atmeydanı Sokak 40; ☺ 7am-1am
Locations don't get much better than this. On the Hippodrome, Sultan Sofrası is a great place to rest after a hectic bout of sightseeing. At night live folk music is played between 7-11pm and there's nothing better than enjoying a nargileh and Turkish coffee (both €2.80) while listening to the plaintive sounds of the *oud* and watching the sound and light show at the **Blue Mosque** (p84). It also serves food – try the spinach *gözleme* (€1.70).

Top Five Bars
- Leb-i Derya (p168)
- 5 Kat (p168)
- KeVe (p167)
- Pano (p169)
- Nu Teras (p169)

YENİ MARMARA
Map pp278-80 *Turkish Café*
Marmara Café; ☎ 212-516 9013; Çayıroğlu Sokak, Küçük Aya Sofya; ☺ 8am-midnight
This is the genuine article: a neighbourhood teahouse packed to the rafters with backgammon-playing locals, who play while sipping tea and puffing on nargilehs. The place has bucket loads of character, and features rugs, wall hangings and low brass tables. Recorded fasıl music in the background adds a nice atmospheric touch. In winter a wood stove keeps the place cosy; in summer patrons sit on the rear terrace and look out over the Sea of Marmara. Tea is €1.10 and a nargileh €2.80.

YENİ YILDIZ
Map pp278-80 *Turkish Café/Restaurant*
☎ 212-518 1257; Cankurtaran Meydanı 18, Cankurtaran; ☺ 7am-11pm
Though not strictly a tea garden or coffee house (it's really a restaurant; p152), this is one of the local population's favourite places to enjoy a Turkish coffee (a bargain basement €0.60) and nargileh (€2.80). Trust us: there are few experiences as pleasant as sitting under the vine-covered awning here and whiling away a few hours.

YEŞİL EV Map pp278-80 *Bar/Outdoor Café*
☎ 212-517 6785; Kabasakal Caddesi 5, Cankurtaran; ☺ noon-10.30pm
Most of the bars in Sultanahmet are rowdy backpacker establishments, so the elegant rear courtyard of this historic hotel is a real oasis for those wanting a quiet drink. In spring flowers and blossom fill every corner; in summer the fountain and shady trees keep the temperature down; and in the cooler months a flower-filled conservatory provides shelter. A beer costs €3.30, a glass of wine €4.40 and a tea €2.20. Forget about eating here – our experience indicates that a drink is a far safer bet.

THE BAZAAR DISTRICT

Like most parts of the Old City, the area around the Grand Bazaar is conservative and there are few places serving alcohol. There are a few *çay bahçesi* and *kahvehanes* that are worth checking out, though, as well as the city's most famous *boza* bar. See if you're brave enough to give this local brew a try!

COLHETI CAFÉ & RESTAURANT
Map pp282-3   *Bar*
☎ 212-512 5094; Sandal Bedesteni 36, Grand Bazaar;
🕑 9am-6.30pm Mon-Sat

Though it's really more restaurant than bar, Colheti is the only place in the bazaar selling alcohol, so we've included it here. To be frank, after a few hours of dealing with touts and putting your bargaining skills to the test, you're probably going to need to grab one of its comfortable cane chairs and down a drink or three… A beer costs €2.20.

DERSAADET CAFÉ
Map pp278-80   *Bar/Café*
Galata Bridge; 🕑 9am-1am

Locals and tourists alike were thrilled when cafés and restaurants opened on the lower floor of the new Galata Bridge, and this place, at the extreme Karaköy end, has been packing customers in ever since. With its live Turkish pop music, stunning views over Topkapı and Old İstanbul, and backgammon-obsessed regulars, it's a good place to check out the local scene. Don't expect quality, though: the tobacco in the nargilehs (€2.90-3.80) is rough and the coffee (€1.10) tastes as if it has been made with water sourced from under the bridge. We'd suggest going for a beer (€1.90).

ERENLER ÇAY BAHÇESİ
Map pp282-3   *Tea Garden/Coffee House*
☎ 212-528 3785; Yeniçeriler Caddesi 36/28, Çemberlitaş; 🕑 7am-midnight, later in summer

Packed to the rafters with students from nearby İstanbul University, who are doing their best to live up to their genetic heritage (ie develop a major tobacco addiction), this nargileh establishment is set in the leafy courtyard of the Çorlulu Ali Paşa Medrese and has a row of carpet shops down its side. Look for the sign saying 'Magic Waterpipe Garden'.

ETHAM TEZÇAKAR KAHVECİ
Map p103   *Tea Garden/Coffee House*
Halıcılar Caddesi, Grand Bazaar; 🕑 8.30am-7pm Mon-Sat

This tiny tea and coffee stop is found smack-bang in the middle of Halıcılar Caddesi. Its traditional brass-tray tables and wooden stools stand in stark contrast to the funky Fes Café opposite, though the fridge with its Coke stickers tarnish the image somewhat.

İLESAM LOKALI
Map pp282-3   *Tea Garden/Coffee House*
☎ 212-511 2618; Yeniçeriler Caddesi 84, Çemberlitaş; 🕑 7am-midnight, later in summer

This club, set in the pleasant courtyard of the Koca Sinan Paşa Medrese, was formed by the enigmatically named Professional Union of Owners of the Works of Science & Literature. Fortunately, members seem happy for strangers to infiltrate their ranks. It's a great place to enjoy a cheap tea (€0.35) and nargileh (€2.80). After entering through the gate to **Koca Sinan Paşa's tomb**, go past the cemetery; İlesam Lokalı is the second teahouse to the right.

LALE BAHÇESİ
Map pp282-3   *Tea Garden/Coffee House*
Sifahane Sokak, Süleymaniye; 🕑 8am-midnight

In a sunken courtyard that was once part of the Süleymaniye *külliye* (mosque complex), this charming outdoor teahouse is always full of students from the nearby theological college and İstanbul University, who come here to sit on cushioned seats under trees and relax while watching the pretty fountain play. It's one of the cheapest places in the area to enjoy a tea and nargileh.

ŞARK KAHVESİ
Map p103   *Tea Garden/Coffee House*
☎ 212-512 1144; Yaglikcilar Caddesi 134, Grand Bazaar; 🕑 8.30am-7pm Mon-Sat

The Şark's arched ceiling betrays its former existence as part of a bazaar street; years ago some enterprising *kahveci* (coffee-house owner) walled up several sides and turned it into a café. The nicotine colour on the walls is testament to its long pedigree as a popular spot for stall-holders to come and enjoy a coffee and a cigarette. These days they have to fight for space with tourists, who love the quirky 'flying dervish' murals, old photographs on the walls, and cheap tea (€0.50) and Turkish coffee (€1.10).

VEFA BOZACISI Map pp282-3   *Boza Bar*
☎ 212-519 4922; Katip Çelebi Caddesi 104/1, Kalenderhane; 🕑 7am-midnight

Worn out by the demands of too much sightseeing? *Boza* is your answer! This famous *boza* bar was established in 1875 and locals still flock here to drink the stuff, which is made from water, sugar and fermented grain, and has a reputation for building up strength and virility. The viscous mucous-coloured beverage won't be to everyone's taste, but the bar itself, with its blue tiles, mirrored columns, marble tables and wooden bar, is worth a visit in its own right. If the *boza* (€0.75 per glass) is too confrontational for you, the bar also serves *şıra*, a fermented grape juice (€0.75 per glass).

NORTH OF THE GOLDEN HORN
BEYOĞLU – GALATA BRIDGE TO İSTİKLAL CADDESİ

This part of town is developing a reputation as the gathering place for the city's arty set, and funky bars are starting to pop up around Galata and Tünel Squares. Be careful around here at night – it can be a bit seedy and bag-snatchers lurk around Galipdede Caddesi.

Though there are few nargileh joints around İstiklal Caddesi itself, you'll find the most popular nargileh spot in the city around the Nusretiye Camii on Necatibey Caddesi in Tophane. There's nothing gained by us singling out one at the expense of the others – they're all packed with locals, redolent with the smell of apple tobacco and great fun.

ANEMON GALATA Map pp284-6   *Bar*
☎ 212-293 2343; cnr Galata Meydani & Büyükhendek Caddesi, Tünel; ☽ 6pm-midnight

As yet undiscovered by the İstanbul bar set, this eyrie on top of a recently restored Ottoman hotel is one of the best places in the city to watch the sun set while enjoying a cocktail. Views over to Old İstanbul and across the Golden Horn are stunning and the surrounds are super-elegant.

CAFÉ GRAMOFON Map pp284-6   *Bar*
☎ 212-293 0786; Tünel Meydani 3, Tünel; ☽ 9am-2am

A tiny café/bar with stylish lounge chairs and large windows opening onto the main square in Tünel, Gramofon is where the older set goes to hear occasional live jazz (Astrid Gilberto covers are a perennial favourite) and drink more than a few glasses of wine. It's very pleasant, though we haven't been impressed by management's attitude – check on the cover charge before you sit down. The place functions as a bar at night and a less-busy café during the day. An espresso costs €1.90 and a glass of wine €2.80.

KEVE Map pp284-6   *Bar*
☎ 212-251 4338; Tünel Geçidi 10, Tünel; ☽ 8.30am-2.30am

Is this the most atmospheric bar in the city? In a plant-filled Belle Epoque courtyard/arcade just opposite the Tünel station, Keve is invariably full of thirty-somethings who've just been to a gallery opening on İstiklal and

Keve (above)

Drinking – Beyoğlu – Galata Bridge to İstiklal Caddesi

167

need a drink before moving on to see a new arthouse release at the cinema. The twinkling lights and wrought-iron tables just add to the atmosphere. A beer costs €2.80 and a glass of wine €4.

Top Five Nargileh Spots

- Yeni Marmara (p165)
- The raft of joints at Tophane (p167)
- Café Meşale (p164)
- Erenler Çay Bahçesi (p166)
- Sultan Sofrası (p165)

BEYOĞLU – ON & AROUND İSTİKLAL CADDESİ

Whether you want to drink a few quiet ales in a cosy pub, down a martini or two in a sophisticated bar or party the night away in its pumping next-door neighbour, the streets and lanes off İstiklal Caddesi will have the right drinking spot for you. This is where the city's barflies and party set hang out when they're not down on the shores of the Bosphorus, and it's great fun. It's even a good place for coffee and cake if you get there before the sun is over the yardarm.

5 KAT Map pp284-6 *Bar*
☎ 212-293 3774; Soğancı Sokak 7/5, Cihangir; ✆ 11am-2am

Run by glamorous red-haired film actress Yasemin Alkaya, 5 Kat is one of the city's best bars. The 'boudoir chic' décor features deep red walls, satin ceiling, velvet chairs and candles galore – it's amusingly over the top. The Bosphorus views from the full-length windows are simply breathtaking and the in-house DJ has an eccentric but very successful touch, with sultry French numbers popping up frequently. In the warmer weather the rooftop terrace bar is a favoured watering place for İstanbul's bohemian set. A beer costs €3.30. The bar also offers food (p156).

BADEHANE Map pp284-6 *Bar*
☎ 212-249 0550; General Yazgan Sokak 5, Tünel; ✆ 9am-2am

This tiny neighbourhood bar is a favourite with Beyoğlu's bohemian set. In fine weather patrons chain smoke and sip beer in the laneway. Dress down and come ready to enjoy an attitude-free evening.

CHARLOTTE Map pp284-6 *Bar*
360-362 İstiklal Caddesi, Passage Markiz; ✆ 10am-10pm

Chocolate and cream tones are the hallmark of this elegant champagne and vodka bar, one of the tenants of the recently opened Passage Markiz. Like everything in the shopping complex, the mood is elegantly subdued and the clientele is mature and moneyed. A good place to recover after a frenzied shopping episode on İstiklal Caddesi.

DULCINEA Map pp284-6 *Bar*
☎ 212-245 1039; Meşelik Sokak 20, Taksim; ✆ 9am-2am

Beyoğlu bars come and go, but Dulcinea just keeps on going… Backlit bottles against burnished gold glass provide a stylish touch in this long room with its enormous bar. Grab one of the popular bar stools and strike up a conversation with a regular – you're bound to enjoy yourself. A beer costs €2.20 and a glass of wine €3.30.

IF BAR Map pp284-6 *Bar*
☎ 212-252 5460; Richmond Hotel, İstiklal Caddesi 445; ✆ 7pm-2am Mon-Sat

Lolling on the If Bar's stylish olive-green banquettes and enjoying the spectacular view of the Bosphorus and Asian shore while drinking a martini is our idea of a damn fine late afternoon. We usually leave before the live band starts, though, as pop covers just don't hold the same attraction. Beers cost €3.30, cocktails €6.

JAMES JOYCE IRISH PUB
Map pp284-6 *Bar*
☎ 212-224 2013; The Irish Centre, Balo Sokak 26, off İstiklal Caddesi; ✆ 1pm-2am Sun-Thu, 1pm-4am Fri & Sat

The only authentic Irish bar in town, this popular place is a good spot to enjoy a pint and a *craik*. There's a mixed crowd and a popular all-day breakfast (€8.80). It occasionally organises live sessions of traditional Irish folk music and performances by Irish singers.

LEB-İ DERYA Map pp284-6 *Bar*
☎ 212-293 4989; Kumbaracı Yokuşu 115/7; ✆ 11am-4am

Without doubt our favourite bar in İstanbul. On the seventh floor of a building off İstiklal Caddesi, it's friendly, stylish and always buzzing. And oh, the views! Sip a Derya Dudağı, the house cocktail (€9.40), while gazing over

Vogue (p170)

to the Asian side and you'll never want to leave. There's also food on offer (p157).

MADRID Map pp284-6 *Bar*
İpek Sokak 15, off İstiklal Caddesi; 🕑 **2pm-2am**
Grab your castanets and get ready for a big night, because this Spanish bar provides cheap beer and a good time for all. There'll always be someone willing to chat about the latest Almodovar flick or accompany you in a drunken tango late in the evening. Watch out for the steep iron staircase.

NU TERAS Map pp284-6 *Bar*
☎ **212-245 6070; Meşrutiyet Caddesi 149/7, Tepebaşı;** 🕑 **6.30pm-2am Mon-Thu, 6.30pm-4am Fri & Sat Jun-Oct only**
You want glam? Well, you'll get it at this ultra-chic rooftop bar. With its glass bar, tables full of beautiful people dining alfresco and panoramic views, Nu Teras is the place to be seen in town. Go at sunset and make sure you frock up.

ORIENT EXPRESS BAR Map pp284-6 *Bar*
☎ **212-251 4560; ground fl, Meşrutiyet Caddesi 98-100, Pera Palace Oteli, Tepebaşı;** 🕑 **10am-2am**
We love the faded, old-fashioned charm of this bar, right down to the lady pianist play-

ing Cole Porter numbers and the centrepiece fish bowl. All of the public spaces in the Pera Palace are impressive and the bar is up there with the best, featuring lovely stained-glass windows, a wood-and-tile bar and comfortable lounge chairs that have been sat on by more than their fair share of luminaries and cads. The gins and tonic (€7.20) go down a treat.

PANO Map pp284-6 *Bar*
☎ **212-292 6664; Hamalbaşı Caddesi 26, Tepebaşı;** 🕑 **11am-1am**
You'll have to fight your way through the throngs at this extraordinarily popular wine bar on a Thursday, Friday or Saturday night. Drinkers prop themselves on the high bar tables at the front and swig the cheap house wine (€7.50 per bottle); others take a table at the back or upstairs and pace themselves while sampling good-quality hot and cold meze (€1.50 to €4.70).

QUEEN Map pp284-6 *Bar*
Zambak Sokak 23, off İstiklal Caddesi; 🕑 **11pm-4am**
The name of this establishment says it all. Late-night revellers are fond of dropping in for a drink and a preen in front of the wall mirrors. Go buffed and ready to party hard. A beer costs €1.70.

SMYRNA Map pp284-6 *Bar*
☎ **212-244 2466; Akarsu Yokuşu Sokak 29, Cihangir;** 🕑 **10.30am-midnight**
This stylish neighbourhood bar is most definitely worth crossing town for. Smyrna is known for its long bar, collection of antique toys, couch-filled back corner and candle-lit tables. The atmosphere is laid back, the music is unobtrusive and the crowd is early 30s 'Beyoğlu Arty'. If you decide to make a night of it here (and many do) there's good simple food available. Beer is €1.90, a glass of wine €2.20.

SODA Map pp284-6 *Bar*
☎ **212-251 6126; Meşrutiyet Caddesi 151, Tepebaşı;** 🕑 **noon-1am Mon-Sat**
This basement bar is a bit of an enigma. Its stark Scandinavian interior is more suited to a quiet cocktail bar than party central, but the loud trance music and Diesel-clad clientele are clearly here to live it up rather than strike poses over an Absolut. There's fusion food and a brunch on Sundays. A beer will set you back €5.

SOHO SUPPER CLUB

Map pp284-6   *Bar*

☎ 212-245 0152; Meşelik Sokak 14, Taksim;
🕒 10am-2am Mon-Thu, 10am-4am Fri & Sat

The designers of this bar were obviously super-impressed by Kubrick's *2001: A Space Odyssey*. A funky cream-and-pink colour scheme and mood lighting lure drinkers off one of Beyoğlu's busiest side streets and into this long, minimalist space. The mixed clientele gets down to house music and punchy cocktails. The food is good, too.

TAKSIM, HARBIYE & NIŞANTAŞI

If you know and wear designer labels, you may like to join the moneyed set drinking at these upmarket establishments. Don't go if you can't cope with too much attitude.

BRASSERIE NIŞANTAŞI

Map p287   *Bar*

☎ 212-343 0443; Abdi İpekçi Caddesi 23, Nişantaşı;
🕒 10am-1am Mon-Sat, noon-1am Sun

We're talking serious glamour here. Loads of beautiful people (men in linen suits and sunglasses, young women in designer jeans so tight we were truly concerned about their reproductive futures) congregate at the street-side tables or strike attitudes underneath the most spectacular chandelier in town to enjoy pricey beers (€5) or espresso (€2.50). Have a botox booster before you go and see p160 for a food review.

TEPE LOUNGE Map p287   *Bar*

☎ 212-251 4696; Marmara Hotel, Taksim Square;
🕒 5pm-1.30am

We think there's something special about bars in five-star hotels. Just picture barfly Bill Murray in *Lost in Translation* and you'll get what we mean. Here the décor is fussy, but the martinis are dry and the views down to the Bosphorus Bridge are wonderful. It's the perfect place to

chill before sunset. There's live jazz on Thursday, Friday and Saturday after 10pm.

BEŞIKTAŞ & ORTAKÖY

The many tiny bars packed along the narrow lanes of Ortaköy around İskele Square are famous for their devotion to Turkish pop music and their casual atmosphere. They're particularly busy on a weekend. Get there by bus No 25E from Eminönü or bus Nos 40, 40A or 40T from Taksim Square; a taxi at the end of the night should cost around €4 to Beyoğlu and €6 to Sultanahmet.

In Beşiktaş you'll find one of the city's most glamorous bars, Vogue.

CENEVIZ KAHVESI Map p288   *Bar*

☎ 212-227 1449; Osmanzade Sokak 13-15, Ortaköy;
🕒 1pm-2am

This laid-back bar is a popular watering spot for gay men in particular, though everyone's welcome. Part cellar, part cave with raw rock/brick finishes and low lighting, its drinks are reasonably cheap and its music is unobtrusive. You'll find it near the Burger King.

VOGUE Map p288   *Bar*

☎ 212-227 4404; BJK Plaza, A Blok Kat 13, Spor Caddesi, Beşiktaş; 🕒 noon-midnight Mon-Sat, noon-11pm Sun

İstanbul's most sophisticated bar/restaurant has a sleek stainless-steel bar, a terrace with stunning views over the Bosphorus to Old İstanbul and the Asian side, and bar staff that look as if they've been outfitted at Armani. You can always rely on two things here: the martinis being dry and the crowd being stylish. See p161 for a food review.

WALL Map p288   *Bar*

☎ 212-236 1903; Kaymakçı Sokak 14; 🕒 noon-3am

You can have a drink on one of the sofas outside, venture in to prop up the downstairs bar or join the locals having a great time dancing to Turkish pop covers upstairs.

Entertainment

Entertainment

You can while away the night in glamorous nightclubs on the Bosphorus where you'll spend your entire holiday budget in the space of one night if you're not careful; attend a musical recital, opera or ballet at one of the city's many top-class performance venues; or drink raki and burst into song with locals while listening to live fasıl music at one of the city's many rowdy meyhanes. Put simply, there's an entertainment option for everyone in İstanbul. With its array of cinemas, almost religious devotion to all forms of music and great love of dance, it's rare to have a week go by when there's not a special event, festival or performance scheduled. And then there are the everyday practices that are performances in themselves, such as a visit to a historic *hamam* or catching a night ferry for next to nothing and admiring the twinkling lights and spectacular city skyline of Old İstanbul as it recedes into the distance. In short, the only thing you can't do in this town is be bored.

Tickets & Reservations

Buying tickets for events in a foreign country can be somewhat daunting when your grasp of the language is limited to 'thank you' and 'sorry, I'm married'. Most venues sell tickets at the box office, which allows you to deal face to face with the seller. This way you can gesticulate (a prerequisite to helping you be understood) and it also means you can check out the advertising literature, photographs and make double-sure the performance (if verbal) is going to be in a language you understand.

If you can't make it to the box office or there isn't one for the venue, try **Biletix** (☎ 216-454 1555, 216-556 9800; www.biletix.com). It's a major ticket seller for all kinds of events from festivals and big-name concerts to football matches. Biletix outlets are found in many spots throughout the city – in Vakkorama in Akmerkez, at the Beyoğlu Ada Kültür in Tünel – but the most convenient for travellers is probably the one at the **İstanbul Hilton** (p213) in Harbiye, a short walk from **Taksim Square** (p123). Alternatively, you could buy your ticket by credit card on Biletix's website and collect the tickets from the venue before the concert, but this usually means standing in long queues.

Ticket costs vary wildly, ranging from €3 to €30 and lots of places in between. Student discounts are available at the Cultural Centres, but not usually at the commercial venues.

HAMAMS

CAĞALOĞLU HAMAMI Map pp278-80

☎ 212-522 2424; Yerebatan Caddesi 34, Cağaloğlu; bath & massage €20, bath €10; ☉ 8am-10pm men, 8am-8pm women

Built over three centuries ago, this is one of the city's most beautiful *hamams*. It boasts (without evidence) that King Edward VIII, Kaiser Wilhelm II, Franz Liszt, Cameron Diaz and Florence Nightingale have enjoyed its pleasures, no doubt at the same time and with Elvis in attendance. It's pricey, but the surroundings are so impressive that they've featured in everything from soap ads to an *Indiana Jones* film. Separate baths each have a large *camekan* (reception area), where it's possible to have a nap or a tea at the end of your bath. There's also a bar/café. The 'Sultan Treatment' costs €30 and includes bath, massage and exfoliation.

ÇEMBERLİTAŞ HAMAMI Map pp278-80

☎ 212-522 7974; Vezir Hanı Caddesi 8, Çemberlitaş; bath & massage €13.80, bath €8.30; ☉ 6am-midnight

There won't be too many times in your life when you'll get the opportunity to have a Turkish bath in a building dating back to 1584, so now might well be the time to do it. Commissioned by Nurbanu Sultan, wife of Selim II and mother of Murat III, this *hamam* was designed by the great architect Sinan and is among the most beautiful in the city. Just off Divan Yolu near the Grand Bazaar, it's a double *hamam* (separate baths for men and women) that's particularly popular with tourists. Although the splendid *camekan* is unfortunately for men only (women must put up with a utilitarian corridor filled with lockers and benches) the *hararet* (hot room) in each section is a glorious space with a large marble *göbektaşı* (raised platform above heating source) and domed ceilings with

Hamams

We run the danger of sounding like your mum here, but frankly, we just don't think it's advisable for you to leave İstanbul without having a bath. A Turkish bath, that is.

The concept of the steam bath was passed from the Romans to the Byzantines and then on to the Turks, who named it the *hamam* and have relished it ever since. They've even exported the concept throughout the world, hence the term Turkish bath. Until recent decades, many homes in İstanbul didn't have washing facilities and, due to Islam's emphasis on personal squeaky-cleanness, the community relied on the hundreds of *hamams* that were constructed throughout the city, often as part of the *külliye* of a mosque. Of course, it wasn't only personal hygiene that was attended to in the *hamam*. It was the perfect place for a prospective mother-in-law to eye off, pinch and prod a prospective daughter-in-law, for instance, and it was equally good for catching up on the neighbourhood gossip. Now that many people have bathrooms in İstanbul, *hamams* are nowhere near as popular as they used to be, but some carry on, no doubt due to their role as local meeting places. Others have become extremely successful tourist attractions.

The city's *hamams* vary enormously. Some are dank dives where you may come out dirtier than you went in (remember – Turks call cockroaches '*hamam* insects'); others are plain and clean, servicing a predominantly local clientele. An increasing number are building a reputation as gay meeting places (we're talking truly steamy here) and a handful are geared exclusively towards tourists. If you're only going to visit one or two when you're in town, we suggest you choose the 'Big Two' – **Cağaloğlu** and **Çemberlitaş** (both opposite). Sure, they're touristy, but they're also gorgeous historic buildings where most of the clientele will be having their first experience of a *hamam*, so you won't feel out of place. They're also clean and have some English-speaking staff.

Bath Procedure

Upon entry you are shown to a *camekan* (entrance hall or space) where you will be allocated a dressing cubicle or locker and given a *peştemal* (bath-wrap) and sandals. Store your clothes and don the *peştemal* and sandals. An attendant will then lead you through the *soğukluk* (intermediate room) to the *hararet* (hot room), where you sit and sweat for a while, relaxing and loosening up, perhaps on the *göbektaşı* (central, raised platform atop the heating source).

Soon you will be half-asleep and as soft as putty from the steamy heat. The cheapest bath is the one you do yourself, having brought your own soap, shampoo and towel. But the real Turkish bath experience is to have an attendant wash and massage you.

If you have opted for the latter, an attendant douses you with warm water and lathers you with a sudsy swab. Next you are scrubbed with a coarse cloth mitten loosening dirt you never suspected you had. After a massage (these yo-yo between being enjoyable, limp-wristed or mortally dangerous) comes a shampoo and another dousing with warm water, followed by one with cool water.

When the scrubbing is over, stay in the *hararet* relaxing or head for the cool room and grab a towel. You then go back to your locker or cubicle to get dressed – if you've got a cubicle you can even have a rest or order something to drink. If you want to nap, tell the attendant when to wake you. The average *hamam* experience takes around one hour.

Modesty

Traditional Turkish baths have separate sections for men and women, or have only one set of facilities and admit men or women at different times. Bath etiquette requires that men remain clothed with the bath-wrap at all times. In the women's section women sometimes wear their underwear (but not their bra). It's up to you – most tourists seem not to do this. During the bathing, everyone washes their private parts themselves, without removing the bath-wrap or underclothes.

In touristy areas, some baths now accept that foreign men and women like to bathe together. No Turkish woman would let a masseur touch her (it must be a masseuse), but masseurs are usually the only massagers available in these foreign-oriented baths. We suggest that women willing to accept a masseur should have the massage within view of male companions or other friends.

Practicalities

Soap, shampoo and towels are provided at all of the *hamams* we've reviewed. Çemberlitaş is the only *hamam* where the price includes tips; others will tell you that tipping is at your discretion, but frankly, you've got as much of a chance of leaving without tipping as you have of approaching the Blue Mosque and being ignored by the touts selling postcards. We suggest giving 10-20% of the total fee (depending on service). You'll get drenched, so make sure you take a comb, toiletries, make-up and (if you choose to wear underwear during the massage) a dry pair of replacement knickers star-like apertures admitting filtered light. In the women's *harare* it's not unusual for one of the masseuses to break into song. For your money you'll get lots of heat and a thorough and very soapy massage. There's a 20% discount for ISIC student-card holders.

ÇUKURCUMA HAMAMI Map pp284-6

☎ 212-243 2401; Çukurcuma Caddesi 57, Çukurcuma; bath & massage €23, bath €11.50; ☷ 9am-8pm

This is, without doubt, the most famous gay *hamam* in the city – stuff happens here that the local imam sure ain't going to approve of. It has even got a bar to get its male clientele in the mood. There's a sauna that functions as a back room and exercise equipment for those looking for a more orthodox type of workout.

GEDİKPAŞA HAMAMI Map pp282-3

☎ 212-517 8956; Hamam Caddesi 65-7, off Gedikpaşa Caddesi, Gedik Paşa; bath & massage €12.40, bath €9; ☷ 6am-midnight

It's old (c 1475 in fact), run down and a bit grubby, but the masseuses at this popular local *hamam* know what they're doing and it costs half the price of some of its competitors.

SÜLEYMANİYE HAMAMI Map pp282-3

☎ 212-519 5569; Mimar Sinan Caddesi 20, Süleymaniye; bath & massage €13.80, bath €8.30; ☷ 7am-midnight

Another *hamam* designed by Sinan, though this one's not as impressive as the Çemberlitaş and is a mixed bath, meaning that everyone gets naked together and all masseurs are men. Most women will not feel comfortable here.

TARİHİ GALATASARAY HAMAMI

Map pp284-6

Historic Galatasaray Turkish Bath; ☎ 212-252 4242; Turnacıbaşı Sokak 24, Çukurcuma; bath & massage €24, bath €19.40; ☷ 6am-10pm men, 8am-8pm women

Though not as pretty as many Old İstanbul *hamams*, this quiet place off İstiklal Caddesi is one of the city's best, with lots of marble decoration, small cubicles for resting and sipping tea after the bath, pretty fountains and even a shoe-shine service. Parts of the building date from 1481, but it has been rebuilt several times. The interiors are much nicer in the men's section than the women's. It's famous for having one of the hottest *hararets* in town (that sounds rude but we mean it literally). Be warned: it's pricey and staff have a reputation for hassling for tips.

Hamam, Süleymaniye (above)

MUSIC

TURKISH MUSIC

Turks are proud of their traditional music and whether young or old will usually be familiar enough with the most popular folk and fasıl numbers to sing along in bars or meyhanes. One of the most entertaining experiences you can possibly have while visiting İstanbul is to have dinner at a fasıl venue such as Despina (below) and see the guests take turns in serenading the restaurant with their favourite song. If you do this, make sure you tip when the musicians come to your table – anything less than €10 per table would be insulting, particularly if the band has a few (or more) members. If you have a drink at a bar where folk music is being played, you don't need to tip the musicians quite so lavishly, but it's obligatory to leave something. When booking at a meyhane (it's not necessary to book at bars), try to opt for a Friday or Saturday night – on other nights restaurant management occasionally tells musicians not to come in if numbers are low.

Multidisciplinary venues such as the **Cemal Reşit Rey Konser Salonu** (p177) or the **Tarık Zafer Tunaya Kültür Merkezi** (p178) occasionally programme Ottoman music. The atmospheric **Basilica Cistern** (p83) is another such venue.

ANDON Map pp284-6

☎ 212-251 0222; Sıraselviler Caddesi 89, Taksim; ⏰ 7pm-3am

In addition to its rooftop restaurant with fine views over the Bosphorus, its wine bar with a rowdy soloist and its ground-floor disco bar, Andon is known for the fasıl music performed nightly in its excellent meyhane. Come prepared to sing along.

BİNBİRDİREK CISTERN Map pp278-80

Binbirdirek Sarnıçı; ☎ 212-517 8725; İmran Ökten Sokak 4, Binbirdirek

Talk about atmosphere! This Byzantine cistern hosts live music in summertime, sometimes featuring big-name acts such as Turkish pop singer Kayahan. Check the board at the exit for the most up-to-date programme and prices.

DESPINA Map pp276-7

☎ 212-247 3357; Açıkyol Sokak 9, Kurtuluş; ⏰ noon-midnight

Established in 1946 by the glamorous Madame Despina, whose stylish photograph greets guests at the entrance, Despina is one of the city's best meyhanes. The Armenian/Greek food is good (it serves the best fava in town), but plays second fiddle to the live fasıl music, which is played by some of the most accomplished musicians in Turkey. Locals join in the singing and everyone has a great time. Highly recommended, particularly on a warm evening when the garden is open. Come by taxi.

OTANTİK CAFÉ & BAR Map pp284-6

☎ 212-293 6515; Balo Sokak 1/3, off İstiklal Caddesi, Beyoğlu; ⏰ noon-2am

One of Beyoğlu's most popular live-music venues, this bar often hosts big-name local folk singers and so is inevitably packed. It's noisy, smoky and lots of fun. The food at **Otantik** (p159) is average – the meze is around €2.80 – but that's not what you're here for. You'll be in the company of middle-aged couples swaying to the music, groups of young people putting in requests and downing lots of beer and extended families catching up over a bottle of raki – in short, the real İstanbul.

ŞAL CAFÉ BAR Map pp284-6

☎ 212-243 4196; Büyükparmakkapı Sokak 18, off İstiklal Caddesi, Beyoğlu; ⏰ noon-2am

This long smoky venue is low on style (unusual for this part of the city), but has loads of atmosphere on a busy night. Most importantly of all, it hosts folk musicians who really know their stuff. Décor and music choices are resolutely Anatolian. You may see patrons get up from the low tables and dance when a lively number is played or weep quietly into their glass of raki when a heart-wrenching number played on a *bağlama* (a stringed instrument, also known as the 'saz') features. A beer costs €1.70.

TÜRKÜ CAFÉ & BAR Map pp284-6

☎ 212-292 9281; İmam Adnan Sokak 9, off İstiklal Caddesi, Beyoğlu; ⏰ noon-2am

From the street it's easy to see and hear the action at this popular bar, which is a favourite place for locals, who come to hear folk music and indulge in raki-induced dance numbers. It is as raucous as it is good fun. On the weekend, the music starts around mid-afternoon, so it's a great place to visit before settling down for dinner at one of the excellent local restaurants.

JAZZ

İstanbul's few dedicated jazz venues feature a smoky atmosphere, unpretentious décor, and patrons who won't leave before the last set is finished. If jazz is your thing, try somewhere like Nardis (below). If all you want is a bit of jazz with your after-dinner drink, try the highly regarded Q Jazz Club (below) or the Tepe Lounge at the Marmara (p213) on a Thursday, Friday or Saturday night. Both are expensive but oh-so-comfortable. Venues such as Roxy (p182) and Babylon (p181) also host occasional jazz acts, particularly during the International İstanbul Jazz Festival (p10) and Akbank Jazz Festival (p10).

JAZZ CAFÉ Map pp284-6
☎ 212-245 0516; Hasnun Galip Sokak 20, Beyoğlu; no cover charge; ⏰ 8pm-4am Mon-Sat
Bathed in mood lighting, this mellow place boasts hosts expats, jazz-heads and mainly 30-somethings. Live music kicks off at 10.30pm. The programme changes and isn't always jazz – Turkish rock legend Bülent Ortaçgil was playing a weekly gig when this book went to print.

NARDIS JAZZ CLUB Map pp284-6
☎ 212-244 6327; www.nardisjazz.com; Galata Kulesi Sokak 14, Galata; cover charge €5.50; ⏰ music 9.30pm-12.30am Mon-Thu, 11.30pm-1.30am Fri & Sat
Just down the hill from the Galata Tower (p118), this new venue, named after a Miles Davis track, is where the real jazz aficionados go. Run by jazz guitarist Önder Focan, it's small and if you want a decent table, you'll need to book. There are a great sound system, good food (pasta €5, mains €8.50) and reasonably priced beer (€2.80). Acts are mainly local, though some international artists pop up on the programme.

Q JAZZ CLUB Map p288
Çırağan Palace Hotel Kempinski; ☎ 212-236 2121; Çırağan Caddesi 32, Beşiktaş; cover charge varies; ⏰ 10pm-4am
This is about as sophisticated as jazz joints come. In the luxury Çırağan Palace Hotel Kempinski (p214), the Q hosts jazz singers (the more sultry the better) and charges a fortune for drinks. Still, we can think of few better ways to blow

Late-Night Transport
Getting home after pumpkin hour (midnight) can be a bit difficult in İstanbul. Most ferries weigh anchor at around 11pm, the buses and trains dry up at midnight and the *dolmuşes* (shared minibuses) an hour or so thereafter. You could always walk and, if you're going out locally, it's usually fine to do so. But although İstanbul isn't a dangerous city, we wouldn't recommend you set out from Beyoğlu to Sultanahmet at 2am, especially after a few drinks. Taxis are the best option. After midnight, the *gece* (night) rate kicks in until 6am; though 50% more than the *gündüz* (day) rate, it's still a bargain. From Taksim to Sultanahmet you should pay between €3.50 and €5.

our budget than spending a night in its cellar bar (winter) and waterside garden (summer).

WESTERN CLASSICAL MUSIC & OPERA
İstanbul has a lively Western classical music scene and its own headline act, the İstanbul State Symphony Orchestra. There are also regular visits by international orchestras and chamber ensembles. The city's major venues are the Atatürk Cultural Centre, İş Sanat, the Lütfi Kırdar Concert Hall and the Cemal Reşit Rey Concert Hall (all opposite).

In summer, concerts are also held at the Italian Cultural Centre (opposite) in Tepebaşı, in the atmospheric amphitheatre at Rumeli Hisarı and in the watery cavern of the Basilica Cistern (p83). During the International İstanbul Music Festival (p10) there is a wealth of classical music and opera on offer, including performances of Mozart's *The Abduction from the Seraglio*, appropriately staged in the grounds of Topkapı Palace (p91).

The İstanbul State Opera & Ballet has a season running from October to May with some extra performances during the International İstanbul Music Festival (p10). Most performances are at the Atatürk Cultural Centre.

CULTURAL CENTRES & MAJOR PERFORMANCE VENUES
There's big money behind the arts in İstanbul, with banks leading the way in funding the major arts companies and festivals. Fortunately, there are enough impressive venues to host opening nights where the sponsors can schmooze and the dignitaries can party

following the performance. Most of these venues are cultural centres hosting a number of different art forms – it's not unusual for these places to host an opera one night, a jazz performance the next, a ballet on the night after that and an exhibition in the foyer all the time.

To get an overview of what's on where, refer to the monthly listings in *Time Out Istanbul*. Tickets are usually available through **Biletix** (☎ 216-454 1555, 216-556 9800; www .biletix.com).

AKBANK CULTURE & ARTS CENTRE

Map pp284-6

☎ 212-252 3500; İstiklal Caddesi 14-18, Beyoğlu

This small venue, funded entirely by the Turkish bank of the same name, hosts classical and jazz music recitals as well as exhibitions of the work of local artists.

ATATÜRK CULTURAL CENTRE

Map pp284-6

AKM, Atatürk Kültür ve Sanat Merkezi; ☎ 212-251 5600; www.idobale.com in Turkish; Taksim Square, Taksim; ☯ box office 10am-6pm

At night the lights of the city's major cultural centre glow behind its stylised steel grill, providing a welcome sight in the otherwise unprepossessing **Taksim Square** (p123). Unfortunately, during the day the building isn't quite as beguiling. Being the home of the city's major theatre, ballet and opera companies, it hosts more than its fair share of opening nights and acclaimed performances. The centre includes five performance halls in addition to a gallery and a cinema. Tickets are always affordable.

BORUSAN ARTS & CULTURE CENTER

Map pp284-6

Borusan Kültür ve Sanat Merkezi; ☎ 212-292 0655; www.borusansanat.com; İstiklal Caddesi 421, Beyoğlu; ☯ gallery 10.30am-7pm Tue-Sat

This well-regarded arts centre has an established gallery showcasing the work of local artists, with the occasional high-profile international show (a recent stunner featured the work of Sophie Calle, Louise Bourgeois and Maria Marshall). It also hosts concerts and recitals by artists of the calibre of world-famous Turkish pianist Fazıl Say.

CEMAL REŞİT REY CONCERT HALL

Map p287

Cemal Reşit Rey Konser Salonu; ☎ 212-232 9830; www.crrks.org in Turkish; Gümüş Sokak, Harbiye; ☯ box office 10am-7.30pm

With its great acoustics and comfortable chairs, this concert hall is a popular venue for

dance (it hosts the annual **International İstanbul Dance Festival**, p9), classical and Ottoman music and the occasional jazz gig. Its handy monthly guides list upcoming events and prices in English, and are available around town (they're everywhere on İstiklal Caddesi).

HAGHIA EIRENE Map pp278-80

Aya İrini Kilisesi, Church of Divine Peace; First Court of Topkapı Palace, Sultanahmet

Big-name classical events make the most of the acoustics in this ancient venue, particularly during the International İstanbul Music Festival. During the festival a board outside lists upcoming events and contact details; tickets are available through **Biletix** (☎ 216-454 1555, 216-556 9800; www.biletix.com).

İŞ ART & CULTURAL CENTRE

İş Sanat Kültür Merkezi; ☎ 212-316 1083; İş Kuleleri 4, Levent; ☯ box office 9am-6pm

This newish venue in the İş Towers hosts international acts such as the Kronos Quartet, jazz, Ottoman concerts and world music. To get here take the metro from Taksim to Levent and ask for directions; alternatively, catch the free shuttle service that leaves from outside the **Atatürk Cultural Centre** (left) at Taksim at 6pm.

ITALIAN CULTURAL CENTRE

Map pp284-6

İtalyan Kültür Merkezi; ☎ 212-293 9848; Meşrutiyet Caddesi 161, Tepebaşı

In summer this centre hosts low-key performances and recitals mainly organised by the **Borusan Arts & Culture Centre** (left).

LÜTFİ KIRDAR CONCERT HALL

Map p287

Convention Centre; Lütfi Kırdar Kongre ve Sergi Salonu; ☎ 212-296 3055; Darülbedai Sokak, Harbiye

Originally built for the 1948 World Wrestling Championships, this huge refurbished concert hall hosts conferences, the Borusan İstanbul Philharmonic Orchestra and events for the **International İstanbul Music Festival** (p10).

TARIK ZAFER TUNAYA KÜLTÜR MERKEZİ Map pp284-6

Tarık Zafer Tunaya Cultural Centre; ☎ 212-293 1270; Şahkulu Bostanı Sokak 8, Tünel

As well as its regular screenings of Turkish flicks and informative lectures on Turkish culture, this centre hosts music, including occasional performances of Ottoman music.

DANCE & THEATRE

FOLK DANCE

Many people immediately think of belly dancing when they hear the term 'Turkish folk dance', but there are other, far more authentic, traditional dance forms in the country. In fact, although belly dancing has a long, wobbly and undulating history, contrary to popular belief it's not strictly a Turkish dance. It's said to have originated in Egypt as a meditative-erotic dance to entertain the elite in life and death (tomb paintings of dancers have been found) and was brought to Turkey during the Ottoman Empire. Today in İstanbul it's mainly tourist fodder, and although it's entertaining – and pretty sexy – the dancers are usually second-rate and you won't see a performance of the art at anywhere near its best.

As well as belly dancing, other dances can be seen at the cheesy, touristy 'Turkish Shows' around town. These provide a snapshot of Turkey's folk dances (with belly dancing), usually accompanied by dinner. Beloved by package-tour operators, they are expensive and the food is usually mediocre at best. Still, if you are keen to see some folk dance while you're in town these are usually the only places you'll be able to do it.

Finally, check with the cultural centres to see if any special folk dance performances are programmed. If you're lucky enough to be in town when they are, snap up a ticket.

DANCE OF COLOURS Map pp282-3

☎ 212-517 8692; www.dancesofcolours.com; FKM Firat Culture Centre, Divan Yolu Caddesi, Çemberlitaş; €20; ☽ Tue & Thu 7.15pm, Sat 5.15pm

This popular performance features dances from eleven different regions of Turkey. If you want to see a Dervish whirl, a belly dancer undulate and lots more, this one-hour show is for you. Colourful costumes and professional dancers make for a good evening's fun, with the added bonus that you don't have to fork out for an indifferent meal. It's possible to arrange a hotel pick-up if you request this when booking.

GALATA TOWER Map pp284-6

Galata Kulesi; ☎ 212-293 8180; Galata Square; €65; ☽ Mon-Sat 8.30pm-midnight

A live band accompanies the belly dancer at this show on the top floor of this historic tower.

Bosphorus Night Cruises

One of the most enjoyable, and certainly most romantic, night-time activities in İstanbul is to take a Bosphorus ferry. It doesn't really matter where, as long as you don't end up on the southern coast of the Sea of Marmara or on the Princes' Islands, because you will find it difficult to get back. Enjoy the view back to Old İstanbul (surely one of the world's great vistas), the twinkling lights, the fishing boats bobbing on the waves and the powerful searchlights of the ferries sweeping the sea lanes. You can even enjoy a cheap glass of tea or a fresh orange juice (a waiter will offer you these).

Perhaps the best ferry to catch for this purpose is the one from Karaköy (just over the Galata Bridge from Eminönü) to Kadıköy. Just go to Karaköy, buy two tokens (for the voyages out and back) and walk on board. When you reach Kadıköy, you could have dinner or a drink at **Denizati** (p162), just next to the ferry terminal, or walk past Denizati and join the legions of young couples and families at one of the myriad çay bahçesi (tea gardens) on the waterfront. Return ferries leave on the hour and half hour, with the last ferry leaving Kadıköy (or the nearby Haydarpaşa stop) for Karaköy at 11pm; make sure you confirm this at the ticket booth when you first arrive.

A similar ride is the one from Eminönü to Üsküdar. Buy your ticket at Eminönü's dock and board the ferry. When you arrive in Üsküdar you could grab a delicious fish sandwich from one of the bobbing boats to the right of the ferry terminal when you alight (these even have seating) or check out one of the çay bahçesi a bit further on past the **Şemsi Paşa Camii** (p133). Past these is a popular waterside promenade going down to the famous **Kız Kulesi** (Maiden's Tower; p132). It's a gorgeous walk on a summer's evening. Return ferries leave on the hour and half hour, with the last ferry leaving Üsküdar at 10.30pm, but again, make sure you confirm this when you first arrive.

You'll have to put up with a dodgy nightclub singer and bland food, but the fabulous view more than compensates.

ORIENT HOUSE Map pp282-3
☎ 212-517 6163; www.orienthouseistanbul.com; Tiyatro Caddesi 27, Beyazıt; adult/student/child €75/50/50; ☯ 8.30pm-midnight

Orient House is popular mainly because it's close to Sultanahmet and its spruikers have sprinkled brochures and the promise of attractive commissions around many Sultanahmet hotels. Still, its live band, belly dancers and folk dancers seem to know what the audience likes, even going to the extent of putting on a traditional costume show with lots of 'local colour'.

KERVANSARAY Map p287
☎ 212-247 1630; www.kervansaraytr.com; Cumhuriyet Caddesi 30/5, Harbiye; €75; ☯ dinner 7.30pm, show 9pm, finish midnight

This place has decent food and a show with live band, belly dancing and folk dancers. Be warned, though: tables are sometimes a long way from the stage. Guests can dress up as a sultan or sultana and have their photo taken (€15). A free shuttle to and from your hotel is available – request this when booking. If you bargain when you book, you should be able to get a ticket for €60.

BALLET

Like opera, ballet has a keen following among the moneyed elite in İstanbul. There are occasional performances by home-grown and international artists, usually at the **Atatürk Cultural Centre** (p177). April sees the **International İstanbul Dance Festival** (p9), with most performances held at the **Cemal Reşit Rey Concert Hall** (p177). The city's major company is the **İstanbul State Opera & Ballet** (☎ 212-251 1023; www.idobale.com in Turkish).

THEATRE

The Turks are enthusiastic theatregoers and have a special genius for dramatic art. The problem for the foreign visitor is language, as most performances are in Turkish. Your best chance of seeing theatre in English is during May's **International İstanbul Theatre Festival** (p10), where some English-language plays are staged, often sponsored by cultural organisations such as the British Council.

One form of theatre that is accessible to foreign visitors is the famous Shadow Puppet Theatre (*Karagöz*). Although the country's main troupe is based in Bursa, it also performs in İstanbul. The puppets (10cm to 50cm tall) are cut from hide pieces, coated with oil to promote translucency and decorated with colourful paints. Most have movable arms and legs, and some have movable heads. During the performances they prance behind a white sheet enacting stories. The best time to see *Karagöz* is in May each year, when the city hosts the **International Ülker Puppet Festival İstanbul** (p10).

CINEMAS

İstiklal Caddesi, between Galatasaray and Taksim, is the centre of İstanbul's cinema (*sinema*) district. During April's **International İstanbul Film Festival** (p9) every corner of Beyoğlu is filled with enthusiastic cinema-goers keen to see the latest Hollywood blockbuster or major European release, as well as home-grown products. Tickets to this festival are hot numbers – you'll need to book way in advance.

During the rest of the year, the enthusiasm for flicks remains. Films are mostly shown in English with Turkish subtitles, but double-check at the box office in case the film has Turkish (*Türkçe*) dubbing, as this sometimes happens with blockbusters. For movie listings, see the *Turkish Daily News*.

When possible, buy your tickets a few hours in advance. Depending on the venue, tickets cost between €2.80 and €6.60 for adults, €2.20 and €5 for students – many places offer reduced rates before 6pm and all day on Monday and Wednesday.

The usher will expect a small tip for showing you to your seat.

AFM AKMERKEZ
☎ 212-282 0505; Akmerkez Shopping Centre, Nispetiye Caddesi 76/1, Etiler

This multiplex is pricey, but its comfortable surrounds are a good place to rest after a big day at the city's best mall.

AFM FITAŞ Map pp284-6
☎ 212-251 2020; İstiklal Caddesi 24-26, Fitaş Pasajı, Beyoğlu

This multiplex has 11 screens and all the Hollywood trimmings. Above the arcade there's a popular expat pub, which is a good place to grab a drink before or after the show.

ALKAZAR SİNEMA MERKEZİ

Map pp284-6

☏ 212-293 2466; İstiklal Caddesi 179, Beyoğlu

First a porn cinema, then an arthouse joint, Alkazar has now given in to Hollywood, though it still occasionally programmes an arthouse hit. There are three screens and a plush and cosy interior.

ATLAS SINEMALAN Map pp284-6

☏ 212-252 8576; İstiklal Caddesi 209, Atlas Pasajı, Beyoğlu

On the first floor of one of the historic arcades along İstiklal, Atlas is always bustling. Three screens are on the first floor and the programming is eclectic.

BEYOĞLU SINEMALAN Map pp284-6

☏ 212-251 3240; İstiklal Caddesi 140, Beyoğlu

This is a good place to check out European and local indie productions.

EMEK Map pp284-6

☏ 212-293 8439; İstiklal Caddesi, Yeşilçam Sokak 5, Beyoğlu

Functioning since the 1920s, this barn of a cinema is one of the oldest in the city. It's not the most comfortable on offer, but has managed to retain a bit of the glamour it had during Pera's heyday.

REXX

☏ 216-336 0112; Sakızgülü Sokak 20-22, Kadıköy

We've sheltered here from bad weather before risking a ferry back to town more than once. On the Asian side of İstanbul, the Rexx's programme usually lacks surprises. The only exception is in April, when it screens part of the International İstanbul Film Festival (p9).

ŞAFAK SİNEMALARI Map pp282-3

☏ 212-516 2660; Divan Yolu Caddesi 134, Çemberlitaş

This seven-screen cinema is the closest to Sultanahmet, only a 10-minute walk along Divan Yolu. Enter via the menswear arcade and go downstairs to the top-quality multiplex screening local, Hollywood and European releases.

SİNEPOP Map pp284-6

☏ 212-251 1176; İstiklal Caddesi, Yeşilçam Sokak 22, Beyoğlu

Sinepop lacks the style of **Emek** (above), close by, but is more comfortable. Its two cinemas are well fitted out and screen mainly Hollywood product.

ART GALLERIES

İstanbul has a thriving art scene. As well as cultural centres (p176), most of which have excellent exhibition spaces (**Borusan Arts & Culture Centre**, p177, in particular), numerous small independent galleries exhibit the work of local and international visual and multimedia artists. Most upmarket private galleries are in the shopping areas of Teşvikiye and Nişantaşı, whereas the high-profile contemporary spaces funded by banks and other companies are on İstiklal Caddesi in Beyoğlu. Small galleries exhibiting the work of young local and international artists are in Asmalımescit, just off İstiklal Caddesi.

The big visual arts event of the year is the International İstanbul Biennal (p11).

ASMALIMESCİT SANAT GALERİSİ

Map pp284-6

Asmalımescit Art Gallery; ☏ 212-249 6979; Sofyalı Sokak 5, Tünel; ⏰ 11am-7pm

Set in an older house, this highly regarded private gallery exhibits local and international artists upstairs and has a stylish bar down below.

GALERİ ARTİST ÇUKURCUMA

Map pp284-6

☏ 212-251 9163; Altı Patlar Sokak 26, Çukurcuma; ⏰ 11am-7pm Mon-Sat

Jammed between antique shops, this tiny gallery shows work by emerging local and international artists, with an emphasis on painting and drawing.

PLATFORM GARANTİ CONTEMPORARY ART CENTRE

Map pp284-6

☏ 212-293 2361; İstiklal Caddesi 276, Beyoğlu; ⏰ Tue-Thu 1-8pm, Fri & Sat 1-10pm

A minimalist space funded by the Garanti Bank, Platform shows the very best of international contemporary art, with an emphasis on installation and multimedia work.

PROJE4L İSTANBUL MUSEUM OF CONTEMPORARY ART

İstanbul Güncel Sanat Müzesi; ☏ 212-281 5150; Harman Sokak, Harmanci Giz Plaza, Levent; ⏰ Tue-Sat 11am-7pm

Established by a local architect and property developer to further the understanding of experimental art in the city, Proje4L is super cool and programmes cutting-edge exhibitions mainly sourced from Europe. It occupies an annex of a tower block in Levent and is well worth a visit. Ring ahead to check what's on.

SCHNEIDERTEMPEL ART CENTRE

Map pp284-6
Schneidertempel Sanat Merkezi; ☎ 212-252 5157; Felek Sokak 1, Karaköy; ⏰ 10.30am-5.30pm Tue-Sat, noon-4pm Sun

Housed in an old synagogue, the Schneidertempel exhibits work by local Jewish artists as well as frequent exhibitions from abroad. Quality varies, but we've seen some excellent photographic exhibitions here, as well as extremely moving exhibitions of historical work from the Holocaust. Since the 2003 bombs, security has been tightened and opening hours are irregular. Treat those given above as a guide only.

TAKSİM SANAT GALERİ Map p287

İstanbul Büyükşehir Belediyesi; ☎ 212-245 2068; Cumhuriyet Caddesi 23, Taksim; ⏰ 10am-7pm Mon-Sat

Run by the municipality, this space exhibits work by local artists. To be frank, the work is usually amateur standard (think of the daubs that your crazy Aunt Yvonne might do), but an occasional show bucks the trend.

YAPI KREDİ BANKASI GALLERY

Map pp284-6
☎ 212-252 4700; İstiklal Caddesi 285, Galatasaray; ⏰ 10am-7pm Mon-Fri, 10am-6pm Sat, 1-6pm Sun

The convenient location just opposite the Galatasaray Lycée makes dropping into this gallery easy; better still, the exhibitions in the large airy space are top notch and usually showcase the work of big-name Turkish artists.

CLUBBING

Who cares if İstanbul's in Europe or Asia? All we know is that it's developing a great club and live-music scene. The horrible 1980s covers and saccharine Turkish pop that used to be inflicted on club-goers is increasingly being replaced by Middle Eastern fusion beats, techno and jazz-influenced tracks. If you're like us, you'll rarely see the daylight during your stay.

When İstanbullus go out clubbing they dress to kill. If you don't do the same, you'll be unlikely to get past the door bitches (usually buffed young hunks) at the mega-venues on the Bosphorus. Fortunately, you'll have no trouble at perennial favourites such as Babylon (below) and Roxy (p182), as these stay proud of their bohemian roots and couldn't give a toss what labels you're wearing.

As is the case with bars and restaurants, most of the clubbing action is in Beyoğlu or along the Bosphorus. The only thing to do at night in Sultanahmet is leave. Clubs are busiest on Friday and Saturday night, and the action doesn't really kick off until 1am. Many of the clubs close down from June or July until the end of September, when the party crowd moves down the coast. Those clubbers who stay in town tend to flock to the Bosphorus clubs such as Laila (p182) and Reina (p182) during this time.

As well as the clubs reviewed here, the Soho Supper Club (p170) and Dulcinea (p168) are safe bets if you want a few drinks and a dance or two.

BABYLON Map pp284-6

☎ 212-292 7368; www.pozitif.info; Şehbender Sokak 3, Tünel; admission varies according to acts; ⏰ 9.30pm-2am Tue-Thu, 10pm-3am Fri & Sat

Babylon is a dance club, a live-music venue, a bar and a city institution. Check the website to get an idea of the eclectic programme, which often features big-name international music acts. During the festival season this place truly heaves. Some advice: it's best to get your ticket in advance via Biletix (☎ 216-454 1555, 216-556 9800; www.biletix.com) or the box office (⏰ noon-11pm Tue-Sat).

Babylon nightclub

Top Five Clubs

- **Babylon** (p181)
- **Roxy** (below)
- **2C** (opposite)
- **Crystal** (below)
- **Laila** (below)

BAR BAHÇE Map pp284-6

☎ 212-243 2879; Soğancı Sokak 7/1, Cihangir; admission free Mon-Thu, Fri & Sat €5.50 (includes 1 drink); ☽ 10pm-2am Sun & Tue- Thu, 10pm-4am Fri & Sat

Glam young gay things love this place to bits. There's a dance bar, two chill-out rooms and always someone to flirt with (only if you're of a particular persuasion, of course).

CRYSTAL Map p288

☎ 212-278 4578; www.clubcrystal.org; Muallim Naci Caddesi 65, Ortaköy; admission free Thu, Fri & Sat €16.60 (includes 1 free drink); ☽ midnight-5.30am Thu-Sat

The home of the city's techno aficionados, who come here to appreciate sets put together by some of the best DJs from Turkey and the rest of Europe. There's a great sound system, a crowded dance floor and a lovely covered garden bar.

GODET Map pp284-6

☎ 212-244 3897; www.soap-system.com; Zambak Sokak 15, Beyoğlu; admission free Wed & Thu, €8 Fri & Sat; ☽ 11pm-4am Wed, Fri & Sat

Two dance floors means that this place can cater for diverse tastes. There may be techno downstairs in the Godet Club and smooth funk or house upstairs in the Red Room. Whatever's spinning, rest assured, the crowd will be jumping.

LAILA

☎ 212-236 3000; Muallim Naci Caddesi 54, Kuruçeşme; admission free Mon-Thu & Sun, Fri & Sat €16; ☽ 7pm-4am

During the summer months this huge outdoor club is the venue for cashed-up beautiful people to party until the wee hours alongside spectacular views of the Bosphorus. Food is available and the dress code is glamour, darlings. The fashionably late arrive just before the serious dance action starts at around 11pm. The DJs know what they're doing, but the crowd couldn't really care – they're more interested in celebrity spotting. Kuruçeşme is

about 1km northeast of Ortaköy or 7km from Sultanahmet; get there by taxi.

REINA

☎ 212-259 5919; Muallim Naci Caddesi 44, Kuruçeşme; admission free Mon-Thu & Sun, Fri & Sat €13; ☽ 6pm-3am

First came Laila, followed by her equally glamorous younger sister, Reina. They could almost be twins, but the music isn't quite as good here, with decidedly Eurovision overtones.

ROXY Map p287

☎ 212-249 1283; www.roxy.com.tr in Turkish; Arslan Yatağı Sokak 1-3, off Sıraselviler Caddesi, Taksim; admission varies according to acts; ☽ 9pm-3am Wed & Thu, 10pm-4am Fri & Sat

The Roxy vies with **Babylon** (p181) for the title of best live-music club in the city. Frankly, we don't care which one is the flavour of any particular month – we love them both. Slightly grungy and always good fun, it's a great place to hear everything from hip- hop to jazz fusion to electronic music. Check the website for who's playing and think seriously about organising tickets ahead of time.

Nightlife Rip-Offs

Foreigners, especially single foreign males, are targets for a classic İstanbul rip-off that works like this:

You're a single male out for a stroll in the afternoon or evening. A well-spoken, well-dressed Turk strikes up a conversation and says he knows a 'good place where we can have a drink and chat' or a 'great nightspot' etc. You enter, sit down and immediately several women move to your table and order drinks. When the drinks come, you're asked to pay – anywhere from €100 to however much money you have with you. It's a mugging and if you don't pay up, they take you into the back office and take it from you.

An exotic variation is a single foreign male having a drink and a meal at the Çiçek Pasajı. Several Turkish friends strike up a conversation, then suggest you all take a taxi to another place. In the taxi, they forcibly relieve you of your wallet.

How do you avoid such rip-offs? As many Turks are generous, hospitable, curious and gregarious, it's difficult to know whether an invitation is genuine (as it most often is) or the prelude to a mugging. Tread carefully if there's any reason for suspicion. As for nightclub recommendations, take them from a trusted source, such as your hotel clerk. And if anything like this happens to you, go straight to a police station afterwards and report it.

2C Map p287

☎ 212-235 6197; Abdülhakhamid Caddesi 19, Taksim; admission free Mon-Thu, Fri & Sat €13.80;

🕙 1am-6am

This huge place pulses to electronic beats and has a reputation as one of the city's best gay venues, though everyone is welcome and the mood is inclusive. One of the longest-running venues around, it just seems to go from strength to strength. Go.

SPORT, HEALTH & FITNESS

SOCCER

There's only one spectator sport that really matters to Turks. And that's soccer.

For the 24 hours preceding a big soccer match, team scarves are worn, flags are aflutter and hotted-up testosterone-motors bounce up and down at red lights before screeching off and dragging team colours behind them. The victorious team has its colours plastered over the city for another day, or two, or three… At the end of the game, traffic around Beyoğlu crawls to a halt as merrymakers head to **Taksim Square** (p123) to celebrate. Shoulder to shoulder the crowds sway, chant club anthems, wave club flags and clamber all over each other, while many still find time to ogle passing women (football is strictly a male concern).

Eighteen teams from all over Turkey compete from August to May. Each season three move up from the second league into the first and three get demoted. The top team of the first league plays in the European Cup (Galatasaray won in 2000). In 2003 the national team made it to the semi-finals of the World Cup, triggering ecstatic celebrations back home. Matches are usually held on the weekend, often on a Saturday night. Tickets are sold at the clubhouses at the stadium (*stadyum*) or at **Biletix** (☎ 216-454 1555, 216-556 9800; www.biletix.com), and usually go on sale between Tuesday and Thursday for a weekend game. For open seating you'll pay around €7; for covered seating – which has the best views – anywhere up to €90. If you miss out on the tickets you can get them at the door of the stadium, but note that they are outrageously overpriced.

Although violence at home games is not unknown, most matches are fine. If you're worried, avoid the Galatasaray and Fenerbahçe clashes, as the supporters of these arch rivals can become overly excited and throw a few punches around.

İstanbul's major soccer teams

- **Beşiktaş** (www.bjk.com/turk) Home stadium: İnönü Stadyumu, Beşiktaş. Colours: black and white.
- **Fenerbahçe** (www.fenerbahce.org.tr) Home stadium: Rüştü Saraçoğlu Stadyam, Kadıköy. Colours: yellow and blue.
- **Galatasaray** (www.galatasaray.org.tr) Home stadium: Ali Sami Yen Stadyum, Mecidiyeköy (about 3km northeast of Taksim). Colours: yellow and red.

SWIMMING & GYMS

Swimming in the Bosphorus is only an option for those who have a death wish. Those with a hankering for the water, head to the beaches at Yeşilköy and Florya (you can get to these by train from Sirkeci Railway Station) – but only to paddle. The water around the Princes' Islands is fairly clean, though the tiny beaches are crammed bottom-to-bottom in summer. The best option, if you really want to go to the beach, is to visit one of the towns along the Black Sea coast: **Kilyos** (p226) and **Şile** (p226), both day trips by bus.

Most of İstanbul's pool facilities are privately owned and open to members only. However, it's possible to organise a pricey day pass to use the leisure facilities at many of the city's luxury hotels, and there's much to be said for the idea of spending a day poolside at one of these places, particularly when good eateries, a health club and Bosphorus views come as part of the package. The best pools are at the **Swissôtel İstanbul the Bosphorus** (p214), the **İstanbul Hilton** (p213) and the **Çırağan Palace Hotel Kempinski** (p214).

Many of the local gyms are testosterone-packed no-go-zones if you're a woman: they're brimming with ogling gents sporting muscles and lots of attitude. The equipment is usually fairly limited too, so it's probably worth forking out a bit more and joining a hotel gym or paying for a day pass. The gyms at the Marmara (p213) and the Swissôtel İstanbul the Bosphorus are particularly well set up.

FLASH GYM Map pp284-6

☎ 212-249 5347; İstiklal Caddesi 212, Aznavur Pasaji, Beyoğlu; day pass €5; ⏱ 10am-10pm Mon-Fri, 10am-9pm Sat

The equipment at this basic gym is a bit dated, but the atmosphere is welcoming for both sexes and it's certainly conveniently situated.

KORUKENT GYM & HOBBY CLUB

☎ 212-274 0668; Korul Sokak, Korulent Sitesi, A Blok, Levent; day pass (gym) Mon-Fri €12, Sat & Sun €8; (gym & pool) Mon-Fri €16.50, Sat & Sun €11; ⏱ 9am-10pm Mon-Fri, 9am-8pm Sat & Sun

It's in Levent, which is a bit of a trek, but this place is worth travelling across town for. Its large indoor and outdoor pools, spas, sauna, aerobics, gym, tennis courts, basketball courts and 10-pin bowling lanes will keep you entertained as well as fit. Get there on the metro from Taksim and then ask for directions.

Shopping

Shopping

For centuries the favourite pastime of İstanbullus has been shopping, and then more shopping. Trading is in their blood and they've turned making a sale or purchase into an art form. Go into any carpet shop and you'll see what we mean – there's etiquette to be followed, tea to be drunk, conversation to be had. And, of course, there's money to be spent and made.

Whether you're after a cheap souvenir or a family-heirloom-to-be, İstanbul is the city to find it in. Rugs (carpets and kilims), textiles, ceramics and jewellery are just a few of the temptations laid out in more arcades, bazaars and stores than you could ever hope to flash a credit card in. There's also fashion, decorative arts and home wares that can hold their own against the stock of any concept store or designer boutique in London, LA or Lisbon. And we won't even begin to rhapsodise about the delectable foodstuffs on offer...

Opening Hours
The most common shopping hours are from 9am to 6pm Monday to Saturday, but this is by no means always the case. We have indicated specific hours in all reviews.

Taxes & Refunds
Turkey has a value-added tax (VAT) known as the *katma değer vergisi* (KDV). This means that 18% tax is added to (and hidden in) the price of most goods and services.

Turkish delight (p50), İstiklal Caddesi

If non-residents buy an expensive item such as a carpet or a leather garment from a shop that participates in the national 'Global Refund: Tax Free Shopping' scheme and then take the item out of the country within three months, they are entitled to a refund of the KDV. Unfortunately, there aren't many shops participating in this scheme. Still, it's always worth asking the shopkeeper if it is possible to get a *KDV iade özel fatura* (special VAT refund receipt). Ask for this when you're haggling over the price, rather than after you've made your purchase. Some shops display a blue, grey and white 'Tax Free Shopping' sign in their window, conveniently signalling that they are participants in the refund scheme.

If the shopkeeper issues the refund receipt, take it with you to the airport when you leave. Before going through immigration, take the receipt and the goods that you have purchased to the 'Global Refund: Tax Free Shopping' desk, where staff will stamp the receipts to confirm that you are leaving the country. You then collect your refund from another booth in the departure lounge food court after you have gone through immigration. The refund is supposedly available in the form of cash (Turkish lira) on the spot, a bank cheque or credit to your chosen credit-card account, but our experiences indicate that the cash option is the only one on offer.

Bargaining

Traditionally, when customers enter a Turkish shop to make a significant purchase, they're offered a comfortable seat and a drink (coffee, tea or a soft drink). There is some general chitchat, then discussion of the shop's goods (carpets, apparel, jewellery etc) in general, then of the customer's tastes, preferences and requirements. Finally, a number of items in the shop are displayed for the customer's inspection.

The customer asks the price; the shop owner gives it; the customer looks doubtful and makes a counteroffer 25% to 50% lower. This procedure goes back and forth several times before a price acceptable to both parties is arrived at. It is considered very bad form to offer an amount, have the shopkeeper agree and then change your mind. If no price is agreed upon, the customer has absolutely no obligation and may walk out at any time.

To bargain effectively you must be prepared to take your time, and you must know something about the items in question, not to mention their market price. The best way to do this is to look at similar goods in several shops, asking prices but not making counteroffers. Shopkeepers will give you a quick education about

Clothing Sizes
Measurements approximate only, try before you buy

Women's Clothing

Aus/UK	8	10	12	14	16	18
Europe	36	38	40	42	44	46
Japan	5	7	9	11	13	15
USA	6	8	10	12	14	16

Women's Shoes

Aus/USA	5	6	7	8	9	10
Europe	35	36	37	38	39	40
France only	35	36	38	39	40	42
Japan	22	23	24	25	26	27
UK	3½	4½	5½	6½	7½	8½

Men's Clothing

Aus	92	96	100	104	108	112
Europe	46	48	50	52	54	56
Japan	S		M	M		L
UK/USA	35	36	37	38	39	40

Men's Shirts (Collar Sizes)

Aus/Japan	38	39	40	41	42	43
Europe	38	39	40	41	42	43
UK/USA	15	15½	16	16½	17	17½

Men's Shoes

Aus/UK	7	8	9	10	11	12
Europe	41	42	43	44½	46	47
Japan	26	27	27½	28	29	30
USA	7½	8½	9½	10½	11½	12½

shopping

What to Buy in İstanbul

While Turkey's rugs have the highest shopping profile, there are plenty of other souvenir possibilities:

Antiques

The grand Ottoman-era houses of İstanbul have given up a lot of fascinating stuff left over from the empire, and you'll find these treasures – furniture in the Ottoman baroque style, jewellery, crockery, paintings and more – in the antique shops of Çukurcuma and Nişantaşı. You'll also occasionally see older relics such as illuminated manuscripts and Greek and Roman figurines.

Ceramics

After carpets and kilims, ceramics would have to be Turkey's most successful souvenir industry. This is for good reason: the ceramics are beautiful and the standard fare fits within most budgets. Many of the tiles you see in the tourist shops have been painted using a silkscreen printing method and this is why they're cheap. One step up are the ubiquitous hand-painted bowls, plates and other pieces; these are made by rubbing a patterned carbon paper on the raw ceramic, tracing the black outline and filling in the holes with colour. The most expensive ceramics for sale are hand-painted – without the use of a carbon- paper pattern – and derived from an original design. Note that many of the ceramics have lead in the glaze, so it's probably safest to use them as ornaments only.

Copper

Some copper vessels on sale in the bazaars are old – occasionally several centuries old – most are handsome and some are still eminently useful. The new copperware tends to be of a lighter gauge; that's one of the ways you tell the new from old. But even the new stuff will have been made by hand. Copper vessels should not be used for cooking in or eating from unless they are tinned inside: that is, washed with molten tin that covers the toxic copper. If you intend to use a copper vessel, make sure the interior layer of tin is intact, or negotiate to have it *kalaylamak* (tinned). If there is a *kalaycı* shop nearby, ask about the price of the tinning in advance, as tin is expensive.

Glassware

İstanbul produces some unique glasswork, a legacy of the Ottoman Empire's affection for this delicate and intricate art. Paşabahçe, a large factory on the Asian side, has been producing glass for 150 years and still churns out some good stuff. If you're after tea sets, the Grand Bazaar (Kapalı Çarşı) has many shops selling plain, colourful and ugly, heavily gilded sets. Note that most of the ornate, curvy perfume bottles you see in the touristy shops are Egyptian, despite what the seller might say.

Inlaid Wood

Local artisans make jewellery boxes, chess and backgammon (*tavla*) boards, and other items that are inlaid with different coloured woods, silver or mother-of-pearl. Make sure the piece really does feature inlay. These days, alarmingly accurate decals exist. Also, check the silver: is it really silver, or does it look like aluminium or pewter? And what about that mother-of-pearl – is it in fact 'daughter-of-polystyrene'?

Jewellery

İstanbul is a wonderful place to buy jewellery, especially antique stuff. New gold work tends to be flashy, featuring yellowy gold and a surfeit of decoration – it won't appeal to everyone. Silverware is more refined and there is an incredible variety of styles and designs, including many inspired by Ottoman and Byzantine jewellery. Gold shops should have a copy of the newspaper that bears the daily price for unworked gold of so many carats. Serious gold buyers should check this price, watch carefully as the jeweller weighs the piece in question, and then calculate what part of the price is for gold and what part for labour. Silver will also be weighed. There is sterling silver jewellery (look for the hallmark), but nickel silver and pewter-like alloys are much more common. Serious dealers don't try to pass

their wares by demonstrating to you what's good about them and telling you what's bad about their competitors' goods. Soon you will discover which shops have the best quality for the lowest asking prices and you can then proceed to bargain. Always stay good humoured and polite when you are bargaining – if you do this, the shopkeeper will too. And remember, shopkeepers know their own bottom line and will only bargain up to a certain point.

off alloy as silver. Some shops will pass off plastic, glass and other stones as real gemstones – if you don't know what you're looking for, steer clear.

Leather
On any given *Kurban Bayramı* (Sacrifice Holiday), more than 2.5 million sheep get the axe in Turkey. Add to that the normal day-to-day needs of a cuisine based on mutton and lamb and you have a huge amount of raw material to be made into leather items, hence the country's thriving leather industry. If you've always wanted a leather coat or jacket, İstanbul may be the place to purchase it, but look out for shoddy workmanship.

Meerschaum
If you smoke a pipe, you know about meerschaum. For those who don't, meerschaum ('sea foam' in German; *lületası* in Turkish) is a hydrous magnesium silicate, a white, soft stone that is porous but heat-resistant. When carved into a pipe, it smokes cool and sweet. Over time, it absorbs residues from the tobacco and turns a nut-brown colour. The world's largest and finest beds of meerschaum are found in Turkey, near the city of Eskişehir. Artful carving of this soft stone into pipes is a tradition and you'll marvel at the artistry of the Eskişehir carvers, displayed in many souvenir stores.

Old Books, Maps & Prints
Collectors will have a field day with İstanbul's wealth of antique books – some immaculate, some moth-eaten. The city and its inhabitants have been immortalised in maps, illustrations and engravings throughout the years, and many of these are available as prints, which make excellent souvenirs. You'll also see illuminated pages, supposedly from Ottoman manuscripts. These are usually modern reproductions, but they're attractive nevertheless and, again, make excellent souvenirs.

Silk
Bursa, south of the Sea of Marmara, is the silk centre of Turkey. Silkworms are raised, their cocoons are sold in Bursa and there the silk is crafted into scarves and other items. Here in İstanbul you can get your hands on Bursa's beautiful scarves; many have ornate hand-painted patterns and/or marbled colouring.

Spices, Potions & Turkish Delight
The Spice Bazaar (Mısır Çarşısı; p191) was once the centre of the spice and medicinal herb trade in İstanbul. It's still an important outlet, though these days locals are more likely to shop in the surrounding streets, leaving the market for tourists. Do what the locals do and shop along Hasırcılar Caddesi for spices, tea, herbs and sweets. Prices are clearly marked and you are encouraged to taste goods before you buy.

Where To Buy It
Every tourist has heard of İstanbul's **Grand Bazaar** (Kapali Çarşı; p191), but few know about the various speciality shopping areas in the city. Those who are serious about their shopping or who want specific items should follow the locals and go to the retail neighbourhood specialising in goods of a particular type.

Antiquarian books Sahaflar Çarşısı (Old Book Bazaar) near the Grand Bazaar; around İstiklal Caddesi in Beyoğlu.
Antiques Çukurcuma in Beyoğlu.
Books (New) Around İstiklal Caddesi in Beyoğlu.
Ceramics Grand Bazaar; Sultanahmet.
Fashion Around Teşvikiye Caddesi in Nişantaşı; İstiklal Caddesi in Beyoğlu; Almerkaz and Galleria Shopping Malls.
Handicrafts Grand Bazaar; Sultanahmet.
Jewellery Nuruosmaniye Caddesi in Cağaloğlu (near the Grand Bazaar).
Leather Grand Bazaar.
Music Galipdede Caddesi in Tünel.
Rugs & textiles Grand Bazaar; Sultanahmet.

When bargaining, you can often get a discount by offering to buy several items at once, by paying in US dollars or another strong major currency, or by paying in cash and not requesting a receipt.

If you don't have sufficient time to shop around, follow the age-old rule: find something you like at a price you're willing to pay, buy it, enjoy it and don't worry about whether or not you received the world's lowest price.

OLD İSTANBUL

SULTANAHMET

ALİ MUHİDDİN HACI BEKİR

Map pp278-80 *Food & Drink*

☎ 212-522 0666; Hamidiye Caddesi 83, Eminönü;
🕑 8am-8pm Mon-Sat, 9am-8pm Sun

It's best to buy *lokum* (Turkish delight) in specialist shops and you can't find one more specialised than this. The stuff was invented by Ali Muhiddin in the 18th century and it's now sold from this (the original) shop by his descendants. Pre-packed gift boxes range in cost from €2.70 to €14. There's another store on İstiklal Caddesi in Beyoğlu and one in Kadıköy.

CAFERAĞA MEDRESESİ

Map pp278-80 *Handicrafts*

☎ 212-513 3601; Caferiye Sokak, near Topkapı
Palace; 🕑 8.30am-7pm

The rooms around this pretty *medrese* (Islamic seminary) are used as art-teaching studios and some of the product – jewellery, miniatures, marbled paper (*ebru*) – is sold here for reasonable prices. There's not much to choose from, but it's certainly worth wandering in for a peek at what's on offer.

COCOON

Map pp278-80 *Textiles & Rugs*

☎ 212-638 6271; Küçük Aya Sofya Caddesi 13, Küçük
Aya Sofya; 🕑 8.30am-7.30pm

There are so many rug and textile shops in İstanbul that isolating individual stores is usually particularly difficult. We had no problems whatsoever in singling this one out, though. In Cocoon four floors of felt hats and antique costumes and textiles from Central Asia are artfully displayed next to rugs from Persia, Central Asia, the Caucasus and Anatolia. The owners here really know their stuff, and most of their sales are international and dealer-based. Put simply, it is one of the most beautiful shops in the city and we love it to bits. There's another, smaller store in the nearby **Arasta Bazaar** (opposite).

DÖSIM

Map pp278-80 *Handicrafts*

☎ 212-513 3134; Babıhümayun Caddesi, Topkapı
Palace; 🕑 9am-5pm Mon & Wed-Sun

To be frank, this place sells high-end souvenirs rather than true handicrafts. Nonetheless, we've listed it for two reasons: it's conveniently near the Topkapı Palace's Imperial Gate

and it's run by the government. This means it charges only what the stuff is worth and marks the prices, a rarity indeed in this part of town. On offer are jewellery, glassware, ceramics, cooking pots, brass, embroidery and much more.

GALERİ CENGİZ

Map pp278-80 *Rugs*

☎ 212-518 8882; Arasta Bazaar 155-157,
Cankurtaran; 🕑 9am-9pm

One of the many rug shops in the **Arasta Bazaar** (opposite), Galeri Cengiz stocks top-quality old and new carpets and kilims, and is well worth a browse.

GALERİ DESEN

Map pp278-80 *Rugs*

☎ 212-517 6801; Arasta Bazaar 173, Cankurtaran;
🕑 9am-9pm

Another of the shops in the **Arasta Bazaar** (opposite), Galeri Deniz stocks a colourful range of carpets and kilims that are sure to place your baggage allowance for the flight home in jeopardy.

GALERİ KAYSERİ

Map pp278-80 *Books*

☎ 212-512 0456; Divan Yolu Caddesi 11;
🕑 9am-9pm

Sultanahmet's most famous bookshop has moved to a super-swish six-floor premises across the road from its old headquarters. The reasons for this store's success are simple: the staff know and love their stock and the stock itself is extensive – over 200,000 English-language titles about Turkey and the Middle East. Serious book browsers will love this place.

HAFİZ MUSTAFA ŞEKERLEMELERİ

Map pp278-80 *Food & Drink*

☎ 212-526 5627; Hamidiye Caddesi 84-86, Eminönü;
🕑 8am-8pm Mon-Sat, 9am-8pm Sun

Opposite **Ali Muhiddin Hacı Bekir** (above), this shop also sells excellent Turkish delight. You can buy a small bag of freshly made treats to sample, plus gift boxes to take home. There are also a small café and **börekçi** (p152).

Top Five Old İstanbul Shops

- Cocoon (above)
- Derviş (p192)
- Muhliş Günbattı (p193)
- Şişko Osman (p194)
- Sofa (p194)

HASEKİ HAMAM CARPET & KILIM
SALES STORE Map pp278-80 *Rugs*
Haseki Hürrem Hamamı; 212-638 0035; Aya Sofya Square 4; 8.30am-5.30pm Tue-Sun

Located in the historic **Baths of Lady Hürrem** (p83), which are worth a visit in their own right, this Ministry of Culture carpet shop sells new carpets replicated from museum pieces. Prices are set and clearly marked.

İSTANBUL HANDICRAFTS MARKET
Map pp278-80 *Handicrafts*
İstanbul Sanatlar Çarşısı; 212-517 6782; Kabasakal Caddesi; 9am-6.30pm

Set in the small rooms surrounding the leafy courtyard of the 18th-century Cedid Mehmed Efendi Medresesi, this handicrafts centre next door to the hotel **Yeşil Ev** (p208) is unusual in that local artisans work here and don't mind if visitors watch while they do so. Their creations are available for purchase; it's a great place to source beautiful calligraphy, embroidery, glassware, miniature paintings, ceramics and fabric dolls.

İZNİK CLASSICS & TILES
Map pp278-80 *Ceramics*
212-517 1705; Arasta Bazaar 67 & 73, Cankurtaran; 9am-8pm

These two shops have the same owners but the stock in each is different. The shop on the Cankurtaran side sells collector-item ceramics, all hand painted by accredited masters including Adnan Hoca. These plates, vases and tiles

---

Top Five Shopping Areas

İstanbul has thousands of shops and many shopping hubs, but a few places will give you a quintessential İstanbul shopping experience.

Grand Bazaar Map p103
Locals know it as the Kapalı Çarşı, and it's the oldest and most atmospheric shopping mall in the city. The Grand Bazaar is a one-stop shop where you can buy everything from belly-dancing outfits to precious antique textiles, leather handbags to top-quality rugs. It's an experience that must not be missed. Have a laugh at the well-rehearsed patter of the touts, eat lunch or have tea at one of the excellent eateries and wander around a complex that is as architecturally interesting as it is historically significant.

Spice Bazaar Map pp282-3
Locals know this historic marketplace as the Mısır Çarşısı and some guidebooks call it the Egyptian Market. Like the Grand Bazaar, it's full of tourists and oozes atmosphere. The centre of a small precinct of spice and food shops on the quay at Eminönü, just near the **Yeni Camii** (p99), it's the place to come and buy love potions, sticky *lokum* (Turkish delight) and the city's most amusing souvenir – Turkish Viagra.

Arasta Bazaar Map pp278-80
Set beside the **Blue Mosque** (p84), the Arasta (Cavalry) Bazaar is a historic open arcade lined with shops. There are plenty of carpet shops (some very good) and occasional ceramic and jewellery shops. It vies with the Grand Bazaar for the dubious honour of having the most touts per square metre of all the city's shopping strips.

Aznavur Pasajı Map pp284-6
This mini-Kapalı Çarşı along İstiklal Caddesi over in Beyoğlu misses the hassle and bustle of its cousin over the Golden Horn, but still has some of the same goods: silver jewellery, ceramics, oils, inlaid woodwork. Upstairs, there are tacky presents plus hippy-ish clothes and handbags. If you can't find what you want here, you may be able to find it at the nearby Avrupa Pasajı (European Passage) leading off the Balık Pazar (Fish Market).

Tahtakale Map pp282-3
No trip to İstanbul would be complete without a stroll through the ancient shopping district of Tahtakale – especially along Uzunçarşı Caddesi and Mahmut Paşa Yokuşu. This is where the locals shop; prepare your elbows and dive in for a look. Although you're not going to find classic tourist souvenirs (unless you think circumcision robes and wedding dresses make great presents), you'll enjoy a walk through this chaotic mess.

are made with real quartz and metal oxides for pigments, and retail for anything between €160 and €3000. On the other side of the bazaar is a shop with mass-produced stock, which is a lot cheaper but still beautiful. You'll be able to take home a lovely platter for as little as €28 if you bargain. There's another store in the İç Bedestan at the Grand Bazaar.

SEDİR Map pp278-80 *Textiles & Rugs*
☎ 212-458 4702; Mimar Mehmet Ağa Caddesi 39, Cankurtaran; 🕑 9am-10pm

There can't be too many rug shops in town with Byzantine mosaics in the basement. After looking through Sedir's excellent and affordable range of kilims from Anatolia, Central Asia, Persia and the Caucasus, ask the staff in this shop if you can have a peek at the mosaics. That way, you can merge your shopping and sightseeing!

VAKKO'S SALE STORE
Map pp278-80 *Remainder Outlet*
Vakko İndirim Mağazası; ☎ 212-522 8941; Yenicamii Caddesi 1/13, Eminönü; 🕑 9.30am-6pm Mon-Sat

If you like Vakko's style, but have concerns about the price tags, this remainder store may be for you. There's a good selection of quality women's, men's and children's clothing, as well as shoes and accessories.

THE BAZAAR DISTRICT
ABDULLA NATURAL PRODUCTS
Map p103 *Homeware*
☎ 212-522 9078; Halıcılar Caddesi 53, Grand Bazaar; 🕑 9am-7pm Mon-Sat

The first of the Western-style designer stores that are starting to appear in this ancient marketplace, Abdulla sells cotton bed linen, handspun woollen throws from Eastern Turkey, cotton *peştemals* (bath wraps) and pure olive-oil soap. It's all quality stuff, but you pay a premium – soap is €2.80, a *peştemal* is €14 and the throws range from €200 to €280.

DERVİŞ Map p103 *Homeware*
☎ 212-514 4525; Keseciler Caddesi 33-35, Grand Bazaar; 🕑 9am-7pm Mon-Sat

The owner of this shop was in partnership with the crew at Abdulla Natural Products before striking out on his own and he is selling almost identical stock, though with a greater emphasis on village textiles. It's a great place to pick up a souvenir *hamam* bowl (€8-€19.40) or dowry

shirts (€19.40 for cotton, climbing to €100 for silk). For a truly fabulous souvenir of your trip, why not take home a felt rug (€110)?

HALITUR Map p103 *Art, Antiques & Rugs*
☎ 212-520 9504; Halıcılar Caddesi 97, Grand Bazaar; 🕑 9am-7pm Mon-Sat

One of the myriad bazaar shops selling a mix of curios and carpets, Halıtur does a nice line in Russian icons, antique İznik tiles (€40-€250) and Anatolian carpets.

HAMDİ BAKLAVA
Map pp282-3 *Food & Drink*
☎ 212-514 1310; Kalçın Sokak 17, off Tahmis Sokak, Eminönü; 🕑 9am-midnight

If you don't get the chance to sample the delicious baklava at the upstairs restaurant, do not fear – the ground-floor pastry shop can help out with a parcel to take home. Shame they don't sell their kebabs to take home as well…

KOÇ DERİ Map p103 *Leather*
☎ 212-527 5553; Kürkçüler Çarşısı 22-46, Grand Bazaar; 🕑 8.30am-8pm

If you fancy a leather jacket or coat, Koç is bound to have something that suits. It's one of the bazaar's busiest stores.

KÜÇÜK KÖŞE
Map p103 *Leather Handbags*
Little Corner; ☎ 212-513 0335; Kalpakçılarbaşı Caddesi 89-91, Grand Bazaar; 🕑 9am-7pm Mon-Sat

If you've always wanted a Kelly or Birkin but can't afford Hermès, this place is for you. Its copies of the work of the big-gun designers are good quality and at around €200 they're a lot more affordable. The next-door store, Pako, is owned by the same people.

KURUKAHVECİ MEHMET EFENDİ MAHDUMLARI
Map pp282-3 *Food & Drink*
☎ 212-522 0080; Tahmis Sokak 66, Eminönü; 🕑 9am-6.30pm Mon-Fri, 9am-2pm Sat

Caffeine addicts are regularly spotted queuing outside this, the flagship store of İstanbul's most famous coffee purveyor. You can join them in getting a fix of the freshest beans in town, and also purchase a cute little set of two signature coffee cups and saucers, a copper coffee pot and a jar of coffee for a very reasonable €15. It's a great gift to take back home.

LAPIS Map pp282-3   *Jewellery & Rugs*
☎ 212-511 0550; Babiali Caddesi 15-17, Cağaloğlu;
🕑 9.30am-6pm

Though touristy (there's inevitably a tourist coach outside), Lapis is worth visiting if you're looking for quality jewellery or rugs. After all, it's been selling the stuff for 30 years. We spent a long time eyeing an Ottoman-influenced goldseed, pearl and sapphire bracelet for €850. Alas, it didn't come home. Don't pay what's on the price-tag – ask for the best price.

M & K GOURMET FOOD
Map pp282-3   *Food*
☎ 212-520 7063; Nuruosmaniye Otoparkı 37, Çemberlitaş; 🕑 9am-7pm Mon-Sat

Just outside one of the Grand Bazaar's gates, this small gourmet shop sells Iranian caviar and Turkish wine, *lokum* and olive-oil products. The shop boasts a limited range, but it's all good-quality stuff.

MEHMET KALMAZ
BAHARATÇI   *Spices & Tonics*
☎ 212-522 6604; Spice Bazaar 41, Eminönü;
🕑 8am-7pm Mon-Sat

One of the few shops in the **Spice Bazaar** (Mısır Çarşısı; p106) that specialises in potions and lotions, this old-fashioned place sells remedies to make women younger, others to make men stronger, and a royal love potion that, we guess, is supposed to combine the two. It also stocks spices, teas and medicinal herbs.

MUHLİŞ GÜNBATTI
Map p103   *Textiles & Rugs*
☎ 212-511 6562; Parçacilar Sokak 48, Grand Bazaar;
🕑 9am-7pm Mon-Sat

One of the most famous stores in the bazaar, Muhliş Günbattı specialises in *suzani* (needlework) fabrics from Uzbekistan. These spectacularly beautiful bedspreads, tablecloths and wall hangings are made from fine cotton embroidered with silk. A bedspread will set you back between €350 and €700. As well as the textiles, it stocks a small range of antique Ottoman fabrics richly embroidered with gold, top-quality carpets and brightly coloured kilims.

SELVİ EL SANATI ARI
Map p103   *Ceramics*
☎ 212-527 0997; Yağlıkçılar Caddesi 54, Grand Bazaar;
🕑 9am-6pm Mon-Sat

The speciality here is *Kütahya faience*. There is a small range of these hand-painted (20cm by 20cm) tiles, which are reasonably priced and make a nice souvenir or gift. There's also a selection of plates, cups and bowls.

Derviş (opposite)

Galeri Alfa (opposite)

ŞİŞKO OSMAN Map p103 *Rugs*

☎ 212-528 3548; Zincirli Han 15, Grand Bazaar; 🕐 9am-6pm Mon-Sat

The Osmans have been in the rug business for four generations and are rated by many as the best dealers in the bazaar. Certainly, their stock is a cut above many of their competitors. Most of the rugs on sale are dowry pieces and all have been hand woven and coloured with vegetable dyes. To get your hands on an antique kilim that will be passed down from one generation of your family to the next, you'll be looking at between €1500 and €2500. You can also visit Şişko Osman's other **store** (Halıcılar Caddesi 49).

SOFA Map pp282-3 *Art & Antiques*

☎ 212-520 2850; Nuruosmaniye Caddesi 85, Cağaloğlu; 🕐 9.30am-7pm Mon-Sat

What a treasure-trove of a shop! As well as its eclectic range of prints, textiles, ceramics, calligraphy and Ottoman miniatures, Sofa sells contemporary Turkish art and books. The range of jewellery made out of antique Ottoman coins and 24-carat gold is extraordinarily beautiful – an heirloom piece will set you back between €330 and €800.

VEFA BOZACISI Map pp282-3 *Food & Drink*

☎ 212-519 4922; Katip Çelebi Caddesi 104/1, Kalenderhane; 🕐 7am-midnight

As well as selling bottles of the vile-looking drink *boza* (p166), a traditional brew made from fermented grain, sugar and water, Vefa Bozacisi is famous for its range of *sirke* (wine vinegars) and sauces (try the delicious pomegranate concoction).

YÖRÜK Map p103 *Rugs*

☎ 212-527 3211; Kürkçüler Çarşısı 16, Grand Bazaar; 🕐 8.30am-7pm Mon-Sat

This narrow store has a selection of top-quality rugs from the Caucasus and Central Asia, most of them dowry pieces. The owners are friendly and knowledgeable – best of all, they refrain from the hard sell.

NORTH OF THE GOLDEN HORN

BEYOĞLU – GALATA BRIDGE TO İSTİKLAL CADDESİ

ARTRIUM

Map pp284-6 *Art, Books & Antiques*

☎ 212-251 4302; Tünel Square 7, Tünel; 🕐 9am-7pm Mon-Sat

This Aladdin's cave of a shop is crammed with antique ceramics, Ottoman miniature paintings, maps, prints and jewellery. It also has occasional pieces of Ottoman clothing and fabric. If you're after anything in particular, ask the owner, as she'll be happy to rummage upstairs in the storage area where excess stock is kept. Pricey but nice.

ELVIS Map pp284-6 *Musical Instruments*

☎ 212-293 8752; Galipdede Caddesi 35; Tünel; 🕐 10am-6pm

If you thought Elvis was hiding in the Bahamas, you're wrong. He's here selling a good range of traditional stringed instruments.

LALE PLAK Map pp284-6 *Music*

☎ 212-293 7739; Galipdede Caddesi 1, Tünel; 🕐 9am-7pm Mon-Sat

This small shop is crammed with CDs of jazz, Western classical and Turkish classical and folk music. It's a popular hang-out for local bohemian types.

BEYOĞLU – ON & AROUND İSTİKLAL CADDESİ

A LA TURCA Map pp284-6   *Rugs*
☎ 212-245 2933; Faikpaşa Sokak 4, Çukurcuma;
🕑 10am-6pm Mon-Sat

If you fancy an antique Anatolian kilim to brighten up your home (and who doesn't?) A la Turca may be the place to get it. In the trendy Çukurcuma district, which is one of the best areas in the city to browse for antiques and curios, A la Turca's small but interesting stock is certainly worth a second or third look.

AMBAR Map pp284-6   *Food & Drink*
☎ 212-292 9272; Kallavi Sokak 12, Tepebaşı;
🕑 9am-7.30pm Mon-Sat, 12.30-7.30pm Sun

This small organic produce store smells as good as it looks. It stocks free-range eggs, tofu, soy milk and other health foods, as well as a range of stylish earthenware pottery and quality olive-oil soap.

ANADOL ANTİK
Map pp284-6   *Art & Antiques*
☎ 212-251 5228; Turnacıbaşı Sokak 65, Çukurcuma;
🕑 9am-7pm Mon-Sat

Fancy a wooden door from an Ottoman house? Or perhaps a ceramic-clad wood stove? This cavernous shop is filled with a hodgepodge of curios and collectables. If you brave the dust and the dim lights you just might find yourself a treasure.

BEYOĞLU HALI EVİ
Map pp284-6   *Rugs & Ceramics*
☎ 212-293 9990; İstiklal Caddesi 388, Tünel;
🕑 9am-8pm

The ceramics and rugs on sale here aren't of the highest quality, but they're well priced and worthy of a browse. Tea glasses and hand-painted ceramic copies of Ottoman originals in the Victoria & Albert gallery are the best bets.

Top Five Beyoğlu Shops
- Leyla Seyhanlı (p196)
- Artrium (opposite)
- Halide D (right)
- Vakko (p198)
- Robinson Crusoe (p198)

DENİZLER KİTABEVİ
Map pp284-6   *Maps, Prints & Books*
☎ 212-249 8893; İstiklal Caddesi 395;
🕑 9.30am-7.30pm

A charmingly eccentric shop specialising in old maps and books, Denizler Kitabevi also stocks antique prints and quirky chess sets with different historical figures (€89).

GALERİ ALFA Map pp284-6   *Antiques*
☎ 212-251 1672; Faikpaşa Sokak 47, Çukurcuma;
🕑 11am-5.30pm

What makes this store special is its range of charming toy Ottoman soldiers and court figures – even Süleyman the Magnificent has been shrunk to 10cm tall. It's worth popping in just to see them. It also stocks old maps and prints.

HALİDE D
Map pp284-6   *Homeware & Accessories*
☎ 212-245 7775; Turnacıbaşı Sokak 71, Çukurcuma;
🕑 1-6pm

The owner has given both her name and her sense of style to this design store, which stocks a select range of home ware, furniture, accessories and *objets d'art*. Check out the spectacular mirrors made with glass squares and decorated with Ottoman-style painting and etching by artist İsmail Acar. Other pieces include leather and felt bags, glassware and lights.

HİKMET + PİNAR Map pp284-6   *Antiques*
☎ 212-293 0575; Çukurcuma Caddesi 74, Çukurcuma;
🕑 10am-6pm Mon-Sat

An opulently decorated store filled to the brim with top-class Ottoman-era furniture, mirrors, glassware, textiles and paintings, Hikmet + Pinar is the type of place you enter only if you're ready to spend the cash equivalent of a second mortgage. We'd bet they furnish more than their fair share of İstanbul mansions.

HOMER KİTABEVİ Map pp284-6   *Books*
☎ 212-249 5902; Yeniçarşı Caddesi 28/A, Galatasaray;
🕑 10am-7.30pm Mon-Sat

Homer has an excellent selection of history, architecture and art books – all about Turkey and İstanbul and all in English. It also has a large range of English-language fiction.

İSTANBUL KITAPÇISI Map pp284-6   *Books*
☎ 212-292 7692; İstiklal Caddesi 379; 🕑 10am-7pm Mon-Sat, 11am-7pm Sun

This bookshop is run by the municipality and as a consequence prices are very reasonable.

A recent check saw Freely and Sumner Boyd's excellent *Strolling Through Istanbul* priced one euro cheaper than every other bookshop in town, for instance. It stocks English-language books on İstanbul, guidebooks, maps and prints.

İYİGÜN OYUNCAK Map pp284-6 *Toys*
☎ 212-243 8910; İstiklal Caddesi 415; ☾ 9am-9pm
These guys know what little kids like. And unlike the other stores in town, stock isn't dominated by toy weapons. There's everything from Brio to Teenage Mutant Ninja Turtles, with a few educational parent-pleasers thrown in for good measure.

LA CAVE WINE SHOP
Map pp284-6 *Food & Drink*
☎ 212-243 2405; Sıraselviler Caddesi 207, Cihangir; ☾ 9am-9pm
Its enormous selection of local and imported wine makes La Cave a good stop for tipplers. The staff can tell a chablis from a chardonnay and will be happy to give advice on the best Turkish bottles to add to your cellar.

LEYLA SEYHANLI
Map pp284-6 *Antique Clothing*
☎ 212-293 7410; Altıpatlar Sokak 10, Cihangir; ☾ 10am-7pm
If you love old clothes, you'll adore Leyla Seyhanlı's boutique. Filled to the brim with piles of Ottoman embroidery and outfits, it's a rummager's delight. On a recent foray we found an 1890s cashmere and velvet coat, and a silk embroidery cushion cover that would have been right at home in Dolmabahçe Palace. Lucky us

MAVİ JEANS Map pp284-6 *Clothing*
☎ 212-249 3758; İstiklal Caddesi 117; ☾ 10am-10pm
The dress code of choice for İstanbul's youth is a pair of worn jeans (usually tight and low-slung) and a fair percentage of these would

A Carpet-Buyer's Primer

There's no right or wrong way to go about buying a carpet when you're in Turkey. There are only two hard-and-fast rules. The first is that you should never feel pressured by anyone to buy – the decision is yours and yours alone. The second is to only ever pay a price that you feel comfortable with. When you return home, you want to do so with a piece that you love and that isn't going to bankrupt you.

A good-quality, long-lasting carpet should be 100% wool *(yüz de yüz yün)*: check the warp (the lengthwise yarns), weft (the crosswise yarns) and pile (the vertical yarns knotted into the matrix of warp and weft). Is the wool fine and shiny, with signs of the natural oil? More expensive carpets may be of a silk and wool blend. Cheaper carpets may have warp and weft of mercerised cotton. You can tell by checking the fringes at either end; if the fringe is of cotton or 'flosh' (mercerised cotton) you shouldn't pay for wool. Another way to identify the material of the warp and weft is to turn the carpet over and look for the fine, frizzy fibres common to wool, but not to cotton. But bear in mind that just being made of wool doesn't guarantee a carpet's quality. If the dyes and design are ugly, even a 100% woollen carpet can be a bad buy.

Check the closeness of the weave by turning the carpet over and inspecting the back. In general, the tighter the weave and the smaller the knots, the higher the quality and durability of the carpet. The oldest carpets sometimes have thick knots, so consider the number of knots alongside the colours and the quality of the wool.

Compare the colours on the back with those on the front. Spread the nap with your fingers and look at the bottom of the pile. Are the colours brighter there than on the surface? Slight colour variations could occur in older carpets when a new batch of dye was mixed, but richer colour deep in the pile is often an indication that the surface has faded in the sun. Natural dyes don't fade as readily as chemical dyes. There is nothing wrong with chemical dyes, which have a long history of their own, but natural dyes and colours tend to be preferred and therefore fetch higher prices. Don't pay for natural if you're getting chemical.

New carpets can be made to look old, and damaged or worn carpets can be rewoven (good work but expensive), patched or even painted. There is nothing wrong with a dealer offering you a patched or repainted carpet, of course, provided they point out these defects and price the piece accordingly. And note that some red Bukhara carpets (Bukhara is a city region in Uzbekistan) will continue to give off colour, even though they're of better quality than cheap woollen carpets that don't.

When you are examining the carpet, look at it from one end, then from the other. The colours will differ because the pile always leans one way or the other. Take the carpet out into the sunlight and look at it there. Imagine where you might put the carpet at home and how the light will strike it.

It's all very well taking measures such as plucking some fibres and burning them to see if they smell like wool, silk, or nylon or rubbing a wet handkerchief over the carpet to see if the colour comes off, but unless you know have been purchased from local company Mavi. They're at least half the price of foreign imports – you'll be looking at around €50.

MEPHISTO Map pp284-6 *Music*
☎ 212-293 5049; İstiklal Caddesi 197;
🕑 9am-midnight

If you manage to develop a taste for local music while you're in town, this popular store is the place to indulge it. As well as a huge CD collection of Turkish popular music, there's a select range of Turkish folk and classical music.

MOR TAKI Map pp284-6 *Jewellery*
☎ 212-292 8817; Turnacıbaşı Sokak 16, off İstiklal Caddesi, Galatasaray; 🕑 10.30am-8.30pm Mon-Sat

The gals of this city love their jewellery, and this funky little store keeps many of their collections topped up with costume pieces designed by Nurettin Ayan and Zeynep Güven, who use materials such as bronze and stone.

MUDO PERA *Clothing & Giftware*
Map pp284-6
☎ 212-251 8682; İstiklal Caddesi 401;
🕑 10am-7.30pm Mon-Sat

Housed on the bottom two floors of an Art-Nouveau building, the interior of this boutique is all gleaming wood and cunning lighting – very 1920s Pera. The stock is simply beautiful: a house line of clothing made from cashmere and fine-quality cottons and silks, and *trés* tasteful gifts and tableware.

OTTOMANIA
Map pp284-6 *Maps, Prints & Books*
☎ 212-243 2157; Sofyalı Sokak 30-32, Tünel;
🕑 9am-6pm Mon-Sat

An old map or print can be a great souvenir to bring home from İstanbul and Ottomania is a perfect place to source one. Pop in and choose from the array of framed stock adorning the walls.

what you're doing you're unlikely to learn much from the exercise – and you may well end up with an irate carpet seller to deal with!

In the end the most important consideration should be whether or not you like the carpet.

Pricing & Payment

When it comes to buying, there's no substitute for spending time developing an 'eye' for what you really like. You also need to be realistic about your budget. These days carpets are such big business that true bargains are hard to come by unless there's something (like gigantic size) that makes them hard to sell for their true value.

Prices are determined by age, material, quality, condition, demand, the enthusiasm of the buyer and the debt load of the seller. Bear in mind that if you do your shopping on a tour or when accompanied by a guide, the price will have been inflated to include a commission of up to 35% for the tour operator or guide.

It may be wiser to go for something small but of high quality rather than for a room-sized cheapie. And it's worth remembering that kilims (pileless woven rugs) are usually cheaper than carpets. Another way to make your money stretch further is to opt for one of the smaller items made from carpet materials: old camel bags and hanging baby's cradles opened out to make rugs on which food would be eaten, decorative grain bags, even the bags that once held rock salt for animals.

Some dealers may take personal cheques but all prefer cash. Most shops take credit cards, but some require you to pay the credit-card company's fee and the cost of the phone call to check your creditworthiness. They will rarely be participants in the Global Refund Scheme (tax-free shopping). A few dealers will let you pay in instalments.

All of this is a lot to remember, but it will be worth it if you get a carpet you like at a decent price. You'll have something to take home that will give you pleasure for the rest of your life.

Beware of the Carpet Bait & Switch

Here's the scenario: you make friends with a charming Turk, or perhaps a Turkish-American/European couple. They recommend a friend's shop, so you go and have a look. There's no pressure to buy. Indeed, your new friends wine and dine you (always in a jolly group with others). Before you leave İstanbul you decide to buy a carpet. You go to the shop, choose one you like and ask the price. So far so good; if you can buy that carpet at a good price, everything's fine. But if the owner strongly urges you to buy a 'better' carpet, more expensive because it's 'old' or 'Persian' or 'rare' or 'makes a good investment', beware. You may return home to find you've paid many times more than it is worth. If the shopkeeper ships the carpet for you, the carpet that arrives may not be the expensive carpet you bought; instead it could be a cheap copy.

To avoid this rip-off, you should choose the carpet, inspect it carefully, compare prices for similar work at other shops, then buy and take it with you or ship it yourself; don't have the shopkeeper ship it.

PANDORA Map pp284-6 *Books*
☎ 212-243 3503; Büyükparmakkapı Sokak 3, off İstiklal Caddesi, Taksim; ☯ 10am-8pm Sun-Thu, 10am-10pm Fri & Sat

Unreconstructed lefties and self-confessed postmodernists are equally at home in this excellent bookshop. Though most of the stock is in Turkish, there are a fair few titles in English, including novels, guidebooks, histories and art and politics texts. If you can't find what you're looking for on the ground floor, climb two floors up.

PAŞABAHÇE Map pp284-6 *Glassware*
☎ 212-244 0544; İstiklal Caddesi 314, Tünel; ☯ 10am-8pm

Established in 1957, this local firm manufactures excellent glassware from its factory on the Bosphorus. Three floors of glassware, vases and decanters feature here and prices are very reasonable. Styles are both traditional and contemporary. There's another branch of **Paşabahçe** (Map p287) on Teşvikiye Caddesi in Nişantaşı.

ROBINSON CRUSOE
Map pp284-6 *Books*
☎ 212-293 6968; İstiklal Caddesi 389; ☯ 9am-9.30pm Mon-Sat, 10am-9.30pm Sun

We can imagine few more pleasant fates than being marooned here for an hour or so. With its classy décor, good magazine selection and wide range of English-language novels and books about İstanbul, it's one of the best bookshops around. Staff speak English and know their books.

ŞAMDAN Map pp284-6 *Art & Antiques*
☎ 212-245 4445; Altıpatlar Sokak 20, Çukurcuma; ☯ 11am-5.30pm

Located on one of Beyoğlu's main antique strips, this small shop stocks quality antique furniture, china and glassware, specialising in Ottoman and Art-Deco pieces.

VAKKO Map pp284-6 *Department Store*
☎ 212-251 4092; İstiklal Caddesi 123-5; ☯ 9.30am-6pm Mon-Sat

Seven floors of luxury goods await you at this drop-down-gorgeous boutique department store. The top-floor **Vakko Fashion Museum** highlights the designer clothing the Vakko label has been producing for over 40 years and the new season stock is for sale on the floors below. As well as clothing, you'll find top-quality fabrics, shoes, bed linen and bath linen, scarves made from Bursa silk and accessories. There's even a house perfume. Clever shoppers investigate the basement sale outlet, where bargains are often sourced. There's another smaller branch of **Vakko** (Map p287) on Adbilpekçi Caddesi in Nişantaşı.

Robinson Crusoe (above)

Markets & Malls

With one foot planted in the East and another in the West, İstanbul's shopping has more than its fair share of contradictions: ritzy shopping plazas dot posh suburbs, while the mass of shoppers elbow for goods at the weekly street markets.

Street Markets

On Tuesday there is a massive market in Kadıköy, on the Asian side. The cheapest clothes in town are on sale here, so if you've been on the road for a while and your underwear needs replenishing, this is the place to do it! To get there, get off the ferry and move straight ahead along the major boulevard of Söğütlüçeşme Caddesi for about 500m until you come to a busy intersection, Altıyol Square. Cross over, take the right fork and continue eastward along Kuşdili Caddesi for another 250m (three cross streets). At Hasırcıbaşı Caddesi turn left and you'll see the tent-city market spread out before you. It's open between 8am and 6pm. On Sunday the market is taken over by stall keepers selling a motley collection of antiques, furniture and jewellery.

On Saturday and Sunday the laneways around the waterfront mosque in Ortaköy host a flea market. Merchandise is tacky – most seems to come from the Subcontinent and Africa and is found in flea markets worldwide – and the handicrafts on offer are firmly in the hippy camp, but it's still a pleasant spot to while away a weekend hour or two.

Ironically, in Etiler, beside **Akmerkez shopping mall** (below), there's a Thursday morning market known as the Ulus Pazarı that sells cheap fakes of the designer labels sold next door. It also sells food and household items.

It seems an odd place to set up a street market, but on Wednesday the grounds and courtyard of the **Fatih Camii** (p110) in the Western Districts is the place to find a great little market selling fresh produce, clothes and household items.

Also on Wednesday, Akbıyık Caddesi in Cankurtaran has a street market all day where a decent range of fruit, vegetables, eggs, pickles, cheese and olives can be purchased.

Malls

The most glamorous of the city's shopping malls, **Akmerkez** (☎ 212-282 0170; Nispetiye Caddesi, Etiler; ☉ 10am-10pm) is the place to find popular global brands such as Zara, Polo Ralph Lauren, Diesel, Marks & Spencer and Benetton, as well as upmarket Turkish stores such as Beyman and Vakko. It's also home to one of the best English-language bookshops in the city, Remzi Kitabevi. If you get tired of shopping, you can recover in the comfortable multiplex cinema, the excellent restaurants or the large food court. It's located in Etiler, well north of Taksim and west of Bebek, and you can get here by the Taksim metro (it's right next to the Levent station), by bus No 58A from Eminönü, or by taxi from Taksim (around €5).

Galleria

Galleria (☎ 212-559 9560; Rauf Orbay Caddesi, Ataköy; ☉ 10am-10pm) was the first of the Western-style shopping malls to open in the city and is still popular with locals. Stores include the big İstanbul names such as Mavi Jeans, Beyman, Mudo, Paşabahçe and Vakko, as well as global brands such as Mothercare and Levi's. Leisure facilities include an ice-skating rink, games arcade and cinemas. It's located on the Marmara shore road at Ataköy, west of the city walls on the way to the airport. To get there you can catch the light rail from Aksaray, get off at Ataköy station and ask directions to walk to the mall; alternatively, catch a suburban train from Sirkeci and get off at Barırköy station. The mall is close by.

TAKSİM, HARBİYE & NİŞANTAŞI

GÖNÜL PAKSOY Map p287 *Clothing*
☎ 212-261 9081; Atiye Sokak 6/A & 1/3, Teşvikiye;
☉ 10am-7pm Mon-Sat

İstanbul's best young fashion designer, Gönül Paksoy, creates pieces that transcend fashion and step into art. She works in a number of forms, too: silk and cotton knits, jewellery based on traditional Ottoman designs, and silk and cotton clothing in rich fabrics with feature trimming. Her shawls and scarves are quite unique – and utterly irresistible. Take it from us: once hooked on this stuff there's no turning back. There are two shops opposite each other in Atiye Sokak – make sure you visit both.

MUDO COLLECTION
Map p287 *Clothing & Accessories*
☎ 212-225 2941; Teşvikiye Caddesi 143, Teşvikiye;
☉ 10am-8pm Mon-Sat, noon-7pm Sun

This sister store to Mudo Pera in Beyoğlu stocks a large range of the house-label clothing – all of

Shopping in Kadıköy

Kadıköy's food and drink shops are particularly good. You'll find them and street stalls selling fresh produce by crossing over Deniz Sokak in front of the ferry terminal and walking right until you almost immediately come to Muvakkithane Sokak. Turn left and you are in the food district. There's also a small pocket of antique shops around Dellalzade Sokak just over Moda Caddesi directly behind the food shops:

Bayaz Fırın (☎ 216-345 4066; Yasa Caddesi 23; ⊙ 6.30am-8pm) You'll have to fight your way through the crowds to pick up the fresh and utterly delicious *simit*, biscuits and pastries sold here. The fifth generation of the same family oversees the business and standards are uniformly high. If you decide to tie the knot while you're in town, this is the place to order a wedding cake.

Baylan Pastanesi (☎ 216-346 6350; Muvakkithane Caddesi 19; ⊙ 7am-8pm) The funky 1960s-style entrance isn't retro – it's the real thing. This neighbourhood patisserie has been satisfying local sweet-tooths for decades. Grab some of the excellent biscuits and pastries to take with you or sit down in the small courtyard at the rear of the shop and scoff on the spot.

Eser Ekmek Fabrıkası (Mühürdar Caddesi; ⊙ 6am-6pm Mon-Sat) This charming small neighbourhood bakery adorned with blue tiles bakes wonderful fresh bread throughout the day. To find it, just follow your nose – you'll see the loaves coming out of the oven.

Galeri Antik (☎ 216-330 9852; Dellalzade Sokak 1; ⊙ 9am-6pm Mon-Sat) One of the many antique shops along this street near the market, Galeri Antik is crammed with lights and other collectables.

it top quality and eminently wearable. The store also stocks a range of accessories to provide the perfect accompaniment to your new threads.

SEMA PAKSOY Map p287 *Jewellery*
☎ 212-241 5533; Atiye Sokak 9, Teşvikiye;
⊙ 10am-7pm Mon-Sat
If your jewellery is more statement than investment, Sema Paksoy is your woman. Her chunky pieces crafted from antique silver and semiprecious stones are Ottoman-inspired and lovely. They're pricey but worth it.

YARGICI Map p287 *Clothing & Accessories*
☎ 212-225 2952; Vali Konaği Caddesi 30, Teşvikiye;
⊙ 9.30am-7.30pm Mon-Sat, 1-6pm Sun
Whether they're aged 15 or 50, İstanbul's men and women love buying clothes, toiletries and accessories at Yargıcı. The clothes are affordable high street styles that are made in Turkey, and the accessories include baubles, bangles and beads. The fact that the super-stylish **Bentley Hotel** (p212) in Harbiye provides Yargıcı toiletries for its guests shows how highly they're prized by local style gurus.

Sleeping

Sleeping

Accommodation Styles

Every possible accommodation style is available in İstanbul. You can live like a sultan in a world-class luxury hotel, doss in an anonymous hostel dorm or relax in a simple but stylish boutique establishment. We've labelled each hotel's type next to its name to help you in your choice. By 'Ottoman Hotel' we mean a small place, often but not always housed in a refurbished Ottoman building, that offers comfortable accommodation with traditional Anatolian decorative touches such as textiles on beds and walls, kilims or carpets on the floor and olive-oil soap in the bathroom. By 'Boutique Hotel' we mean a stylish modern hotel that places great emphasis on décor (usually with Ottoman or Anatolian touches) and services. The 'Hotel' tag alone means that the place would be at home in any international city, and doesn't make any real gestures to traditional Turkish decoration or services (eg *hamams* – Turkish steam baths).

All hotels reviewed have rooms with en suite bathroom and airconditioning. Most have satellite TV and minibars or fridges. The prices we've given include breakfast, usually of the Turkish variety (fresh bread, jams, sheep's milk, cheese, olives, tomatoes, cucumber and tea or coffee). Exceptions to these norms are noted in the reviews.

Keep in mind that the appearance of a hotel's lobby doesn't always reflect the quality of its rooms. Look at several rooms if possible. If the first one you see won't do, ask *'Başka var mı?'* ('Are there others?')

Price Ranges

You can bag a mattress on a roof terrace for as little as €5 per night or splurge on the Presidential Suite at the Four Seasons Hotel for €2400. Most of us will opt for something between the two.

A double room in an Ottoman or Boutique hotel in Sultanahmet will cost from €45 to €75; in Beyoğlu you'll pay a bit more. To qualify as one of our 'Cheap Sleep' listings, hotels must charge no more than €40 per double. Most are considerably cheaper than this.

All prices in this book have been cited in euros, are high season prices and include the 18% KDV. During the low season (October–April, but not the Christmas period) you should be able to negotiate a discount of at least 20% on the room price.

It's almost always cheapest to book rooms via the hotel's own website. Before you confirm a booking, ask if the hotel will give you a discount for a cash payment (this will usually be 10% but can be up to 18%), whether a pick-up from the airport is included (it often is if you stay more than three nights) and whether discounts are offered for extended stays. Many of the luxury hotels offer special packages; ask when you make reservations.

We recommend that you refrain from booking accommodation at the airport hotel booking desks, as you'll inevitably pay a premium if you do so. If you arrive at the airport and have no accommodation booked, the **Tourist Information Office** (☽ 24 hr) is usually happy to let you use its phone to call one of the hotels reviewed in this chapter and see if a room is available.

OLD İSTANBUL

SULTANAHMET

The Sultan Ahmet Camii, more commonly known as the **Blue Mosque** (p84), gives its name to the quarter surrounding it. This is the heart of Old İstanbul and the city's premier sightseeing area, so the hotels here, and in the adjoining neighbourhoods to the east (Cankurtaran), west (Küçük Aya Sofya) and north (Binbirdirek), are supremely convenient. The area's only drawbacks are the number of carpet touts around and the lack of decent places to eat and drink.

Akbıyık Caddesi in Cankurtaran is the backpacker hub, home to thumping bars and drunken carousing by night and street cafés by day. Other streets in the area are low key. Küçük Aya Sofya is a charming, old-fashioned and quiet area, just downhill from the southwestern end of the Hippodrome; while just uphill and to the west, Binbirdirek is a quiet residential district named after the Byzantine cistern of that name.

New or refurbished hotels are popping up in the nearby Topkapı district, mostly around busy Hüdavendigar Caddesi. The rest of the neighbourhood is established and very quiet, particularly around the palace. If you're after a good sleep and close proximity to the major sights, these places could be what you're looking for.

Every imaginable hotel type can be found around this neighbourhood: the city's best luxury hotel (the Four Seasons); innumerable boutique Ottoman hotels decorated in a pleasing style that we've dubbed 'Cankurtaran Modern'; comfortable but relatively characterless mid-range options; and a host of budget choices, including most of the city's hostels. Almost every place has a roof terrace with views of the Blue Mosque, **Aya Sofya** (p79) or the Sea of Marmara.

AYASOFYA PANSİYONLARI

Map pp278-80   *Ottoman Hotel*
☎ 212-513 3660; www.ayasofyapensions.com;
Soğukçeşme Sokak; s/d €99/115

If you're keen to play out Ottoman fantasies, come here. A row of 19th-century wooden houses occupying an entire cobbled street abutting **Topkapı Palace** (Topkapı Sarayı; p91), Ayasofya Pansiyonları is about as authentic as the Ottoman boutique hotel comes and it's picturesque to boot. Choose from a total of 52 rooms, all of which are charmingly decorated with brass beds, and enjoy the most glamorous breakfast in town, served in a glass conservatory complete with chandeliers. When the airconditioning units are installed in 2005, this place will be hard to beat. We suggest you consider the Pasha Suite here (US$250) – after all, it's not often you get your own private *hamam*.

DERSAADET OTELİ

Map pp278-80   *Ottoman Hotel*
☎ 212-458 0760; www.dersaadethotel.com;
Kapıağası Sokak 5, Küçük Aya Sofya; s/d €65/75

Roughly translated, the name of this hotel means 'The Place of Happiness' in Turkish, and we're sure that guests will be more than happy with this comfortable mid-sized hotel. In a painstakingly restored Ottoman wooden house, the interior features exquisitely painted ceilings and custom-designed wooden furniture throughout. Rooms, which have four-star amenities, are extremely comfortable, sporting a gold and russet-red colour scheme that gives a sense of luxury. Those with views cost a little bit extra. There's a roof terrace with Sea of Marmara and **Blue Mosque** (p84) views, as well as a comfortable breakfast café.

EMPIRE PALACE Map pp278-80   *Hotel*
☎ 212-514 5400; www.hotelempirepalace.com;
Hüdavendigar Caddesi 17-19, Sirkeci; s/d €55/70

We've included the Empire Palace for three reasons: it's one of the few hotels in the city to have a lift all the way to the roof terrace; it's new and very well appointed; and it's got some of the most friendly staff in the city. Comfortable but characterless décor reflects its Best Western pedigree – if you're looking for Ottoman flourishes this isn't for you. Ask for rooms 506, 503 or 504, which are larger than the others.

FOUR SEASONS HOTEL İSTANBUL

Map pp278-80   *Luxury Hotel*
☎ 212-638 8200; www.fshr.com; Tevkifhane Sokak 1,
Cankurtaran; s/d €349/378

This used to be the infamous Sultanahmet prison (remember *Midnight Express*?), and boy oh boy, we couldn't imagine anything better than being forced to do some serious time here these days. A regular entry in 'Best Hotel in the World' lists, this place oozes quality and comfort. Rooms are country club–elegant, with king-sized beds, enormous marble bathrooms and antique-style work desk. Location is ideal – the hotel is literally in the shadow of the **Blue Mosque** (p84) and **Aya Sofya** (p79). With only 65 rooms and a staff of around 200, the place has only one problem: there aren't enough rooms for everyone who wants one. Breakfast costs an extra €23.

HANEDAN HOTEL

Map pp278-80   *Ottoman Hotel*
☎ 212-516 4869; www.hanedanhotel.com; Adliye
Sokak 3, Cankurtaran; s/d €35/55

A 2003 renovation has endowed this small hotel with the ubiquitous 'Cankurtaran aesthetic', and it is very pleasant as a result. Pale lemon walls and marble floors give a light and elegant feel. Two rooms have Sea of Marmara views, and the roof terrace squeezes in **Aya Sofya** (p79) as well.

HOTEL ARARAT

Map pp278-80   *Ottoman Hotel*
☎ 212-516 0411; www.ararathotel.com; Torun Sokak 3, Cankurtaran; s/d €75
Another hotel decorated by Nikos Papadakis, who did such an inspired job with the **Empress Zoe** (right), the Ararat is tiny, but its charming host Haydar Sarigul and cosy rooftop terrace-bar in the shadow of the **Blue Mosque** (p84) make it a popular choice. Dark wooden floors, textile bedspreads and a clever space-enhancing mirrors are the decorative hallmarks; quality linen and olive-oil soaps are quality touches. The trick here is to pick the right room – otherwise you'll feel as if you're sleeping in a coffin. Request number six or number 12 for a bit of space and fabulous views. Rooms without views are €10-20 cheaper.

HOTEL ARCADIA Map pp278-80   *Hotel*
☎ 212-516 9696; www.hotelarcadiaistanbul.com; Dr İmran Öktem Caddesi 1, Binbirdirek; s/d €66/90
The piped Michael Bolton music in the Arcadia's ugly foyer was disconcerting, but all was forgiven when we were shown the amazing rooftop restaurant with its views of the **Blue Mosque** (p84), **Aya Sofya** (p79), **Topkapı Palace** (p91) and the Sea of Marmara. Room décor

---

---

is unfortunate – when will hotel owners realise that distressed walls and floral dadoes are past their use-by date? – but all have four-star appointments. Request an upper-floor room with view.

HOTEL ARMADA Map pp278-80   *Hotel*
☎ 212-638 1370; www.armadahotel.com.tr; Ahırkapı Sokak, Cankurtaran; s/d €75/85
Fresh flowers and sugared *lokum* (Turkish delight) greet guests when they check in to this comfortable hotel. Rooms feature pale green furnishings and are very well equipped. Ask for one at the front on the top floor and you'll get a sea view. Though the location – very near the Cankurtaran suburban train station and a few steps from the Bosphorus shore – isn't great, it's only a 10-minute walk uphill to Sultanahmet. The hotel's major selling point is the rooftop **Sera Restaurant** (p151) with its wonderful view and very pleasant surrounds. Two rooms have been especially designed for guests in wheelchairs.

HOTEL AYASOFYA

Map pp278-80   *Ottoman Hotel*
☎ 212-516 9446; www.ayasofyahotel.com; Demirci Reşit Sokak 28, Küçük Aya Sofya; s/d €40/60
This 1980s-renovated Ottoman house is looking a bit worse for wear these days, but it's still very comfortable and has a real 'home away from home' feel. Rooms are light, with poky bathrooms, and there's a small roof terrace with views. The surrounding area is quiet and central to all the Sultanahmet sights. Those booking seven nights get one night free.

HOTEL EMPRESS ZOE

Map pp278-80   *Ottoman Hotel*
☎ 212-518 2504; www.emzoe.com; Adliye Sokak 10, Cankurtaran; s/d €65/85
Named after the feisty Byzantine Empress whose portrait adorns the gallery at Aya Sofya, this fabulous place is owned by American Ann Nevens, who really knows her stuff when it comes to running a hotel. The prototype for 'Cankurtaran Modern', the now almost ubiquitous decorative style utilised in myriad Sultanahmet boutique hotels, the Empress Zoe is unusual in that it is constantly being changed and improved – hence the opening of the supremely stylish Chez Zoe garden suites (€115 to €150) in 2002. From the atmospheric underground lobby (once part of a *hamam*) to the gorgeous flower-filled garden where breakfast is served, this place is a gem. Some rooms are tiny, but these

Hotel Nomade (below)

are available at discounted rates (s/d €40/60). All rooms are individually and charmingly decorated – go for the 'petite suite' (€100) or the similarly priced double with private terrace. The rooftop lounge-terrace has excellent views.

HOTEL ERBOY
Map pp278-80   *Hotel*
☎ 212-513 3750; www.erboyhotel.com; Ebussuut Caddesi 32, Sirkeci; s/d €33/41

The Vegas-style furniture and marble floors in its lobby are the Erboy's only attempts at glamour. The rest of the place is resolutely mom-and-pop style, with small rooms that are clean but without frills. On the plus side, the location, near Topkapı, is central and quiet, and the rooms are reasonably priced. There's a roof terrace with so-so views and a pleasant restaurant spilling into the cobbled street.

HOTEL HALI
Map pp278-80   *Hotel*
☎ 212-516 2170; www.halihotel.com; Klodfarer Caddesi 20, Çemberlitaş; s/d €40/65

All the rugs in Turkey couldn't hide this hotel's institutional feel. That said, it's worth considering due to its roof terrace, which has amazing views, and its huge bathrooms and its quiet position. If you can ignore the horror of the décor (every time we remember the colour of the bathroom tiles we feel queasy), it's a reasonable choice. Third and fourth-floor rooms have views of the Sea of Marmara and **Aya Sofya** (p79).

HOTEL NOMADE
Map pp278-80   *Boutique Hotel*
☎ 212-513 2404; www.hotelnomade.com; Ticarethane Sokak 15, Alemdar; s/d €60/70

Mega style and budget pricing don't often go together, but the Nomade bucks the trend. The owners recently brought in French designer Dan Beranger to give the place a total overhaul and all we can say is 'ooh la la'. Just a few steps off busy Divan Yolu, the hotel's 16 small rooms and three suites are tres, tres chic, with great bathrooms and comfortable beds. With one of the best roof-terrace bars in town (smack-bang in front of **Aya Sofya**; p79) and a Philippe Stark feel, this place is about as hip as Sultanahmet gets.

HOTEL ORIENT EXPRESS
Map pp278-80   *Hotel*
☎ 212-520 7161; www.orientexpresshotel.com; Hüdavendigar Caddesi 34, Sirkeci; s/d €53/70

Its location isn't the best, but there's something quite endearing about this small hotel. Décor is around an Orient Express theme – the downstairs Wagon Bar is disarmingly tacky and the tiny but well-appointed rooms, with their capsule-like bathrooms, aren't much bigger than you'd get on the rails. The strongest selling points are the terrace, with great views, and the small indoor pool in the basement. Ask for a room with a Golden Horn view.

HOTEL PENINSULA

Map pp278-80   *Ottoman Hotel*

☎ 212-458 6850; www.hotelpeninsula.com; Adliye Sokak 6, Cankurtaran; s/d €35/45

We've included this hotel chiefly because the management is new, enthusiastic and very friendly. In fact, its enthusiasm has engendered two new ideas when it comes to Cankurtaran hotel amenities – bravo! This is the only roof terrace we found with hammocks for guests (great for enjoying sunset over the Sea of Marmara) and the only breakfast room that uses traditional low stools and brass tables to great (and comfortable) effect. The home-made yogurt and freshly baked cakes get big ticks as well. Rooms are characterless but comfortable.

HOTEL ŞEBNEM

Map pp278-80   *Ottoman Hotel*

☎ 212-517 6623; www.sebnemhotel.com; Adliye Sokak 1, Cankurtaran; s/d €35/50

Simplicity is the rule at the Şebnem, and it works a treat. Run by an extended family (son manages the hotel, mum cooks breakfast etc), its rooms, which are clearly inspired by the **Empress Zoe** (p204), **Ararat** (p204) et al, have rose-pink walls, canopy beds and wooden floors. Stylish linen and plentiful textiles provide a touch of class. The large terrace upstairs has views over the Sea of Marmara, and downstairs rooms, though a tad dark, have a private courtyard garden. There's also a very nice family room (€65). At the time of writing, airconditioning is scheduled to be installed in early 2005.

HOTEL SOKULLU PAŞA

Map pp278-80   *Ottoman Hotel*

☎ 212-518 1790; www.sokullupasahotel.com; Şehit Mehmet Paşa Sokak 5/7, Küçük Aya Sofya; s/d €49/62

'Ye Olde Guesthouse' décor is taken to the max here, with Laura Ashley–like bedspreads and curtains, and floral wallpaper. Rooms are comfortable, though the singles are tiny and the faux-floorboard lino is awful. What makes the place special is the gorgeous courtyard garden at the back and the hotel's wine bar–cum-restaurant, set in an atmospheric adjoining cellar (set menu with wine €15).

HOTEL SULTAN'S INN

Map pp278-80   *Ottoman Hotel*

☎ 212-638 2562; www.sultansinn.com; Mustafa Paşa Sokak 50, Küçük Aya Sofya; s/d €42/50

This relative newcomer to the competitive Sultanahmet hotel scene is poised to become one of the most successful, largely due to its remarkably friendly and professional staff. Getting the right balance between comfort and style helps too. Seventeen pristine rooms feature beds with textile canopies, lace curtains and sand-coloured walls and rugs. The roof terrace is home to flowerpots, plants galore and a birdhouse; both it and the indoor winter terrace feature great views. Two rooms that are more expensive have views of the **Blue Mosque** (p84) and the Sea of Marmara.

HOTEL TURKOMAN

Map pp278-80   *Ottoman Hotel*

☎ 212-516 2956; www.turkomanhotel.com; Asmalı Çeşme Sokak 2, Binbirdirek; s/d €60/75

You'll feel as if you've booked into a private club when you walk into the Turkoman. In a fantastic position up the hill a few steps off the **Hippodrome** (p86), this renovated 19th-century building features spacious rooms that are simply but tastefully decorated with kilims, reproduction antique furniture and brass beds. Ask for room 4a, which has a balcony and **Blue Mosque** (p84) view. The roof terrace has good views and the husband-and-wife managers are friendly and helpful.

İBRAHIM PAŞA OTELI

Map pp278-80   *Ottoman Boutique Hotel*

☎ 212-518 0394; www.ibrahimpasha.com; Terzihane Sokak 5, Binbirdirek; s/d €79/89

We can't say enough good things about this small designer hotel. In a great position just up from the **Hippodrome** (p86), its owners have managed to straddle the divide between sleek modernist and antique Ottoman with great success. Parquet floors, crisp white linen, marble bathrooms and gold mirrors make the smallish rooms distinctive, and the building's marble spiral staircase and central ornamental lightwell are super classy. After enjoying the excellent breakfast, served in the downstairs kitchen with its stainless-steel bench and olive-green walls, guests often have to be encouraged to leave the building – the alternative option of sinking into one of the foyer lounge's leather couches and enjoying a quiet read is just too tempting. There's also a small roof terrace with views.

KONUK EVI

Map pp278-80   *Ottoman Hotel*

☎ 212-513 3660; www.ayasofyapensions.com; Soğukçeşme Sokak; s/d €99/115

Part of the **Ayasofya Pansiyonlari** (p203), this annex set in a spectacular private garden overlooking the **Caferağa Medresesi** (p85) is even more impressive than its parent. Rooms are large and extremely elegant, with parquet floors, luxurious rugs and velvet-upholstered furniture. The building itself is a replica of a large Ottoman house that was on this site, so it has all the mod cons as well as more than its fair share of period charm. The foyer features gilt mirrors and a grand piano. A classy option that is a bargain at this price. You can also sample the food (p150) and drink (p164) here.

KYBELE HOTEL

Map pp278-80 — *Ottoman Hotel*
☎ 212-522 7347; www.kybelehotel.com; Yerebatan Caddesi 35, Alemdar; s/d €60/70

The gilded exterior of this small hotel (peacock blue with loads of gold) reflects the décor inside, which features hundreds of coloured lights, wooden floors covered in rugs, and antique furniture and curios. The owners are nearly as eccentric as the décor, but have given up previous careers as circus performers to run this place in a personable and professional style. Its location near **Aya Sofya** (p79) is fabulous, and the rooms, which feature cute marble bathrooms, are smallish but comfortable. There's no roof terrace, but a charming patio compensates.

MAVİ EV Map pp278-80 — *Ottoman Hotel*

Blue House; ☎ 212-638 9010; www.bluehouse.com.tr; Dalbastı Sokak 14, Cankurtaran; s/d €99/115

We were in two minds as to whether we should include this hotel, and did so only because of its unrivalled position directly across from the **Blue Mosque** (p84). The views of this, **Aya Sofya** (p79) and the Sea of Marmara from the summer-only roof terrace are exceptional, too. Not as impressive are the rooms, which, though well appointed, have a tiny bathroom and the worst décor imaginable (our mums always told us that if we couldn't say anything nice we shouldn't say anything at all, so with this in mind we are refraining from commenting on the 1970s yellow leather furniture in the foyer).

SARI KONAK OTELI Map pp278-80 — *Hotel*

☎ 212-638 6258; www.sarikonak.com; Mimar Mehmet Ağa Caddesi 42-46, Cankurtaran; s/d €57/74

Apparently the American Ambassador to Turkey stayed here for months before setting up his own place in town, and we can understand why. The type of place that could fit just as easily in Washington as this city of sultans, the Sarı Konak is more *Home Beautiful* than *Hip Hotel*, but those wanting a clean and comfortable

Kybele Hotel (left)

base could do worse than check in here. The jade-coloured décor is as soothing as the sea views from the roof terrace. Added extras are the pleasant courtyard and the tiny balconies in some rooms.

SARNIÇ HOTEL Map pp278-80 — *Hotel*

☎ 212-518 2323; www.sarnichotel.com; Küçük Aya Sofya Caddesi 26, Küçük Aya Sofya; s/d €70/85

Food lovers in particular will adore this small hotel just around the corner from the **Blue Mosque** (p84). Dutch owner Eveline Zoutendijk was a chef before entering the hotel business and runs highly regarded cooking classes from the hotel kitchen (see Courses, p51). Rooms have a grandma-style floral décor that won't appeal to everyone; avoid the ones in the middle, as they have no windows to the street. Breakfasts, which are served on the comfortable roof terrace, are served with home-made jams that are a house speciality. Perfect for those looking for a home away from home in İstanbul.

SUDE KONAK

Map pp278-80 — *Boutique Hotel*
☎ 212-513 2100; www.sudekonak.com; Ebussuut Caddesi 24, Sirkeci; s/d €50/60

Making a valiant if ultimately unsuccessful attempt to be a Jasper Conrad–style hip hotel, the Sude Konak raises hopes with its stylish foyer and mezzanine, but deflates them with its uncomfortable beds and miniscule bathrooms. There's a roof terrace with bar. Go for rooms ending in 5 – they're large and light.

YEŞİL EV Map pp278-80 *Ottoman Hotel*
☎ 212-517 6785; www.istanbulyesilev.com;
Kabasakal Caddesi 5, Cankurtaran; s/d €107/148

This place has either a proud history or a lot to answer for – it depends on your point of view. The model for hundreds of boutique 'Ottoman hotels' in Turkey, it has been one of the city's most famous places to sleep since it opened in 1984. Brass beds and chintz furnishings feature. Tea- and coffee-making facilities provide a nice touch. Unfortunately the bathrooms are a bit cramped. In all, we prefer the slightly cheaper **Ayasofya Pansiyonlari** (p203), which was restored and is run by the same organisation.

Cheap Sleeps
AMPHORA HOSTEL (BOBBY'S PLACE)
Map pp278-80 *Hostel*
☎ 212-638 1554; www.hotelsinturkey.net/amphora;
Terazisi Sokak 8, Küçük Aya Sofya; dm/d €8/25

This place offers basic accommodation enlivened by touches of traditional Anatolian decoration. Join the friendly owners and resident dog in the downstairs lounge when traditional live music is being played, or chill out over a backgammon board throughout the day. It's reasonably clean (bathrooms only just make the grade) and rooms are small but light. Breakfast is served on the rooftop terrace, which overlooks the Sea of Marmara.

İSTANBUL HOSTEL Map pp278-80 *Hostel*
☎ 212-516 9380; info@valide.com; Kutlugün Sokak 35, Cankurtaran; dm/d without bathroom €7/17

We think this is the pick of the Cankurtaran hostels, but party animals might disagree. It has a lovely outdoor terrace on the roof with great views and a very pleasant downstairs bar, neither of which have the jungle atmosphere of nearby hostels. Rooms are light and nicely painted, though the carpet's overdue for replacement. Bathrooms are clean. In all it's a good choice, particularly for those wanting to sleep soundly. A Turkish breakfast costs €1.60 (it's included in the price during the winter months). Internet is expensive (€1.60 per hour), but the beer is cheap (€1.40).

KÜÇÜK AYASOFYA HOTEL
Map pp278-80 *Budget Hotel*
☎ 212-458 2985; Şehit Mehmet Paşa Sokak 25, Küçük Aya Sofya; s/d €14/17

Though in a good position and undoubtedly cheap, this place is dark in its communal areas

and staff don't speak English. Rooms are light and pretty clean, though bathrooms only just pass inspection. Rooms at the back on the top floor have Sea of Marmara views.

MAVİ GUESTHOUSE
Map pp278-80 *Budget Hotel/Hostel*
☎ 212-516 5878; www.maviguesthouse.com;
Kutlugün Sokak 3, Cankurtaran; dm/s/d €8/16/20

Mavi's management is very friendly and the hotel has the added bonus of a kitchen for guests, which is just as well since some rooms are cramped and windowless, and the whole place is pretty run down. The small rooms and lack of airconditioning or fans doesn't make a summer stay all that attractive, either. Mattresses on the rooftop cost €5 (including breakfast) but the best value is provided by front rooms, one of which has an **Aya Sofya** (p79) view. Breakfast is served downstairs or at streetside tables.

NOBEL HOTEL & GUESTHOUSE
Map pp278-80 *Budget Hotel*
☎ 212-516 3177; info@hotelnobel.com; Mimar Mehmet Ağa Caddesi 32, Cankurtaran; s/d €15/25

This family-run place wouldn't win any awards, but it's had a recent makeover and is relatively clean and comfortable. And its prices are about as cheap as you can get without resorting to a hostel. There's a roof terrace with great views. Cheaper rooms without bath are available.

ORIENT INTERNATIONAL HOSTEL
Map pp278-80 *Hostel*
☎ 212-518 0789; www.orienthostel.com; Akbıyık Caddesi 13, Cankurtaran; dm/d without bathroom/ double with bathroom €9/20/35

Always packed to the rafters with young backpackers wanting to see a few sights, drink more than a few beers and then get laid, the Ori-

Top Five Sleeps
- **Best Boutique Hotel** Bentley Hotel (p212)
- **Best Apartments** İstanbul Holiday Apartments (p210)
- **Best Cheap Sleep** Side Hotel & Pension (opposite)
- **Best Luxury Hotel** Four Seasons Hotel İstanbul (p203)
- **Best Ottoman Hotel** It's neck and neck between the Empress Zoe, the Anemon Galata and the İbrahim Paşa Oteli, but the Empress Zoe wins by a whisker (p204).

ent should only be considered if you're young, don't care about creature comforts and are ready to party. The rooftop terrace bar has fabulous views and a relaxed atmosphere (great for meeting people), while the downstairs bar really gets going on Monday, Wednesday and Friday nights, when there is a free belly-dancing show. Breakfast is included in the above price and is pretty good, though you can arrange a slight discount if you forgo it. Don't consider the 'delux' double rooms with bathroom – they're radically overpriced for what you get.

SİDE HOTEL & PENSION

Map pp278-80 *Budget Hotel & Apartments*
☎ 212-517 2282; www.sidehotel.com; Utangaç Sokak 20, Cankurtaran; hotel s/d €33/41, pension s/d €17/29, apt €47-75
A sprawling place that has built a reputation for providing cheap, clean and comfortable rooms, the Side has hotel rooms with TV, airconditioning and en suite; pension rooms with shared bathroom; and fully equipped but dark apartments sleeping one to six people. The pick of the bunch is the front triple hotel room with private balcony overlooking the **Blue Mosque** (p84) and **Aya Sofya** (p79). Avoid rooms at the rear, some of which are dark and blighted by noisy airconditioning units on a nearby building. The rooftop garden-lounge has wonderful views and a welcoming atmosphere. The pension rooms and apartments provide the best value.

SULTAN HOSTEL Map pp278-80 *Hostel*
☎ 212-516 9260; www.sultanhostel.com; Akbıyık Sokak 21, Cankurtaran; dm/s/d €8/16/22
Next door to – and clearly in hot competition with – the Orient, this place is perhaps a tad more comfortable than its neighbour but doesn't have its raffish charm or party reputation. Though the open rooftop restaurant has good views, the downstairs bar can't compete with the atmosphere on the roof at the Orient. On the plus side, Internet access is free, the bathrooms are very clean, the water is very hot and the beds are quite comfortable. Breakfast costs €3, but is included in the price during the winter months.

TÜRKMEN HOTEL & PENSION

Map pp278-80 *Budget Hotel*
☎ 212-517 1355; www.turkmenhotel.com.tr;
Dizdariye Çeşmesi Sokak 27, Çemberlitaş; s/d €16/25
The exterior's only distinguishing feature is

its touch of concrete cancer, but it's worth coming inside for the well-priced rooms, a few of which have balconies overlooking the Sea of Marmara. Though run down, the place is clean and management is friendly. Avoid the depressing pension at the rear – rooms reminded us of Brad Davis' cell in *Midnight Express*. Rooms with balconies or views are slightly more expensive.

YÜCELT INTERYOUTH HOSTEL

Map pp278-80 *Hostel*
☎ 212-513 6150; www.yucelthostel.com; Caferiye Sokak 6/1; dm/s/d €9/20/26
Opened in 1976, this was the country's first youth hostel, and showing admirable staying power, it's still going strong. A warren of basic, clean rooms feature comfortable beds – some even have Aya Sofya views. Bathrooms are clean, modern and relatively plentiful. With its cheap-eats restaurant (breakfast €2.20) garden bar (beer €1.90) and Internet facilities (€1.10 per hour) this is a good choice, if a long way from backpacker central in Cankurtaran. Singles and doubles have a hand basin but no en suite.

THE BAZAAR DISTRICT

There's only one choice in this area, and we can't imagine why anyone would choose it. This part of town is noisy and it lacks the charm of the rest of Old İstanbul.

MERİT ANTIQUE HOTEL

Map pp282-3 *Hotel*
☎ 212-513 9300; www.merithotels.com; Ordu Caddesi 226, Laleli; s/d €132/165
This would have to be the ugliest conversion of a historic building in the entire city. What was once an architecturally progressive apartment block housing 124 families made homeless by fires is now an ultra-tacky international hotel designed around a brass-and-glass extravaganza of an atrium foyer. If we say that this was the preferred accommodation for the 2004 Eurovision contestants, you'll no doubt get the picture. We include it here only because travel agents seem seduced by its close proximity to the **Grand Bazaar (Kapali Çarşı)** (p102) and consequently often recommend it. The rooms are bland but comfortable, though many of them are located off balconies directly above the hotel's noisy foyer areas. There's a gym and an indoor pool.

WESTERN DISTRICTS

Another strange choice when it comes to hotel location, but this part of town has the attraction of the Kariye Museum (p111) as well as two fine boutique hotels, one of them with an exceptional restaurant.

HOTEL DAPHNIS

Map p281   *Ottoman Hotel*
☎ 212-531 4858; www.hoteldaphnis.com; Sadrazam Ali Paşa Caddesi 26, Fener; s/d €40/55
Its position on a busy road along the Golden Horn is pretty well in the middle of nowhere, but this small hotel is worth considering due to its excellent restaurant (p154) and simple, stylish decor. Rooms upstairs at the rear have small balconies looking over the Ecumenical Orthodox Patriarchate (p109). Some have airconditioning, and all have tea and coffee-making facilities and satellite TV.

KARİYE OTELİ Map p281   *Ottoman Hotel*
☎ 212-635 7979; www.kariyeotel.com; Kariye Camii Sokak 18, Edirnekapı; s/d €49/57
What a shame the beautiful foyer of this small hotel next to the Kariye Müzesi, (kilim-strewn wooden floors, comfortable couches, large picture windows overlooking a courtyard garden) isn't indicative of the rest of the spaces. If it were, we'd stay here next time. Rooms are undeniably pretty, featuring parquet floors, pale-pink walls and framed Ottoman prints, but bathrooms are tiny and the general feel is a bit faded. Still, prices are reasonable and one of the best restaurants in the city, Asitane (p154), is located in its basement. On reflection, perhaps we *will* stay here next time we're in town…

NORTH OF THE GOLDEN HORN
BEYOĞLU – GALATA BRIDGE TO İSTİKLAL CADDESİ

In many ways, this is the best location in İstanbul. Halfway between the major sights of Old İstanbul and the main entertainment and eating strip of İstiklal Caddesi, it's rapidly building a reputation as the city's new bohemian centre, with art galleries, cafés, bars and funky boutiques starting to sprout.

It's also home to two of the best apartment hotels in town.

ANEMON GALATA

Map pp284-6   *Ottoman Hotel*
☎ 212-293 2343; www.anemonhotels.com; cnr Galata Meydani & Büyükhendek Caddesi, Karaköy; s/d €82/99
Small hotels don't come much better than this, particularly around Beyoğlu. Located on the attractive new square that's been built around Galata Tower, this wooden building dates from 1842 but has been almost completely rebuilt inside. Individually decorated rooms are super elegant and feature ornate painted ceilings, king-sized beds and antique-style desks. Large bathrooms have baths and marble basins. Frankly, we're not sure which of the hotel's features is the best. Is it the classically beautiful foyer with its chandeliers, marble floors and luxurious rugs? Or the stylish modern bar/restaurant sheathed in glass that's been built on the rooftop? Ask for a room with a view.

GALATA RESIDENCE APART HOTEL

Map pp284-6   *Apartment Hotel*
☎ 212-292 4841; www.galataresidence.com; Hacı Ali Sokak, Karaköy; 1-bed/2-bed apartments per day €60/100, per week €350/630
Buried in the maze of narrow streets down from the Galata Tower (p118), this historic building was built in the late 19th century by the wealthy Kamondo family to house indigent Jewish families. It's now an apartment-hotel with a Greek restaurant on the top floor and a modern annex (for the one-bedroom apartments) next door. Perfectly situated between İstiklal Caddesi and Eminönü (to find it, ask taxi drivers to drop you in front of the Yaşar Bank at the corner of Voyvova Caddesi and Haraçci Ali Sokak and walk up the steep stairs – the hotel is right at the top), the fully-equipped apartments are a bit run down but comfortable, with large rooms and a reasonable amount of light. Top marks go to the daily servicing and the helpful staff. To avoid listening to renditions of *Zorba the Greek* late into the night, avoid the top-floor rooms. Monthly rates are available.

İSTANBUL HOLIDAY APARTMENTS

Map pp284-6   *Apartments*
☎ 212-251 8530; www.istanbulholidayapartments .com; Camekar Sokak & Galata Kulesi Sokak, Tünel; per week €450-750
Saying that holiday apartments in İstanbul are easy to find is like saying the sultans were celi-

bate – it just ain't true. This is why the recent opening of these apartments in two separate buildings just down from Galata Tower is something to be wholeheartedly celebrated. When we saw the penthouse apartment in the Glorya building we seriously considered packing up our normal lives and moving here permanently. We imagine guests who book for a week or two will have a similar reaction. These apartments in residential blocks near the Galata Tower have undergone a quality renovation and are beautifully fitted out with washer/drier, fully equipped kitchen (dishwasher), CD player and every other mod con you may need. Décor features kilims and antique furniture. There's weekly maid service. The Glorya building has three apartments – two with one bedroom and fabulous views and one bedsit with a lovely private courtyard – and the Berekte apartments have two bedrooms (no airconditioning). Though on the pricey side, these places are worth it, particularly for families.

BEYOĞLU – ON & AROUND İSTİKLAL CADDESİ

If you're in town to party at the nightclubs or do business in Beyoğlu, this is a good choice of location. There's a reasonable choice of budget types, though none of the hotels on offer are as impressive as the best that Sultanahmet or Taksim have to offer.

BÜYÜK LONDRA OTELİ

Map pp284–6   *Historic Hotel*
☎ 212-245 0670; www.londrahotel.net; Meşrutiyet Caddesi 117, Tepebaşı; s/d €50/68
The Büyük's 'gothic house of horrors' feel may not be for everyone. Though it dates from the same era as the **Pera Palas Oteli** (p121), it is nowhere near as elegant, has much smaller rooms and bathrooms and is decidedly worse for wear. The good news is that three rooms on the fourth floor have been renovated and are now quite comfortable. We'd suggest booking in only if the hotel guarantees that you can have one of these. The remaining rooms are musty and very scuffed around the edges, with tiny bathrooms and no airconditioning.

PERA PALAS OTELİ

Map pp284–6   *Historic Hotel*
☎ 212-251 4560; www.perapalace.com; Meşrutiyet Caddesi 98-100, Tepebaşı; s/d €124/140
The Pera's 145 faded rooms vary from high-ceilinged chambers, with period furnishings and bathrooms to match, to cramped upper-floor servants' quarters and uninspiring annexe rooms. You're paying a premium for nostalgia here, much of which you can enjoy at huge savings just by having a coffee in the patisserie or a drink at the bar, and frankly, that's what we'd suggest. Common areas are pretty fantastic, though. If you decide to book in, ask for a room with a balcony and Golden Horn view.

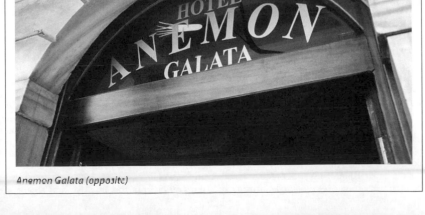

Anemon Galata (opposite)

RICHMOND HOTEL Map pp284-6 *Hotel*

☎ 212-252 5460; www.richmondhotels.com.tr;
İstiklal Caddesi 445; s/d €135/165

Next to the palatial Russian consulate, this is one of only two hotels on İstiklal. Behind its 19th-century facade, the place is modern, quite comfortable and well run. The sleek bar/restaurant has great views over the Bosphorus. Standard rooms are comfortable if characterless, but the suites (€230) are knock outs, with modernist décor, excellent views, great workstation, Jacuzzi and plasma TV. A mainly business clientele keeps the place busy – book ahead.

YENİŞEHİR PALAS Map pp284-6 *Hotel*

☎ 212-252 7160; www.yenisehirpalas.com; Oteller Sokak 1-3, Tepebaşı; s/d €58/82

You could do a lot worse than book into one of the large front rooms here, which are clean and comfortable. The exterior is unprepossessing, but the interior can hold its own with most of the city's business hotels. There's an English-style pub downstairs where guests unwind after a hard day at work.

Cheap sleeps
BAHAR APARTMENT HOTEL

Map pp284-6 *Apartment Hotel*
☎ 212-245 0772; fax 212-244 1708; İstiklal Caddesi 61; 1/2/3 person €25/40/58

Attracted by the idea of sitting in your own apartment with a bottle of wine and viewing the early-evening *passagiata* along İstiklal? You can do this at the Bahar. These basic apartments, which sleep up to four, are quite large, reasonably clean (shame about the showers) and cheap for this side of town. The location is great if you're planning to party in the surrounding nightclubs, but hopeless if you want any sleep. There are tiled floors, ceiling fans, a small kitchen (equipped only with tea and coffee-making gear) and a bathroom. Breakfast is served in the downstairs Café Berlin.

CHILLOUT HOTEL Map pp284-6 *Hostel*

☎ 212-249 4784; www.chillouthc.com; Balyoz Sokak 17, Tepebaşı; dm/s/d €7/9/25

The Chillout is building up a reputation with the backpacking set as a friendly and decent alternative to the Sultanahmet hostels. Its colourful paint scheme, wooden floorboards and cosy downstairs lounge/café are certainly attractive, but the general grubbiness and confrontational bathrooms (shower over squat toilet) made us

want to gross out rather than chill out. Doubles come with a miniscule en suite.

HOTEL RESIDENCE

Map pp284-6 *Budget Hotel*
☎ 212-252 7685; www.hotelresidence.com.tr; Sadri Alışık Sokak 19, off İstiklal Caddesi; s/d €25/37

This place is directly opposite a large police station, so guests will feel extremely safe when returning from a heavy night of partying at the nearby nightclubs. It's very old-fashioned and not at all stylish, but at these prices, who's complaining? Rooms are light, have a small bathroom and also have airconditioning. Most have twin beds. You'll need to negotiate to get these prices.

SAYDAM HOTEL

Map pp284-6 *Budget Hotel*
☎ 212-251 8116, fax 212-244 0366; cnr Asmalımescit & Sofyalı Sokaks, Asmalımescit; s/d €15/25

This place may well win the prize for offering the smallest rooms in the city. However, it's in a great spot on a cobbled street in the middle of a restaurant strip just off İstiklal Caddesi. Rooms are clean and quiet. It's certainly worth considering as an alternative to a hostel.

TAKSİM, HARBİYE & NİŞANTAŞI

Close to Taksim Square (p123), the symbolic and commercial heart of the city, the hotels in this area are invariably comfortable, clean and well-equipped – perfect for the business traveller. You'll also find a couple of the city's most glamorous boutique accommodation choices around here, no doubt due to the neighbourhood's reputation for high-end shopping.

BENTLEY HOTEL

Map p287 *Boutique Hotel*
☎ 212-291 7730; www.bentley-hotel.com; Halaskargazi Caddesi 75, Harbiye; s/d €124/165

It's hip, it's hot and it's sure to make you very, very happy if you stay here. Yes, the Bentley has it all: luxurious rooms that look as if they're straight from the pages of *Wallpaper* magazine, sleek suites for those in the mood to splurge (€280) and enough staff to cater to your every whim. If you over-indulge in the classy foyer bar, don't worry – the health club and sauna will help you recover. Just around the corner from the Teşvikiye and Nişantaşı shopping strips, this is the perfect place to spend an indulgent few days in İstanbul.

CENTRAL PALACE

Map p287   *Boutique Luxury Hotel*
☎ 212-313 4040; www.thecentralpalace.com;
Lamartin Caddesi 18, Taksim; s/d €164/185
Opened in 2004, this boutique hotel has been designed around a 'wellness' concept. Parquet floors feature instead of asthma-inducing carpets, therapeutic fruit juices for every possible complaint are available at the flick of a room-service switch, the restaurant food is all organic and massage showers and Jacuzzis are installed in every bathroom. Ten rooms even have their own exercise bike. We feel healthy even *thinking* about checking in. The joy is that the place is not at all hippy-dippy: appointments are super-luxurious, all fabrics are from **Vakko** (p198), İstanbul's poshest store, and the décor is opulent, with oodles of gilt and marble. The only things missing are views and an impressive exterior (the guys wearing epaulettes just didn't do it for us). As well as large standard rooms, there are suites, family rooms and apartments.

FAMILY HOUSE Map pp284-6   *Apartments*
☎ 212-249 7351; familyhouse@ihlas.net.tr; Kutlu Sokak 53, Gümüşsuyu; per day €79, per week €493
This 1970s apartment building is in a residential quarter off Taksim Square. The area is hilly, so you must be fit. Five small apartments offer two single beds and one double bed, telephone, digital TV, bathroom and a fully furnished kitchen. They are spotlessly clean but quite small. Forget about Internet, airconditioning or other modern amenities. To find it, walk down Osmanlı Caddesi from Taksim and turn left at Pembe Sokak. This doesn't have a street sign – it's the street with the Közde Kebab House opposite. Alternatively, walk down İnönü Gümüşuyu Caddesi from Taksim, walk beneath the large red Chinese gate and down the steps, then down another flight.

İSTANBUL HILTON

Map p287   *Luxury Hotel*
☎ 212-315 6000; www.hilton.com, Cumhuriyet Caddesi, Harbiye; s/d with garden view €214, with Bosporus view €247
Designed way back in 1952 by SOM and Sedad Hakkı Eldem, who were among the first architects to introduce International style into the city, the Hilton is wearing well. Set in a 5.6 hectare park overlooking the Bosphorus, its health club, tennis courts and swimming pool are perhaps its best features, though the large rooms with balcony can hold their own against any brash newcomers. Harried staff and a constant stream of package tours and conference guests are the major drawbacks to staying here. Breakfast costs an extra €22.

MARMARA İSTANBUL

Map p287   *Luxury Hotel*
☎ 212-251 4696; www.themarmaraistanbul.com; Taksim Square; s/d €189/214
Right beside busy Taksim Square, the Marmara is an İstanbul institution, having opened to great acclaim in 1976. Its splendid views (10th floor and up) and extremely comfortable rooms make it a good choice for tourists and business people alike, though the frequency of public events on the square necessitating the presence of riot police, tanks and sharpshooters might be off-putting for some. Rooms are large with a classy décor enlivened with royal-blue and gold Ottoman touches. There are a highly regarded rooftop restaurant and bar, a pool, a gym and a *hamam*. Breakfast costs an extra €17.

RIVA HOTEL Map p287   *Hotel*
☎ 212-256 4420; www.rivahotel.com.tr; Aydede Caddesi 8, Taksim; s/d €41/58
One of a host of similar places around Taksim, the Riva knows that its heyday is far behind it and so charges accordingly. The rooms are clean, light and roomy, with comfortable beds and a tiny bathroom. There's a bar downstairs and a welcoming breakfast room on the mezzanine. In all, this is a good choice.

TAKSİM HILL HOTEL Map p287   *Hotel*
☎ 212-334 8500; www.taksimhill.com; Sıraselviler Caddesi 9, Taksim; s/d €99/124
This hotel has a lovely exterior with curliced iron balconies and casement windows. The interior isn't quite as impressive, but rooms are quite large and the owners have made an effort to decorate in a sleek 'Istanbul Moderne' style. It's not entirely successful but we'll give them kudos for effort. Some downstairs rooms are dark, so specify an upstairs room with a Bosphorus view. The hotel will negotiate on price.

TAKSİM SQUARE HOTEL Map p287   *Hotel*
☎ 212-292 6440; info@taksimsquarehotel.com.tr; Sıraselviler Caddesi 15, Taksim; s/d €50/66
This glass-fronted building matches the ugly Taksim surrounds, but inside you'll be pleasantly surprised by the large rooms, which feature a

stylish autumn-leaf décor. Most rooms have views (Square or Bosphorus); corner rooms from the fourth floor up have views of both sides at a nice price, so request one of these. The top-floor breakfast salon is a great place to prepare for the day. In all, a bargain four-star choice.

TAKSİM SUITES

Map p287 *Boutique Apartment Hotel*
☎ 212-254 7777; fax 212-256 2021; Cumhuriyet Caddesi 49, Taksim; per night €136-340

This is a showcase for the Ikea aesthetic. The 14 hotel suites, all with well-equipped kitchens, feature light wooden floors and white furniture: very minimal and about as far away from 'Cankurtaran Modern' as you can get, which is a welcome change. Front suites on the fourth to seventh floors have Bosphorus views, but overlook manic Cumhuriyet Caddesi and so are very noisy – consider requesting one at the rear. All feature sitting areas, workdesks and large beds. The larger suites have a Jacuzzi in the bedroom, which is a bit too Hugh Heffnerish for us but might take the fancy of some. There's a downstairs breakfast room, a small gym on the roof and daily maid service.

VARDAR PALACE HOTEL

Map pp284-6 *Hotel*
☎ 212-252 2888; www.vardarhotel.com; Sıraselviler Caddesi 54, Taksim; s/d €58/74

Dried flower arrangements and faded carpets may remind you of your grandma's house, but this small hotel just off Taksim offers good value for money and so is worth considering. Rooms at the rear are darkish but quiet, front rooms are light but face onto a noisy nightclub strip. It's super clean and very friendly.

Cheap Sleep

HOTEL AVRUPA Map p287 *Budget Hotel*
☎ 212-250 9420; otelavrupa@superonline.com; Topçu Caddesi 32, Taksim; s/d €25/32

You'll be greeted by Casper the resident cocker spaniel when you check into this unpretentious place. The owners live on site and so are always around to make sure that guests are happy and rooms are kept spanking clean. While the lime-green walls, lurid yellow drapes and terracotta tiles won't be to everyone's taste, those on the corner, with their large windows overlooking the street, are universally pleasing. Rates cited are for rooms with en suite; those with shared bathroom are even cheaper. There are also a few rooms with airconditioning (€37).

Top...
- **Roof Terrace Bar** Hotel Ararat (p204) or Hotel Nomade (p205)
- **Interior** The Central Palace Hotel (p213)
- **Garden** Konuk Evi (p206)
- **Hotel Restaurant** Kariye Oteli (p210)
- **Rooftop Views** Anemon Galata (p210) or Hotel Arcadia (p204)

BEŞİKTAŞ & ORTAKÖY

If you have cash to spare and don't mind catching taxis everywhere, these suburbs near the Bosphorus could be what you're looking for. One thing is sure: the views and hotel restaurants are damn fine.

ÇIRAĞAN PALACE HOTEL KEMPINSKI

Map p288 *Luxury Hotel*
☎ 212-326 4646; www.ciragan-palace.com; Çırağan Caddesi 32, Beşiktaş; r €291-766

Housed in a palace constructed by Sultan Abdülaziz and rebuilt as a hotel in the 1980s, most of the guest rooms in this five-star place are in a modern annexe next door. The wedding cake–style palace holds meeting rooms, VIP suites, a ballroom and restaurants. The best thing about the place is its location, right on the Bosphorus down from Yıldız Parkı (p127). East-facing rooms look out on the water, but west-facing 'park-view' rooms look onto a stone wall and should be avoided. All are comfortable, but don't reach the heights of indulgence that could be expected at these prices. Two things that Abdülaziz would no doubt have approved of are the waterside pool surrounded by manicured lawns, and the hotel boat, which ferries guests from Ataköy near the airport across the water to the hotel's private landing place. We doubt he would have got his head around the concept of the hotel's wellness spa.

SWISSÔTEL İSTANBUL THE BOSPHORUS Map p288 *Luxury Hotel*
☎ 212-326 1100; Bayıldım Caddesi 2, Maçka, Beşiktaş; r €234-366

On a wooded hilltop overlooking the Bosphorus, Asian shore and Old İstanbul, this modern hotel has every amenity you could possibly require. Rooms are light, mega-comfortable and luxuriously appointed. The super-swish foyer, two highly regarded restaurants and excellent leisure facilities are all classic five-star accoutrements.

Sleeping – Beşiktaş & Ortaköy

Excursions

Excursions

If you can bear to tear yourself away from the manifold delights of the city, there are a number of alluring options for day and overnight excursions, including the ubiquitous (but no less fabulous) ferry trip along the Bosphorus.

BOSPHORUS HIGHLIGHTS
A trip along the Bosphorus offers treats galore. See how many times you can make your way to Asia from Europe and back! Highlights include **Beylerbeyi Sarayı** (p218), **Küçüksu Kasrı** (p220), **Rumeli Hisarı** (p220), **Hıdiv Kasrı** (p221) and the **Sadberk Hanım Müzesi** (p221). See p222 for two suggested itineraries

ISLANDS & BEACHES
The serene **Princes' Islands** (p223) are the top pick here, though swimmers may choose to make day trips to the Black Sea beaches of **Kilyos** (p226), **Ağva** (p226) and **Şile** (p226).

OTTOMAN GLORY
The Ottoman capital before İstanbul, **Edirne** (p226) offers architecture and history buffs plenty to see, including the most famous Ottoman mosque of all, the sublimely beautiful **Selimiye Camii** (p226).

BATTLEFIELDS
The sites of monumental battles over three millennia apart – **Troy** (p233) and **Gallipoli** (p230) – make a fascinating overnight trip.

BOSPHORUS TOUR
Divan Yolu and İstiklal Caddesi are always awash with people, but neither is the major thoroughfare in İstanbul. That honour goes to the mighty Bosphorus Strait, which runs from the Sea of Marmara (Marmara Denizi) at the Galata Bridge (Galata Köprüsü) all the way to the Black Sea (Karadeniz), 32km north. Over the centuries it has been crossed by conquering armies, intrepid merchants and many an adventurous spirit. These days, thousands of İstanbullus commute daily along its length, fishing vessels try their luck in its waters and tourists ride its ferries from Eminönü to Anadolu Kavağı and back.

The strait's name is taken from ancient mythology. Bosphorus roughly translates from the ancient Greek as the 'place where the cow crossed'. The cow was Io, a beautiful lady with whom Zeus, king of the gods, had an affair. When his wife Hera discovered his infidelity, Zeus tried to atone by turning his erstwhile lover into a cow. Hera, for good measure, provided a horsefly to sting Io on the rump and drive her across the strait. Proving that there was no justice in Olympus, Zeus managed to get off scot-free.

In modern Turkish the strait is the Boğaziçi or İstanbul Boğazı (from *boğaz,* throat or strait). On one side is Asia, on the other Europe. Both shores are densely populated and have attractions galore for the day visitor.

The Bosphorus has certainly figured in history. It is thought that Ulysses' travelled through here and Byzas, founder of Byzantium, explored these waters before the time of Jesus. Mehmet the Conqueror built two mighty fortresses at the strait's narrowest point to close it off to allies of the Byzantines. After İstanbul fell to the Turks, enormous Ottoman armies would take several days to cross the Bosphorus each spring on their way to campaigns in Asia. At the end of WWI, the defeated Ottoman capital cowered under the guns of Allied frigates moored here; and when the republic was proclaimed, the last Ottoman sultan walked down to the Bosphorus and sailed into exile.

For millennia, crossing the strait meant a boat trip – the only exceptions were the few occasions when it froze. Late in 1973, the Bosphorus Bridge, the fourth-longest suspension bridge in the world, was opened. For the first time there was a physical link across the straits from Europe to Asia. Traffic was so heavy over the bridge that it paid for itself in less than a decade. Now there is a second bridge, the Fatih Bridge (named after Mehmet the Conqueror, Mehmet Fatih), just north of Rumeli Hisarı. A third bridge, even further north, is planned.

Eminönü to Ortaköy

As you start your trip up the Bosphorus, watch out for the small island **Kız Kulesi**, just off the Asian shore near Üsküdar. Just before the first stop at Beşiktaş, you'll pass the grandiose **Dolmabahçe Palace**, built on the European shore of the Bosphorus by Sultan Abdül Mecit between 1843 and 1856. Shortly after Beşiktaş, **Çırağan Sarayı**, once home to Sultan Abdül Aziz and now a luxury hotel, looms up on the left. On the Asian shore is the **Fethi Ahmet Paşa Yalı**, built in the late 18th century. The word *yalı* comes from the Greek word for 'coast', and describes the waterside wooden summer residences along the Bosphorus built by Ottoman aristocracy and foreign ambassadors in the 17th, 18th and 19th centuries, now all protected by the country's heritage laws. This one is known as the 'pink *yalı*'. To your left a little further on is the pretty **Ortaköy Camii**, its dome and two minarets dwarfed by the adjacent **Bosphorus Bridge**, the symbol of modern İstanbul.

Beylerbeyi Sarayı

On the waterfront across the bridge is the grand **Beylerbeyi Sarayı**. Look for its whimsical marble bathing pavilions on the shore, one was for men, the other for the women of the harem.

Every sultan needed a little place to get away to, and the 30-room Beylerbeyi Sarayı was the place for Abdül Aziz (r 1861–76). An earlier wooden palace had burned down here, so Abdül Aziz wanted stone and marble.

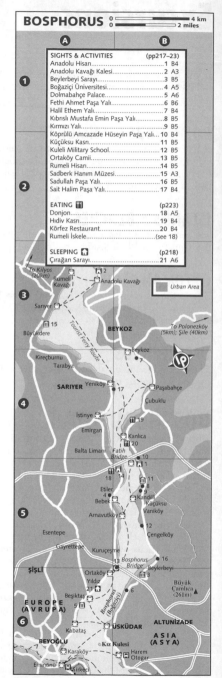

BOSPHORUS   0 ___ 4 km   0 ___ 2 miles

SIGHTS & ACTIVITIES	(pp217–23)
Anadolu Hisarı	1 B4
Anadolu Kavağı Kalesi	2 A3
Beylerbeyi Sarayı	3 B5
Boğaziçi Üniversitesi	4 A5
Dolmabahçe Palace	5 A6
Fethi Ahmet Paşa Yalı	6 B6
Halil Ethem Yalı	7 B4
Kıbrıslı Mustafa Emin Paşa Yalı	8 B5
Kırmızı Yalı	9 B5
Köprülü Amcazade Hüseyin Paşa Yalı	10 B4
Küçüksu Kasrı	11 B5
Kuleli Military School	12 B5
Ortaköy Camii	13 B5
Rumeli Hisarı	14 B5
Sadberk Hanım Müzesi	15 A3
Sadullah Paşa Yalı	16 B5
Sait Halim Paşa Yalı	17 B4

EATING	(p223)
Donjon	18 A5
Hıdiv Kasrı	19 B4
Körfez Restaurant	20 B4
Rumeli İskele	(see 18)

SLEEPING	(p218)
Çırağan Sarayı	21 A6

He ordered architect Sarkis Balyan, brother of Nikoğos, architect of Dolmabahçe, to get to work. Balyan came up with a building that delighted the many foreign dignitaries who visited, including Empress Eugénie of France; Nasruddin, shah of Persia; and Nicholas, grand duke of Russia. The palace's last imperial 'guest' was the former sultan, Abdül Hamit II, who was brought here to spend the remainder of his life (1913–18) under house arrest. He had the dubious pleasure of gazing across the Bosphorus and watching the empire he had ruled for over 30 years crumble before his eyes.

These days Beylerbeyi is musty but still impressive, particularly on sunny afternoons when light floods the rooms. A compulsory guided tour whips you past room after room of Bohemian crystal chandeliers, French (Sèvres) and Ming vases and sumptuous carpets. It's reminiscent of Dolmabahçe, though not quite as ostentatious.

Ortaköy to Bebek

Past the small village of Çengelköy on the Asian side is the imposing Kuleli Military School, built in 1860 and immortalised in Irfan Orga's wonderful memoir, *Portrait of a Turkish Family*.

Opposite Kuleli on the European shore north of Ortaköy is Arnavutköy, a village boasting a number of frilly Ottoman-era wooden houses, including numerous *yalıs*. On the hill above it are buildings formerly occupied by the American College for Girls. Its most famous alumni was Halide Edib Adıvar, who wrote about the years she spent here in her

Transport

The most popular way to explore the Bosphorus is by ferry. Most day-trippers take the Eminönü-Kavaklar Boğaziçi Özel Gezi Seferleri (Eminönü-Kavaklar Bosphorus Special Touristic Excursions) ferry up its entire length. These depart from the Boğaz Hattı dock (No 3) at Eminönü daily at 10.35am. From June to September there is an extra service at noon and from May to September there is another at 1.35pm. A ticket costs €3.60 return, €1.80 one way. The ferry stops at Beşiktaş, Kanlıca, Yeniköy, Sarıyer, Rumeli Kavağı and Anadolu Kavağı (the turnaround point). It is not possible to get on and off the ferry at stops along the way using the same ticket.

The boats fill up early in summer – especially on weekends – so buy your ticket and walk aboard at least 45 minutes (preferably an hour) prior to departure to get a seat outside or next to a window. During the trip waiters will offer you fresh orange juice, tea and other drinks. An orange juice costs €1.70, other drinks are cheaper.

Most day-trippers take the ferry all the way to Anadolu Kavağı, but some go only as far as Sarıyer, on the European shore. They then make their way back to the city on the bus, stopping at Rumeli Hisarı and perhaps at Ortaköy, Çırağan Sarayı or Dolmabahçe Palace on the return trip. From Sarıyer, bus No 25E makes the slow trip back to Eminönü, No 40 to Taksim Square and No 40B to Beşiktaş. *Dolmuşes* (shared minibuses) also ply this route. The ferry arrives at Sarıyer at 11.45am, 11.10pm (June to September) and 2.45pm (May to September).

The trip to Anadolu Kavağı takes 1¾ hours and the ferry returns at 3pm and 5pm. If you decide to catch the ferry to Anadolu Kavağı and make your way back by bus, catch the No 15A, which leaves from just east of the ferry terminal en route to Kavacik Aktarma. These depart at 12.55pm, 1.30pm, 2.50pm, 3.30pm, 4.15pm and then every hour or so until 8.30pm. The timetable is slightly different on weekends. Get off at Kanlıca and catch the No 101 bus to Beşiktaş. Alternatively, catch the infrequent Nos 15 or 15P to Üsküdar, from where you can catch a ferry to Eminönü; or catch a taxi across the Fatih Bridge to Rumeli Hisarı and catch a bus back to Eminönü, Taksim Square or Beşiktaş.

From Kanlıca it's also possible to catch a passenger ferry back to towards İstanbul. These stop at Anadolu Hisarı, Kandilli, Bebek and Arnavutköy. Departures from Kanlıca are at 8.40am, 10.10am, 1.30pm, 2.40pm, 4.10pm, 5.40pm, 5.05pm and 7pm. The trip to Bebek takes 25 minutes. These are winter times (departure times vary with the seasons).

There is also a passenger ferry service between Sarıyer and Anadolu Kavağı with 15 ferries a day from 7.15am to 10.15pm; eight of these ferries stop at Rumeli Kavağı on the way.

Yet another option is a private Bosphorus boat tour. Ticket touts are always to be found around dock No 3 at Eminönü flogging the tickets for these, which cost €10 (try bargaining). Tours are on smaller boats (60 to 100 people), each with a small sun deck. They only travel as far as Rumeli Hisarı (without stopping) where they stop for lunch for an hour before returning. The whole trip takes about three hours. The advantage of these trips is they take less time and the boat goes closer to the shore; the disadvantages are the higher price and the fact that you don't get to see the whole of the Bosphorus. These boats leave on the half-hour starting at around 10.30am and finishing at 6pm from May to September (4pm at other times).

1926 autobiographical work, *The Memoir of Halide Edib*.

Arnavutköy runs straight into the glamorous suburb of **Bebek**, famous for upmarket restaurants such as **Poseidon** and waterside cafés. Its shops surround a small park and a mosque; to the east of these is the ferry dock, to the south is the **Egyptian consulate**. The consulate is a gorgeous Art Nouveau mini-palace built by the last khedive of Egypt, Abbas Hilmi II, who also later built Hıdiv Kasrı above Kanlıca on the Asian side of the Bosphorus. You'll see its mansard roof and ornate wrought-iron fence from the ferry. Above Bebek you'll notice the New England 19th-century-style architecture of the **Boğaziçi Üniversitesi** (Bosphorus University). Founded by American missionaries in the mid-19th century as Robert College, the college had an important influence on the modernisation of political, social, economic and scientific thought in Turkey. It was donated to the Turkish Republic in the early 1970s.

Dolmabahçe Palace (p218)

Bebek to Kanlica

Opposite Bebek on the Asian shore is **Kırmızı Yalı** (Red *Yalı*), constructed in 1790 and one of the oldest still standing; a bit further on, also past the village of Kandilli, is the long, white **Kıbrıslı Mustafa Emin Paşa Yalı.**

Next to the Kıbrıslı *Yalı* are the Büyük Göksu Deresi (Great Heavenly Stream) and Küçük Göksu Deresi (Small Heavenly Stream), two brooks that descend from the Asian hills into the Bosphorus. Between them is a fertile delta, grassy and shady, which the Ottoman elite thought perfect for picnics. Foreign residents, referred to the place as 'The Sweet Waters of Asia'.

If the weather was good, the sultan joined the picnic, and did so in style. Sultan Abdül Mecit's answer to a simple picnic blanket was the wedding cake–like **Küçüksu Kasrı**, an ornate lodge built in 1856–57. Earlier sultans had wooden kiosks here, but architect Nikoğos Balyan designed a Rococo gem in marble for his monarch.

Just before the Fatih bridge are the majestic structures of **Rumeli Hisarı** (Fortress of Europe) and **Anadolu Hisarı** (Fortress of Anatolia).

Mehmet the Conqueror had Rumeli Hisarı built in a mere four months during 1452, in preparation for his siege of Byzantine Constantinople. For its location, he chose the narrowest point of the Bosphorus, opposite Anadolu Hisarı, which Sultan Beyazıt I had built in 1391. By doing so Mehmet was able to control all traffic on the strait, so cutting the city off from re-supply by sea.

To speed Rumeli Hisarı's completion (he was impatient to conquer Constantinople), Mehmet ordered each of his three viziers to take responsibility for one of the three main towers. If the tower's construction was not completed on schedule, the vizier would pay with his life. Not surprisingly, the work was completed on time. The mighty fortress' useful military life lasted less than one year. After the conquest of Constantinople, it was used as a glorified Bosphorus toll booth for a while, then as a barracks, a prison, and finally as an open-air theatre. Its amphitheatre still functions as a performance venue during the summer months, particularly during the International İstanbul Music Festival (p10).

Within Rumeli Hisarı's walls are park-like grounds, an open-air theatre and the minaret of a ruined mosque. Steep stairs (with no barriers, so beware!) lead up to the ramparts and towers; the views of the Bosphorus from here are magnificent. Just next to the fortress is a clutch of cafés and restaurants, including the hip eatery/bar, **Donjon**, and the long-standing favourite **Rumeli İskele**.

Though not open as a museum, visitors are free to wander about Anadolu Hisarı's ruined walls.

Just past Anadolu Hisarı (almost directly under the Fatih Bridge) is **Köprülü Amcazade Hüseyin Paşa Yalı**, built right on the water in 1698. It is the oldest on the Bosphorus and is in a deplorable state of repair.

Past the bridge, still on the Asian side, is the charming village of **Kanlıca**, famous for its rich and delicious yoghurt. You'll be offered some on the ferry and can sample it in the **Asırlık Kanlıca Yoğurdu** on the shady waterfront village square. The small **Gâzi İskender Paşa Camii** in the square dates from 1560 and was designed by Sinan.

Kanlıca to İstinye

One of İstanbul's most famous seafood restaurants, **Körfez**, is on Kanlıca's outskirts, almost directly under the bridge. This is the perfect place to spend a weekend afternoon, eating lunch on its outdoor terrace while watching the ferries and boats sail past. Just near Körfez is the late 19th century **Ethem Pertev Yalı**, with its boathouse and ornate wooden decoration.

High on a promontory above Kanlıca is **Hıdiv Kasrı**, a grand Art Nouveau villa built by the last khedive of Egypt as a summer residence for use during his family's annual visits to İstanbul.

Having ruled Egypt for centuries, in 1805 the Ottomans lost control to an adventurer named Muhammed Ali (also known as Mehmet Ali), who defied the sultan in İstanbul to dislodge him. The sultan, unable to do so, gave him quasi-independence and had to be satisfied with reigning over Egypt rather than ruling. This was left to Muhammed Ali and his line, and the ruler of Egypt was styled *hıdiv*, 'khedive' (not 'king', as that would be unbearably independent). The khedives of Egypt kept up the pretence of Ottoman suzerainty by paying tribute to İstanbul.

The Egyptian royal family, which looked upon itself as Turkish, often spent its summers in a traditional *yalı* on the Bosphorus shore at Bebek (now the Egyptian consulate). In 1906, Khedive Abbas Hilmi II built himself this palatial villa on the most dramatic promontory on the Bosphorus. In the 1930s it became the property of the municipality.

Restored after decades of neglect, the Hıdiv Kasrı now functions as a restaurant and garden café, much to the delight of İstanbullus and tourists alike. The villa is a gem and the view from the extensive and lovely garden is superb.

On the opposite shore is the wealthy suburb of **Emirgan**. In late April to early May, Emirgan Park, just above the town, is decked out in tulips. North of Emirgan, there's a ferry dock near the small yacht-lined cove of **İstinye**.

İstinye to Sarıyer

Just north of İstinye, **Yeniköy** is on a point jutting out from the European shore. It was first settled in classical times and later became a favourite summer resort, as indicated by the lavish 19th-century Ottoman *yalı* of the one-time grand vizier, Sait Halim Paşa. Look for its two small stone lions on the quay. On the opposite shore is the village of **Paşabahçe**, famous for its glassware factory. A bit further on is the fishing village of **Beykoz**, which has a graceful ablutions fountain **İshak Ağa Çeşmesi**, dating from 1746, near the village square, as well as several fish restaurants. Much of the land along the Bosphorus shore north of Beykoz is a military zone.

Originally called Therapeia for its healthy climate, the little cove of **Tarabya** on the European shore has been a favourite summer watering place for İstanbul's well-to-do for centuries, though contemporary development has poisoned some of its charm.

North of the village are some of the old summer embassies of foreign powers. When the heat and fear of disease increased in the warm months, foreign ambassadors would retire to palatial residences, complete with lush gardens, on this shore. The region for such embassy residences extended north to the village of **Büyükdere**, notable for its churches, summer embassies and the **Sadberk Hanım Müzesi**.

Named after the wife of the late Vehbi Koç, founder of Turkey's foremost commercial empire in 1926, the museum is her private collection of Anatolian antiquities and

Ottoman heirlooms. Labels are in English and Turkish.

The original museum building is a graceful old *yalı*, once the summer residence of Manuk Azaryan Efendi, an Armenian who was speaker of the Ottoman parliament. It houses artefacts and exhibits such as worry beads of solid gold; bejewelled tobacco boxes and watches (one bears the sultan's monogram in diamonds); beautiful İznik and Kütahya pottery; and even a table that once belonged to Napoleon. A number of rooms in the great old house have been arranged and decorated in Ottoman style.

The collections in the new building, which is beside the original *yalı*, include artefacts dating from the 6th century BC, and from Roman and Byzantine times. There's also a well-chosen collection of Chinese celadon ware from the 14th to 16th centuries, later Chinese blue-and-white porcelain and some 18th-century Chinese porcelain made specifically for the Ottoman market.

A Day on the Bosphorus

If you only have one day to explore the Bosphorus, think about following one of these itineraries:

Catch the 10.35am Bosphorus excursions ferry to Anadolu Kavağı. After exploring this small fishing village and the ruined castle on the hill above it, take the No 15A bus down to Kanlıca. Enjoy lunch at Hıdiv Kasrı or Körfez restaurants and then take the 2.40pm ferry to Bebek, from where you can catch a bus or taxi to Rumeli Hisarı, the fortress of Europe. After clamouring over the ramparts, take a bus from outside the nearby restaurants back to town.

Another possibility is to take the 10.35am ferry as far as Sarıyer, wander around the town and visit the Sadberk Hanım Müzesi. After this, catch the No 25E, 40 or 40B bus to Rumeli Hisarı and have lunch at Donjon or Rumeli İskele restaurants. After lunch explore the fortress and then catch a bus back to town, perhaps stopping at Ortaköy on the way.

The residents of **Sarıyer**, the next village up from Büyükdere on the European shore, have occupied themselves for most of their history by fishing. This is still a pastime and the main livelihood here, and Sarıyer is justly noted for its good fish restaurants. It's a busy place. Turn right as you leave the ferry dock, stay as close to the shore as possible, and you will pass the seabus terminal and several fish restaurants before coming to the **Tarihi Balıkçılar Çarşısı**, the village's historic fish market.

Sarıyer to Anadolu Kavağı

The ferry's second-last stop is **Rumeli Kavağı**, a sleepy place that only gets excited with the arrival and departure of the ferry. A public beach named **Altınkum**, near the village, has a small restaurant serving meze and beer, but not much else. To the south of the town is the shrine of the Moslem saint Telli Baba, reputed to be able to find suitable husbands for young women who pray there.

Anadolu Kavağı is where the Bosphorus excursions ferry finishes its journey. It's a pleasant spot in which to wander and have a seafood lunch. The two best restaurants are probably **Kavak & Doğanay Restaurant** and **Yedigül Restaurant**, both of which are located on the square in front of the ferry terminal.

Perched above the village are the ruins of **Anadolu Kavağı Kalesi**, a medieval castle that originally had eight massive towers in its walls. First built by the Byzantines, it was restored and reinforced by the Genoese in 1350, and later by the Ottomans. Two more fortresses built by Sultan Murat IV in the 17th century are north of here. It will take you 30 to 50 minutes to walk up to the fortress from the town. Alternatively, taxis wait near the fountain in the town square just east of the ferry dock; they charge €5.60 for the return trip with 30 minutes waiting time. Whichever way you get there, it's worth the effort for the spectacular Black Sea views. Unfortunately, the site is strewn with litter discarded by picnickers.

Sights

Beylerbeyi Sarayı (Map p218; ☎ 216-321 9320; Abdullah Ağa Caddesi, Beylerbeyi; adult/student €3.30/1.70; ☯ 9.30am-4pm Tue, Wed & Fri-Sun) This palace is a few kilometres north of Üsküdar. Catch bus No 15A or a *dolmuş* north along the shore road from Üsküdar's main square, and get out at the Çayırbaşı stop, just north of Beylerbeyi and the Asian pylons of the Bosphorus Bridge.

Hıdiv Kasrı (Map p218; Khedive's Villa; ☎ 216-413 9644; Çubuklu Yolu 32, Kanlıca; admission free, parking €1.40; ☯ 8am-11pm) The villa is a few minutes by taxi (€2) uphill from Kanlıca or a 20-minute walk. To walk, go north from Kanlıca's main square and mosque and turn right at the first street (Kafadar Sokak), which winds up towards the villa car park. Turn left at Dere Sokak and shortly you'll come to a fork in the road. Take the left fork and walk up past Kanlıca Hekimler Sitesi on the corner. You'll soon see the villa's car park and extensive wooded garden.

Küçüksu Kasrı (Map p218; ☎ 216-332 3303; Küçüksu Caddesi; admission €3.30; ☼ 9.30am-5pm Tue, Wed & Fri-Sun Apr-Oct; 9.30am-4pm Tue, Wed & Fri-Sun Nov-Mar) Take bus No 15A or a *dolmuş* along the shore road north from Beylerbeyi and Üsküdar to reach the Küçüksu Kasrı bus stop, then walk the 300m to the shore and the pavilion.

Rumeli Hisarı (Map p218; ☎ 212-263 5305; Yahya Kemal Caddesi 42, Rumeli Hisarı; admission €2.20; ☼ 8.30am-noon & 12.30-5pm Thu-Tue) Catch bus No 25E, 40, 40B or 42 from Beşiktaş or Yeniköy and get off at the stop in front of the cafés next to the fortress.

Sadberk Hanım Müzesi (Map p218; Sadberk Hanım Museum; ☎ 212-242 3813; Büyükdere Caddesi 27-9, Sarıyer; admission €1.70; ☼ 10.30am-6pm Thu-Tue Apr-Sep, 10am-5pm Thu-Tue Oct-Mar) Walk south from the ferry docks in Sarıyer for approximately 15 minutes.

Eating

Asırlık Kanlıca Yoğurdu (İskele Square, Kalıca; yogurt with honey €1.50, tea €1; ☼ 9am-midnight) This simple café on the water next to the ferry terminal is the best place to sample the stuff that has made Kanlıca famous.

Donjon (Map p218; ☎ 212-287 2910; Yahya Kemal Caddesi 40, Rumeli Hisarı; beer €3, espresso €2.50, pasta €6; ☼ 8am-4am) Hip young things loll on the beanbags downstairs and listen to the in-house DJ spin his stuff; others

seek out the pleasant roof balcony and terraces with views over the Bosphorus. It's the second café from the fortress.

Hıdiv Kasrı (Map p218; ☎ 216-320 2036; sandwiches €1.70-3, cakes €1-2, grills €8; ☼ 8am-11pm) Choose from the simple menu at the charming café next to the rose garden or the more extensive choice in the grand dining room and adjoining marble terrace. The food is average but the surroundings are drop-dead gorgeous. No alcohol is served.

Kavak & Doğanay Restaurant (☎ 216-320 2036; Yalı Caddesi 13, Anadolu Kavağı; meze €2-4.50, fish €5.50-14; ☼ 11am-midnight) Right on the water, the outdoor terrace is a pleasant place to enjoy basic but fresh dishes with a glass of wine or beer.

Körfez Restaurant (Map p218; ☎ 216-413 4314; Körfez Caddesi 78, Kanlıca; mains €16-44; ☼ 11am-4pm Tue-Sun, 6pm-midnight daily) Famous for its sea bass baked in salt, Körfez is the perfect place for a special meal in İstanbul. To make it even more special, organise for the restaurant's own motor launch to pick you up from Rumeli Hisarı across the strait and drop you back after your meal. Book ahead.

Poseidon (☎ 212-263 3823; Cavdat Paşa Caddesi 58, Bebek; mains €10-18; ☼ noon-1am) Super stylish seafood restaurant with fabulous outdoor terrace on the water.

Rumeli İskele (Map p218; ☎ 212-263 2997; Yahya Kemal Caddesi 1, Rumeli Hisarı; meze €2-5, mains €5-42; ☼ noon-1am) The location is as good as the food at this long-standing favourite. It's next to the bus stop.

Yedigül Restaurant (☎ 216-320 2180; İskele Square 4, Anadolu Kavağı; meze €2-4.50, fish €5.50-14; ☼ 9am-midnight) The view from the upstairs dining room of this waterside eatery is pleasant and the service is excellent.

PRINCES' ISLANDS

Most İstanbullus refer to the Princes' Islands (Kızıl Adalar or 'Red Islands') as 'The Islands' (Adalar), as they are the only islands around the city. They lie about 20km southeast of the city in the Sea of Marmara, and make a great destination for a day escape from the city.

In Byzantine times, refractory princes, deposed monarchs and troublesome associates were interned here in convents and monasteries, hence the name the 'Princes' Islands'. A ferry service from İstanbul was started in the mid-19th century and the islands became popular summer resorts with Pera's Greek, Jewish and Armenian communities. Many of the fine Victorian villas built by these wealthy merchants survive, and make the larger islands, Büyükada and Heybeliada, charming places to explore.

Only a few minutes after landing, you'll realise the Islands' surprise: there are no cars! Except for the necessary police, fire and sanitation vehicles, transportation is by bicycle, horse-drawn carriage and foot, as in centuries past. After the hustle and bustle of İstanbul, this comes as a very pleasant change indeed.

All of the islands are busy in summer, particularly weekends. For that reason, avoid a Sunday visit. If you wish to stay overnight during the summer months, book ahead. Many hotels are closed during winter. There are nine islands in the Princes' Islands group; five are populated. The ferry stops at four of these; the fifth, Sedef, has only recently attracted a resident population. Year-round there are 20,000 permanent residents scattered across the five, but numbers swell to 120,000 during summer when İstanbullus – many of whom have holiday homes on the islands – escape the city heat. The small islands of Kınalıada and Burgazada are the ferry's first stops. **Kınalıada**, which is a favourite holiday spot for İstanbul's Armenian population, is sprinkled with white houses, all sporting red-tiled roofs and oriented towards the water. Ugly communications towers mar the rest of the landscape. The island has a few pebble beaches, a modernist mosque and an Armenian church to the left of the ferry station.

Burgazada has always been favoured by İstanbullus of Greek heritage. It is green and has heavily cultivated hills. Sights include a church, mosques, a synagogue, and the home of the late writer Sait Faik, now a museum. On the island's western shore, a 20-minute walk from the ferry station, is an unpretentious restaurant and a swimming spot. Frankly, neither island offers much reward for the trouble of getting off the ferry

In contrast, the charming island of **Heybeliada** (Heybeli for short) has much to offer the visitor. Home to the Turkish Naval Academy (you'll see it to the left of the ferry dock), it has a number of restaurants and a thriving shopping strip with bakeries and delicatessens selling picnic provisions to day-trippers, who come here on weekends to walk in the pine groves and swim from the tiny (but crowded) beaches. The island's major landmark is the hilltop **Haghia Triada Monastery.** Perched above a picturesque line of poplar trees, the monastery functioned as a Greek Orthodox theological school until the 1970s, when it was closed on the government's orders. There are strong signs that it may re-open soon.

Heybeliada has a couple of hotels, including the comfortable **Merit Halki Palace**, perched at the top of Rafah Şehitleri Caddesi with wonderful water views. The delightful walk up to this hotel passes a few antique shops and a host of large wooden villas set in lovingly tended gardens. Many laneways and streets leading to picnic spots, and lookout points are located off the upper reaches of this street. To find the hotel, turn right as you leave the ferry and head past the waterfront restaurants and cafés to the plaza with a central newsstand. From here walk up İsgüzar Sokak, veering right until you hit Rafah Şehitleri Caddesi. If you don't feel like walking up to the hotel (it's uphill, but not too steep), you can hire a bicycle from one of the shops in the main street (€1.40 per hour) or a *fayton* (horse-drawn carriage) to take you around the island. A 25-minute tour *(küçük tur)* costs €8.30 and a one-hour tour *(büyük tur)* costs €11.07. Some visitors spend the day by the pool at the Merit Halki Palace, which is a good idea, as the waters around the island aren't clean. Towels and chaise longues are supplied, and there's a pleasant terrace restaurant for meals or drinks. The charge for non-guests to use the pool is €13.90 on weekdays and €19.40 on weekends.

The largest island in the group, **Büyükada** (Great Island) shows is impressive from the ferry, with gingerbread villas climbing up the slopes of the hill and the bulbous twin cupolas of the Splendid Otel providing an unmistakable landmark. It's a lovely spot to spend an afternoon, though perhaps not quite as pretty as Heybeliada.

Transport

At least nine ferries run to the islands each day from 7am to 11pm, departing from Sirkeci's 'Adalar İskelesi' dock, east of the dock for car ferries to Harem. The most useful departure times for day-trippers are 9am, 10.30am and noon. On summer weekends, board the vessel and grab a seat at least half an hour before departure time unless you want to stand the whole way. The trip costs €1.20 to the islands and the same for each leg between the islands and the return trip. The cheapest and easiest way to pay is to use your Akbil.

You can also take a fast catamaran from Eminönü or Kabataş to Bostancı on the Asian shore, then another from Bostancı to Heybeliada and Büyükada, but you save little time, and the cost is much higher. These leave Bostancı twice a day, at 7.20am and 5.20pm, returning from Büyükada at 8.25am and 6.30pm.

The ferry steams away from Sirkeci, out of the Golden Horn (Haliç) and around Seraglio Point (Saray Burnu), offering fine views of Topkapı Palace (Topkapı Sarayı), Aya Sofya and the Blue Mosque (Sultan Ahmet Camii) on the right, and Üsküdar and Haydarpaşa on the left. After 25 minutes the ferry makes a quick stop at Kadıköy on the Asian side before making its way to the first island, Kınalıada. This leg takes 30 minutes. After this, it's another 15 minutes to Burgazada; another 15 minutes again to Heybeliada, the second-largest island; and another 10 minutes to Büyükada, the largest island in the group.

Most day-trippers stay on the ferry until Heybeliada, stop there for an hour or so and then hop on another ferry to Büyükada, where they have lunch and spend the rest of the afternoon. On the trip back to Eminönü it's often possible to spot dolphins in the Sea of Marmara from the left-hand side of the ferry when approaching Seraglio Point.

The **ferry terminal** is a lovely building in the Ottoman kiosk style. Inside there's a pleasant tile-decorated café with an outdoor terrace, as well as a Tourist Information Office. Eateries serve fresh fish to the left of the ferry terminal, next to an ATM. These places are all of a similar standard, though the **Kalamar** and **Alibaba Restaurants** pull most of the crowds, largely because they employ touts at the ferry terminal at Eminönü.

The island's drawcard is the Greek **Monastery of St George**, in the 'saddle' between Büyükada's two highest hills. To get there, walk from the ferry straight ahead to the clock tower in İskele Square (Dock Square). The shopping district is left along Recep Koç Sokak. Bear right onto 23 Nisan Caddesi, then head along Kadıyoran Caddesi up the hill to the monastery. The walk (at least 50 minutes) takes you past a long progression of impressive wooden villas set in gardens. About halfway up on the left is the **Büyükada Kültür Evi**, a charming spot to enjoy a

Ferry to Princes' Islands (p224)

tea or coffee in the garden. After 30 minutes or so you will reach a reserve called 'Luna Park' by the locals. The monastery is a 20-minute walk up an extremely steep hill from here. Some visitors hire a donkey to take them up the hill and back for €5.60. As you ascend, you'll see countless pieces of cloth tied to the branches of trees along the path – each represents a prayer, most made by female supplicants visiting the monastery to pray for a child.

There's not a lot to see at the monastery. A small and gaudy church is the only building of note, but there are fabulous panoramic views from the terrace, as well as a small **restaurant** with outdoor seating. It's possible to see all the way to İstanbul and the nearby islands of Yassıada and Sivriada.

Bicycles are available for rent in several of the town's shops, and shops on the market street can provide picnic supplies, though food is cheaper on the mainland. Just off the clock tower square there is a *fayton* stand. Hire one for a long tour of the town, hills and shore (one hour, €13) or a shorter tour of the town (€10). It costs €5.60 to be taken to Luna Park. A shop just near the *fayton* stand hires out bicycles for €1.10 per hour.

Information

Tourist Information Office (Ferry Terminal, Büyükada; ☉ 10am-4pm) Staffed by volunteers, this office offers advice, but no maps or brochures.

Sleeping

Halki Prenset Pansiyon (☎ 216-351 0039; www .halkiprenset.com in Turkish; Ayyıldız Caddesi 40-2, Heybeliada; r €50) A friendly but shabby place that is a bit overpriced for what it offers, probably because there's only one other hotel in town.

Hotel Princess Büyükada (☎ 216-382 1628; fax 216-382 1949; İskele Square 2, Büyükada; s/d €42/58) This hotel is right on the clock tower square, so can be noisy if you want. Rooms are large but characterless, with uncomfortable beds. Sea-view rooms are 40% more expensive.

Merit Halki Palace (☎ 216-351 0025; www.merithotels .com; Refah Şehitleri Caddesi 94, Heybeliada; s/d €74/91) This comfortable hotel is the perfect place for a weekend break. Sea-view rooms cost €16.60 extra. The pool area is particularly impressive.

Splendid Otel (☎ 216-382 6950; www.splendidhotel .net; Nisan Caddesi 23, Büyükada; s/d €50/66) This landmark building is indeed splendid. Rooms aren't quite as impressive as the exterior, but are comfortable enough. Front ones have small balconies and sea views. There's a pool and a restaurant.

Eating

Alibaba Restaurant (☎ 216-382 3733; Gülistan Caddesi 20, Büyükada; meze €2.20, fish €8-25; ☉ noon-11pm) One of the many licensed waterside restaurants next to the ferry terminal.

Kalamar Restaurant (☎ 216-382 1245; Gülistan Caddesi 16, Büyükada; meze €2.20, fish €8-25; ☺ noon-11pm) Next to Alibaba, this place is almost a carbon copy.

Merit Halki Palace (☎ 216-351 0025; Refah Şehitleri Caddesi 94, Heybeliada; mains €17, beer €2.80) This hotel restaurant serves meals and drinks on its poolside terrace.

Monastery of St George Restaurant (Büyükada; meze €1.30, grills €1.90, beer €1.70; ☺ noon-9pm) Simple but appetising food served at outdoor tables.

BLACK SEA BEACHES

KİLYOS

İstanbul's coastal resort of Kilyos is a former Greek fishing village now popular with İstanbullus for swimming in the chilly waters of the Black Sea. Unfortunately, the beach, though sandy, is grubby and the place is being built up to such an extent that it holds few reminders of its former village charm. It's crowded on summer weekends.

Dolmuşes and buses from Sarıyer make the trip over the hills to Kilyos in about 20 minutes, passing small open-air roadside restaurants featuring *kuzu çevirme* (spit-roasted lamb) and clusters of Lego-like holiday homes.

Transport

Heading to Kilyos, 10km north of İstanbul, *dolmuşes* and the İETT bus No 151 leave Sarıyer from a stop about 1km inland from the seabus stop. To find it, head inland along Sular Caddesi for about 700m until you come to the *belediye* (town hall). Turn right into Eski Kilyos Caddesi soon after the *belediye* and you'll see the Kilyos bus stand 100m or so ahead. The bus to Kilyos takes about 20 minutes. It leaves Sarıyer every 30 minutes from 6am (every hour after 2pm). The last return bus departs Kilyos at 10.30pm.

ŞİLE & AĞVA

Şile, a small fishing town 72km northeast of Üsküdar on the Black Sea coast, has long sand beaches and a fairly laid-back atmosphere – on weekdays at least. Visitors enjoy wandering around the remains of a Genoese castle on an island off the beach, swimming and enjoying fish lunches.

Known as Kalpe in classical times, Şile was a port of call for ships sailing east from the Bosphorus. It was visited by Xenophon and his Ten Thousand on their way back to Greece from their disastrous campaign in Persia in the 4th century BC. Unable to find ships to sail them to Greece, Xenophon and his men marched to Chrysopolis (Üsküdar) along the route now followed by the modern road.

Şile's other claim to fame is *Şile bezi*, an open-weave cotton cloth with hand embroidery, usually made into shirts and skirts that are cool in the summer heat.

Ağva, 50km further along the coast, isn't as crowded or developed as Şile. Here the Göksu and Yeşilçay Creeks flow into the sea and visitors relax in gardens and hammocks along their banks. Canoes and boats of all descriptions can be hired to explore the creeks, and nearby trekking trails lead to waterfalls and caves. Five hundred metres outside town there is a long sand beach.

Transport

A bus departs from Doğancilar Caddesi in Üsküdar (right from the ferry terminal and across the road) on the hour from 9am to 4pm for the 70-minute journey to Şile, continuing on the hour-long trip to Ağva. The last bus leaves Ağva for Üsküdar via Şile at 6pm. In winter it leaves earlier.

EDİRNE

Edirne, 235km (2½ hours) northwest of İstanbul, is known for its mosques and oil-wrestling festival. Statues of oil wrestlers grace many of its public squares, only outnumbered by the minarets of grand Ottoman mosques. It's an odd but potent combination. Recently, locals were horrified when the truth behind the growing international recognition of the town's headline event – the **Kırkpınar oil wrestling festival** – became clear. Conservative Muslims that they are, the realisation that the festival had become a leading event on the gay travelling circuit nearly caused the town's musclemen to surrender their wrestling leathers en masse. Tradition won out, though, and the festival, which is held around July each year, continues.

Edirne has a rich history. The Roman emperor Hadrian founded it in the 2nd century as Hadrianopolis. The town's name was later shortened by Europeans to Adrianople, and later by the Turks to Edirne.

By the 1300s the fledgling Ottoman empire expanded from its heartland in northwest Anatolia looking for conquests. The mighty walls of Constantinople were beyond its power, but the Ottomans crossed the Dardanelles and captured Adrianople in 1362, making it their capital. For almost 100 years, this was the city from which the Ottoman sultan set out on his campaigns to Europe and Asia. When the time was ripe for the final conquest of the Byzantine Empire, Mehmet the Conqueror rode from Edirne on the Via Ignatia to Constantinople.

Those interested in the Ottomans and their buildings – mosques, bridges, bazaars, caravansaries and *hamams* – will find a visit here extremely rewarding. Others should probably give it a miss.

Edirne's **Kaleiçi** (Old Town) retains its original medieval plan, which had streets laid out on a grid. Walk south along Maarif Caddesi to pass some fine old **Ottoman wooden houses**, designed in an ornate style known as Edirnekâri. At the southern end of Maarif Caddesi you will come to what's left of Edirne's **Great Synagogue**. There are other fine houses along Cumhuriyet Caddesi, which crosses Maarif Caddesi north of the synagogue. Fragments of **Byzantine city walls** are still visible on the edges of Kaleiçi, down by the Tunca River. If you follow Saraçlar Caddesi south and out of town across the river, you'll find a swathe of pleasant **çay bahçesi** (tea gardens) and **restaurants** between and beyond two attractive **Ottoman bridges**.

The jewels of the city are its magnificent Ottoman mosques. These include the **Üçşerefeli Camii**, which owes its name to its 'three galleries' or balconies on one of the mosque's four quite different minarets. The Üçşerefeli's design shows the transition from the Seljuk-style mosques of Konya and Bursa to a truly Ottoman style, which would be perfected by architects such as Mimar Sinan later in İstanbul. The courtyard, with its central *şadırvan* (ablutions fountain), was an innovation that became standard in the great Ottoman mosques. Across the street from the mosque is the still-functioning **Sokollu Mehmet Paşa Hamamı**, built in the late 1500s and designed by Sinan. Despite its pleasant proportions, the *hamam* is a minor work compared with his masterpiece, the nearby **Selimiye Camii**. Considered the most architecturally significant Ottoman mosque in the country, the Selimiye was constructed for Sultan Selim II between 1569 and 1575, and is similar to Sinan's earlier (1557) Süleymaniye Camii in İstanbul. It crowns its small hill and is easily visible from across the rolling

Transport

From İstanbul, the quickest way to get to Edirne is to take a bus from the *otogar*. Express buses depart for Edirne from the Volkan Turizm office at 7am, 8.15am, 9.15am and then every hour until 11pm. Radar Turizm buses follow a similar timetable. The journey takes around 2.5 hours and tickets on both bus lines cost €6.70 one way. The buses terminate at Edirne's *yeni otogar* (new bus station), which is approximately 8km out of town. If you haven't already purchased a return ticket, do so when you arrive here, as the buses back to İstanbul fill up fast. And make sure that the service is express, or else you'll be in for a long return trip. From the Edirne *otogar*, there's a free shuttle bus into the centre of town. Ask the bus driver to drop you outside the Eski Camii, near Hürriyet Meydanı (Freedom Square). Leaving Edirne, catch the shuttle bus from the bus stop along Mimar Sinan Caddesi. You'll need to show your return ticket, and you should make sure that you allow at least 30 minutes to get back to the *otogar*. Buses to İstanbul leave the *otogar* at 5.15pm, 6.15pm and then every hour until 10.30pm.

Trains between Edirne and İstanbul are slow and inconvenient. The bus is a much better option.

EDİRNE

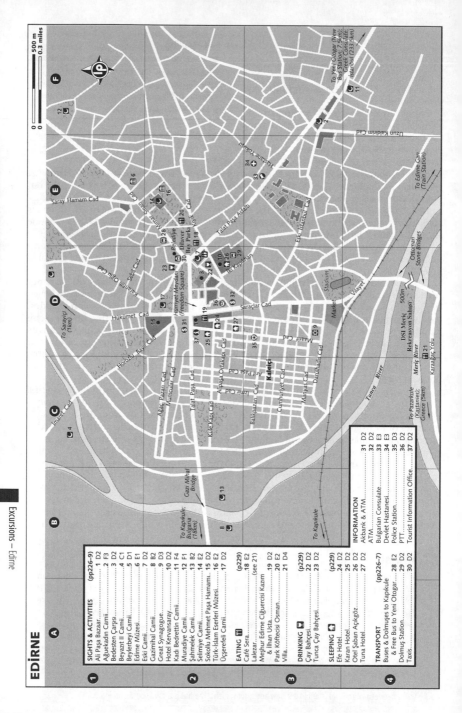

SIGHTS & ACTIVITIES (pp226–9)
Ali Paşa Bazaar..................................1 D2
Ağuekadin Camii...............................2 F3
Bedesten Çarşısı...............................3 D2
Beyazıt II Camii.................................4 C1
Beylerbeyi Camii...............................5 D1
Edirne Müzesi....................................6 E1
Eski Camii...7 D2
Gaziminal Camii................................8 B2
Great Synagogue...............................9 D3
Hotel Kervansaray.............................10 D2
Kadi Bedrettin Camii..........................11 F4
Muradiye Camii.................................12 F1
Şahmelek Camii................................13 B2
Selimiye Camii...................................14 E2
Sokollu Mehmet Paşa Hamamı........15 D2
Türk-Islam Eserleri Müzesi.................16 E2
Üçşereteli Camii.................................17 D2

EATING 🍴 (p229)
Café Sera...18 E2
Lalezar...(see 21)
Meşhur Edirne Ciğurcisi Kazim
 & İlhan Usta......................................19 D2
Park Köftecisi Osman..........................20 E2
Villa...21 D4

DRINKING ▶ (p229)
Çay Bahçesi..22 D2
Tunca Çay Bahçesi..............................23 D2

SLEEPING 🛏 (p229)
Efe Hotel..24 D2
Karan Hotel..25 D2
Otel Şaban Açıkgöz............................26 D2
Tuna Hotel...27 D2

TRANSPORT (pp226–7)
Buses & Dolmuşes to Kapikule
 & Free Bus to Yeni Otogar...............28 E2
Dolmuş Station...................................29 D2
Taxis..30 D2

INFORMATION
Akbank & ATM....................................31 D2
ATM..32 D2
Bulgarian Consulate............................33 E3
Devlet Hastanesi.................................34 E3
Police Station......................................35 D3
PTT...36 D2
Tourist Information Office....................37 D2

Thracian landscape. To fully appreciate it, enter from the west, as the architect intended. Walk up the street and through the courtyard rather than through the park and the *arasta* (shops), an obtrusive later addition made during the reign of Murat III. The serenity of the interior is quite remarkable.

The Selimiye's *medrese* now houses the **Türk-İslam Eserleri Müzesi** (Turkish & Islamic Arts Museum), an eclectic (dare we say eccentric?) collection of knitted socks, armour and hand embroidery. The most interesting exhibit is the room devoted to oil wrestling: here you'll see photographs of champions since 1924 (the year of the first festival), most of whom are sporting moustaches nearly as impressive as their muscles.

The **Eski Camii** (Old Mosque), built in 1414, has rows of arches and pillars supporting a series of small domes. Inside, there's a marvellous mihrab. Huge calligraphic inscriptions adorn the walls inside and out. Look out for the Roman columns at the front of the mosque; incorporating architectural remnants was a common practice over the centuries.

Near the Eski Camii is the *bedesten* (covered market). Dating from 1418, it's now known as the **Bedesten Çarşısı**, or Bedesten Bazaar, and is still filled with shops selling homewares and clothing. Nearby is the **Ali Paşa Bazaar**, designed by Sinan in 1569. Opposite is the **Hotel Kervansaray**, a restored Ottoman han that now functions as a sleazy and overpriced hotel.

The **Edirne Müzesi** (Archaeological & Ethnological Museum) behind the Selimiye Camii has a small collection, including some impressive textiles and costumes and three slightly naff ethnographic displays.

Other mosques of note in town include the **Muradiye Camii**, built on the orders of Sultan Murat II and completed in 1436, and the **Beyazit II Camii**, which has an intact *külliye* (mosque complex) built from 1484 to 1488. Buildings include a *tabhane* (hostel for travellers), *medrese*, bakery, *imaret* (soup kitchen), *tımarhane* (asylum) and *darüşşifa* (hospital).

Information

Tourist Information Office (Map p228; ☎ /fax 284-213 0208; Talat Paşa Caddesi; ⏱ 8.30am-7pm Mon-Fri summer 8.30am-5.30pm Mon-Fri winter) Advice and brochures are available. Unfortunately, it doesn't supply maps of the town.

Sights

Türk İslam Eserleri Müzesi (Map p228; Turkish & Islamic Arts Museum; ☎ 284-225 1120; Mimar Sinan Caddesi; admission €1.10; ⏱ 8.30am-noon & 1-5.30pm Tue-Sun)

Edirne Müzesi (Map p228; Archaeological & Ethnological Museum; Kad Pa Mek Sokak; admission €1.10; ⏱ 8.30am-noon & 1-5.30pm Tue-Sun)

Sleeping

Otel Şaban Açıkgöz (Map p228; ☎ 284-213 0313; www .acikgoz.com in Turkish; Tahmis Meydanı 9; s/d €20/34) Basic but comfortable rooms with friendly management. Ask for a front room, as these are larger and lighter.

Tuna Hotel (Map p228; ☎ 284-214 3340; fax 284-214 3323; Maarif Caddesi 17; s/d €17/25) Only a few years old, this clean and comfortable place is a bargain at these prices.

Efe Hotel (Map p228; ☎ 284-213 6080; www.efehotel .com in Turkish; Maarif Caddesi 13; s/d €30/40) The 'olde English manor' touches (including an English pub) are odd, but the Efe's rooms are reasonably comfortable. Ask for one of the rooms at the front – those at the back are dark.

Karan Hotel (Map p228; ☎ 284-225 1555; fax 284-225 1556; Maarif Caddesi, Garanti Bankası Sokak 6; s/d €31/42) In a restored Ottoman house, the Karan offers large rooms and a friendly atmosphere. Breakfast is served in the sunny courtyard or hotel restaurant.

Eating

Edirne has many small eateries, especially simple *köftecis* (serving grilled lamb meatballs) and *ciğercis* (serving fried liver). There are also a number of pleasant *çay bahçesis* in the centre of town.

Café Sera (Talat Paşa Caddesi) Located in the park opposite the Eski Camii. A great place to sit and people-watch; it also has a small children's playground. Unfortunately, the service was the worst we've encountered in Turkey.

Meşhur Edirne Ciğercisi Kazım & İlhan Usta (Map p228; ☎ 284-212 1280; tava ciğeri €2.20) If you're game to try some fried liver, this is the best place to do it. You'll find this place at the southeast side of the Ali Paşa Bazaar on the opposite side of the street.

Park Köftecisi Osman (Map p228; ☎ 284-7725; köfte €2.20) This establishment has built a reputation for serving the best *köfte* (meatballs) in town. You'll find it behind Café Sera in a street on the eastern boundary of the park.

For atmosphere and views, the eateries out by the Meriç River, south of the town, are your best bets. The most popular of these are **Villa** and **Lalezar**.

GALLIPOLI & TROY

Few places resonate with history as strongly as Troy and Gallipoli. Both are the locations of great battles and have been the subjects of major works of literature, countless school history texts and Hollywood feature films both good and bad (Brad Pitt as Achilles just didn't do it for us we're afraid). Together, they make a trip to the Dardanelles from İstanbul an enticing prospect. As they are a six-hour drive away, it's best to allow two days for your visit, and stay overnight in the small university town of **Çanakkale**, on the Dardanelles. It was here that Leander swam across what was then called the Hellespont to his lover Hero, and here too that Lord Byron emulated the feat in 1810. The town of Eceabat, though closer to the battlefields, is nowhere near as pleasant.

GALLIPOLI

The slender peninsula that forms the northwestern side of the Dardanelles (Çanakkale Boğazı), across the water from the town of Çanakkale, is called Gallipoli (Gelibolu in Turkish). For a millennium it has been the key to İstanbul – the navy that could force the straits had a good chance of capturing the capital of the eastern European world. Many fleets have tried to do so. Most, including the mighty Allied fleet mustered in WW1, have failed. Today, the Gallipoli battlefields are peaceful places covered in scrubby brush, pine forests and fields. But the battles fought here nearly a century ago still live in the memories of many people, both Turkish and foreign, and the annual pilgrimage that Australians and New Zealanders make here on Anzac Day (25 April) has become one of the major events on the Turkish tourism calendar.

Most people know the tragic story of the Gallipoli offensive. With the intention of capturing the Ottoman capital and the road to Eastern Europe during WWI, Winston Churchill, British First Lord of the Admiralty, organised a naval assault on the Dardanelles. A strong Franco-British fleet tried first to force them in March 1915 but failed. Then, in April, British, Australian, New Zealand and Indian troops were landed on Gallipoli, and French troops near Çanakkale. Both Turkish and Allied troops fought desperately and fearlessly. After months of ferocious combat with little progress, the Allied forces were withdrawn.

The Turkish success at Gallipoli was partly due to bad luck and bad leadership on the Allied side, and partly due to the timely provision of reinforcements aiding the Turkish side under the command of General Liman von Sanders. But a crucial element in the defeat was that the Allied troops landed in a sector where they faced Lieutenant-Colonel Mustafa Kemal (Atatürk).

At this time Atatürk was a relatively minor officer, but he had General von Sanders' confidence. He guessed the Allied battle plan correctly when his commanders did not, and disobeyed an order from his commanders to send his troops south to Cape Helles, instead stalling the invasion by bitter fighting that wiped out his division. Though suffering from malaria, he commanded in full view of his troops and of the enemy, and miraculously escaped death several times. His brilliant performance made him a folk hero and paved the way for his promotion to pasha (general).

The Gallipoli campaign lasted until January 1916, and resulted in a total of more than half a million Allied and Turkish casualties.

Transport

Çanakkale is the logical base for visits to the Gallipoli battlefields and/or Troy. Truva Turizm and Radar Turizm buses depart Kadıköy and then İstanbul's main *otogar* at Esenler hourly between 5am and 1am. The only time you'll need to book ahead is around Anzac Day. The trip (six hours, 340km) costs €12.20, with a small discount for children. Buses stop for one rest break. If you're heading back to İstanbul, you can buy bus tickets and board buses from near the ferry docks rather than going to the Çanakkale *otogar*. Truva Turizm buses leave at 1am, 3am, 5am, 7am and then every hour until 7pm, with one later service at 11pm. Radar Turizm buses follow a similar timetable. Most buses to/from İstanbul travel on the Eceabat–Çanakkale ferry and along the Thracian side of the Sea of Marmara coast.

If you are travelling in your own car, there are car ferries between Gelibolu and Lapseki; Eceabat and Çanakkale; and Kilitbahir and Çanakkale. Most depart hourly between 6am and midnight; they cost approximately €3.30 per car and €0.60 per person.

Touring the Battlefields

Gallipoli is a fairly large area to tour: It's over 35km as the crow flies from the northernmost battlefield to the southern tip of the peninsula. The principal battles took place on the western shore of the peninsula near Anzac Cove and Arıburnu Cemetery, and in the hills just to the east.

With a car you can easily tour the major battlefields in a day and be in a Çanakkale hotel by nightfall. If you're in a hurry, a morning or afternoon will be enough time to see the main sites. Most of the tours run by companies in Çanakkale and Eceabat take half a day. The best of these tours are run by **Hassle Free** in Çanakkale and **TJs Tours** in Eceabat.

If you're a hiker, and you have lots of time, take a ferry from Çanakkale to Eceabat and a *dolmuş* or taxi to Kabatepe, and follow the trail around the sites described in an excellent map sold at the **Kabatepe Information Centre** (Kabatepe Tanıtma Merkezi).

Gallipoli National Historic Park (Gelibolu Yarımadası Tarihi Milli Parkı) covers much of the peninsula and all of the significant battle sites. To get to the Information Centre, head north of Eceabat. After about 3km you'll see a road marked for Kabatepe; follow it until you come to the info centre, just east of Kabatepe. As well as selling maps of the battlefields, the centre has a small **museum** with a collection of period uniforms, soldiers' letters and other battlefield finds.

From the information centre, head west and then north for 3km to the **Beach (Hell Spit) Cemetery**; a bit further on a road goes inland to the Shrapnel Valley and **Plugge's Plateau Cemeteries**.

Further north from the inland turn-off is **Anzac Cove** (Anzac Koyu). The ill-fated Allied landing was made here on 25 April 1915, beneath and just south of the Arıburnu cliffs. As it is a memorial reserve, the beach here is off limits to swimmers and picnickers.

A few hundred metres beyond Anzac Cove is the **Arıburnu Cemetery** and, further along, the **Canterbury Cemetery**. Less than 1km further along the seaside road are the cemeteries at **No 2 Outpost** set back inland from the road, and the **New Zealand No 2 Outpost** right next to the road. The **Embarkation Pier Cemetery** is shortly beyond them.

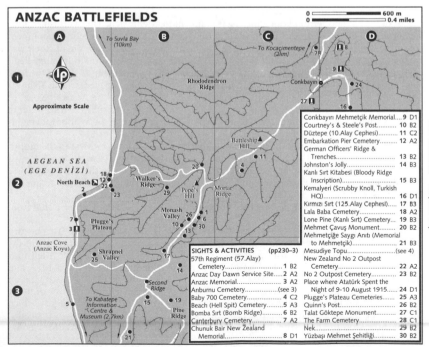

ANZAC BATTLEFIELDS

600 m
0.4 miles

SIGHTS & ACTIVITIES	(pp230–3)
57th Regiment (57.Alay) Cemetery	1 B2
Anzac Day Dawn Service Site	2 A2
Anzac Memorial	3 A2
Arıburnu Cemetery	(see 3)
Baby 700 Cemetery	4 C2
Beach (Hell Spit) Cemetery	5 A3
Bomba Sırt (Bomb Ridge)	6 B2
Canterbury Cemetery	7 A2
Chunuk Bair New Zealand Memorial	8 D1
Conkbayırı Mehmetçik Memorial	9 D1
Courtney's & Steele's Post	10 B2
Düztepe (10.Alay Cephesi)	11 C2
Embarkation Pier Cemetery	12 A2
German Officers' Ridge & Trenches	13 B2
Johnston's Jolly	14 B3
Kanlı Sırt Kitabesi (Bloody Ridge Inscription)	15 B3
Kemalyeri (Scrubby Knoll, Turkish HQ)	16 D1
Kırmızı Sırt (125.Alay Cephesi)	17 B3
Lala Baba Cemetery	18 A2
Lone Pine (Kanlı Sırt) Cemetery	19 B3
Mehmet Çavuş Monument	20 B2
Mehmetçiğe Saygı Anıtı (Memorial to Mehmetçik)	21 B3
Mesudiye Topu	(see 4)
New Zealand No 2 Outpost Cemetery	22 A2
No 2 Outpost Cemetery	23 B2
Place where Atatürk Spent the Night of 9-10 August 1915	24 D1
Plugge's Plateau Cemeteries	25 A3
Quinn's Post	26 B2
Talat Göktepe Monument	27 C1
The Farm Cemetery	28 C1
Nek	29 B2
Yüzbaşı Mehmet Şehitliği	30 B2

Turkish cemetery, Gallipoli (p233)

Retrace your steps and follow the signs up the hill for **Lone Pine (Kanlı Sırt) Cemetery.** It's along the same inland road that passes Shrapnel Valley. Another 3km uphill will take you to the **Chunuk Bair New Zealand Memorial.** This area, which saw the most bitter fighting of the campaign, was later cloaked in pines, but a fire in 1994 denuded the hills. Reforestation efforts are under way.

At Lone Pine, 400m uphill from the **Kanlı Sırt Kitabesi** (Bloody Ridge Inscription), Australian forces captured Turkish positions on 6 August. In the few days of the August assault 4000 men died. The trees that shaded the cemetery were swept away by the 1994 fire, leaving only one: a lone pine planted as a memorial years ago from the seed of the original tree that stood here during the battle. The small tombstones carry touching epitaphs: 'Only son', 'He died for his country' and 'If I could hold your hand once more just to say well done'.

The trenches were separated only by the width of the modern road at **Johnston's Jolly,** 300m beyond Lone Pine; **Courtney's & Steele's Post,** another 300m along; and especially at **Quinn's Post,** another 400m uphill. On the western side at Johnston's Jolly is the Turkish monument to the soldiers of the 125th Regiment who died here on 'Red Ridge' (Kırmızı Sırt/125 Alay Cephesi). At Quinn's Post is the memorial to Sergeant Mehmet, who fought with rocks and his fists after he ran out of ammunition; and the Captain Mehmet Cemetery.

Just over 1km uphill from Lone Pine is a monument to 'Mehmetçik' (the Turkish equivalent of GI Joe) on the west side of the road and, on the east side, the cemetery and monument for officers and soldiers of the Ottoman 57th Regiment. As the Anzac troops made their way up the slopes towards Chunuk Bair on 25 April, Atatürk brought up the 57th Infantry Regiment and gave them his famous order: 'I order you not just to attack, but to die. In the time it takes us to die, other troops and commanders will arrive to take our places.' The 57th was wiped out, but held the line and inflicted equally heavy casualties on the Anzacs below.

The statue of an old man showing his granddaughter the battle sites portrays veteran Hüseyin Kaçmaz, who fought in the Balkan Wars, in Gallipoli and in the War of Independence at the fateful Battle of Dumlupınar. He died in 1994 at the age of 110.

A few hundred metres past the 57th Regiment Cemetery, a road goes west to the monument to **Mehmet Çavuş** (another Sergeant Mehmet) and the **Nek.** It was at the Nek on 7 August 1915 that the 8th (Victorian) and 10th (West Australian) regiments of the 3rd Light Horse Brigade vaulted out of their trenches into withering fire and certain death. Their action was immortalised in Peter Weir's film *Gallipoli.*

Baby 700 Cemetery on the site of the other object of the assault, is 300m further uphill from Mehmet Çavuş.

At the top of the hill, past the **monument to Talat Göktepe,** is a 'T' intersection. A right turn takes you to the spot where, having stayed awake for four days straight, Atatürk spent the night of 9–10 August, and to the **Kemalyeri** (Scrubby Knoll), his command post. A left turn leads after 100m to **Chunuk Bair,** the first objective of the Allied landing in April 1915, and now the site of the **New Zealand memorial.** Chunuk Bair was at the heart of the struggle on 6–9 August 1915, when 28,000 men died on this ridge. The peaceful pine grove of today makes it difficult to imagine the battlefield of old. The Anzac attack on 6–7 August, which included the New Zealand Mounted Rifle Brigade and a Maori contingent, was deadly, but the attack on the following day was of a ferocity which, according to Atatürk, 'could scarcely be described'.

To the east a road leads up to the Turkish **Conkbayırı Mehmetçik Memorial.** Here are five gigantic tablets with inscriptions (in Turkish) describing the progress of the battle.

Memorials on the Southern Peninsula can be reached via the road that goes south from near the Kabatepe Information Centre. It's about 18km to the village of **Alçıtepe,** formerly known as Krythia or Kirte. In the village, signs point out the road southwest to the cemeteries of **Twelve Tree Copse** and **Pink Farm** and north to the Turkish cemetery **Sargı Yeri** and the **Nuri Yamut monument.**

Heading south, the road passes the **Redoubt Cemetery.** About 5.5km south of Alçıtepe, just south of the **Skew Bridge Cemetery,** the road divides, the right fork leading to the village of **Seddülbahir** and several Allied memorials.

The initial Allied attack was two-pronged, with the southern landing taking place here at the tip of the peninsula on **'V' Beach.** Yahya Çavuş was the Turkish officer who led the first resistance to the Allied landing on 25 April 1915, causing heavy casualties. The cemetery named after him, **Yahya Çavuş Şehitliği,** is between the Helles Memorial and 'V' Beach.

Follow the signs for Yahya Çavuş Şehitliği to reach the **Cape Helles British Memorial,** 1km beyond the Seddülbahir village square. From the Helles Memorial there are fine views of the Dardanelles, with ships cruising by placidly. **Lancashire Landing Cemetery** is off to the north along a road marked by a sign.

Retrace your steps to the road division and go east. For Abide and/or Çanakkale Şehitleri Abidesi follow the signs east at Morto Bay. Along the way you pass the **French War Memorial and Cemetery.** French troops, including a regiment of Africans, attacked Kumkale on the Asian shore in March 1915 with complete success, then re-embarked and landed in support of their British comrades-in-arms at Cape Helles.

Çanakkale Şehitleri Abidesi (Çanakkale Martyrs' Memorial) commemorates all of the Turkish soldiers who fought and died at Gallipoli. It's a gigantic four-legged stone table (almost 42m high and surrounded by landscaped grounds) standing above a war museum. At the foot of the Turkish monument hill is a fine pine-shaded picnic area.

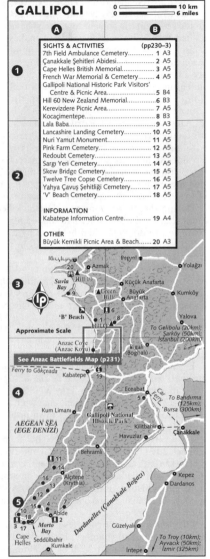

GALLIPOLI

SIGHTS & ACTIVITIES	(pp230–3)
7th Field Ambulance Cemetery	1 A3
Çanakkale Şehitleri Abidesi	2 A5
Cape Helles British Memorial	3 A5
French War Memorial & Cemetery	4 A5
Gallipoli National Historic Park Visitors' Centre & Picnic Area	5 B4
Hill 60 New Zealand Memorial	6 B3
Kerevizdere Picnic Area	7 A5
Kocaçimentepe	8 B3
Lala Baba	9 A3
Lancashire Landing Cemetery	10 A5
Nuri Yamut Monument	11 A5
Pink Farm Cemetery	12 A5
Redoubt Cemetery	13 A5
Sargı Yeri Cemetery	14 A5
Skew Bridge Cemetery	15 A5
Twelve Tree Copse Cemetery	16 A5
Yahya Çavuş Şehitliği Cemetery	17 A5
'V' Beach Cemetery	18 A5

| INFORMATION | |
| Kabatepe Information Centre | 19 A4 |

| OTHER | |
| Büyük Kemikli Picnic Area & Beach | 20 A3 |

TROY

The approach to Troy (Truva), 30km from Çanakkale, is across rolling grain fields. This is the ancient Troad, all but lost to legend until German-born Californian treasure-seeker and amateur archaeologist Heinrich Schliemann (1822–90) excavated it in 1871. He uncovered four superimposed ancient towns, destroying three others in the process.

There are few structures here, but visitors can clearly trace the excavations and can get an idea of what the ancient town must have looked like. With a good guide, it makes a fascinating excursion. The views around the countryside and over to the Dardanelles are a bonus, too.

In Homer's *Iliad,* Troy was the town of Ilium. The Trojan War took place in the 13th century BC, with Agamemnon, Achilles, Odysseus (Ulysses), Patroclus and Nestor on the Achaean (Greek) side, and Priam with his sons Hector and Paris on the Trojan side. Rather than suggesting commercial rivalries as a cause for the war, Homer claimed that Paris had kidnapped the beautiful Helen from her husband Menelaus, King of Sparta (his reward for giving the golden apple for most beautiful woman to Aphrodite, goddess of love), and the king asked the Achaeans to help him get her back.

During the decade-long war, Hector killed Patroclus and Achilles killed Hector. Paris knew that Achilles' mother had dipped her son in the River Styx to make him invincible. However, to do so she had held him by his heel, the one part of his body that remained unprotected. Hence Paris shot Achilles in the heel and bequeathed a phrase to the English language.

When 10 years of carnage couldn't end the war, Odysseus came up with the idea of the wooden horse filled with soldiers, against which Cassandra warned the Trojans in vain. It was left outside the west gate for the Trojans to wheel inside the walls. At the site there is a wooden replica that children love to climb.

One theory has it that the earthquake of 1250 BC aided the Achaeans by bringing down Troy's formidable walls and allowing them to battle their way into the city. In gratitude to Poseidon, the earth-shaker, they built a monumental wooden statue of his horse. So there may well have been a Trojan horse, even though Homer's account is not historical.

Excavations by Schliemann and others have revealed nine ancient cities, one on top of another, dating back to 3000 BC. The first people lived here during the early Bronze Age. The cities called Troy I to Troy V (3000–1700 BC) had a similar culture, but Troy VI (1700–1250 BC) had a different character, with a new population of Indo-European stock related to the Mycenaeans. The town doubled in size and carried on a prosperous trade with Mycenae.

Troy VII lasted from 1250 to 1050 BC, then languished for four centuries. It was revived as a Greek city (Troy VIII, 700–85 BC) and then as a Roman one (Troy IX, 85 BC–AD 500).

The Kazı Evi (Excavation House) near the wooden horse replica was used by earlier archaeological teams. Today it holds exhibits on work in progress, as well as historical interpretations and a history of the site's excavation that is particularly unkind to Schliemann. The models and illustrations should help you understand what Troy looked like at different points in its history.

Of the remaining structures at the site, the oldest still-standing wall in the world; the bouleuterion (council chamber) built c 800 BC; the stone ramp from Troy II; and the Temple of Athena from Troy VIII, rebuilt by the Romans, are of particular interest.

Transport

Troy is only 25 minutes (30km) by car or *dolmuş* from Çanakkale. The *dolmuş* station is under a small bridge opposite the fairground on Atatürk Caddesi. In high summer, *dolmuşes* go to the small village of Tevfikiye, just outside Troy, every 30 to 60 minutes. These cost less than €1. At other times of the year, you should plan to visit early in the day to be sure of getting a return *dolmuş.*

Information

In Çanakkale there are banks, a PTT and shops.

Kabatepe Information Centre (Map p233; Kabatepe Tanıtma Merkezi, Gallipoli; museum admission €0.60; ⏱ 8.30am-5pm)

Keyif Café & Internet (Map p235; ☎ 286-212 0671; per hr €0.55; ⏱ 24hr) Fast Internet connections.

Tourist Information Office (Map p235; ☎ 286-217 1187; ⏱ 8.30am-7.30pm Mon-Fri, 10.30am-6pm Sat & Sun May-Sep; 8.30am-5.30pm Mon-Fri Oct-Apr).

Tours

Hassle Free (Map p235; ☎ 286-213 5969; www .anzchouse.com; Cumhuriyet Meydanı 61, Çanakkale) Based in the Anzac House hostel, Hassle Free runs Gallipoli tours for €20 and Troy tours for €13.30. The three-hour Troy tour leaves at 8.30am; the six-hour Gallipoli tour

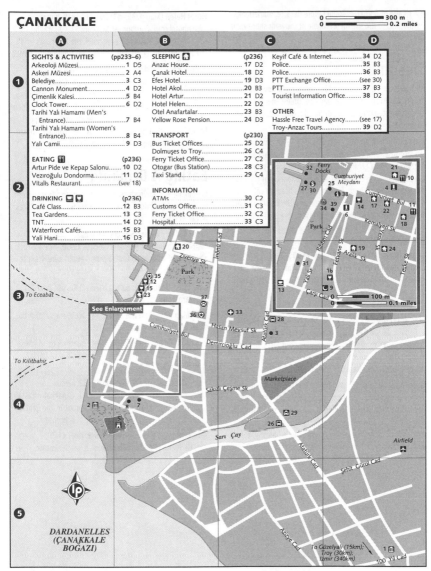

ÇANAKKALE

0 — 300 m
0 — 0.2 miles

SIGHTS & ACTIVITIES	(pp233–6)
Arkeoloji Müzesi	1 D5
Askeri Müzesi	2 A4
Belediye	3 C3
Cannon Monument	4 D2
Çimenlik Kalesi	5 B4
Clock Tower	6 D2
Tarihi Yalı Hamamı (Men's Entrance)	7 B4
Tarihi Yalı Hamamı (Women's Entrance)	8 B4
Yalı Camii	9 D3

EATING	(p236)
Artur Pide ve Kepap Salonu	10 D2
Vezıroğulu Dondorma	11 D2
Vitalis Restaurant	(see 18)

DRINKING	(p236)
Café Class	12 D2
Tea Gardens	13 D2
TNT	14 D2
Waterfront Cafés	15 B3
Yali Hani	16 D3

SLEEPING	(p236)
Anzac House	17 D2
Çanak Hotel	18 D2
Efes Hotel	19 D3
Hotel Akol	20 B3
Hotel Artur	21 D2
Hotel Helen	22 D2
Otel Anafartalar	23 B3
Yellow Rose Pension	24 D3

TRANSPORT	(p230)
Bus Ticket Offices	25 D2
Dolmuşes to Troy	26 C4
Ferry Ticket Office	27 C2
Otogar (Bus Station)	28 C3
Taxi Stand	29 C4

INFORMATION	
ATMs	30 C2
Customs Office	31 C2
Ferry Ticket Office	32 C2
Hospital	33 C3

Keyif Café & Internet	34 D2
Police	35 B3
Police	36 B3
PTT Exchange Office	(see 30)
PTT	37 B3
Tourist Information Office	38 D2

OTHER	
Hassle Free Travel Agency	(see 17)
Troy-Anzac Tours	39 D2

0 — 100 m
0 — 0.1 miles

To Eceabat

To Kilitbahir

DARDANELLES
(ÇANAKKALE
BOGAZI)

leaves at 11.30am and includes lunch at the Maydos Restaurant in Eceabat. It's possible to do both tours in one day. The English-speaking guides are very good. Hassle Free also organises round-trip Gallipoli tours from İstanbul including transport, a Troy tour and one night's accommodation in Çanakkale. There is a tour for the dawn service on Anzac Day. Check the website.

TJ Tours (☎ 286-814 3121; www.anzacgallipolitours .com; Cumhuriyet Caddesi 5/A, Eceabat) TJ runs a six-hour Gallipoli tour leaving at 11.45am and including a lunch

box for €17; its three-hour Troy tour costs the same. The company is based at TJ's Hostel in Eceabat and has an alliance with the Yellow Rose Pension in Çanakkale. Its Gallipoli tour has a good reputation.

Sights

Troy Archaeological Site (☎ 286-283 0536; admission €5.60; plus per car €1.10; ☉ 8.30am-6.30pm) The window where you buy your admission ticket is just past the village of Tevfikiye, 500m before the site. Guidebooks (with map) to the site are available at souvenir shops near the ticket box.

Sleeping

All hotels are heavily booked in summer; the town is insanely crowded around Anzac Day. Unless mentioned, all places listed offer air-conditioned rooms with en suite bathroom.

Anzac House (Map p235; ☎ 286-213 5969; www .anzachouse.com; Cumhuriyet Meydanı 61, Çanakkale; dm/s/d €4.20/8/12) Rooms are clean, but some don't have windows. Ask for a discount if management tries to put you in one of these. The downstairs licensed café is a backpacker hotspot where *Gallipoli* and *The Fatal Shore* are screened nightly. A Turkish breakfast costs €2.50. There's no air-conditioning, but hot water is available all day in the shared bathrooms.

Çanak Hotel (Map p235; ☎ 286-214 1582; canakhotel@superonline.com; Dibek Sokak 1, Çanakkale; s/d €25/38) This recently built place offers extremely comfortable rooms at very reasonable prices. There's a pleasant rooftop restaurant and bar.

Efes Hotel (Map p235; ☎ /fax 286-217 3256; Aralık Sokak 5, Çanakkale; s/d €11/14) This place is a gem. Run by Mrs Yetimoğlu, it's spotlessly clean, has very comfortable beds and is extremely quiet. Two rooms have air-conditioning; the rest have fans. Breakfast costs €1.50.

Hotel Akol (Map p235; ☎ 286-217 9456; www.hotelakol .com; Kordonboyu, Çanakkale; s/d €45/66.50) This place has large rooms with all the mod cons and is popular with tour groups as a consequence. Though getting on in years it's aging quite gracefully. All rooms have a balcony, some with water views. There's a pool, bar and restaurant.

Hotel Helen (Map p235; ☎ 286-212 1818; www .helenhotel.com; Cumhuriyet Meydanı 57, Çanakkale; s/d €37/49) Another relatively new hotel, the Helen has small but comfortable rooms and a restaurant fronting the street.

Yellow Rose Pension (Map p235; ☎ 286-217 3343; www.yellowrose.4mg.com; Yeni Sokak 5, Çanakkale; dm/ s/d €4.40/8.30/14) All rooms in this hostel have windows, plus shower, sink and toilet. The dorm sleeps 15. It's clean and much quieter than Anzac House, its major competitor. Facilities – including film screenings – are similar. There's no air-conditioning. Breakfast costs €1.50.

Eating & Drinking

Çanakkale is a university town, so has quite a few student bars and cafés. Unfortunately there are few decent places to eat in town.

Artur Pide ve Kebap Salonu (Map p235; ☎ 286-212 6726/8; Cumhuriyet Meydanı; kebabs €2.50, *pide* €1.70; ⏰ 8.30am-midnight) Grab a *pide* (kebab) here. Next to Hotel Artur.

Café Class (Map p235; Balıkçı Barınağı Karşısı; Beer €2; ⏰ 9am-1am)

TNT (Map p235; Fetvane Sokak; ⏰ 10.30am-1am) A bar often hosting live music.

Vezıroğlu Dondurma (Cumhuriyet Square) A good place to enjoy ice-cream, *fırın sütlaç* (rice pudding) or baklava after your meal.

Vitalis Restaurant (☎ 286-214 1582; canak hotel@superonline.com; Dibek Sokak 1, Çanakkale; pasta €2.50, salads €3.80) The rooftop restaurant at the Çanak Hotel, for something more upmarket. It is licensed.

Yali Hani (Map p235; Fetvane Sokak; beer €1.70; ⏰ 10.30am-midnight) This bar also has live music.

Directory

Directory

TRANSPORT

AIRLINES

Most of İstanbul's airline offices are in the suburbs around **Taksim Square** (p123), but Turkish Airlines has offices around the city. Travel agencies can also sell air tickets and make reservations. The two major airlines flying domestic routes are Turkish Airlines and newcomer Onur Air. Onur Air is in many cases cheaper than its long-established rival.

The following airlines have offices in İstanbul:

Air France (☎ 212-310 1919; www.airfrance.com; Emirhan Caddesi 145, Dikilitaş); **Atatürk International Airport** (☎ 212-663 0600)

Alitalia (www.alitalia.com; ☎ 212-315 1900; Valikonağı Caddesi 73, Nişantaşı); **Atatürk International Airport** (☎ 212-663 0577)

American Airlines (☎ 212-219 8223; Halaskargazi Caddesi, Mısırlı Han 121, Harbiye)

British Airways (Map p287; ☎ 212-234 1300; www .britishairways.com; Cumhuriyet Caddesi 10, Elmadağ); **Atatürk International Airport** (☎ 212-663 0574)

Emirates Airlines (☎ 212-293 5050; www.emirates.com; İnönü Caddesi 96, Gümüşsuyu); **Atatürk International Airport** (☎ 212-663 0825)

Japan Airlines (JAL; Map p287; ☎ 212-233 0840; www .jal.co.jp; Cumhuriyet Caddesi 107/2, Elmadağ); **Atatürk International Airport** (☎ 212-663 6871)

KLM-Royal Dutch Airlines (☎ 212-230 0311; www.klm .com; Valikonağı Caddesi 73/7, Nişantaşı); **Atatürk International Airport** (☎ 212-663 0603)

Lufthansa Airlines (☎ 212-315 3434; www.lufthansa .com; Maya Akar Centre, B Blok Kat 3, Büyükdere Caddesi 100-102, Esentepe); **Atatürk International Airport** (☎ 212-663 0594)

Olympic Airlines (Map p287; ☎ 212-247 3701; www .olympicairlines.com; Cumhuriyet Caddesi 171/A, Elmadağ); **Atatürk International Airport** (☎ 212-663 0820)

Onur Air (Map p287; ☎ 212-233 3800; www.onurair .com.tr; Cumhuriyet Caddesi 141/147, Elmadağ); **Atatürk International Airport** (☎ 212-663 0773)

Singapore Airlines (☎ 212-232 3706; Halaskargazi Caddesi 113, Harbiye); **Atatürk International Airport** (☎ 212-663 0710)

Turkish Airlines (THY; Map p287; ☎ 212-1106, reservations 212-663 6363; www.thy.com; Cumhuriyet Caddesi, Taksim & Gezi Dükkanları Sokak 7, Taksim)

AIRPORT

Atatürk International Airport (Atatürk Hava Limanı) is in Yeşilköy, 23km west of Sultanahmet (the heart of Old İstanbul). The **international terminal** (Dış Hatlar; flight information ☎ 212-663 6400) is polished and organised. Close by, the domestic terminal (İç Hatlar) is smaller but no less efficient. Another airport, Sabiha Gokçen International Airport at Kurtköy on the Asian side of the city, opened in early 2001, though most flights still arrive at and depart from Atatürk International Airport.

There are car-hire desks, exchange offices, a pharmacy, ATMs and a PTT at the international arrivals area. There is also a 24-hour **Tourist Information Office** (☎ 212-663 0793) that can supply maps, advice and brochures. All food and drink outlets at the international terminal are ridiculously overpriced. The 24-hour Left Luggage service charges €4.50 per suitcase per 24 hours; you'll find the booth to your left as you exit customs.

One of the few annoying things about the airport is that travellers must pay €1.10 to use a trolley on either side of immigration. You can pay in Turkish lira, euros or US dollars; fortunately, attendants give change.

To/From Atatürk Airport

A taxi from the airport to Sultanahmet or Taksim Square costs around €10, more if it's between midnight and 6am or if there's heavy traffic. Instead of a tip, just round the amount up to the closest TL1,000,000.

There's a quick, cheap Light Rail Transit (LRT) service from the airport to Aksaray, from where it's easy to connect with the tram to Sultanahmet and Eminönü. The station is on the lower ground floor beneath the international departures hall – follow the 'Rapid Transit' signs down the escalators and right to the station. A ticket to Aksaray costs a mere €0.60 and the trip takes 30 minutes. Services depart every 10 minutes or so from 6am (Mon-Fri), 6.15am (Sat) and 6.30am (Sun) until midnight. When you get

Akbil

İstanbul's public transport system is excellent and the Akbil system is one of its best features. If you're staying in the city for a week or more you should consider getting yourself one of these computerised debit fare tags and save yourself time and money when hopping on and off trams, trains, ferries and buses all around the city. Daily (*günlük*), weekly (*haftalık*), 15-day and monthly (*aylık*) Akbil tags are available at the Akbil Gişesi booths at Sirkeci, Eminönü, Aksaray or Taksim Square bus stands for a deposit of €2.20 (daily), €11.10 (weekly), €19.40 (15-day) and €33.30 (monthly). When you have your tag, you can charge it with any amount from €2.80 at any Akbil booth or at machines at the Tünel or metro stations. Press the card's metal button into the fare machine on a bus, ferry, LRT, train or tram and – beep – the fare is automatically deducted from your line of credit. Akbil fares are 10% lower than cash or ticket fares. You'll get your €3.30 deposit back when you return the device.

off the light rail, exit the station, cross over busy Adnan Menderes Bulvarı and turn right at the Murat Paşa mosque. A short walk will bring you to another major street, Turgut Özal Caddesi (Millet Caddesi), where the Yusufpaşa tram stop is located. Cross to the stop near the opposite side of the road. Ticket kiosks are located at the tram stop; a token costs €0.60. The tram makes its way down Divan Yolu to Sultanahmet and then terminates at Eminönü.

If you are staying near Taksim Square, the **Havaş airport bus** (☎ 212-243 3399) is your best bet. This departs from outside the arrivals hall, then goes to Yenikapı (30 minutes) and on to Taksim Square (45 to 60 minutes). Buses leave at 5am, 7am and then every 90 minutes until 10pm. Tickets cost €4.10 and the bus stops outside the Havaş ticket office on Cumhuriyet Caddesi just off Taksim Square. Another Havaş airport bus runs from the airport to Etiler (**Akmerkez shopping centre**, p199), every half-hour from 7am to 9pm.

The Havaş bus departs Cumhuriyet Caddesi for the airport at 5am, 6am and then every 30 minutes until 11pm. The trip takes about an hour.

BOAT
Cruise Ships

Cruise ships arrive at the **Karaköy International Maritime Passenger Terminal** (☎ 212-249 5776) just near the Galata Bridge.

Ferries & Seabuses

The most enjoyable way to get around town is by ferry or *deniz otobüsü* (fast catamaran or seabus). Crossing to and from the Asian and European shores, these vessels are as efficient as they are popular with locals.

The major ferry docks are at the mouth of the Golden Horn (Eminönü, Sirkeci and Karaköy) and at Kabataş, 2km northeast of the Galata Bridge, just south of **Dolmabahçe Palace** (p124).

Information regarding ferry service times is found in the Transport boxes in the Neighbourhoods (pp76–134) and Excursions (pp215–236) chapters. The ferries run to two annual timetables: winter (mid-September to mid-June) and summer (mid-June to mid-September). Printed timetables are available from all ferry terminals and an online timetable (in Turkish) is available at www.tdi.com.tr. Tickets (*jetons*) are cheap (usually less than €0.50) and it's possible to use Akbil on most routes.

Major seabus docks on the European side are at Yenikapı and Kabataş, with less frequently served docks at Eminönü, Karaköy and several Bosphorus docks such as İstinye and Sarıyer. On the Asian side, major docks are at Bostancı and Kartal, and minor docks are at Büyükada and Heybeliada.

Fares for the seabuses are more expensive than the ferries. Like the ferries, the seabuses run to summer and winter timetables. The

Ferry Travel

Ferries ply the following routes:
- Eminönü–Üsküdar
- Eminönü–Kadıköy (some stop at Haydarpaşa)
- Sirkeci–Harem (daily car ferry from 7am, then every half-hour until 9.30pm)
- Üsküdar–Eminönü–Kasımpaşa–Fener–Balat–Ayvansaray–Sütlüce–Eyüp
- Sirkeci–Kadıköy–Kınalıada–Burgazada–Heybeliada–Büyükada (Princes' Islands ferry)
- Eminönü–Moda–Bostancı
- Eminönü–Anadolu Kavağı (Bosphorus Excursions Ferry)
- Kabataş–Üsküdar
- Beşiktaş–Üsküdar
- Beşiktaş–Kadıköy
- Karaköy–Kadıköy (some stop at Haydarpaşa)
- Karaköy–Üsküdar
- Kanlıca–Anadolu Hisarı–Kandilli–Bebek–Arnavutköy
- Sarıyer–Rumeli Kavağı–Anadolu Kavağı

Seabus Travel

Seabus routes include the following:
- Kadıköy–Bostancı
- Yenikapı–Kadıköy–Bostancı
- Eminönü–Kadıköy
- Üsküdar–Bakırköy
- Yenikapı–Bakırköy
- Sarıyer–Beykoz–İstinye–Beşiktaş–Üsküdar–Karaköy–Eminönü–Kadıköy–Bakırköy
- Sarıyer–Kadıköy
- Beykoz–Kadıköy
- Eminönü–Karaköy–Beykoz
- Kabataş–Karaköy–Eminönü
- Bostancı–Heybeliada–Büyükada–Kartal (Princes' Islands ferry)

İstanbul Deniz Otobüsleri (www.ido.com.tr) has fare and timetable information or you can pick up a printed timetable at any of the seabus docks.

BUS

The **International İstanbul Bus Station** (Uluslararası İstanbul Otogarı; Map p290; ☎ 212-658 0505) is the city's main bus station for both intercity and international routes. Called simply the 'otogar', it's in the western district of Esenler, just south of the expressway and about 10km west of Sultanahmet or Taksim. The LRT service from Aksaray stops here (Otogar stop) on its way from the airport; you can catch this to Aksaray and then connect with a tram to Sultanahmet. Alternatively, bus 830 leaves from the centre of the *otogar* and takes about an hour to reach Taksim Square; and bus 910 goes to Eminönü. A taxi from Sultanahmet or Taksim Square will cost around €5.50.

Many bus companies offer a free service bus to or from İstanbul's *otogar*. If you're booking a ticket out of İstanbul from a bus office in Taksim (or elsewhere) ask about this service. You'll be asked to front up at the bus office around an hour before your bus is due to leave and a minibus will pick you up and take you from the office to your bus at the *otogar*. If you've just arrived by bus in İstanbul, ask your bus driver about the service bus. One should be waiting close by to drop you at Sultanahmet or Taksim Square.

There's a smaller bus station on the Asian shore of the Bosphorus at **Harem** (Map p290; ☎ 216-333 3763), south of Üsküdar and north of Haydarpaşa train station. If you're arriving in İstanbul by bus from anywhere on the Asian side of Turkey, it can be quicker to get out at Harem and take the car ferry to Sirkeci/Eminönü or a *dolmuş* to Kadıköy or Üsküdar and a ferry from there; if you stay on the bus until the *otogar*, you'll add at least an hour to your journey. If you're going the other way, you may want to *catch* your bus here, instead of at the *otogar*; check if this is possible at the bus office.

City Buses

The bus system in İstanbul is extremely efficient. The major bus stands are at Taksim Square, Beşiktaş, Aksaray, Rüstempaşa (Eminönü), Kadıköy and Üsküdar, and most services run between 6.30am and 11.30pm. Destinations and main stops on city bus routes are shown on a sign on the right (kerb) side of the bus (*otobus*) or on the electronic display at its front. The ubiquitous İETT buses are run by the city. You must have a ticket (€0.60) before boarding. Buy tickets from the white booths near major stops and bus, tram and metro stations, or from some nearby shops for a small mark-up (look for 'İETT *otobüs bileti satılır*'). Think about buying enough to last you throughout your stay in the city. You can also use your Akbil and save some money. Private buses, called Özel Halk Otobüsü and regulated by the city, run the same routes; these accept cash (pay the conductor) and some accept Akbil.

The most useful bus for travellers is the **T4 bus** (Map pp278-80) that runs between Sultanahmet and Taksim Square. It leaves from outside the **Sultanahmet Tourist Information Office** (Map pp278-80) and stops at Karaköy and Dolmabahçe en route to Taksim.

Intercity & International Buses

Many bus offices are in Beyoğlu near Taksim Square on Mete and İnönü Caddesis. The following are the top national lines:

Kamil Koç (Map pp284-6; ☎ 444 0562; www.kamilkoc .com.tr in Turkish; İnönü Caddesi 31) Services most major cities throughout Turkey.

İETT

İstanbul Elektrik Tramvay ve Tünel (İETT) is responsible for running the public bus, tram, LRT and metro systems in the city. Its excellent website (www.iett. gov.tr) has useful timetable and route information in Turkish and English. The site also has information on the Akbil system.

Ulusoy (Map pp284-6; ☎ 244 6375; www.ulusoy.com
.tr; İnönü Caddesi 59) Ulusoy runs twice-weekly buses to
and from Greece, Germany and France, as well as services
to most major cities in Turkey.

Varan Turizm (Map pp284-6; ☎ 212-251 7474; www
.varan.com.tr; İnönü Caddesi 29/B) Varan is a premium line
with routes to major Turkish cities and to several points in
Europe, including Athens.

CAR
Driving

It makes no sense to drive in İstanbul. The
traffic is hectic, free parking is scarce and drivers can be aggressive. If you have a car, we
suggest leaving it at your hotel or in a car park
(otopark) and using public transport, except
perhaps for excursions out of the city.

Drivers must have a valid driving licence. An
International Driving Permit (IDP) is required
for stays of more than three months, or if your
licence is from a locality that a Turkish police officer is likely to find obscure. Drive on the right-
hand side of the road. The speed limit is 50km/h
in urban areas and 120km/h on motorways.

The **Türkiye Turing ve Otomobil Kurumu** (Turkish
Touring & Automobile Club; ☎ /fax 212-282
8140/212-282 8042; Oto
Sanayi Sitesi Yanı, Çamlık Caddesi 4, Levent)
has licence and other information you'll need
to hire a car or bring your own vehicle into
the country. Between 9am and 5pm it offers a
breakdown service (☎ 212-278 6214).

Rental

You need to be at least 21 years old, with a
year's driving experience, to be able to rent a
car. You must pay with a major credit card, or
you will be required to make a large cash deposit. Most rental cars have standard gearshift;
you'll pay more to have automatic transmission
and air-conditioning.

Rental cars are moderately expensive in Turkey, partly due to huge excise taxes paid when
the cars are purchased. A week's rental will be
between €260 and €330 for a model such as a
Ford Fiesta, depending on the company and
the time of year. Child safety seats are usually
available for around €5 per day.

Mandatory third-party liability insurance
and KDV (value-added tax) are included in the
standard charge. Optional collision damage
waiver, theft protection and SOS personal accident and health insurance are also offered by
all companies for an extra cost.

If your car incurs any accident damage, or
if you cause any, do not move the car before
finding a police officer and asking for a kaza
raporu (accident report). The officer may ask
you to submit to a breath-alcohol test. Contact your car-rental company within 48 hours.
Your insurance coverage may be void if it can
be shown that you were operating under
the influence of alcohol or other drugs, were
speeding, or if you did not submit the required
accident report within 48 hours.

The agencies listed below have 24-hour
booths at the arrivals hall in Atatürk Airport's
international terminal:

Avis (Map p287; head office ☎ 212-368 6868;
www.avis.com.tr; Hilton Hotel Arcade, Cumhuriyet
Caddesi 107, Elmadağ); **Atatürk International Airport**
(☎ 212-663 0646)

Budget (Map p287; head office ☎ 212-296 3196;
www.budget.com; Cumhuriyet Caddesi 19, Gezi
Apartımanı, Elmadağ); **Atatürk International Airport**
(☎ 212-663 0858)

Hertz (head office ☎ 216-349 3040; www.hertz.com;
Bağdat Caddesi 146, Feneryolu, Kadıköy);
Atatürk International Airport (☎ 212-663 7063)

National (Map p287; Taksim office ☎ 212-254 7719;
www.nationalcar.com; Şehit Muhtar Mah Aydede
Sokak 1/2, Taksim); **Atatürk International Airport**
(☎ 212-663 7119)

DOLMUŞ

A dolmuş is a shared minibus; it waits at a
specified departure point until it has a full
complement of passengers (in Turkish, dolmuş
means full), then follows a fixed route to its
destination. Destinations are displayed in the
window of the dolmuş. Passengers flag down
the driver to get on and indicate to the driver
when they want to get off, usually by saying 'inecek var'. Fares vary (pay on board) and
are slightly more expensive than those on the
municipal buses, but dolmuşes are almost as
comfortable as taxis, run later into the night
in many instances and sometimes ply routes
that buses don't service.

LIGHT RAIL TRANSIT (LRT)

A new LRT service connects Aksaray with
the airport, stopping at 18 stations including
the otogar along the way. Trains leave every
10 minutes or so from 6am to midnight on
weekdays, 6.15am to midnight on Saturday
and 6.30am to midnight on Sunday. There are
plans to extend the service to Yenikapı.

METRO

İstanbul's underground metro system is a work in progress. From Taksim there is a service stopping at Osmanbey, Şişli, Gayrettepe, Levent and Levent 4. This is being extended north to Ayazağa and south to the seabus jetty at Yenikapı. Another line goes from the western side of Aksaray, northwestward under Adnan Menderes Bulvarı through the Bayrampaşa and Kartatepe districts. Then it turns south past the *otogar* in Esenler and terminates at Havaalani (Airport). Services run every five minutes or so from 6.15am to 12.30am Monday to Thursday, 6.15am to 1am on Friday and Saturday and 6.30am to 12.20am on Sunday.

See p117 for details of the one-stop Tünel underground system between Karaköy and İstiklal Caddesi in Beyoğlu.

TAXI

İstanbul is full of taxis. Some drivers are lunatics; others are con artists – most are neither. If you're caught with the first category and you're about to go into meltdown, say *'yavaş gidin!'* (slow down!). Drivers in the second of these categories – the con artists – are unfortunately reasonably common. All taxis have digital meters and must run them, but some of these drivers ask for a flat fare, or pretend the meter doesn't work so they can gouge you at the end of the run. The best way to counter this is to tell them no meter, no ride. Other drivers take advantage of the many zeros on Turkish currency to charge hapless tourists 10 times what the meter reads, to short-change them, or to try a common scam whereby they tell the passenger that he/she gave the wrong denomination note in payment, eg a TL500,000 note rather than a TL5,000,000 note. In reality, he has switched the note before giving it back and demanding 'correct payment'. All you can do to prevent this happening is to make yourself familiar with the different notes and be sure to proffer the correct one. Then stand your ground.

A base rate (drop rate, flag fall) is levied during the daytime *(gündüz);* the night-time *(gece)* rate, from midnight to 6am, is 50% higher. Meters, with LCD displays, flash *'gündüz'* or *'gece'* when they are started. Occasionally, drivers try to put the night-time *(gece)* rate on during the day, so watch out.

Few taxis have seatbelts. If you catch a taxi over either of the Bosphorus Bridges, it is your responsibility to cover the toll. The driver will add this to your fare.

TRAIN
Long-Distance Trains

All trains from Europe terminate at **Sirkeci Railway Station** (Map pp278-80; ☎ 212-527 0051; Ankara Caddesi, Sirkeci), right next to Eminönü. Outside the station's main door there's a convenient tram up the hill to Sultanahmet, Beyazıt and Aksaray. Buses leave from the nearby Rüstempaşa/Eminönü bus stand to many other destinations around town, including Taksim Square.

International services from Sirkeci include the daily Bosfor Ekspresi service leaving at 10pm every night going to Sofia (14 hours), Bucharest (18 hours) and Budapest (33 hours). There is also a slow daily service to Thessaloniki (16 hours) departing at 8.30am, where you can connect with trains to Athens. Sirkeci Railway Station has a restaurant but few other facilities.

Trains from the Asian side of Turkey, and from points east and south, terminate at **Haydarpaşa Railway Station** (Map pp276-7; ☎ 216-336 4470; Haydarpaşa Istasyon Caddesi, Kadıköy), on the Asian shore of the Bosphorus close to Kadıköy. Ignore anyone who suggests you should take a taxi to or from Haydarpaşa. The ferry from the station is cheap, convenient, pleasant and speedy. Taxis across the Bosphorus are expensive and slow.

Services from Haydarpaşa include eight daily departures to Ankara. To book a ticket to Ankara, call ☎ 216-336 4470; tickets can also be purchased from Sirkeci Railway Station. International services from Haydarpaşa include the Trans-Asya Espressi to Iran, leaving at 10.55pm on Wednesday; and the Toros Espressi to Syria, leaving at 8.55pm on Thursday.

Haydarpaşa has a left-luggage room *(emanet)*, a restaurant serving alcoholic beverages, numerous snack shops, bank ATMs and a small post office (PTT).

Local Trains

There are two suburban train lines *(banliyö treni)* in İstanbul. The first rattles along the Sea of Marmara shore from Sirkeci Railway Station, around Seraglio Point to Cankurtaran, Kumkapı, Yenikapı and a number of stations before it terminates past Atatürk International Airport at Halkala. The second runs from Haydarpaşa railway station to Gebze via Bostancı. The trains are a bit decrepit, but are reliable (nearly every half-hour) and cheap (€0.60). Akbil can be used.

TRAM

A street tram runs from Eminönü to Gülhane, Sultanahmet, and then along Divan Yolu to Çemberlitaş, Beyazıt (for the Grand Bazaar) and Aksaray (to connect to the *otogar* and airport), then out through the city walls to Zeytinburnu. Trams run every five minutes from 5.30am to midnight. On Sunday the service doesn't start until 6.10am. The fare is €0.60 and Akbil can be used. Works are currently under way to extend the line in both directions. The most useful of these extensions for travellers will be past Eminönü over the Galata Bridge and then on to Kabataş, where the tram will connect with a funicular to Taksim Square. The second is from Zeytinburnu to Bağcılar.

A tram running between Kadıköy Square and the exclusive residential suburb of Moda recently commenced operation.

See p120 for details of the two-stop antique tram that runs between Tünel and Taksim Square in Beyoğlu.

PRACTICALITIES

ACCOMMODATION

Accommodation choices in the Sleeping chapter (pp201–214) are ordered by neighbourhood and then arranged in alphabetical order, with mid-range and top-end places followed by budget options under a 'Cheap Sleeps' heading. All prices are for rooms in the high season (May to September) and include the KDV tax. Unless otherwise indicated, hotels included in the main body of listings (not Cheap Sleeps) have rooms with bathroom and air-con. Breakfast is included in the price – exceptions are noted. Room prices can be discounted by up to 20% during the low season (October to April, but not the Christmas period) – negotiate this directly with the hotel when making your booking.

BUSINESS HOURS

Opening hours vary wildly across businesses and services in İstanbul. Actual opening hours are cited with every restaurant, bar, shop and museum listing throughout this book. The following is a very general guide:

Banks 8.30am-noon and 1.30-5pm Mon-Fri.

Grocery shops 6am or 7am to 7pm or 8pm.

Offices Government and business hours are usually 8am or 9am to noon and 1.30-5pm Mon-Fri; however, during the holy month of Ramazan the work day is shortened.

Post Offices 8.30am-12.30pm and 1.30-5pm.

Shops 9am to 6pm or 7pm Mon-Sat; some shops close for lunch (noon to 1.30pm or 2.30pm); some stay open late and others are open seven days.

CHILDREN

Your child (*çocuk*) or children (*çocuklar*) will be treated indulgently in İstanbul. Given the high Turkish birth rate, they'll have lots of company, too. The larger hotels can arrange for daycare (*kreş*) and baby-sitting services. Charges are usually negotiated directly with the childcare centre or babysitter. Chains such as Mothercare have opened large stores in major shopping malls such as Galleria and Akmerkez, and stock everything you could possibly need. Disposable nappies (*bebek bezi*) are available in supermarkets and formula is sold at pharmacies.

For recommendations of activities in the city that children will enjoy, see 'Max's İstanbul' (p99).

Lonely Planet's *Travel with Children* offers useful general advice for families travelling with children.

CLIMATE

The best times to visit İstanbul are around spring and autumn, roughly from April to May and from September to October, when the climate is perfect. During July and August it is hot and steamy; a lot of İstanbullus head for the west and south coasts over these months. Chill winter winds and snow are common in winter

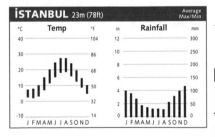

CONSULATES

Embassies (*büyükelçiliği*) are in Ankara, the national capital. The following countries have consulates (*konsolosluğu*) in İstanbul.

Australia (☎ 212-257 7050; Tepecik Yokuşu 58, Etiler)

Canada (Map pp284-6; ☎ 212-251 9838; İstiklal Caddesi 373, Beyoğlu)

Egypt (☎ 212-263 6038; Cevdet Paşa Caddesi, Bebek)

France (Map pp284-6; ☎ 212-334 8730; İstiklal Caddesi 8, Taksim)

Germany (Map pp284-6; ☎ 212-334 6100; İnönü Caddesi 16/18, Taksim)

Greece (Map pp284-6; ☎ 212-245 0596; Turnacıbaşı Sokak 32, Galatasaray)

Iran (☎ 212-513 8230; Ankara Caddesi 1, Cağaloğlu)

Ireland (Map p287; ☎ 212-259 6979; Acısu Sokak 5/4, Harbiye)

Israel (☎ 212-317 6500; Yapı Kredi Plaza, Blok C, Kat 7, Levent)

Italy (Map p276-8; ☎ 212-243 1024; Palazzo di Venezia, Tomtom Kaptan Sokak 15, Galatasaray)

Japan (☎ 212-393 2010; İnönü Caddesi 24, Gümüşsuyu)

Netherlands (Map pp284-6; ☎ 212-393 2121; İstiklal Caddesi 393, Tünel)

Spain (☎ 212-270 7410; Karanfil Aralığı Sokak 16, Levent)

Syria (Map p287; ☎ 212-232 6721; Maçka Caddesi 59, Ralli Apt 3, Nişantaşı)

UK (Map pp284-6; ☎ 212-293 7540; Meşrutiyet Caddesi 34, Tepebaşı) Temporarily closed at the time of research.

USA (Map pp284-6; ☎ 212-335 9000; Kaplıcalar Mevkii 2, Istinye)

COURSES
Cooking

See p51 for details of cooking courses in İstanbul.

Handicrafts

The historic **Caferağa Medresesi** (p85; ☎ 212-513 3601; Caferiye Sokak) is the home of the Turkish Cultural Services Foundation, which runs courses for locals and travellers in techniques such as calligraphy, miniature painting, marbling, binding and glass painting. Courses are organised into four-hour sessions one day per week over three months and cost €100.

Language

The most popular Turkish-language courses for native English speakers are run by **Taksim Dilmer** (Map p287; ☎ 212-292 9696; www.dilmer.com; Tarık Zafer Tunaya Sokak 18, Taksim). On offer are eight-week intensive (daily) courses costing €560; eight-week regular (three days per week) courses costing €276; and four-week intensive courses costing €230. Choose between morn-

ing, afternoon, evening or weekend classes. Classes have a maximum of 14 students.

CUSTOMS

İstanbul's Atatürk International Airport uses the red and green channel system, randomly spot-checking passengers' luggage. Items valued over US$15,000 must be declared and may be entered in your passport to guarantee that you take the goods out of the country. You're allowed to bring two bottles of wine, one carton (200) of cigarettes, 1.5kg of coffee and 10 cigars (100 cigars if they are purchased from the duty-free shop at the airport arrivals hall). There's no limit to the amount of Turkish liras or foreign currency you can bring into the country. It's illegal to take antiquities out of the country. Check www.gumruk.gov.tr for more information.

DISABLED TRAVELLERS

İstanbul has severely limited accessibility for mobility-impaired travellers. Roads are potholed and pavements – if they exist at all – are crooked and cracked. Airlines and some top hotels have meagre provisions for wheelchair access; and ramps are beginning to appear (ever so slowly) in a few buildings and streets, though most are dangerously steep and narrow. Neither public toilets nor public transport are wheelchair friendly.

ELECTRICITY

Electricity in İstanbul is supplied at 220V, 50Hz, as in Europe. Plugs (fiş) are of the European variety, with two round prongs. There are infrequent power cuts across the city, so it's a good idea to travel with a torch (flashlight) in your bag or pocket.

EMERGENCY

Ambulance (☎ 112)

Fire (☎ 110)

Police (☎ 155)

GAY & LESBIAN TRAVELLERS

Homosexuality is legal in Turkey, but there's an ambivalent attitude towards it among the general population. There are sporadic reports of violence towards gays and conservative İstanbullus frown upon open displays of affection between persons of the same sex.

The following websites may be of interest: www.absolutesultans.com, www.eshcinsel.net/ in Turkish, www.trgi.info/ in Turkish and www.istanbulgay.com.

Lambda (☎ 212-245 7068; www.lambdaistanbul.org; Büyükparmakkapı Sokak, Halas Bldg 20/4 Kat 3, Beyoğlu) is the Turkish branch of the international Gay, Lesbian, Bisexual and Transgender Liberation Group. It organises weekly meetings (in Turkish) and film afternoons (Saturday, 5pm) at its **information centre** (☻ 3-8pm weekdays, 1-8pm weekends), and has its sights firmly fixed upon seeing a homophobia-free Turkey.

The monthly *Time Out İstanbul* mag includes gay and lesbian listings. **Kaos GL** (www.geocities.com/kaosgl) is the country's only gay and lesbian magazine; it's published in Turkish only.

HEALTH
Food & Water
Travellers in Turkey experience a fair amount of travellers diarrhoea ('the sultan's revenge') and it's possible that you will pick up a bout in İstanbul, particularly if you eat street food (see 'Fancy Some Bacteria?' on p47).

DINING PRECAUTIONS
In lokantas choose dishes that look freshly prepared and sufficiently hot.

Beware of milk products and dishes containing milk that have not been properly refrigerated. If you want a rice pudding (*sütlaç*) or some such dish with milk in it, choose a shop that has lots of them in the window, meaning that a batch has been made recently. In general, choose things from trays, pots etc that are fairly full rather than almost empty. Eating some fresh yogurt every day can also help to keep your digestive system in good condition.

DRINKING PRECAUTIONS
Tap water in İstanbul is chlorinated, but is still not guaranteed to be safe (most locals don't drink it). Spring water is sold everywhere in 0.33L, 1.5L and 3L plastic bottles and is very cheap.

Illnesses
FOOD POISONING & TRAVELLERS DIARRHOEA
Food poisoning symptoms are headaches, nausea and/or stomach-ache, diarrhoea, fever and chills. If you get food poisoning, go to bed

and stay warm. Drink lots of fluids; preferably hot tea without sugar or milk. Chamomile tea (*papatya çay*) can ease a queasy stomach.

Simple things like a change of water, food or climate can all cause a mild bout of diarrhoea, but a few rushed toilet trips with no other symptoms is not indicative of a major problem.

Dehydration is the main danger with any diarrhoea, particularly in children or the elderly, as dehydration can occur quite quickly.

Gut-paralysing drugs such as loperamide or diphenoxylate can be used to bring relief from the symptoms, although they do not actually cure the problem. Only use these drugs if you do not have access to toilets, eg if you *must* travel. Note that these drugs are not recommended for children under 12 years.

If you experience diarrhoea with blood or mucus (dysentery), any diarrhoea with fever, profuse watery diarrhoea, persistent diarrhoea not improving after 48 hours or severe diarrhoea, antibiotics may be required. These symptoms suggest a more serious cause of diarrhoea and in these situations gut-paralysing drugs should be avoided. A stool test may be necessary to diagnose what bug is causing your diarrhoea, so seek medical help urgently.

Fluid replacement is important. Weak black tea with a little sugar, soda water, or soft drinks allowed to go flat and diluted 50% with bottled water are all good. You need to drink at least the same volume of fluid that you are losing in bowel movements and vomiting. Urine is the best guide to the adequacy of replacement – if you have small amounts of concentrated urine, you need to drink more. Keep drinking small amounts often. Stick to a bland diet as you recover.

Other Health Risks
Turks smoke like chimneys. If you are asthmatic or allergic and have difficulty coping with cigarette smoke, you'll find İstanbul challenging because there are so few places to escape it. Non-smoking restaurants and bars are almost unknown, taxi drivers smoke incessantly and few hotels have designated non-smoking rooms.

Vaccinations
You need no special inoculations before entering Turkey unless you're coming from an endemic or epidemic area. However, do discuss your requirements with a doctor. Consider typhoid fever and hepatitis A and B vaccinations if you plan to travel off the beaten track in Turkey;

also make sure that your tetanus/diphtheria and polio vaccinations are up to date (boosters are necessary every 10 years).

A rabies vaccination should be considered for those who plan to stay for a month or longer in Turkey, where rabies is common. Rabid dogs have been a problem in İstanbul in the recent past, but the council now vaccinates dogs (the yellow tag on the ear shows they've been vaccinated) and the danger seems to have been alleviated somewhat.

HOLIDAYS

The official Turkish calendar is the Gregorian (Western) one. Friday is the Muslim holy day, but it is not a holiday. The day of rest, a secular one, is Sunday.

Secular Holidays

Banks, offices and government services close for the day on the five secular public holidays per year. These are New Year's Day (1 January), National Sovereignty & Children's Day (23 April), Youth & Sports Day (19 May), Victory Day (30 August) and Republic Day (29 October).

Religious Holidays

Religious festivals, two of which (Şeker Bayramı and Kurban Bayramı) are public holidays, are celebrated according to the Muslim lunar Hejira calendar. As the lunar year is about 11 days shorter than the Gregorian one, Muslim festivals occur 11 days earlier each year.

Muslim days, like Jewish ones, begin at sundown. Thus a Friday holiday will begin on Thursday at sunset and last until Friday at sunset.

For major religious and civic holidays there is also a half-day vacation for preparation, called *arife*, preceding the start of a festival; shops and offices close about noon, and the festival begins at sunset.

Day-to-day business in İstanbul shuts down during religious holidays, and roads and flights out of town are full of locals escaping to the coast or mountains. Hotels in town and flights into the city can be busy with people from other parts of Turkey and the Middle East who have decided to escape to İstanbul.

RAMAZAN

During the Holy Month, called Ramadan in other Muslim countries, a good Muslim lets *nothing* pass the lips during daylight: no eating, drinking or smoking.

The fast is broken traditionally with flat *pide* (bread). Lavish *iftar* ('breaking of the fast') dinners are given and may last far into the night. Before dawn, drummers circulate throughout the town to awaken the faithful so they can eat before sunrise.

Although many İstanbullus observe the fast, most restaurants and cafés open to serve non-Muslims and locals who are not. It's polite to avoid ostentatious public smoking, eating, drinking and drunkenness during Ramazan.

Ramazan starts on 5 October 2005, 24 September 2006, and 13 September 2007. The 27th day of Ramazan is *Kadir Gecesi* (Night of Power) when the Quran was revealed and Mohammed appointed the Messenger of God.

ŞEKER BAYRAMI

This is a three-day festival at the end of Ramazan. *Şeker* (shek-*ehr*) is sugar or candy. During this festival children traditionally go door to door asking for sweet treats, Muslims exchange greeting cards and pay social calls, and everybody enjoys drinking lots of tea in broad daylight after fasting for Ramazan. The festival is a national holiday when banks and offices are closed, and hotels, buses, trains and planes are heavily booked.

KURBAN BAYRAMI

Called Eid al-Adha in Arabic countries, this is the most important religious holiday of the year. Meaning Sacrifice Holiday, it is a four-day festival commemorating Abraham's near-sacrifice of his son on Mt Moriah (Genesis 22; Quran, Sura 37). Right after the early morning prayers on the actual day of Bayram, the head of the household sacrifices a sheep. A feast is prepared, with much of the meat going to charity. Almost everything closes, including banks. Transport may be packed.

INTERNET ACCESS

There are Internet cafés all over İstanbul, usually filled with truant pimply adolescents playing computer games. Look for Internet cafés that advertise having an ADSL connection; other places can be frustratingly slow. Most hostels and hotels also offer Internet access for their guests.

When in a local Internet café, you may have to use a Turkish keyboard, in which case you need to be aware that Turkish has two 'i's: the familiar dotted 'i' and the less-familiar dotless 'ı'. Unfortunately the one in the usual place is the dotless 'ı' on a Turkish keyboard; you will need to make sure you use the correct dotted 'i' when typing in a web or email address. To create the @ symbol, hold down the 'q' and the right-hand ALT keys at the same time.

The following places have relatively fast connections and staff who know what they're talking about; all but Sinera have English-speaking staff. Café Turka and Otantik have some English keyboards.

Café Turka Internet Café (Map pp278-80; ☎ 212-514 6551; Divan Yolu Caddesi 22/2, Sultanahmet; per hr €1.40; ☙ 9am-2am) This place is always full of backpackers and Sultanahmet locals, who come to check their email and drink tea on the couches overlooking Divan Yolu. It's on the second floor above Trek Travel International.

Otantik Internet Café (Map pp278-80; ☎ 212-511 2433; Alayköşkü Caddesi 2/B, Sultanahmet; per hr €1.70; ☙ 9am-midnight) A busy place in a basement in a street off Yerebatan Caddesi.

Robin Hood Internet (Map pp284-6; ☎ 212-244 8959; Yeni Çarşı Caddesi 24/4, Galatasaray; per hr €0.80; ☙ 9am-11.30pm) Opposite the Galatasaray Lycée, this friendly place has lots of terminals. Coffee, tea and sandwiches are available. It's on the fourth floor up a steep flight of stairs.

Sinera Internet (Map pp284-6; ☎ 212-292 6899; Mis Sokak 6/1, Beyoğlu; per hr €0.80; ☙ 10am-midnight) Just off İstiklal Caddesi and next door to the pleasant Bir Kahve café.

In four- and five-star hotels, most telephone connections are made using the American-style small clear plastic RJ11 plug, so it's easy to plug in a laptop. Many of these hotels also have Ethernet ports and LANs. In cheaper or older hotels, the phones often use a larger white or beige three-prong Turkish plug. In such cases you'll need to find an electrical shop, and buy a cable with one of these plugs on one end and an RJ11 plug on the other.

Local Internet access kits are available at all computer shops and some large music shops. The most popular local ISP is probably Super-online.

MAPS

Lonely Planet produces a handy, laminated *İstanbul* city map that includes a walking tour.

Free maps in several different languages are usually available from tourist information offices. English maps are sometimes available in the arrivals hall at **Atatürk International Airport** (p238). For more detailed guidance, look for *Sokak Sokak İstanbul (İstanbul Street by Street)* in bookshops. It costs €16.70.

MEDICAL SERVICES

The fact that Turkey doesn't have reciprocal health-care arrangements with other countries means that having travel insurance is highly advisable.

For minor problems, it's customary to ask at a chemist/pharmacy *(eczane)* for advice. Sign language usually suffices to communicate symptoms and the pharmacist will prescribe treatment on the spot. Drugs requiring a prescription in Western countries are often sold over the counter (except for the most dangerous or addictive ones) and will often be cheaper, too. Ensure you know the generic name of your medicine; the commercial name may not be the same in Turkey. See p256 for a list of medical terms; for a more comprehensive list, get a copy of Lonely Planet's *Turkish Phrasebook*. The word for hospital is '*hastanesi*'.

Most doctors in Turkey speak English and half of all the physicians in İstanbul are women. If a woman visits a male doctor, it's customary to have a companion present during any physical examination or treatment, as there is not always a nurse available to serve in this role.

If it's an emergency and you want to try a public hospital, consider **Taksim Hastanesi** (Emergency Hospital; Map pp284-6; ☎ 212-252 4300; Sıraselviler Caddesi, Cihangir; ☙ 24hr) The doctors speak English and its charges are the same whether or not you're a foreign visitor/resident or a Turkish citizen.

Though they are expensive, it's probably easiest to visit one of the private hospitals listed below if you need medical care when in İstanbul. The standard of care given by these places is excellent and you will have no trouble finding staff who speak English.

Alman Hastanesi (Map pp284-6; ☎ 212-293 2150; Sıraselviler Caddesi 119, Taksim; ☙ 8.30am-6pm Mon-Fri, 8.30am-5pm Sat) This hospital is a few hundred metres south of Taksim Square on the left-hand side. It has eye and dental clinics, German administration and English-speaking staff. A consultation costs €48. Credit cards are accepted.

American Hastanesi (☎ 212-311 2000; Güzelbahçe Sokak 20, Nişantaşı ☙ 24hr emergency dept) About 2km northeast of Taksim Square, this hospital has a US administration (all doctors speak English) and a dental clinic. It offers an excellent service. A consultation costs €53. Credit cards are accepted.

Metropolitan Florence Nightingale Hastanesi (☎ 212-288 3400; Cemil Aslan Guder Sokak 8, Gayrettepe; ☙ 24hr emergency dept) This modern facility has a well-respected paediatrics department. Staff speak English. Credit cards are accepted.

MONEY

The unit of currency is the Turkish *lira,* or TL. Coins come in amounts of 50,000, 100,000 and 250,000 lira. Banknotes come in amounts of 250,000 (being phased out), 500,000, one million, five million, 10 million and 20 million lira.

With all those zeroes, it's often difficult to make sure you're trading the correct notes. Beware! Shopkeepers and taxi drivers may sometimes try to give you a 500,000 lira note in place of a five million, or a one million note instead of a 10 million.

When the government undertakes the inevitable elimination of some zeroes on the currency (slated for January 2005, but we're not holding our breath) the confusion will be far greater, as old lira notes with all the zeroes will remain in circulation with new notes for a time. Take your time and be sure of amounts.

See p17 for a discussion of inflation and the ever-fluctuating value of the lira. The exchange rate table in the Quick Reference section on the inside front cover has pegged the euro to TL1,600,000 and the US$ to TL1,484,030; these exchange rates have been used when citing prices throughout this book.

ATMs

Automated teller machines (ATMs, cashpoints) are common in İstanbul. Virtually all of them offer instructions in English, French and German and will pay out Turkish liras when you insert your bank debit (cash) card. ATMs will also pay cash advances on most major credit cards (especially Visa). The limit on cash withdrawals is generally the equivalent of about €300 per day, though this varies from bank to bank.

All of the major Turkish banks and some smaller banks have ATMs; Akbank and Yapı Kredi are the most common. The specific machine you use must be reliably connected to the major ATM networks' computers via telephone lines. Look for stickers with the logos of these services (Cirrus, Maestro, Plus Systems etc) affixed to the machine. If the connection is not reliable, you may get a message saying that the transaction was refused by your bank (which may not be true) and your card will (hopefully) be returned to you.

Changing Money

There are 24-hour exchange bureaux *(döviz bürosu)* in the arrivals hall at Atatürk International Airport that offer rates comparable to those offered by bureaux in the city. Count the money you're given carefully and save your currency exchange receipts *(bordro),* as you may need them to reconvert Turkish liras at the end of your stay.

US dollars and euros are easily changed at exchange bureaux. They are also often accepted as payment without being changed. Other currencies such as French francs and Australian, Canadian or New Zealand dollars are fairly easily changed too, though it's better to stick with the major currencies. Rates are similar whichever bureau you go to, with the possible exception of those in the tourist precinct of Sultanahmet. Bureaux are open long hours (at a minimum, between 9am and 7pm). You will usually need to show your passport when changing cash.

As Turkish liras are fully convertible, there is no black market.

Credit Cards

Most hotels, car-rental agencies, shops, pharmacies, entertainment venues and restaurants will accept major credit cards. Budget hostels and hotels, and basic eateries such as lokantas, pidecis, *kebabçıs* and börekçis usually accept cash only.

Travellers Cheques

If you have travellers cheques, you will have to change them at a bank or post office. Exchange bureaux do not handle them. You'll need to show your passport.

NEWSPAPERS & MAGAZINES

Local daily newspapers are in full lurid colour featuring scantily clad women squeezed between the advertisements. The journalistic content is best left unmentioned. Of prime interest to visitors is the *Turkish Daily News,* an English-language daily newspaper published in Ankara and sold for €0.70 in İstanbul. It has some international news and an oversupply of self-important editorial opinion.

The Guide İstanbul is published bi-monthly and runs listings of restaurants, shops and other services. Features can be interesting, but often read as advertorial. It costs €2.30.

There are monthly Turkish and English editions of the *Time Out İstanbul* magazine. Like *The Guide İstanbul,* this has a large listings section and some articles that read as advertorial. Its features are more interesting, though, and it is the best source of details about upcoming events in town. It costs €1.40. Time Out also publishes an annual shopping guide (in Turkish).

The glossy magazine *Cornucopia* has excellent restaurant reviews and articles on Anatolian arts, culture, history and literature. It's published three times per year and costs €8.40.

You can also buy the big international papers such as the *International Herald Tribune, Le Monde* and *The Guardian* from newsstands. Be sure to check the date on any international paper before you buy it. The best selection of international magazines can be found at the Remzi Kitabevi bookshop at Akmerkez.

POST

Post offices, marked by black-on-yellow signs, are traditionally known as PTTs (peh-teh-teh; *Posta Telefon, Teleğraf*). **İstanbul's Central Post Office** (Merkez Postane; Map pp278-80; Şehinşah Pehlevi Caddesi, Eminönü) is several blocks southwest of Sirkeci Railway Station. It has a section open 24 hours a day, where you can make phone calls, buy stamps and send and receive faxes. All post restante mail should be sent here (c/o Post Restante, Büyük Postane, Büyük Postane Caddesi, Sirkeci, İstanbul).

There's a **PTT booth** (Map pp278-80) outside Aya Sofya on Aya Sofya Meydanı in Sultanahmet, which is open 9am to 4pm Tuesday to Sunday. There are PTTs in the **law courts** (Map pp278-80) on İmran Öktem Caddesi in Sultanahmet; off İstiklal Caddesi at **Galatasaray Square** (Map pp284-6); near the **Galata Bridge** (Map pp284-6) in Karaköy; and in the southwestern corner of the **Kapalı Çarşı** (Map p103) near the Havuzlu Lokantası on Gani Çelebi Sokak.

The *yurtdışı* slot is for mail to foreign countries, *yurtiçi* is for mail to other Turkish cities, and *şehiriçi* is for mail within İstanbul. Mail delivery is fairly reliable. All PTTs sell stamps; a stamp for a postcard to Europe costs €0.40 and to the US or Australia €0.50.

The easiest way to send a parcel is by courier; there is a **DHL office** (Map p287; ☎ 212-444 0040) conveniently located on Cumhuriyet Caddesi just north of Taksim Square. Be prepared for a hefty charge, though.

SAFETY
Pedestrian Safety
As a pedestrian, give way to cars and trucks in all situations, even if you have to jump out of the way. The sovereignty of the pedestrian is recognised in law but not out on the street.

Police
Blue-clad officers are part of a national force designated by the words *polis* or *emniyet* (security). Under normal circumstances you will have little to do with them. If you do encounter them, they will judge you partly by your personal appearance. If you look tidy and 'proper', they'll be on your side. If you're dressed carelessly they may not be as helpful.

Other blue-clad officers with peaked caps are market inspectors *(belediye zabıtası)*. You won't have much to do with them.

Racial Discrimination
Turkey is not ethnically diverse. Its racial mix is mostly among subgroups of the Caucasian group, with admixtures (sometimes ancient) of Asian races. Recent immigration has largely been from Russia and Eastern Europe. This means that travellers who are Asian or Black stand out as being different and can be treated unacceptably as a consequence. As well as harassment, there have been isolated incidents of violence towards Blacks, allegedly at the hands of individual members of the police force.

Theft & Robbery
Theft is not generally a big problem and robbery (mugging) is comparatively rare, but don't let İstanbul's relative safety lull you. Take normal precautions. Areas to be particularly careful in include Aksaray/Laleli, the city's red-light district; the Grand Bazaar (pickpocket central); İstiklal Caddesi in Beyoğlu; and Galipdede Caddesi in Tünel, where bag snatching occurs regularly.

Traffic Accidents
It's worth mentioning that Turkey has one of the world's highest motor-vehicle accident rates. Drive very defensively. A massive safety campaign is under way, but its full effects will not be felt for some years.

TELEPHONE

Country code (☎ 90)

European İstanbul (☎ 212)

Asian İstanbul (☎ 216)

Code to make an intercity call (☎ 0 plus local code)

International access code (☎ 00)

Directory inquiries (☎ 118)

International operator (☎ 115)

Türk Telekom (☎ 212-444 1444; www.telekom .gov.tr) has a monopoly on phone services. You'll find most public phones in clusters, often near PTTs. International calls can be made from most of these phones. You pay for calls with a prepaid telephone card (telefon kartı); some newer phones also take credit cards. There are two types of telefon kartı, the regular floppy version (manyetik kart) or a rigid 'smart kart'. Manyetik karts come in denominations of 30, 60 and 100 usage units and cost €1.20, €2.40 and €4, respectively. Smart karts come in denominations of 50, 100 and 200 usage units and cost €2, €4 and €8. You can buy them from booths near clusters of phones or from PTTs. In general, a 30-unit card is ample for local calls; 60 units for a short, domestic intercity call; and 100 units for longer domestic calls. You'll need a 200-unit card to make an international call of more than a couple of minutes. Rates for local and intercity domestic calls are moderate. Reduced rates for international calls are in effect from 10pm to 9am and all day Sunday.

If you are in European İstanbul and wish to call a number in Asian İstanbul, you must dial 0, followed by ☎ 216. If you are in Asian İstanbul and wish to call a number in European İstanbul use ☎ 212. Do not use a prefix (that is, don't use the 0 or 212/6) if you are calling a number on the same shore.

Fax

Most PTTs will send and hold faxes for you. The **Central Post Office** (Map pp278-80) in Sirkeci has a fax centre open 24 hours.

Mobile Phones

Mobile reception is very good in İstanbul and locals have embraced the technology wholeheartedly. At the time of research there were four local GSM networks:

Aria (☎ 414 1155; www.aria.com.tr in Turkish)

Telsim (☎ 444 0542; www.telsim.com.tr)

Turkcell (☎ 444 0532; www.turkcell.com.tr in Turkish)

These all offer prepaid subscriptions. You can also invest in prepaid SIM cards (hażr kart) at any Turkcell dealer (these are thin on the ground). You'll need to show your passport.

TIME

İstanbul time is East European Time, two hours ahead of Coordinated Universal Time (UTC, alias GMT), except in the warm months, when clocks are turned ahead one hour. Daylight saving (summer) time usually begins at 1am on the last Sunday in March and ends at 2am on the last Sunday in October.

Turks use the 24-hour clock.

TIPPING

Restaurants & cafés 10%.

Taxis To the closest TL1,000,000.

Hotel porters €1.

Hamams 10-20% (unless included in fee).

Musicians at meyhanes €10 per table.

See p149 for more information.

TOILETS

In most public toilets you must pay around €0.25. Instead of providing toilet paper, these toilets are equipped with a tap and receptacle for water or a little copper tube that spurts water where needed. Some toilets are tiled holes in the ground rather than sit-down numbers.

Basic public toilets can be found near the big tourist attractions and transport hubs. Some are dirty, others quite acceptable. Every mosque also has a toilet.

TOURIST INFORMATION

The **Ministry of Culture & Tourism** (www.touris mturkey.org, www.turizm.gov.tr) runs the following tourist information offices:

Atatürk International Airport (☎ 212-573 4136; ☽ 24hr) In the international arrivals area.

Beyazıt Square (Hürriyet Meydanı; Map pp282-3; ☎ 212-522 4902; ☽ 9am-5pm Mon-Sat)

Elmadağ (Map 279; ☎ 212-233 0592; ☽ 9am-5pm Mon-Sat) In the arcade in front of the İstanbul Hilton Hotel, just off Cumhuriyet Caddesi near Taksim Square.

Karaköy International Maritime Passenger Terminal (Map pp284-6; ☎ 212-249 5776; ☽ 9am-5pm Mon-Sat)

Sultanahmet (Map pp278-80; ☎ 212-518 8754; ☽ 9am-5pm) At the northeastern end of the Hippodrome.

The Sultanahmet office is most helpful. All usually stock free maps and brochures. Be mindful that hotel, entertainment and other recommendations from tourist offices may not be impartial, as commissions may be involved.

VISAS

Nationals of the following countries (among others) may enter Turkey for up to three months with only a valid passport (no visa is required): Denmark, Finland, France, Germany, Greece, Israel, Japan, Malaysia, New Zealand, Singapore, Sweden and Switzerland.

Nationals of the following countries (among others) may enter for up to three months upon purchase of a visa sticker at their point of arrival (ie not at an embassy in advance): Australia, Austria, Belgium, Canada, Ireland, Italy, Netherlands, Portugal, Spain, UK and USA.

Nationals of Norway, Hungary and many Eastern European and Central Asian countries may enter for up to one month upon purchase of a visa sticker at their point of arrival.

Your passport must have at least three months' validity remaining, or you may not be admitted into Turkey. If you arrive at Atatürk International Airport, get your visa from the booth to the left of the 'Other Nationalities' counter in the customs hall before you go through immigration. Officially, you can pay in Turkish lira, pounds sterling, euros or US dollars, but we know of instances where customs officials refused payment in one or other of these currencies, insisting that Britons pay in sterling, Americans in US dollars etc. They may also insist on correct change. An ATM machine dispensing Turkish liras is next to the counter, but it's not always working. The fees change (when the Iraq War broke out, visa fees for US citizens skyrocketed to US$100 in what was thought to be a Turkish protest against the US-led invasion), but at the time of research Australians and Americans paid US$20, Canadians US$45, Britons UK£10 or €15 and Spaniards US$10.

Visa Extensions

There are single- and multiple-entry visas. Single-entry visas are valid for three months from the day of entry; multiple-entry visas are valid for three-month blocks during a one-year period. Depending on your nationality, you may be able to extend your visa. Most visitors wanting to extend their stay for a few months avoid bureaucratic tedium by taking a quick overnight trip to Greece (Thessaloniki or Rhodes), returning to Turkey the next day with a new three-month stamp in their passports.

WOMEN TRAVELLERS

As is the case in most Muslim countries, Western women often attract the sort of attention they (thankfully) never would at home. Most of this attention will be innocent and friendly. Inevitably, however, some of it won't be. Though serious assault is far less common in İstanbul than in London, Paris or New York, harassment such as rude noises and touching are more common – especially in the more conservative sections of the city such as Old İstanbul.

You may find men converse with your breasts, instead of your face, burst into song as you pass, or throw a pathetic handful of foreign words your way. Many of these embarrassing attempts at seduction are due to cultural misunderstandings bred by European and American films and different cultural norms. In general, keep your dealings with Turkish men formal and polite, not friendly. Avoid casual eye contact and dress modestly. Ignore noises or advances on the street. Also avoid walking alone at night, especially in Aksaray/Laleli, Karaköy and the back streets of Beyoğlu. It's a good idea to sit in the back seat of taxis. If approached by a Turkish man in circumstances that upset you, try saying *Ayıp!* (ah-*yuhp*), which means 'Shame on you!'

You'll have no trouble finding tampons, sanitary napkins and condoms in pharmacies and supermarkets in İstanbul. Bring a shawl to cover your head when visiting mosques.

Aile Salonu

Women are welcome in all public establishments, but the overwhelmingly male clientele of many places makes some Turkish women uncomfortable. Many restaurants have rooms set apart for use only by women, couples and mixed groups. Called the *aile salonu* (family room), it allows women to escape unwanted attention. Look for the sign *Aile Salonumuz Vardır* (We Have a Family Room) in the windows of cheap and mid-range restaurants. Sitting in the *aile salonu* is optional, of course. If you'd rather sit in the main dining room, do so.

Resources

The following İstanbul-based organisations work to promote women's rights in Turkey:

İstanbul Barosu Kadın Hakları Uygulama Merkezi (İstanbul Bar Association Women's Rights Enforcement Center; ☎ 212-292 7739; ihm@istanbulbarosu.org.tr) Operates as a counselling centre and participates at hearings on behalf of women who can't afford legal representation.

Kadının İnsan Hakları Projesi (KIHP, Women for Women's Human Rights (WWHR); ☎ 212-251 0029; wwhrist@superonline.com; İnönü Caddesi, Saadet Apt 37/6, Gümüssuyu) Involved in advocacy and lobbying, documentation and dissemination of materials, legal literacy groups.

Pazartesi (☎ 212-292 0739; pazartesidergi@superonline .com; Abdullah Sokak 9, Beyoğlu) A feminist newspaper for women.

Women's Library and Information Centre Foundation (Kadın Eserleri Kütüphanesi ve Bilgi Merkezi Vakfı; ☎ 212-534 9550; Fener Mahallesi, Fener Vapur Iskelesi Karşısı, Fener-Haliç; ⏰ 9am-5.30pm Mon-Sat) This is the only women's library and information centre in Turkey. Paid and volunteer staff collect, preserve and present information about women's history and the current status of women in Turkey and elsewhere.

Women's Studies Association Necla Arat (☎ 212-511 9826; Kuşkonmaz Sokak 5/8, Yeşilyurt)

WORK

After sampling the manifold delights of İstanbul, many travellers decide to stay. Jobs aren't all that easy to find (Turkey has a very high unemployment level) and most of these people end up teaching English at one of the many private colleges or schools; others get work as nannies or in the hospitality industry.

If you want to get a job at one of the well-paid private schools, you'll need to have a Teaching English as a Foreign Language (TEFL) certificate, or an equivalent, and a graduate degree (it doesn't matter what it's in). Other jobs are advertised in the *Turkish Daily News*.

Doing Business

Turkish companies have a gloss of Western-style business manners and practices, but doing business here can be different to doing so in Western Europe or North America. Most risks are greater, but as a rapidly developing country the rewards may be greater as well.

Government cooperation cannot be assumed until the project is completed and actively operating. In part, this is because of frequent changes in the endless succession of fairly weak ruling coalitions, and the subsequent uncertainty among the ministries regulating business and financial activity. An astute Turkish business partner is usually essential; finding a suitably ethical one is important.

GETTING STARTED

Contact the commercial attaché at the nearest Turkish embassy or consulate. The attaché can put you in touch with local trade and business groups in your home country, and can suggest useful government contacts in Turkey.

The *Executive's Handbook Turkey Almanac* is a useful book published annually (supposedly) in İstanbul. It has articles about the economy, markets and policies for the previous year, and other general information about Turkey's business world. You can buy it at bookshops in İstanbul for €8.30 or contact the publishers, **Intermedia** (☎ 212-279 6402; www.intermedia .com.tr). Intermedia also publishes *Turkey Weekly*, a newsletter covering significant economic and political developments in the country that is emailed or faxed to subscribers every Monday.

IBS Research, a corporate advisory service, publishes *Doing Business in Turkey*, which details regulations and the climate of the Turkish business world. Order it online at the publisher's website (www.ibsresearch.com) – which also has heaps of useful info – or try ☎ 212-252 2460. An annual subscription (one edition plus three quarterly updates) costs €1227.

The monthly *Turkish Business World* is available in bookshops and newspaper stands around the city. It has a collection of articles and advertisements that may be of interest. Check out www .turkishbusinessworld.com.

DEIK (Dış Ekonomik İlişkiler Kurulu; ☎ 212-243 4180; www.deik.org.tr; İstiklal Caddesi 286/9, Beyoğlu) is the Foreign Economic Relations Board of Turkey. Its website has useful links and economic and business information.

Work Visas

It's best to obtain a *çalışma vizesi* (work visa) from the Turkish embassy or consulate in your home country before you leave. You must have a job lined up before a work visa will be issued and your employment must be approved by the relevant Turkish ministry (eg the Ministry of Education for a teaching job). Your prospective employer will organise this approval and provide you with the permission letter. You must submit this letter as part of your work-visa application along with the completed visa form, your passport and two photos of yourself. If your visa is granted (most are), you must pay a fee. Your passport will be returned with the visa stamped inside; it usually takes around a month.

If you're not at home and you want a work visa, you must apply for it outside Turkey. The Turkish consulate in Komotini, Greece, is accustomed to such requests. It usually grants the visa within a few hours.

Possession of a work visa automatically qualifies you for an *ikamet tezkeresi* (residence permit, most commonly known as a 'pink book'), valid for two years.

Language

Language

It's true – anyone can speak another language. Don't worry if you haven't studied languages before or that you studied a language at school for years and can't remember any of it. It doesn't even matter if you failed English grammar. After all, that's never affected your ability to speak English! And this is the key to picking up a language in another country. You just need to start speaking.

Learn a few key phrases before you go. Write them on pieces of paper and stick them on the fridge, by the bed or even on the computer – anywhere that you'll see them often.

You'll find that locals appreciate travellers trying their language, no matter how muddled you may think you sound. So don't just stand there, say something! If you want to learn more Turkish than we've included here, pick up a copy of Lonely Planet's comprehensive but user-friendly *Turkish Phrasebook*.

PRONUNCIATION

Once you learn a few basic rules, you'll find Turkish pronunciation quite simple to master. Despite oddities such as the soft 'g' (ğ) and undotted 'i' (ı), it's a phonetically consistent language – there's generally a clear one-letter/one-sound relationship.

It's important to remember that each letter is pronounced; vowels don't combine to form diphthongs and consonants don't combine to form other sounds (such as 'th', 'gh' or 'sh' in English). It therefore follows that **h** in Turkish is always pronounced as a separate letter. For example, your Turkish friend Ahmet is 'ahh-met' not 'aa-met', and the word *rehber* (guide) is pronounced 'rehber' not 're-ber'.

Here are some of the letters in Turkish which may cause initial confusion:

â	a faint 'y' sound in the preceding consonant
İ, i	a short 'i', as in 'hit' or 'sit'
I, ı	a neutral vowel; as the 'a' in 'ago'
Ö, ö	as the 'e' in 'her' said with pursed lips (but with no 'r' sound)
U, u	as the 'oo' in 'book'
Ü, ü	an exaggerated rounded-lip 'you'
C, c	as the 'j' in 'jet'
Ç, ç	as the 'ch' in 'church'
G, g	always hard as in 'garden' (not as in 'gentle')
Ğ, ğ	silent; lengthens preceding vowel
J, j	as the 'z' in 'azure'
Ş, ş	as the 'sh' in 'show'

SOCIAL
Meeting People

Hello.
Merhaba.
Goodbye.
Allaha ısmarladık. (said by one departing)
Güle güle. (said by one staying)
Please.
Lütfen.
Thank you (very much).
Çok teşekkür ederim.
Yes/No.
Evet/Hayır.
Do you speak English?
Inglizce konuşuyor-musunuz?
Do you understand (me)?
Anlıyormusunuz?
Yes, I understand.
Anlıyorum.
No, I don't understand.
Anlamıyorum.

Could you please ...?
Lütfen ...?

repeat that	tekrarlar mısınız
speak more slowly	daha yavaş konuşur musunuz
write it down	yazar mısınız

Going Out

What's on ...?
... görülecek neler var?

locally	Yerel olarak
this weekend	Bu hafta sonu

| today | Bugün |
| tonight | Bu gece |

Where are the ...?
... nerede?

clubs	Klüpler
gay venues	Gey klüpleri
places to eat	Yemek yenilebilecek yerler
pubs	Birahaneler

Is there a local entertainment guide?
Buranın yerel eğlence rehberi var mı?

PRACTICAL
Question Words

Who?	Kim?
What?	Ne?
When?	Ne zaman?
Where?	Nerede?
How?	Nasıl?

Numbers & Amounts

1	bir
2	iki
3	üç
4	dört
5	beş
6	altı
7	yedi
8	sekiz
9	dokuz
10	on
11	on bir
12	on iki
13	on üç
14	on dört
15	on beş
16	on altı
17	on yedi
18	on sekiz
19	on dokuz
20	yirmi
21	yirmi bir
22	yirmi iki
30	otuz
40	kırk
50	elli
60	altmış
70	yetmiş
80	seksen
90	doksan
100	yüz
1000	bin
2000	iki bin
1,000,000	milyon

Days

Monday	Pazartesi
Tuesday	Salı
Wednesday	Çarşamba
Thursday	Perşembe
Friday	Cuma
Saturday	Cumartesi
Sunday	Pazar

Banking

I'd like to ...
... istiyorum.

cash a cheque	Çek bozdurmak
change money	Para bozdurmak
change a travellers cheque	Seyahat çeki bozdurmak

Where's the nearest ...?
... nerede?

| ATM | Bankamatik/ATM |
| foreign exchange office | Döviz bürosu |

Post

Where is the (main) post office?
(Merkez) Postane nerede?

I want to send a ...
Bir ... göndermek istiyorum.

fax	faks
parcel	paket
postcard	kartpostal

I want to buy ...
... satın almak istiyorum.

an aerogram	Telsiz telgraf
an envelope	Zarf
a stamp	Pul

Phones & Mobiles

I want to buy a phone card.
Telefon kartı istiyorum.

I want to make ...
... istiyorum.

| a (local) call | (Yerel) bir görüşme yapmak |
| reverse-charge/ collect call | Ödemeli görüşme yapmak |

I'd like a/an ...
... istiyorum.

| charger for my phone | Cep telefonum için şarj aleti |

mobile/cell phone for hire	Cep telefonu kiralamak
prepaid mobile/ cell phone	Kontörlü cep telefonu
SIM card for your network	Buradaki şebeke için SİM kart

Internet

Where's the local Internet café?
En yakın internet kafe nerede?

I'd like to ...
... istiyorum.

| check my email | E-postama bakmak |
| get Internet access | İnternete girmek |

Transport

What time does the ... leave?
... ne zaman kalkacak?

bus	Otobüs
ferry	Feribot
plane	Uçak
train	Tren

What time's the ... bus?
... (otobüs) ne zaman?

first	İlk
last	Son
next	Sonraki

Is this taxi free?
Bu taksi boş mu?
Please put the meter on.
Lütfen taksimetreyi çalıştırın.
How much is it to ...?
... ne kadar?
Please take me to (this address).
Lütfen beni (şu adrese) götürün.

FOOD

breakfast	kahvaltı
lunch	öğle yemeği
dinner	akşam yemeği
snack	hafif yemek

| eat | yemek |
| drink | içmek |

Can you recommend a ...
İyi bir ... tavsiye edebilir misiniz?

bar	bar
café	kafe
restaurant	restoran

Is service included in the bill?
Hesaba servis dahil mi?

For more detailed information on food and dining out, see p42.

EMERGENCIES

It's an emergency!
Bu acil bir durum!
Could you please help?
Yardım edebilir misiniz lütfen?
Call the police/a doctor/an ambulance!
Polis/Doktor/Ambulans çağır(ın).
Where's the police station?
Polis karakolu nerede?

HEALTH

Where's the nearest ...?
En yakın ... nerede?

chemist (night)	(nöbetçi) eczane
dentist	diş hekimi
doctor	doktor
hospital	hastane

I need a doctor (who speaks English).
(İngilizce konuşan) bir doktora ihtiyacım var.

Symptoms

I have (a) ...
... var.

diarrhoea	Ishalim
fever	Ateşim
headache	Ibaş ağrısı
pain	Ağrım/sancım

Glossary

Here, with definitions, are some useful words and abbreviations. See p34 for a more extensive list of architectural terms and p51 for more food terms.

ada(sı) – island
aile salonu – family room; for couples, families and women in a Turkish restaurant
altgeçidi – pedestrian subway/underpass

arabesk – music that blends folk, classical and *fasıl* traditions
aşik – Turkish troubadours
Asya – Asian İstanbul
Avrupa – European İstanbul
ayran – a yogurt drink

bahçe(si) – garden
balık – fish

banliyö treni (s), banliyö trenleri (pl) – suburban (or commuter) train

belediye – town hall

bey – 'Mr'; follows the name

birahane – beer hall

boğaz – strait

bordro – exchange receipt

börek – flaky pastry that can be sweet or savoury

büfe – snack bar

bulvarı – often abbreviated to 'bul'; boulevard or avenue

büyük tur – long tour

caddesi – often abbreviated to 'cad'; street

caïque – long, thin rowboat

çalışma vizesi – work visa

çamaşır – laundry, underwear

camii – mosque

çarşı(sı) – market, bazaar

çay bahçesi – tea garden

cicim – embroidered mat

çift – pair

çocuk – child

çorba – soup

darüşşifa – hospital

deniz – sea

deniz otobüsü – catamaran, sea bus

Dikkat! Yavaş! – Careful! Slow!

dolmuş – shared taxi (or minibus)

dondurma – ice cream

döner kebap – meat roasted on a revolving, vertical spit

döviz bürosu – currency exchange office

eczane – chemist, pharmacy

ekmek – bread

emanet – left luggage

emniyet – security

eyvan – vaulted hall opening onto a central court in a medrese or mosque

ezan – the Muslim call to prayer

fasıl – energetic folk music played in taverns or *meyhanes*

fayton – horse-drawn carriage

feribot – ferry

fiş – electricity plug

gazino – open-air Turkish nightclub (not for gambling)

gece – night

gişe – ticket booth

göbektaşı – hot platform in Turkish bath

gözleme – Turkish pancake

gündüz – daytime

hamam(ı) – Turkish steam bath

harem – family/women's quarters of a residence

hat(tı) – route

hazır yemek lokanta – ready-made-food restaurant

hısar(ı) – fortress or citadel

ikamet tezkeresi – residence permit, known as 'pink book'

imam – prayer leader; Muslim cleric; teacher

imaret – soup kitchen

iskele(si) – landing-place, wharf, quay

jeton – token (for telephones)

kadın – wife

kale(si) – fortress, citadel

kapı(sı) – door, gate

Karagöz – shadow-puppet theatre

kat – storey (of a building)

KDV – katma değer vergisi;value-added tax (VAT)

kebapçı – place selling kebaps

kilim – pileless woven run

köfte – Turkish meatballs

köfteci – place selling grilled meatballs

köprü – bridge

köy(ü) – village

küçük tur – short tour

kürsü – prayer-reader's platform

kuru temizleme – dry cleaning

lahmacun – Arabic soft pizza

liman(ı) – harbour

lokanta – restaurant

lokum – Turkish delight

mahalli hamam – neighbourhood Turkish bath

mahfil – high, elaborate chair

Maşallah – Wonder of God! (said in admiration or to avert the evil eye)

menba suyu – spring water

merkez postane – central post office

mescit – prayer room, small mosque

mevlevi – whirling dervish

meydan(ı) – public square, open place

meyhanes – wine shops, taverns

müezzin – the official who sings the *ezan*, or call to prayer

müze(si) – museum

nargileh – water pipe

ocakbaşı – grill

oda(sı) – room

otel – hotel

otogar – bus station

otopark – car park

otostop – hitch

otoyol – multilane toll highway

padişah – Ottoman emperor, sultan

pansiyon – pension, B&B, guesthouse

pastane – also pastahane; pastry shop, patisserie

pazar(ı) – weekly market, bazaar

pide – Turkish pizza

pideci – pizzeria

polis – police

PTT – Posta, Telefon, Telğraf; post, telephone and telegraph office

rakı – aniseed-flavoured grape brandy

saz – traditional Turkish long-necked string instrument

sebil – fountain

sedir – low sofa

şehir – city; municipal area

sema – Sufic religious ceremony

servis ücreti – service charge

servis yolu – service road

sıcak şarap – mulled wine

şile bezi – a type of open-weave cotton cloth with hand embroidery

şiş kebap – grilled, skewered meat

sinema – cinema

sokak, sokağı – often abbreviated to 'sk' or 'sok'; street or lane

su – water

Sufi – Muslim mystic, member of a mystic ('dervish') brotherhood

sultan – sovereign

sumak – flat-woven rug with intricate detail

sünnet odası – circumcision room

tabhane – hostel

tarikat – a Sufic order

tatıcı – specialist dessert place

TC – Türkiye Cumhuriyeti (Turkish Republic); designates an official office or organisation

telekart – telephone debit card

tuğra – sultan's monogram, imperial signature

ücretsiz servis – free service

valide sultan – queen mother

yardımcı – assistant

yeni otogar – new bus station

yıldız – star

yol(u) – road, way

Behind the Scenes

THE LONELY PLANET STORY

The story begins with a classic travel adventure: Tony and Maureen Wheeler's 1972 journey across Europe and Asia to Australia. There was no useful information about the overland trail then, so Tony and Maureen published the first Lonely Planet guidebook to meet a growing need.

From a kitchen table, Lonely Planet has grown to become the largest independent travel publisher in the world, with offices in Melbourne (Australia), Oakland (USA) and London (UK). Today Lonely Planet guidebooks cover the globe. There is an ever-growing list of books and information in a variety of media. Some things haven't changed. The main aim is still to make it possible for adventurous travellers to get out there – to explore and better understand the world.

At Lonely Planet we believe travellers can make a positive contribution to the countries they visit – if they respect their host communities and spend their money wisely. Every year 5% of company profit is donated to charities around the world.

THIS BOOK

This 4th edition of *İstanbul* was researched and written by Virginia Maxwell. The 3rd edition was revised and updated by Verity Campbell. The 1st and 2nd editions were written by Tom Brosnahan. This guidebook was commissioned in Lonely Planet's Melbourne office and produced by:

Commissioning Editor Will Gourlay
Coordinating Editor Simon Williamson
Coordinating Cartographer Amanda Sierp
Coordinating Layout Designer Jim Hsu
Assisting Editors & Proofreaders David Andrew, Evan Jones, Craig Kilburn & Kate McLeod
Assisting Layout Designer Jacqui Saunders
Cover Designer Gerilyn Attebery
Cover Artwork Wendy Wright
Managing Cartographer Shahara Ahmed
Managing Editor Kerryn Burgess
Layout Manager Adriana Mammarella
Mapping Development Paul Piaia
Project Manager Fabrice Rocher
Language Content Coordinator Quentin Frayne

Cover Photographs Spice display at the Spice Bazaar, Greg Elms/Lonely Planet Images (top); a reflection extends the minarets on İstanbul's Blue Mosque, Richard Hamilton Smith/Australian Picture Library/Corbis (bottom); detail of Turkish slippers at a market, Wayne Walton/Lonely Planet Images (back).

Internal photographs by Phil Weymouth/Lonely Planet Images except for the following: p67 (#2) Greg Elms; p72 (#3) Susan Storm; p72 (#4), p220, p232 Izzet Keribar; p225 Diana Mayfield. All images are the copyright of the photographers unless otherwise indicated. Many of the images in this guide are available for licensing from Lonely Planet Images: www.lonelyplanetimages.com.

ACKNOWLEDGMENTS

Many thanks to the following for use of their content:

Akşit Kültür Turizm Sanat Ajans (İstanbul): plan of Kariye (Chora) Museum from *The Museum of Chora – Museum and Frescoes*, İlhan Akşit (2002).
David Ball (translator): Excerpt from Pierre Loti, *Constantinople in 1890*, Ünlem Basim Yayıncılık Ltd (Istanbul, 2002).

THANKS
VIRGINIA MAXWELL

My greatest thanks, as always, go to my all-time favourite travelling companions, Peter and Max Handsaker. Big thanks also go to Jill Hollingworth, Kate Gray, Catherine Hannebery, Elizabeth Maxwell, Matthew Clarke, Janet Austin, Dave McClymont, Ahmet and Marc, Derya and Dara at the Galata Residence, and Ann at the Empress Zoe.

Sincere thanks to Pat Yale, who showed me her favourite places in the city, shared lots of information and refrained from laughing at my attempts to speak Turkish.

At Lonely Planet, thanks go to publishing manager Kate Cody, as well as the long-suffering and ever-charming Will Gourlay and the totally unflappable Shahara Ahmed and Mandy Sierp.

OUR READERS

Many thanks to the travellers who used the last edition and wrote to us with helpful hints, useful advice and interesting anecdotes. Your names follow:

Carlos Arroyo, Gary Arthur, Periklis Atzampos, Steve Bade, Eric Ball, Hugh Barker, Basak Basoglu, Robert Beattie, Natalie Becker, Nicole Bellefleur, Barry Benda, Jim Berry, Alain Bertallo, Eliza Bird, Katerina Bojanova, Truman Bradley, Susan Bush, Simon Butcher, Mario Cams,

Gilon Catibog, Lee Choong, Karen Chorny, April Chow, Rosie Cohan, Daniel Cohen, Doug Cook, Jane Cook, Meg Cook, Ursula Cornu, Claire Dannenbaum, Kris Darby, Alard de Boer, Don de Greef, Lenart de Regt, Bert D'Hooghe, Vojtech Dobias, Moray Easdale, Tadd Fernee, John Fogg, Judy Forge, Wendy Fox, Jeffrey Jay Foxx, Diana Gabanyi, Joshua C Gambrel, Brett Gardner, Jean & John Glenister, Ela Glowicka, Robert Godbe, Gerald Goldstein, Damian Goodburn, Ed Gramlich, Sally Hall, Mike Hancock, Michael Hanna, Rachael Harding, Ton Harfst, Freddie Hart, Shohei Hasegawa, Patricia Havekost, Jane Hennessy, Francesca Hilbron, Parker Holden, Fred Hood, Erik Hoogcarspel, Chris Hunt, Melis Iler, Andrew Johnson, Lisa Johnson, Alex Jones, Gairn Kalla, Aileen Kennedy, Andre Khougaz, Kim King, Jakob & Charlotte Knudsen, Eric Koh, David Koistinen, Piet Kooijman, Rob & Nelleke Kool, Cherry Kovoor, Rod Latham, Joe Leach, Karen Lindquist, Miklos Lipcsey, Luba Malin, C Van Manen, Debbie Manuel, Jim Manuel, Melvin Mazur, Betty McGeever, Elizabeth McWhorter, Ron Miller, Conor Morris, Simon Motz, Lelde Muehlenbachs, Shusha Niederberger, Stefano Nikolaou, James Oehlcke, Michael Palij, Philip Pearson, Michaël Pecheux, Saadet Perrigon, Carlo Pezza, Joachim Pruefer, Marco Ranieri, Chris Reiher, Jorge Reparaz, Ran Reshef, Ildiko Ribeiro, Kim Richardson, Miffy Robb, Geoff Robinson, Geoff & Shirley Robinson, Anne Rout, Trevor Russell, Wouter Rutten, Bob Schofield, Adam Schreck, Alison Simmons, Andrea Simonetta, Koen Simons, Bennett Sloan, Maaike Sluis, David K Smith, Owen Smith, Michael Snyder, Joseph T Stanik, Marla Stepanek, Joy & Peter Stirling, Richard Stoller, Brett Tappin, Alessandra Testoni, Hakon Tolleshaug, Stephane Valorge, Chris Vickery, Dawn Walker, Bronwyn Wellings, Patricia West, Anna Belle Whiting O'Brien, Jorien Wiersum, Anna Wright, John Yatczyshyn, Lyu Younghoon

SEND US YOUR FEEDBACK

We love to hear from travellers – your comments keep us on our toes and help make our books better. Our well-travelled team reads every word on what you loved or loathed about this book. Although we cannot reply individually to postal submissions, we always guarantee that your feedback goes straight to the appropriate authors, in time for the next edition. Each person who sends us information is thanked in the next edition – and the most useful submissions are rewarded with a free book.

To send us your updates – and find out about Lonely Planet events, newsletters and travel news – visit our award-winning website: www.lonelyplanet.com/feedback

Note: We may edit, reproduce and incorporate your comments in Lonely Planet products such as guidebooks, websites and digital products, so let us know if you don't want your comments reproduced or your name acknowledged. For a copy of our privacy policy visit www.lonelyplanet.com/privacy.

Notes

Notes

Notes

Notes

Notes

Notes

Index

See also the separate indexes for Eating (p273), Drinking (p273), Shopping (p274) and Sleeping (p274).

Index

269

Index

Index

000 map pages
000 photographs

MAP LEGEND

ROUTES

Tollway	One-Way Street
Freeway	Mall/Steps
Primary Road	Tunnel
Secondary Road	Walking Tour
Tertiary Road	Walking Tour Detour
Lane	Walking Trail
Under Construction	Walking Path
Track	Pedestrian Overpass
Unsealed Road	

TRANSPORT

Ferry	Bus Route
Metro	Rail
Monorail	Tram

HYDROGRAPHY

River, Creek	Canal
Intermittent River	Water
Swamp	Lake (Dry)
Mangrove	Lake (Salt)
Reef	Mudflats
Glacier	

BOUNDARIES

International	Regional, Suburb
State, Provincial	Ancient Wall
Disputed	Cliff
Marine Park	

AREA FEATURES

Airport	Forest
Area of Interest	Land
Beach, Desert	Mall
Building, Featured	Park
Building, Information	Reservation
Building, Other	Rocks
Building, Transport	Sports
Cemetery, Christian	Urban
Cemetery, Other	

POPULATION

○ CAPITAL (NATIONAL)	◉ CAPITAL (STATE)
● Large City	○ Medium City
○ Small City	○ Town, Village

SYMBOLS

Sights/Activities
- Beach
- Castle, Fortress
- Christian
- Islamic
- Jewish
- Monument
- Museum, Gallery
- Ruin

Eating
- Eating

Drinking
- Drinking
- Café

Entertainment
- Entertainment

Shopping
- Shopping

Sleeping
- Sleeping
- Camping

Transport
- Airport, Airfield
- Border Crossing
- Bus Station
- Parking Area
- Taxi Rank

Other
- Other Site
- Picnic Area

Information
- Bank, ATM
- Embassy/Consulate
- Hospital, Medical
- Information
- Internet Facilities
- Police Station
- Post Office, GPO
- Telephone
- Toilets

Geographic
- Lighthouse
- National Park
- Pass, Canyon
- River Flow

Map Section

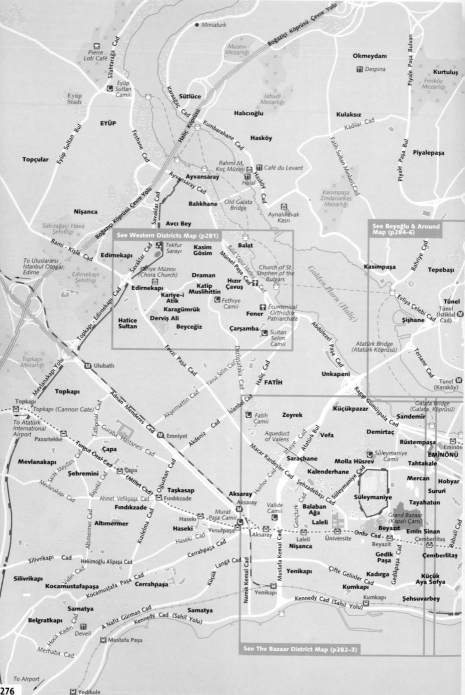

Miniatürk

Pierre Loti Café

Musevi Mezarlığı

Boğaziçi Köprüsü Çevre Yolu

Okmeydanı

Despina

Piyale Paşa Bulvarı

Kurtuluş

Ferikóy Mezarlığı

Silahtarağa Cad

Eyüp Sultan Camii

Sütlüce

Halıcıoğlu

Kulaksız

Kadılar Cad

Piyalepaşa

Piyale Paşa Bul

Eyüp Stadı

Karağaç Cad

Haliç Köprüsü

Kumbarahane Cad

Hasköy

Fatih Sultan Mehmet Cad

EYÜP

Feshane Cad

Eyüp Sultan Bul

Topçular

Rahmi M. Koç Müzesi

Café du Levant

Kasımpaşa Zindanarkası Mezarlığı

Ayvansaray

Halaİ

Hasköy Cad

Ayvansaray Cad

Balıkhane

Old Galata Bridge

Aynalıkavak Kasrı

See Beyoğlu & Around Map (p284–6)

Nişanca

Savaklar Cad

Avcı Bey

Balat

Golden Horn (Haliç)

Kasımpaşa

Bahriye Cad

Tepebaşı

Sakızağacı Hava Şehitliği

Rami - Kışla Cad

Boğaziçi Köprüsü Çevre Yolu

Tekfur Sarayı

See Western Districts Map (p281)

Kasım Gösim

Balat Vapur İskelesi

Mürsel Paşa Cad

Church of St. Stephen of the Bulgars

Evliya Çelebi Cad

Tünel (İstiklal Cad)

Edirnekapı

Savaklar Cad

Kariye Müzesi (Chora Church)

Draman

Hızır Çavuş

Ecumenical Orthodox Patriarchate

Abdülezel Paşa Cad

Şişhane

To Uluslararsı İstanbul Otogar; Edirne

Edirnekapı Şehitliği

Edirnekapı

Katip Muslihittin

Fethiye Camii

Fener

Tünel (Karaköy)

Kariye-i Atik

Karagümrük

Topkapı - Edirnekapı Cad

Hatice Sultan

Derviş Ali

Beyceğiz

Çarşamba

Sultan Selim Camii

Tersane Cad

Topkapı Mezarlığı

Fevzi Paşa Cad

Yavuz Selim Cad

Darüşşafaka Cad

Haliç Cad

Ragıp Gümüşpala Cad

Ulubatlı

FATİH

Unkapani

Galata Bridge (Galata Köprüsü)

To Atatürk International Airport

Mevlanakapı Yolu

Topkapı

Adnan Menderes Cad

Akşemsettin Cad

Akdeniz Cad

İstanbul Cad

Fatih Camii

Zeyrek

Küçükpazar

Sarıdemir

Topkapı (Cannon Gate)

Tatlıpınar Cad

Emniyet

Aqueduct of Valens

Vefa

Hayre Cad

Atatürk Bul

Demirtaş

Rüstempaşa

Emínönü

Pazartekke

Turgut Özal Cad

Çapa

Guraba Hastanesi Cad

Macar Kardeşler Cad

Hohor Cad

Sarachane

Molla Hüsrev

Süleymaniye Camii

Tahtakale

Mevlanakapı

Şehremini

Çapa (Millet Cad)

Oğuzhan Cad

Taşkasap

Şehzadebaşı Cad

Kalenderhane

Süleymaniye Cad

Süleymaniye

Mercan

Hobyar

Sururi

Saray Meydanı Cad

Bayezit Cad

Fındıkzade

Aksaray

Gençturk Cad

Balaban Ağa

Tayahatun

Ahmet Vefikpaşa Cad

Fındıkzade

Murat Paşa Camii

Valide Camii

Laleli

Beyazıt

Emin Sinan

Altınmermer

Fındıkzade

Haseki

Yusufpaşa

Ordu Cad

Beyazit

Çemberlitaş

Hekimoğlu Alipaşa Cad

Haseki

Haseki Cad

Aksaray

Nişanca

Üniversite

Gedik Paşa

Çemberlitaş

Silivrikapı Cad

Kızılelma Cad

Cerrahpaşa Cad

Küçük Langa Cad

Laleli

Çifte Gelinler Cad

Kadırga

Gedikpaşa Cad

Küçük Aya Sofya

Silivrikapı

Vidin Cad

Altınmermer Cad

Namık Kemal Cad

Yenikapı

Mustafa Kemal Cad

Kumkapı

Şehsuvarbey

Kocamustafapaşa

Cerrahpaşa

Kocamustafa Paşa Cad

Yenikapı

Kennedy Cad (Sahil Yolu)

Kumkapı

Samatya

A Nafiz Gürman Cad

Samatya

Belgratkapı

Hoca Kadın Cad

Develi

Kennedy Cad (Sahil Yolu)

Merhaba Cad

Mustafa Paşa

See The Bazaar District Map (p282–3)

To Airport

Yedikule

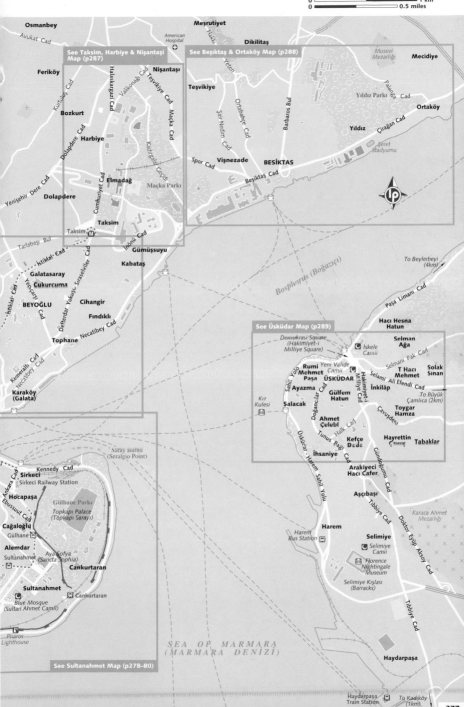

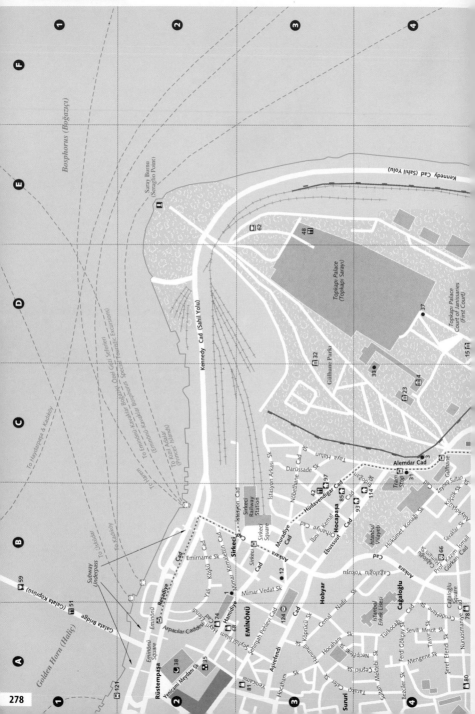

WESTERN DISTRICTS

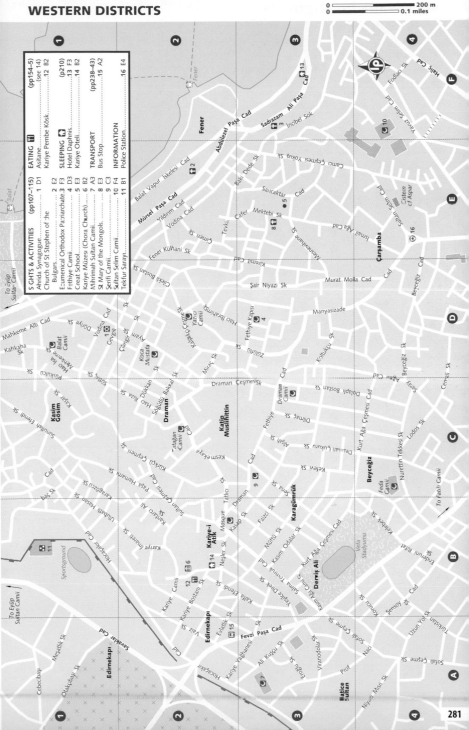

THE BAZAAR DISTRICT

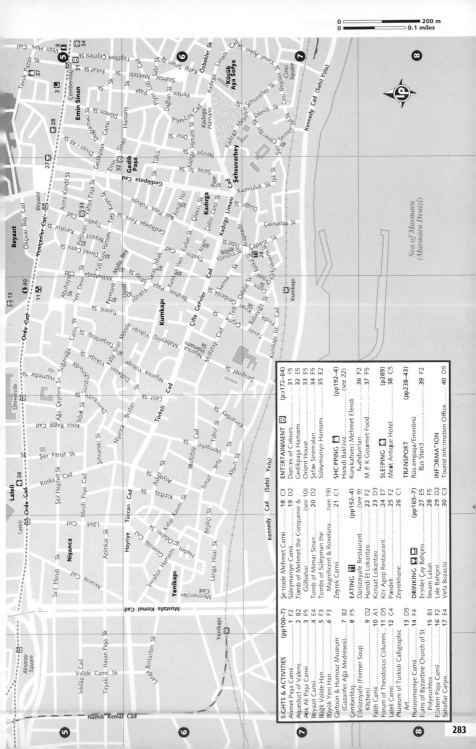

A **B** **C** **D**

1

Paşa Yokuşu Sk
Avuk Cad
Tahtakadı Sk
Hakim Sk
Bayramyeri Sk
Cad
Şirürü Çeşme
Emin
Aynalı Çeşme Cad
Işık Çık
Darack Sk
Balık Sk
Hamalbaşı Cad
Kalyoncu Kulluğu
Bulvarı
Arslan Sk
139
58

Seyh Veli Sk
Arkası Sk
Değirmen
Kızılay Meydanı Cad
Dereboyu
Kasap Zekeriya Sk
Turşucu Bayram Sk
K Bostanı Sk
Sipahi
Firını
Işığı
Meydanı
Tarlabaşı
Cad
Haçapulo Çk
Galatasaray Square
94
88

2
Paşakapısı Cad
Hoca Ahmet Sk
Tabakhane Sk
Başhane Sk
Başhane Aralığı
Potinciler
Neva Sk
Aşıklar
Çay Danlık Sk
Deniz
Çivici Sk
Cad
Kasımpaşa Stadı
Tepebaşı
Meşrutiyet
120
8
22
91
Kallavi Sk
Acar Sk
10

Kasımpaşa
Bahriye Cad
Demir
Bülent Sk
Ankan Sk
Tatlı Sk
Akarca Sk
Tepebaşı Cad
Refik Saydam Cad
Tepebaşı Parkı
157
80
35
41
60
127
140
96
76
113
115
102
İstiklal Cad
131
121
Balyoz Sk
Piremeci Sk
141
110
103
71
9
Postacılar Sk

3
To Fener Kasımpaşa
Havuz Kapısı Cad
Hasan Paşa Parkı
Havuzbaşı Değirmen Sk
Anbar Arkası Sk
Avni Sk
Lobut Sk
Hayriye Sk
Tatlı Sk
Tepebaşı
Kuyu Sk
Şimal Sk
Ali Baba Sk
154
Asmalımescit
Gönül Sk
Asmalımescit
Minare Sk
Jurnal Sk
51
129
69
21
150
13
30
66
49
128
47
95
6
To Eminönü

Tünel
111
Sümbül Sk
50
40
Tünel Geçidi
39
Kumbaracı
93
Negris Sk
54
36
105
Şahkulu Bostanı Sk
Bedrettin Sk
Tünel (İstiklal Cad)
72
17
86
Evliya Çelebi Cad
Paşa Çırpak Sk
Müellif Cad
Galipdede Cad
97
7

4
Şişhane
Yolcuzade İskender Cad
Şişhane Sk
Şişhane Square
Büyük Hendek Sk
İlk Belediye Cad
Küçük Hendek Sk
Serdar Ekrem Sk
Hoca Dibek Sk

5
Golden Horn (Haliç)
Atatürk Bridge
Atatürk Köprüsü
Dik Sk
Tutsuk Sk
Okçu Musa Cad
19
Harput Sk
Mürver Sk
Yolcuzade
Yanıkkapı Sk
Deve Dikani Sk
Tersane Cad
Buğulu Sk
Hoca Hanım Sk
Galita Sk
Mahkemesi Sk
5
Şair Ziya Paşa Cad
Lalefi Çeşme Cad
32
14
118
Camekan Sk
Tatar Beyi Sk
Ali Hoca Aralığı Sk
Lüleci Hendek Cad
78
126
125
Cad
Alageyik Sk
11
Galata Kulesi
Camii Sk
1
Yüksek Kaldırım
Zürafa Sk
Kemeraltı Cad
31
Kart Çınar Sk
123
83
Büyük Hendek
Yemenciler Cad
Yelkenciler Sk
Sırmalı Nafe Sk
Bakıt Sk
Samul Sk
Perçemle Pazarı Sk
Zincirli Hân
16
18
Voyvoda Cad
Banker Sk
Maliye Cad

6
Ziyalı Sk
Arap Kayyum Sk
Yüzbaşı Sabahattin
Bereketzade Sk
Tünel (Karaköy)
Büyük Mertebani Sk
Perçemli Sk
Evren Cad
Harköy Cad
Karaköy Cad
Necatibey
Karaköy (Galata)
Fermeneciler Sk
148
Karaköy Square
Gümrük Sk
Fish Market
Rıhtım Cad
Ferries to Üsküdar
Ferries to Kadıköy

TAKSİM, HARBİYE & NİŞANTAŞI

0 ——————— 200 m
0 ——————— 0.1 miles

SIGHTS & ACTIVITIES (pp122–3)
Askeri Müzesi.............................1 B2
Cumhuriyet Anıtı (Republic
  Monument).............................2 A6
Nişantaşı Marker........................3 C6
Taksim Dilmer...........................4 C6

EATING 🍴 (p160)
Banyan: Food for the Soul..........5 D2
Brasserie Nişantaşı....................6 C1
Mado......................................7 D2
Saray Muhallebicisi....................8 D1

DRINKING (p170)
Tepe Lounge..........................(see 23)

ENTERTAINMENT 🎭 (pp172–84)
Cemal Reşit Rey Concert Hall......9 C2
Kervansaray.............................10 B3
Taksim Sanat Galeri..................11 B5

SHOPPING 🛍 (pp199–200)
Gönül Paksoy Shop 1................12 D2
Gönül Paksoy Shop 2................13 D2
Mudo Collection.......................14 C1
Paşabaçhe..............................15 D1
Sema Paksoy...........................16 D1
Vakko....................................17 D1
Yargıcı..................................18 C1

SLEEPING 🛏 (pp212–14)
Bentley Hotel..........................19 B2
Central Palace..........................20 A5
Hotel Avrupa...........................21 A5
İstanbul Hilton.........................22 B4
Marmara.................................23 B6
Riva Hotel...............................24 A5
Taksim Hill Hotel......................25 A6
Taksim Square Hotel.................26 B6
Taksim Suites..........................27 B5

TRANSPORT (pp238–43)
Air France...............................28 A6
Aksaray Dolmuş.......................29 A6
Avis..30 B4
Bakırköy Dolmuş......................31 A5
British Airways.........................32 B4
Budget Car Rental....................33 B5
Bus Turistik Ticket Box.........(see 47)
Buses to Eyüp.........................34 A5
Dolmuşes to Beşiktaş.................35 B2
Europcar.................................36 A5
Havaş Airport Bus Stop.............37 B5
Japan Airlines..........................38 B5
Kadıköy-Bostancı Dolmu...........39 B6
Kadıköy-Şişli-Beşiktaş Dolmuş....40 A5
Karaköy-Eminönü-Sirkeci
  Dolmuş.................................41 A5
Nev Tur Bus Ticket Office..........42 B6
Olympic Airlines..................(see 53)
Onur Air..................................43 B3
Pamukkale Bus Ticket Office......44 B6
Sarıyer Dolmuş.........................45 C5
Sixt (Sun Rent a Car)................46 B4
Taksim Bus Stand.....................47 B6
Taksim Square Bus Stops...........48 B6
Topkapı Dolmuş.......................49 A6
Turkish Airlines........................50 B6
Yeşilköy-Ataköy-Florya-Hava
  Limanı Dolmuş.......................51 A5

INFORMATION
Bamka Döviz Exchange Office...52 B5
Irish Consulate.........................53 B3
PTT.......................................54 B6
Syrian Consulate......................55 D2
Tourist Information Office...........56 B4
Türkiye İş Bankası....................57 A5
Yapı Kredi Bankası...................58 A6

OTHER
DHL Couriers...........................59 B5

SIGHTS & ACTIVITIES	(pp123–8)
Çadır Köşkü	1 D2
Çırağan Sarayı	2 D3
Deniz Müzesi	3 B4
Dolmabahçe Palace	4 A4
Ihlamur Kasrı	5 A1
Istanbul Museum of Painting & Scuplture	6 B4
Ortaköy Camii	7 F2
Yıldız Şale	8 C1

EATING	(pp160–1)
Çınar	9 F2
Ilhami'nin Yeri	10 F2
Mado	11 F2
Vogue	12 A3

DRINKING	(p170)
Cenevız Kahvesi	13 F2

ENTERTAINMENT	(pp172–84)
Q Jazz Club	(see 2)
Wall	14 F2

SLEEPING	(p214)
Çırağan Palace Hotel Kempinski	(see 2)
Swissôtel Istanbul the Bosphorus	15 A4

TRANSPORT MAP

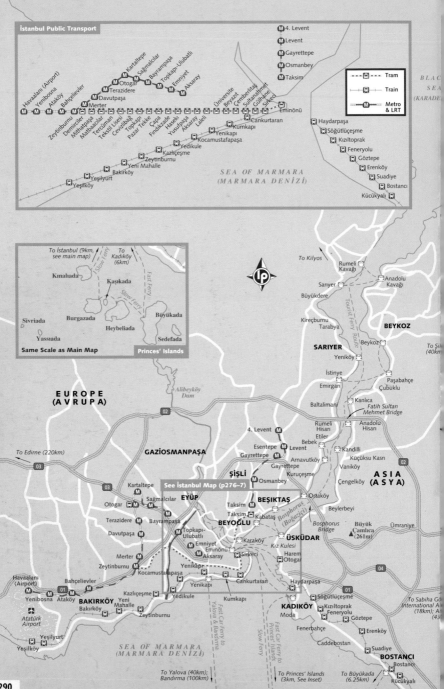